LATTER-DAY PROPHETS AND THE DOCTRINE AND COVENANTS VOL.1

COMPILED BY
ROY W. DOXEY

LATTER-DAY PROPHETS AND THE DOCTRINE AND COVENANTS VOL. 1

Deseret Book Company
Salt Lake City, Utah
1978

To our children—Douglas Allen, Clarke Benson, Kimball LeRoy, and Cheryl Diane—in the hope that they will seek by the Spirit to learn the way to eternal life through the scriptures and the teachings of the latter-day prophets.

Library of Congress Cataloging in Publication Data

Doxey, Roy Watkins, 1908-   ed.
    Latter-day prophets and the Doctrine and covenants.

    Bibliography: p.
    Includes index.
    1. Smith, Joseph, 1805-1844. Doctrine and covenants.
2. Mormons and Mormonism—Doctrinal and controversial
works. I. Smith, Joseph, 1805-1844. Doctrine and
covenants. II. Title.
BX8628.D69 1978   230′.9′33   78-17475
ISBN 0-87747-704-3 (v. 1)

CONTENTS

PREFACE

There are two main reasons that have stimulated me to produce this book. First, many years of study and teaching of the Doctrine and Covenants have convinced me of a conscious need for more Latter-day Saints to become acquainted with this marvelous book of scripture. The second stems out of inspiration received in listening to sermons of the General Authorities in general and stake conferences of the Church, which has also suggested this kind of commentary on the Doctrine and Covenants.

The gospel of Jesus Christ was restored through the Prophet Joseph Smith, and the same keys, powers, authorities, and callings received by him have continued with The Church of Jesus Christ of Latter-day Saints. The power and spirit of the prophets, seers, and revelators of this dispensation, as reflected in their printed works, have attested to this fact and also that the Holy Ghost continues to enlighten and edify the Church as it has done in all ages.

The Lord has declared that scripture is made when his servants are moved upon by the Holy Ghost. Their utterances then become the will, mind, word, voice of the Lord "and the power of God unto salvation." (D&C 68:4.) It is the inspiring power of the Holy Ghost that carries the words of scripture into the hearts of the listener or reader. (2 Nephi 33:1-2.) These truths and the blessings received from heeding the inspiration of the Spirit are stated in the following revelation:

> Therefore, why is it that ye cannot understand and know, that he that receiveth the word by the Spirit of truth receiveth it as it is preached by the Spirit of truth?
>
> Wherefore, he that preacheth and he that receiveth, understand one other, and both are edified and rejoice together.
>
> And that which doth not edify is not of God, and is darkness.
>
> That which is of God is light; and he that receiveth light, and continueth in God, receiveth more light; and that light groweth brighter and brighter until the perfect day. (D&C 50:21-24.)

To what better source may the Latter-day Saints go than to the living oracles for instruction and edification? Although the standard works (Bible, Book of Mormon, Doctrine and Covenants, and Pearl of Great Price) are of great worth in pointing the way to salvation, both in the past and the present, it may be maintained, and rightly so, that one could lose the sacred writings, yet the work of the Lord would continue through the inspired men who are his prophets, seers, and revelators. Hence scripture can be made today the same as in times past, by revelation to living oracles.

In addition to the President of the Church, who actively holds all of the keys and authorities of the priesthood, and *only* to whom revelation *for* the Church is given (D&C 28:2; 43:3-7; 90:9, 12-16; 107:8, 65-66, 91-92), the counselors in the First Presidency, the Twelve Apostles, and the Patriarch to the Church are sustained by the members in general and stake conferences as prophets, seers, and revelators. Concerning the members of the Council of the Twelve Apostles, President Joseph Fielding Smith wrote:

> Each of the apostles when he is ordained has conferred upon him all the keys and authorities which were given by Joseph Smith to the apostles before his death. These brethren, however, cannot exercise these authorities except when the occasion arises that they come to the presidency. Before that time the powers lie dormant. This is the reason why they are sustained as prophets, seers and revelators in the Church, but there can be but one revelator for the Church at a time [the president of the Church]. (*Church History and Modern Revelation*, series 2, page 151, 1948.)

President Brigham Young said concerning the calling of an apostle:

> Now, brethren, the calling of an Apostle is to build up the kingdom of God in all the world: it is the Apostle that holds the keys of his power, and nobody else. If an Apostle magnifies his calling, he is the word of the Lord to this people all the time, or else he does not magnify his calling; — either one or the other.
>
> If he magnifies his calling, his words are the words of eternal life and salvation to those who hearken to them, just as much so as any

written revelations contained in these three books (Bible, Book of Mormon, and Doctrine and Covenants). There is nothing contained in these three books that is any more revelation than the words of an Apostle that is magnifying his calling. (*Journal of Discourses*, 6:282.)

It is apparent that when the Saints require an understanding of the teachings of the gospel, their hearts and ears should be attuned to the words of those who have this calling. Anciently, as today, apostles and prophets were placed in the Church of Jesus Christ to perfect the lives of the Saints through their instruction, and thereby to avoid being shifted about by every teaching or doctrine heard. (Eph. 4:11-14.) Elder Mark E. Petersen of the Council of the Twelve has written:

The solid truth of the gospel is what converts. The scriptures provide that instruction. In order that mankind need not be tossed to and fro with every wind of doctrine, the Lord put in his Church Apostles and prophets as guides for the people. They teach the doctrines of truth. They are inspired men. The Lord guides them that they in turn may guide his people. That is what prophets and Apostles are for. (*Your Faith and You*, p. 241.)

President Reuben Clark, Jr., well stated the calling of the prophets, seers, and revelators:

It should be in mind that some of the General Authorities have had assigned to them a special calling, they possess a special gift; they are sustained as prophets, seers, and revelators, which gives them a special spiritual endowment in connection with their teaching of the people. They have the right, the power, and authority to declare the mind and will of God to his people, subject to the over-all power and authority of the President of the Church. Others of the General Authorities are not given this special spiritual endowment and authority covering their teaching; they have a resulting limitation, and the resulting limitation upon their power and authority in teaching applies to every other officer and member of the Church, for none of them is spiritually endowed as a prophet, seer, and revelator. Furthermore . . . the President of the Church has a further and special spiritual endowment in this respect, for he is the Prophet, Seer, and Revelator for the whole Church. (Address to Seminary and Institute Faculty, July 7, 1954.)

By abiding the counsel of the General Authorities, the Latter-day Saint fulfills his covenant responsibility in working for the cause of Zion. (D&C 6:6-7; 11:6; 12:6; 14:6.) Otherwise he pollutes the holy ordinances and revelations and will be removed out of his place. (D&C 124:45-46.) The opportunity and obligation of the Saints to sustain the leadership of the Church comes periodically in the appointed conferences. (D&C 20:61-62; 124:143-44.) Regarding this solemn procedure, Elder James E. Talmage said:

> Do you ever think of the inconsistency of raising your right hand in solemn witness before God that you will sustain certain men who have been called and ordained, in the manner appointed of God, as your leaders, as prophets unto the people, verily as revelators, and then, though perchance you come together and hear their words, going away and pay no attention to them? When one speaks with the power of his Priesthood, and in the authority of his office, then what he speaks is binding upon himself and all who hear. . . .
>
> You cannot, we cannot, pass by lightly the words that come by way of counsel and instruction from the ordained servants of God, and escape the inevitable penalty of that neglect. Nevertheless, we have our agency; we may choose to disobey, but we must take the consequences of that choice. (*Conference Report,* October 1921, pp. 187-88.)

In what areas of life is counsel given? The spiritual welfare of the Latter-day Saint includes the temporal affairs of life. (D&C 29:34-35.) Basic to this truth is the truth that the gospel is an everyday religion. (D&C 59:11.) The sermons and writings of the prophets, seers, and revelators deal with the practical, everyday application of the eternal truths found in the books of scripture. *Latter-day Prophets and the Doctrine and Covenants* abounds in the application of truth to everyday living.

With many years of teaching and study of the Doctrine and Covenants and the works of the "prophets, seers, and revelators" of this dispensation, there has come to me a greater understanding of these truths: Joseph Smith is a true prophet of God; the heavens were opened to him and the truths of eternal worth were made known; and this generation is still receiving the Lord's word through the books of scripture brought forth by him. (D&C 5:10.) My testimony, also born of the Holy Ghost, is that Joseph Smith's successors who are the Presidents of the Church, together with the other prophets, seers, and revelators, have given counsel and instruction by revelation as a continuation of the onward destiny of "the only true and living church upon the face of the whole earth." (D&C 1:30.) It is equally true that the only way to real happiness in this life and eternal life in the world to come is dependent upon obedience to the words of the prophets, living and dead. (D&C 59:23.)

BACKGROUND INFORMATION ON THE DOCTRINE AND COVENANTS

What were the major events in the dispensation preceding the publication of the first compilation of revelations?

1. The vision of God the Father and his Son, Jesus Christ to Joseph Smith in the spring of 1820. This event opened the last dispensation of the gospel by revealing that Joseph Smith should not join any of the churches of the day, for their "creeds were an abomination in his sight." (Joseph Smith — History 1-26.)

2. The visitations of the Angel Moroni, the last prophet-historian of the former inhabitants of the American continent, who, as a resurrected being, revealed the depository of the gold plates of the Book of Mormon and gave instructions to Joseph Smith (September 21-22, 1823).

3. The translation of these ancient records as well as many other matters relating to the restoration of the fulness of the gospel. (Joseph Smith — History 27-54.)

4. The restoration of the Aaronic Priesthood to Joseph Smith and Oliver Cowdery on May 15, 1829. The restoration of the Melchizedek Priesthood in the same year by the ancient apostles, Peter, James, and John.

5. The organization of The Church of Jesus Christ of Latter-day Saints on April 6, 1830, at Fayette Township, Seneca County, New York.

How did we get the book known as the Doctrine and Covenants?

1. In the summer of 1830, Joseph Smith began to arrange and compile some of the revelations he had received to that time.

2. At the conference on November 1, 1831, it was decided to print 10,000 copies to be known as A Book of Commandments. It was later decided to print 3,000 copies.

3. Oliver Cowdery and John Whitmer took the compiled revelations to Jackson County, Missouri, to have them printed.

4. On July 20, 1833, a mob destroyed the W. W. Phelps & Co. printing press and most of the printed revelations. A number of copies of the incomplete work of 65 chapters survived this mob action.

5. On September 24, 1834, arrangements were made by the high council in Kirtland, Ohio, to prepare another volume of revelations.

6. On August 17, 1835, a general assembly accepted, from a committee composed of Joseph Smith, Sidney Rigdon, Oliver Cowdery, and Frederick G. Williams, the manuscript of revelations to be printed. This edition of 102 sections, named the Doctrine and Covenants, is known as the 1835 edition.

7. On June 27, 1844, the Prophet Joseph Smith was martyred. An edition comprising 111 sections was printed after the martyrdom.

8. The next edition, enlarging the Doctrine and Covenants to 136 sections, was printed in 1876 under the direction of Orson Pratt. The revelations were divided into verses in this edition.

9. The current edition was issued in 1921, with the omission of the Lectures on Faith, published in earlier editions. Added to the volume were introductions to sections, double-column pages, and revised footnote references and index.

What are the Lectures on Faith?

These lectures were prepared for use in the School of the Elders conducted in Kirtland, Ohio, during the winter of 1834-35. These lessons, edited by the Prophet Joseph Smith, were never intended as revelations, but only as theological lessons. The Kirtland high council bore record through Elder John Smith that "the revelations in said book [Doctrine and Covenants] were true, and that the lectures judiciously were written and compiled, and were profitable for doctrine." (HC 2:176, footnote.)

During what years was the greatest number of sections in the Doctrine and Covenants given?

The years 1829 to 1833 were the most productive,

probably because these were the years of restoration, when the doctrine, organization, and foundation principles were made known because of the growth of the Church. The following table gives the number of revelations received during each year:

1 1823	16 1832	1........1837	4........1843
2 1828	13 1833	8........1838	1........1844
14 1829	5 1834	3........1839	1........1847
19 1830	3 1835	3........1841	
37 1831	3 1836	2........1842	

In which state were most of the sections given?

The answer is found in the following table showing the number of sections given in each state:

25—New York	1—Massachusetts
15—Pennsylvania	10—Illinois
64—Ohio	1—Nebraska
20—Missouri	

Why was the title of the revelations changed from A Book of Commandments to the Doctrine and Covenants?

The reason is not given in the *History of the Church*, but with the additional revelations added to the 1835 edition, it is possible that a more comprehensive title was necessary. *Doctrine* means *instruction, belief,* and *covenant* means a contract or arrangement between God and man. In speaking of a time subsequent to November 1831, the Prophet Joseph Smith referred to the compilation of revelations as "the book of Doctrine and Covenants." (HC 1:229.)

Who is the Giver of revelations?

The Giver of all revelations for this earth is Jesus Christ. (D&C 76:12-13.) He was Jehovah of the Old Testament (Ex. 6:3), identified as such in modern revelation (D&C 110:1-4). All revelations given in the Doctrine and Covenants were given by Jesus Christ (D&C 10:57; 27:1; 29:1; 62:1) or under his immediate direction (D&C 2). Jesus speaks for the Father (John 5:43; 3 Ne. 28:10; D&C 50:43); therefore Doctrine and Covenants 29:1 and 42 were given by the same personage, Jesus Christ.

By what ways were some of the revelations received, according to the Doctrine and Covenants?

1. By an angel(s) — Sections 2; 13; 27:1-4; 110.

2. The Urim and Thummim — Sections 3, 6, 7, 11, 14, 15, 16, 17.

3. By the spirit of prophecy and revelation (HC 1:64) — Section 20.

4. Vision — Sections 76; 107:93.

5. By the "still small voice" — Section 85.

6. By a "voice" — Section 130:12-13.

In what manner did the Prophet Joseph Smith give the revelations?

Parley P. Pratt said regarding section 50:

"After we had joined in prayer in his translating room, he dictated in our presence the following revelation: — (Each sentence was uttered slowly and very distinctly, and with a pause between each, sufficiently long for it to be recorded, by an ordinary writer, in long hand.)

"This was the manner in which all his written revelations were dictated and written. There was never any hesitation, reviewing, or reading back, in order to keep the run of the subject, neither did any communications undergo revisions, interlinings, or corrections. As he dictated them so they stood, so far as I have witnessed; and I was present to witness the dictation of several communications of several pages each." (*Autobiography of Parley P. Pratt*, p. 62.) [The Prophet made revisions in some early revelations published in the Book of Commandments in 1833. Errors made by scribes and publishers were also corrected. HC 1:173.]

What types of materials are found in the Doctrine and Covenants?

Types	Sections
Preface	1
Translation scripture	7
Prayers	13, 65, 109
Letters	127, 128
Items of instruction	130, 131

What sections in the current edition of the Doctrine and Covenants were added after Joseph Smith's martyrdom?
Sections 2, 13, 77, 85, 87, 103, 105, 108-32, 135, 136.

In what languages has the complete Doctrine and Covenants been printed?

Armenian	1941
Chinese	1975
Danish	1852
Dutch	1908
English	1833, 1835, 1844, 1876, 1921
Finnish	1955
French	1958
German	1876
Hawaiian	1914
Indonesian	1977
Italian	1965
Japanese	1957
Korean	1968
Maori	1919
Norwegian	1957
Portuguese	1950
Samoan	1963
Spanish	1948
Swedish	1888
Tahitian	1965
Tongan	1959
Welsh	1851

Additional foreign language editions are in process of translation. In 1948 the Doctrine and Covenants was printed in Braille for the use of the blind.

There were three special and eight other witnesses to the authenticity of the Book of Mormon, but what about the Doctrine and Covenants?

The testimony of the Twelve Apostles of the Church was formulated, signed, and presented to the assembly [August 17, 1835] in the form following:

TESTIMONY OF THE TWELVE APOSTLES

The Testimony of the Witnesses to the Book of the Lord's Commandments, which commandments He gave to His Church through Joseph Smith, Jun., who was appointed by the voice of the Church for this purpose:

We, therefore, feel willing to bear testimony to all the world of mankind, to every creature upon the face of all the earth, that the Lord has borne record to our souls, through the Holy Ghost shed forth upon us, that these commandments were given by inspiration of God, and are profitable for all men and are verily true.

We give this testimony unto the world, the Lord being our helper; and it is through the grace of God the Father, and His Son, Jesus Christ, that we are permitted to have this privilege of bearing this testimony unto the world, in the which we rejoice exceedingly, praying the Lord always that the children of men may be profited thereby.

Thomas B. Marsh	Parley P. Pratt
David W. Patten	Luke S. Johnson
Brigham Young	William Smith
Heber C. Kimball	Orson Pratt
Orson Hyde	John F. Boynton
Wm. E. M'Lellin	Lyman E. Johnson

KEY TO ABBREVIATIONS

Abbreviations are used for those sources quoted most exten-sively in Latter-day Prophets and the Doctrine and Covenants. Titles of other publications are given in full following quotations. A bibliography giving publishing data for all publications is found in the back of volume 4.

AF   *Articles of Faith,* by James E. Talmage

C   *The Contributor*

CHMR   *Church History and Modern Revelation,* by Joseph Fielding Smith

CR   *Conference Report*

DN   *Deseret News*

DNCS   *Deseret News* Church Section

DW   *Deseret Weekly*

EMS   *Evening and Morning Star*

HC   *History of the Church,* by Joseph Smith

I   *Instructor*

IE   *Improvement Era*

JD   *Journal of Discourses*

JI   *Juvenile Instructor*

LEJ   *Liahona,* or *Elder's Journal*

MS   *Millennial Star*

RSM   *Relief Society Magazine*

TPJS   *Teachings of the Prophet Joseph Smith*

TS   *Times and Seasons*

YWJ   *Young Women's Journal*

SECTION 1

Revelation given through Joseph Smith the Prophet, during a special conference of Elders of the Church of Jesus Christ of Latter-day Saints, held at Hiram, Ohio, November 1, 1831. Many revelations had been received from the Lord prior to this time; and the compilation of these for publication in book form was one of the principal subjects passed upon at the conference. See History of the Church, vol. 1, page 222. This Section constitutes the Lord's Preface to the doctrines, covenants, and commandments given in this dispensation. – Proclamation of warning and commandment to the Church and to the inhabitants of the earth at large – The authority of the Priesthood in this dispensation attested – Second advent of the Lord Jesus Christ foretold – Authenticity of the Book of Mormon affirmed.

1. Hearken, O ye people of my church, saith the voice of him who dwells on high, and whose eyes are upon all men; yea, verily I say: Hearken ye people from afar; and ye that are upon the islands of the sea, listen together.

2. For verily the voice of the Lord is unto all men, and there is none to escape; and there is no eye that shall not see, neither ear that shall not hear, neither heart that shall not be penetrated.

3. And the rebellious shall be pierced with much sorrow; for their iniquities shall be spoken upon the housetops, and their secret acts shall be revealed.

4. And the voice of warning shall be unto all people, by the mouths of my disciples, whom I have chosen in these last days.

5. And they shall go forth and none shall stay them, for I the Lord have commanded them.

6. Behold, this is mine authority, and the authority of my servants, and my preface unto the book of my commandments, which I have given them to publish unto you, O inhabitants of the earth.

7. Wherefore, fear and tremble, O ye people, for what I the Lord have decreed in them shall be fulfilled.

8. And verily I say unto you, that they who go forth, bearing these tidings unto the inhabitants of the earth, to them is power given to seal both on earth and in heaven, the unbelieving and rebellious;

9. Yea, verily, to seal them up unto the day when the wrath of God shall be poured out upon the wicked without measure—

10. Unto the day when the Lord shall come to recompense unto every man according to his work, and measure to every man according to the measure which he has measured to his fellow man.

11. Wherefore the voice of the Lord is unto the ends of the earth, that all that will hear may hear:

12. Prepare ye, prepare ye for that which is to come, for the Lord is nigh;

13. And the anger of the Lord is kindled, and his sword is bathed in heaven, and it shall fall upon the inhabitants of earth.

14. And the arm of the Lord shall be revealed; and the day cometh that they who will not hear the voice of the Lord, neither the voice of his servants, neither give heed to the words of the prophets and apostles, shall be cut off from among the people;

15. For they have strayed from mine ordinances, and have broken mine everlasting covenant;

16. They seek not the Lord to establish his righteousness, but every man walketh in his own way, and after the image of his own God, whose image is in the likeness of the world, and whose substance is that of an idol, which waxeth old and shall perish in Babylon, even Babylon the great, which shall fall.

17. Wherefore, I the Lord, knowing the calamity which should come upon the inhabitants of the earth, called upon my servant Joseph Smith, Jun., and spake unto him from heaven, and gave him commandments;

18. And also gave commandments to others, that they should proclaim these things unto the world; and all this that it might be fulfilled, which was written by the prophets—

19. The weak things of the world shall come forth and break down the mighty and strong ones, that man should not counsel his fellow man, neither trust in the arm of flesh—

20. But that every man might speak in the name of God the Lord, even the Savior of the world;

21. That faith also might increase in the earth;

22. That mine everlasting covenant might be established;

23. That the fulness of my gospel might be proclaimed by the weak and the simple unto the ends of the world, and before kings and rulers.

24. Behold, I am God and have spoken it; these commandments are of me, and were given unto my servants in their weakness, after the manner of their language, that they might come to understanding.

25. And inasmuch as they erred it might be made known;

26. And inasmuch as they sought wisdom they might be instructed;

27. And inasmuch as they sinned they might be chastened, that they might repent;

28. And inasmuch as they were humble they might be made

strong, and blessed from on high, and receive knowledge from time to time.

29. And after having received the record of the Nephites, yea, even my servant Joseph Smith, Jun., might have power to translate through the mercy of God, by the power of God, the Book of Mormon.

30. And also those to whom these commandments were given, might have power to lay the foundation of this church, and to bring it forth out of obscurity and out of darkness, the only true and living church upon the face of the whole earth, with which I, the Lord, am well pleased, speaking unto the church collectively and not individually—

31. For I the Lord cannot look upon sin with the least degree of allowance;

32. Nevertheless, he that repents and does the commandments of the Lord shall be forgiven;

33. And he that repents not, from him shall be taken even the light which he has received; for my Spirit shall not always strive with man, saith the Lord of Hosts.

34. And again, verily I say unto you, O inhabitants of the earth: I the Lord am willing to make these things known unto all flesh;

35. For I am no respecter of persons, and will that all men shall know that the day speedily cometh; the hour is not yet, but is nigh at hand, when peace shall be taken from the earth, and the devil shall have power over his own dominion.

36. And also the Lord shall have power over his saints, and shall reign in their midst, and shall come down in judgment upon Idumea, or the world.

37. Search these commandments, for they are true and faithful, and the prophecies and promises which are in them shall all be fulfilled.

38. What I the Lord have spoken, I have spoken, and I excuse not myself; and though the heavens and the earth pass away, my word shall not pass away, but shall all be fulfilled, whether by mine own voice or by the voice of my servants, it is the same.

39. For behold, and lo, the Lord is God, and the Spirit beareth record, and the record is true, and the truth abideth forever and ever. Amen.

Joseph Smith: *Introduction*

I returned from the conference at Orange, to Hiram; and as Oliver Cowdery and John Whitmer were to start for Independence, Missouri, a special conference was appointed for the first of November, at which I received the following: [Section 1, quoted.] (*HC* 1:221-22; Hiram, Ohio.)

Ezra Taft Benson: 1-5

A hundred and thirty years ago, when the elders were assembled in conference to determine whether the revelations should be published to the world, the Lord saw fit to give revelation to his Church, which was also directed to the world. He referred to it as his "Preface" or his "Introduction to His Book of Commandments," and it is the first section of the Doctrine and Covenants from which I quote these words: (Note them carefully.) [Sec. 1:1-2, 4-5, quoted.]

So our message is a world message. It is intended for all of our Father's children. When God the Father and his Son Jesus Christ saw fit to come here to earth and appear to a boy prophet, surely such a visitation was intended to bless all of our Father's children. (*CR*, April 1961, pp. 113-14.)

Joseph Fielding Smith: 1:5

We may wonder how that will come to pass [Sec. 1:1-5] because we understand that with the best efforts we can make in sending forth and publishing this word there are many who do not hear it. Our two thousand missionaries who are scattered over the face of the earth preaching the Gospel are very few in comparison with the millions unto whom this Gospel is to be proclaimed. But the Lord will reach the hearts of the people, his word will not fail. And I do not understand even from this wording that it is necessary that every heart be penetrated and every ear hear in this life. But if they have not heard, if this opportunity has not come to them through the preaching of the elders and through the things that have been published in the word of the Lord that has gone forth by revelation, the opportunity is going to come to them and they must hear it in the spirit world.

And so the Lord in his kindness and mercy intends to

bring these truths of this restored Gospel to every soul, living or dead. In this manner every heart shall be penetrated and every ear shall hear. (CR, October 1931, p. 16.)

Joseph Fielding Smith: 1-3

The Lord has given so many revelations in our own day. We have this Doctrine and Covenants full of them, all pertaining unto the Latter-day Saints and to the world. For this is not our book alone. This Doctrine and Covenants is my book and your book; but more than that, it belongs to all the infidels, to the Catholics; to the Presbyterians, to the Methodists, to the infidel, to the non-believer. It is his book if he will accept it, if he will receive it. The Lord has given it unto the world for their salvation. If you do not believe it, you read the first section in this book, the preface, and you will find that the Lord has sent this book and the things which it contains unto the people afar off, on the islands of the sea, in foreign lands, and his voice is unto all people, that all may hear. (CR, October 1919, p. 146.)

Joseph Smith: 2
There is none to escape

You cannot go anywhere but where God can find you out. All men are born to die, and all men must rise; all must enter eternity. (HC 6:366, May 13, 1844.)

George Albert Smith: 6
This is mine authority

This preface [Section 1] is worthy of your earnest consideration. It is the admonition of the Father of all of us. It is the living advice of a tender parent who knows what we require, as he said in the chapter [Sec. 1] just read, that knowing what was about to come upon the inhabitants of the earth, he gave these commandments. The Bible, Book of Mormon, Doctrine and Covenants, and Pearl of Great Price do not contain the wisdom of men alone, but of God. While they do not find their way into the homes of many people, they contain the word of the Lord. What mattereth it though we understand Homer and Shakespeare and Milton, and I might enumerate all the great writers of the world; if we have failed to read the scriptures we have missed the better part of this world's literature. (CR, October 1917, p. 43-44.)

Wilford Woodruff: 7
For what I . . . have decreed in them shall be fulfilled

We live in a very important age and generation; we live in the day and time when God has set his hand to fulfill a measure of prophecy and revelation to man, in the great dispensation of all dispensations. . . . I also believe that the saying of every Prophet or Apostle spoken under the inspiration of the Holy Ghost will have its fulfillment, and as Paul said, no prophecy of Scripture hath any private interpretation, but holy men of old spake as they were moved upon by the Holy Ghost. [2 Pet. 1:20-21.] They spake the mind and word of the Lord, and none of their sayings will fail to be fulfilled, for the Lord hath said—"Though the heavens and the earth pass away, my word shall not fail, but shall be fulfilled." That is the way I read prophecy and revelation. (JD, June 27, 1875, 18:38.)

Joseph F. Smith: 10
Every man according to his work

Every man will be judged according to his works, whether they be good or whether they be evil, and that is a doctrine that was advanced and taught by the Prophet Joseph Smith in plainness that cannot be ignored; every man will be judged according to his works, whether they be good or whether they be evil. [Sec. 76:110-111.] Anything short of that would not and could not be of God, if God is just, if God is righteous, if God is impartial; then this principle of justice is a righteous principle, and it certainly has emanated from God, and not from Joseph Smith, nor from man. (CR, October 1911, pp. 8-9.)

Joseph Smith: 13
And the anger of the Lord is kindled

I prophesy, in the name of the Lord God of Israel, anguish and wrath and tribulation and the withdrawing of the Spirit of God from the earth await this generation, until they are visited with utter desolation. This generation is as corrupt as the generation of the Jews that crucified Christ; and if he were here today, and should preach the same doctrine He did then they would put Him to death. (HC 6:58, October 15, 1843.)

Joseph F. Smith: 14

Obedience is a requirement of heaven and is therefore a principle of the Gospel. [Sec. 82:10; 130:20-21.] Are all required to be obedient? Yes, all. What, against their will? O no, not by any means. There is no power given to man nor means lawful to be used to compel men to obey the will of God, against their wish, except persuasion and good advice, but there is a penalty attached to disobedience which all must suffer who will not obey the obvious truths or laws of heaven. (JD, September 30, 1877, 19:193.)

James E. Talmage: 16
Every man walketh... after the image of his own God

The great trouble with the world today, as I understand it, is that it has become idolatrous. We read of idolatry and think of it as a practice or series of practices in the past. This is an idolatrous generation, defying the commandment written by the finger of God—"Thou shalt have no other Gods before me" [Ex. 20:3], and an idolatrous generation is an adulterous generation.... Men are praising the gods of silver and of gold and of all the other valuable commodities that make up wealth, and the God in whose hand their breath is and whose are all their ways they will not recognize. Do you wonder that wickedness and crime have increased to terrifying proportions under those conditions? The prophets of old foresaw it. They spoke of the days of wickedness and vengeance immediately precedent to the second coming of the Lord, which I reiterate, for it has been spoken before, is near at hand. [2 Tim. 3:1-6; Matt. 24:36-39.]

The Israelites were distinguished in the first place as worshipers of a living God, a personal God, in whose image they had been created and made. [Gen. 1:26-27; Ex. 33:21-

23.] No other nation on the face of the earth recognized the living God. That was a sign by which the covenant people, descendants of Abraham, through Isaac and Jacob, were known. Another sign was this: they observed every seventh day as the Sabbath of the Lord their God [Ex. 20:8-11]; and the Lord has said: This shall be a sign between thee and the nations: They shall know that ye are my people because ye observed my Sabbath. [Ex. 31:12-18.] And the third sign I mention is that they were tithed of all they possessed. [Lev. 27:30; Mal. 3:8] Those were set forth prominently as the banners of Israel, by which all nations should know that they were covenant people of God. . . .

Where do we stand with respect to those signs? Are we worshipping the true and living God, or are we going idolatrously after the gods of gold and silver, of iron and wood, and brass, diamonds and other idols of wealth? Are we worshipping our farms, our cattle and sheep? Who is our God? To whom are we yielding homage, allegiance and worship? Not worship by means of words only, in ritualistic form, but worship in action, devotion, and sacrificial service? (CR, October 1930, pp. 71, 73.)

First Presidency (Brigham Young, Heber C. Kimball, Willard Richards): 17-23

The first light of the morning of this age, and the time referred to by the Savior, was the Angel who had the everlasting Gospel, which was to be preached to all people, preaching and ministering to Joseph Smith, Jun., and commanding Joseph to preach and administer to others even as he had received of the Angel; and the light continued to shine and spread, as others believed, on the testimony of Joseph; for they repented of their sins, were baptized by him, and he, having received the Holy Priesthood from the Angels, conferred the same Priesthood on the believers; and they in turn went forth proclaiming the same Gospel, administering the same ordinances, calling on all the faithful to gather themselves together, to the upholding of Zion, until the light has already been seen in the four quarters of the earth, and is fast being reflected over every nation and people; and this, the Gospel, the plan of salvation, is the true light that must shine from the East to the West — that is, to every nation, kindred, tongue, and people on the earth, before the end will come; and the faithful, the Saints, must be gathered together in holy places and build Temples and do all necessary works to open up the way of life and salvation to the dead as well as the living, before they can complete the work which is given them to do in this dispensation and probation. (MS, January 15, 1852, 14:17-25.)

Wilford Woodruff: 17-23

At the commencement of the Church, the Lord gave revelations to the Church and to individuals, through the Prophet, to tell them what to do — be baptized, ordained, go on missions, and anything that was required at their hands; and hence you can see in the Book of Doctrine and Coven-ants revelations given to Martin Harris [Sec. 19], Parley P. Pratt [Sec. 32; 50:37], Orson Pratt [Sec. 34], the Whitmers [Sec. 14, 15, 16], and many others, calling them to go forth and preach the Gospel to the world. In those revelations are promised many great and glorious things, and the pattern is given and the foundation laid for a great and mighty work — a work not to be accomplished in ten, twenty, thirty, forty or fifty years, but a work that embraces the gathering together of all things which are to be saved, both in heaven and on earth, and the establishing of the kingdom of God, to remain forever; and the Lord said, You are laying the foundations for a great and mighty work. [Sec. 64:33.] But we did not understand or comprehend its extent. He called upon us to go forth and warn the world of the judgments to come, and to call upon them to learn the ways of righteousness, and to walk therein; and what has been the result?

Every man that has embraced it, whose heart was hon-est before God, has been inspired by the Spirit of God; he has been ready to engage in the work to shoulder the knapsack, and go forth and preach this Gospel to all people whenever an opportunity presented itself; and the first Elders of this

Church did preach diligently and faithfully, and many received the word with gladness and rejoiced in the truth. (*JD*, January 10, 1858, 7:102.)

Melvin J. Ballard: 17-18

I understand from this [Sec. 1:17-18, 22-24] that the Lord plainly knew the condition of the world, what it was in 1830, and what it would be today in the year 1923. Knowing the calamities that were coming to his children, unless they changed their course, knowing their disposition that there would be no repentance in their hearts, and yet with a great desire to save them, he called upon his servant, Joseph Smith, to warn men, to call repentance, and others to join in this great proclamation to all men: "Repent, for the kingdom of God is at hand." [Sec. 33:10; 42:7.] And not only to warn men that there was peril and danger ahead, but to offer the means of escape from the perils that would come. . . .He has always in ample time given his sons and daughters full and complete warning of the perils and dangers that are ahead of them, and has, in that connection, clearly pointed out the way of escape. That has been true in this dispensation, and the warning has been proclaimed on the islands of the sea, in the continents of the world, and through the states of the United States, and among even Pagan nations, the warning voice of the servants of the Lord has been heard, for nearly one hundred years, and it is a warning voice that also comes with a kind of invitation to all the Father's children, showing the means of escape, which is the Gospel of the Lord Jesus Christ, restored again among men. . . .The law must take its course, and when men refuse the offer and tender the Lord has given by which they may be saved, they cannot blame the Lord if calamities, judgments and destructions come upon them. The Lord cannot avert it, it must take its course, and yet our Father in his kindness and mercy has offered the way and the means of escape. [Sec. 5:18-19; 133:16.] (*CR*, October 1923, pp. 30-31.)

Stephen L Richards: 17

I rebuke the members of the Church who cast aspersion

upon the honored name of the Prophet Joseph Smith, and who in any manner disparage his noble work. By doing so they destroy faith, their own and that of others, and the Lord will hold them accountable.

I repeat what I have said on this pulpit before: My grandfather [Willard Richards; Sec. 135:2] was a close friend and companion of this man. He knew him as intimately as one man may know another. He had abundant opportunity to detect any flaws in his character and discover any deceit in his work. He found none, and he has left his testimony to his family and to all the world that this man was true, that he was divinely commissioned for the work he had to do, and that he gave his life to the fulfillment of his mission. I have complete assurance that Willard Richards did not lie about his friend, and on my own account, independent of my grandfather's testimony, borne out of the spirit within me, I know that Joseph Smith was a prophet of the living God, and the work he was instrumental in setting upon the earth is the veritable kingdom of our Father in heaven.

Having that knowledge and deep reverence for his illustrious name, I deplore and resent the miserable attempts made to discredit him; and I predict that they will all come to naught, that he will survive every attack, that he will yet win the esteem and respect of all good men, and that the Father has already glorified him. (CR, October 1951, pp. 117-18.)

Stephen L Richards: 23
That the fulness of my gospel might be proclaimed

The work is not new to us. We, and our predecessors, have carried it forward for more than one hundred years. It was the first enterprise undertaken by those of sacred memory who initiated the lofty cause to which we give our allegiance. So soon as the first revelation of the latter days came to them, they lost no time in carrying the message to neighbors and adjacent communities. When the Church was organized, they accepted most literally the revelation that its mission should be to preach the Gospel " . . . unto every nation, and kindred, and tongue, and people." (D&C 133:37.) That was their work. In their poverty and weakness they accepted it with such boldness and enthusiasm, fortitude and sacrifice, as history has seldom recorded.

Their faith and confidence were marvelous. They trusted God, and they did not trust in vain. They knew that he had said that "The weak things of the world shall come forth and break down the mighty and strong ones" (D&C 1:19), and that "the fulness of my gospel might be proclaimed by the weak and the simple unto the ends of the world, and before kings and rulers." (D&C 1:23.) With this assurance our forebears went forth. They assumed their obligation and it superseded everything else. Families were left without a competence, ofttimes in the care of relatives and neighbors and friends. Businesses were sacrificed. Such accumulations as they had were expended for the cause. If I were asked to name the outstanding, distinctive, organized accomplishment of the restored Church of Christ in the last century, I would without hesitation set forth its phenomenal missionary labors. Nothing more truly characterizes the altruism of the gospel that it teaches; nothing more deeply signifies the devotion and sincerity of its members.

The enormous cost of the service has been widely distributed, shared by nearly every family in the Church. Many families have sent forth more than one missionary, and not infrequently has a home kept one or more missionaries in the field continuously for ten or a dozen years, sometimes for a quarter of a century. I know of no way of securing comparable data from other religious bodies, but I venture the assertion that no such church at any period in history for a century of time has ever given to a missionary service such a proportion of its membership and its available resources. (CR, October 1945, p. 53.)

Joseph Fielding Smith: 24
That they might come to understanding

It is the duty of the members of this Church to make themselves familiar with the revelations as they have been given and with the commandments as they have been taught in these revelations, or have been presented in them and given to the people, that they might know the truth which makes us free. And if we will study them, if we will put them into practice, if we will keep the commandments of the Lord, we will know the truth and there shall be no weapon formed against us that shall prosper. [Sec. 71:9-11.] There shall be no false doctrines, no teaching of men that will deceive us. There are many cults and many false faiths, there are many strange ideas in the world, but if we will search these revelations then we will be fortified against errors and we will be made strong. False teachings will have no effect upon us, for we will know the truth which makes us free. . . .

Let me read to you this key that the Lord gave to his disciples when he was in his ministry. Speaking of the last days, the days just preceding his coming, he said:

And whoso treasureth up my word shall not be deceived, for the Son of Man shall come, and he shall send his angels before him with the great sound of a trumpet, and they shall gather together the remainder of his elect from the four winds, from one end of heaven to the other. . . . [Joseph Smith 1:37.]

If you treasure up the word of the Lord, if you study these revelations, not merely those that are in the Doctrine and Covenants, but those that are in all the standard works of the Church, and you put into practice the commandments that are here found, you will not be deceived in these perilous times, but you shall have the spirit of discernment and you will know the truth and shall know falsehood, for you shall have power to know the spirits of men and to understand the Spirit of the Lord. (CR, October 1931, pp. 17-18.)

James E. Talmage: 30

In the first section of the Doctrine and Covenants — I pray you read for yourself — after reciting his purposes and plans and the partial realization of such in the bringing forth of this Gospel in this age, he speaks of those who were charged with authority in that day to administer the affairs of the Church, those to whom these commandments were given, and explains that the commandments were given that his servants might have power to lay the foundation of this

Church and to bring it forth out of obscurity and out of darkness. Please mark his words: "The only true and living church upon the face of the whole earth, with which I the Lord am well pleased." But that is not the end of the sentence or paragraph: "with which I the Lord am well pleased, *speaking unto the church collectively and not individually."*

There lies a vital distinction. It is expressed, but we often overlook it. It is a distinction that should be heeded in all our organizations within the Church and without; the difference between the collective status or conditions or achievements and the work of the individual. . . .

We as individuals are not doing all that could be done, all that should be done. I have no concern for the Church as a whole; its destiny is foretold, it is going on to glorious victory. [Sec. 65.] But that does not say that each of us who are members of the Church will go on to glorious victory; we may be left behind entirely. What are we doing individually? I repeat. (CR, October 1928, p. 118.)

Joseph F. Smith: 30

I believe in the Latter-day Saints. I believe they are a people who will do their duty, as a general thing. That there are delinquents, that there are those who are slothful, that there are those who are indifferent, and that there are those who have not the faith they should have, we know; we understand that; and that there are some, occasionally, who go wrong entirely, do wrong entirely; we know and understand that. But the vast majority of the Latter-day Saints are good and faithful members of the Church. God blesses them, and they are in fellowship with him and with each other. (CR, April 1912, p. 9.)

James E. Talmage: 30
The only true and living church upon the face of the whole earth

We are aware that at the present time there is in progress a great world movement having for its object the federation of denominations and sects professing belief in Christianity. It is known as the Inter-Church World Movement. . . .

It is a very important question to ask: Just where does The Church of Jesus Christ of Latter-day Saints stand in relation to that matter. I answer, it stands aloof and alone.

Intimations have been given out that this Church is trying to get in; that it is trying to curry favor with the sects in order that it may have a place in the great combination that has been planned. Why, to think such a thing would be sacrilege on our part. We have not derived our authority to administer in the ordinances of the Gospel from the church of Rome. We are no outgrowth of any of the Protestant denominations. We constitute a Church that has been organized and named by the Lord Jesus Christ. So far as these combinations go, we wish the participants well. They have been foolishly, as they profess and declare, spending vast sums of money for the erection of meetinghouses, chapels, churches that they could not use; and they say they can save money by what they are proposing to do, though they are trying to raise a great sum by a world-wide drive in order to bring about the saving.

If they can do anything better for the common good by joining together, let them join. These churches were formed by men, and men have the right to do with them as they please; we shall not interfere with them. But this Church was not formed on man's initiative, it was not called into being because of some brilliant leader who stepped forward with a new plan; and therefore we cannot, we have not the power nor the authority to make any kind of affiliation with any other church; let me say with equal earnestness, no other denomination, no sect can ever affiliate as such with this, The Church of Jesus Christ of Latter-day Saints. There have been overtures made by some religious bodies to find out the terms under which they probably could come in with us; and the answer has been: Come in as every member of this Church has come in through the door; and note that the door is just wide enough to admit you, one at a time, the door of baptism, that ye may receive the Holy Ghost by the laying on of hands. [Sec. 20:37; 22; 33:11-13.] (CR, April 1920, pp. 103-4.)

George Albert Smith: 31

I am reminded of a portion of the 28th chapter of II Nephi, indicating the attitude of the evil doer, which I read as follows:

> And there shall be also many which shall say: Eat, drink, and be merry; nevertheless, fear God — he will justify in committing a little sin. (v. 8.)

Think of that — the suggestion that a little sin will be justified, yet in the very first revelation contained in the Doctrine and Covenants, that which is known as the Preface, we find these words: [Sec. 1:31, quoted.]

Yet there are those who would say that because it is a little sin our Heavenly Father does not care. Continuing the quotation from II Nephi:

> Yea, lie a little, take advantage of one because of his words. (v. 8.)

Think of what that means, the whispering of the adversary to lie a little. Whether it be a lie intended to effect a religious organization, a business organization, a political organization, or an individual, the lie will brand the one who tells it, and sooner or later he will have to account for the wrong he has committed.

> Yea, lie a little, take advantage of one because of his words, dig a pit for thy neighbor; there is no harm in this; and do all these things, for tomorrow we die; and if it so be that we are guilty, God will beat us with a few stripes, and at last we shall be saved in the kingdom of God. (v. 8.)

That is what the adversary of righteousness is saying to the children of men. That is what Lucifer, who goes out defiling the people, is breathing in their souls. That is the kind of doctrine that is being disseminated in the world by some of those who ought to be the leaders of morality and also of righteousness. . . .

We read further:

> Yea, and there shall be many which shall teach after this manner, false and vain and foolish doctrines, and shall be puffed up in their

hearts, and shall seek deep to hide their counsels from the Lord; and their works shall be in the dark. (v. 9.)

And then further:

> And others will he pacify and lull them away into carnal security, that they will say: All is well in Zion, yea, Zion prospereth, all is well — and thus the devil cheateth their souls, and leadeth them away carefully down to hell.
>
> And behold, others he flattereth away, and telleth them there is no hell; and he saith unto them: I am no devil, for there is none — and thus he whispereth in their ears, until he grasps them with his awful chains, from whence there is no deliverance.
>
> Yea, they are grasped with death, and hell; and death, and hell, and the devil, and all that have been seized therewith must stand before the throne of God, and be judged according to their works, from whence they must go into the place prepared for them, even a lake of fire and brimstone, which is endless torment. (vs. 21-23.)

That is the word of a prophet of the Lord, spoken hundreds of years ago, of what would exist in the world, and I bear you my witness today . . . that that is a condition that does exist in the world in that day and age in which we live. And as your brother, I plead with you that in the dignity of your membership in the great Church of the Lamb of God, you resist the insidious temptations of the adversary and that in your homes and elsewhere you teach and exemplify virtue and righteousness. (CR, October 1932, pp. 28-30.)

George Teasdale: 32
He that repents and does the commandments of the Lord shall be forgiven

He hath said to the sinner, "When the wicked man turneth away from his wickedness that he hath committed, and doeth that which is lawful and right, he shall save his soul alive." [Ezek. 18:27.] This is a precious promise to the erring children of the Father. Our message to the sinner is that if he will repent, cease to do evil and learn to do well, he shall receive a remission of his sins, through obedience to the Gospel and dedicating the rest of his life to the service of God. What a bright and glorious outlook, to be redeemed from sin and to have the privilege of walking in the light, receiving salvation and obtaining a glorious resurrection! (CR, October 1903, p. 50.)

Hyrum G. Smith: 32

In Section 1 of the Doctrine and Covenants we read these distinctive words: [Sec. 1:31-32, quoted.]

Now he does not say how soon the forgiveness shall come, but he does make it plain that he will forgive those who repent and keep the commandments of the Lord. (CR, October 1918, p. 71.)

Harold B. Lee: 32

If the time comes when you have done all that you can to repent of your sins, whoever you are, wherever you are, and have made amends and restitution to the best of your ability; if it be something that will affect your standing in the Church and you have gone to the proper authorities, then you will want that confirming answer as to whether or not the Lord has accepted of you. In your soul-searching, if you seek for and you find that peace of conscience, by that token you may know that the Lord has accepted of your repentance. [Mosiah 4:2-3.] Satan would have you think otherwise and sometimes persuade you that now having made one mistake, you might go on and on with no turning back. That is one of the great falsehoods. The miracle of forgiveness is available to all of those who turn from their evil doings and return no more, because the Lord has said in a revelation to us in our day: " . . . go your ways and sin no more; but unto that soul who sinneth [meaning again] shall the former sins return, saith the Lord your God." (D&C 82:7.) Have that in mind, all of you who may be troubled with a burden of sin. (CR, April 1973, pp. 177-78.)

James E. Talmage: 33
And he that repents not

Because there is hope of repentance beyond the veil, procrastinate not the day of your repentance; for, as the Prophet Alma has pointed out [Alma 13:27; 34:33-35] you may find that the gift of repentance will be withheld from you there for a long, long time because of your unworthiness. For repentance is a gift from God, and when man forfeits it he loses the power to repent; he can't turn away from his sins with a contrite heart and with a desire to forsake them, once and forever. O, Latter-day Saints, ye men and women of Israel, listen to the voices of those who speak to you under the inspiration of the power of God, and heed them, for by hearing we are condemned if we follow not in the path that is pointed out to us as the path of our duty. (CR, October 1913, p. 121.)

Melvin J. Ballard: 34-36

The Lord knew there would be only a few who would accept that message. The majority would reject it. He provided for the few a refuge of peace; but so far as the world is concerned, he said — (I am reading from the 1st Section of the Doctrine and Covenants): [vv. 34-36, quoted.]

Peace taken from the earth, and the devil having power over his dominion. During the last one hundred years, or since these words were spoken, more light and knowledge has come into the world in the realm of science, through the laboratory, and otherwise, than in all the ages that have preceded it, and if this were all used for the alleviation of human suffering, peace and prosperity could be here, and poverty abolished.

But when we see men and nations spending their wealth to use the gas engine, the laboratory, the airplane, as means of human destruction, surely the devil has seized the blessings and privileges the Almighty intended to use to bring about peace, and is using them to destroy that which he presently shall lose the right to rule over. If the devil is not in the character of warfare that goes over the front-line trenches, swoops down upon the poor helpless women and children, drops its deadly bombs and assassinates them, then I do not know anything that has ever happened in this world that is so like the work of the devil as that. He is ruling in the midst of them. (CR, October 1938, pp. 105-6.)

George Q. Cannon: 34-36

This revelation [Section 87 on war] was made known at that time to the Saints and was a subject of constant remarks in the Church; in 1851 it was published to the world and obtained a somewhat wide circulation nearly twenty-nine years after its date; its wondrous fulfillment began when the first gun was fired at Fort Sumter, South Carolina. [Sec. 130:12-13.] Since that time wars and rumors of wars have prevailed throughout the world. Peace has fled, and in view of all the Lord has said, it is not too much to expect it has fled no more to return till the reign of righteousness shall begin. [Sec. 97:22-23.]

It is strange that the solemn warning uttered by Joseph in 1832 should have gone unheeded. His prophecy was not without its purpose. The Lord inspired his mind with visions of the future and with power to view the paths by which the nation might escape the impending disasters, but, like other parts of his message of salvation to the human race, this warning also was rejected. (*Life of Joseph Smith*, 1907, pp. 126-27.)

First Presidency (Brigham Young, Heber C. Kimball, Willard Richards): 34-36

Since our last Epistle, of October 13, 1852, we know of but few particulars that have transpired among the various nations of the earth. But we know that the revelations of Jesus Christ are true, and that peace is taken from the earth, and that those who will not receive and obey the Gospel of Jesus Christ, when they hear it, will grow worse and worse, in evil passions, strife, war, and blood, until the wicked shall have overthrown the wicked and destroyed themselves from the face of the earth [Sec. 63:32-33; 87:6], that Jesus may have the privilege to reign unmolested in the midst of those that love him. (MS, July 9, 1853, 15:437.)

Joseph Fielding Smith: 35
For I am no respecter of persons

The Lord is no respecter of persons. However, let us not misinterpret this saying. It does not mean that the Lord does not respect those who obey him in all things more than he does the ungodly. Without question the Lord does respect those who love him and keep his commandments more than he does those who rebel against him. [Sec. 76:5; 1 Nephi 17:35.] The proper interpretation of this passage is that the Lord is not partial and grants to each man, if he will repent, the same privileges and opportunities of salvation and exaltation. He is just to every man, both the righteous and the wicked. He will receive any soul who will turn from iniquity to righteousness and will love him with a just love and bless him with all that the Father has to give; but let it not be thought that he will grant the same blessings to those who will not obey him and keep his law. If the Lord did bless the rebellious as he does the righteous, without their repentance, then he would be a respecter of persons. His justice and his mercy are perfect. Justice, says Alma, "Exerciseth all her demands, and also mercy claimeth all which is her own; and thus, none but the truly repentant are saved. What, do ye suppose that mercy can rob justice? I say unto you, Nay; not one whit. If so, God would cease to be God." (Alma 42:24-25.) (CHMR, 1948, 2:27.)

Harold B. Lee: 35
The devil

In a revelation to the Prophet Joseph Smith, his preface to his commandments in this dispensation, the Lord said this, making it still clearer to the nature of this force of evil. [Sec. 1:35, quoted.]

Satan's dominion, as the Lord has further explained, was the dominion of those who do wickedly in and throughout the world. . . .

Satan, or the devil, is known by various terms. He is called the dragon; he is called the serpent; he is called perdition; he is called Lucifer; and he is called the adversary or the prince of darkness. After an encounter with Moses with this master of darkness, the Lord appeared and told Moses who Satan was, that he was one of the sons of God who came to Elohim with a proposition before this world was, that would have destroyed the agency of man. [Moses

4:1-4.] Satan was cast out with all those who followed after him, and they became those striving in this earth in a further effort to destroy the agency of man. [Sec. 29:36-38.] (CR, October 1949, pp. 55-56.)

Harold B. Lee: 36
The Lord . . . shall come down

In our day, we have been told some similar things about the power of the Lord among his peoples. In the very first revelation, or the preface to the revelations, the Lord said: [Sec. 1:35-36, quoted.]

One of the ways by which "he comes down among his people" is clearly explained in the revelation in which he defines certain gifts of the Spirit. He enumerates some of the gifts of the Spirit which men might enjoy; knowledge, and faith, and discernment, and the gift of tongues, and the testimony of knowledge that Jesus is the Son of God, and then he says this:

. . . unto such as God shall appoint and ordain to watch over the church, . . . are to have it given unto them to discern all those gifts. . . . (*Ibid.* 46:27.)

Previously he had said: ". . . given for the benefit of those who love me and keep my commandments." (*Ibid.* 9.)

In our day he sounded a warning . . . when he said to those to whom these gifts are committed:

And in nothing doth man offend God, or against none is his wrath kindled, save those who confess not his hand in all things, and obey not his commandments. [*Ibid.* 59:21.] (CR, October 1960, p. 16.)

Joseph F. Smith: 37-38

The Kingdom of God is here to grow, to spread abroad, to take root in the earth and to abide where the Lord has planted it by his own power and by his own word, in the earth, never more to be destroyed or to cease, but to continue until the purposes of the Almighty shall be accomplished, every whit that has been spoken of by the mouths of the holy prophets since the world began. [Sec. 65:2; 27:6; 128:20-21.] (CR, April 1902, p. 2.)

Wilford Woodruff: 38

I am not ashamed to acknowledge myself a firm believer in the literal fulfilment of the Bible, as well as every communication of God to man, although I am well aware that the Scriptures have been more or less spiritualized by the whole Christian world, especially during the last hundred years....The Lord has taught us in a modern revelation contained in this book, the "Doctrine and Covenants," that it matters not whether he speaks from heaven by his own voice, or by the ministration of angels, or by the mouth of his servants when they are moved upon by the Holy Ghost, it is all the same the mind and will of God; and although the heavens and the earth pass away, my words would not fall unfulfilled. (JD, September 16, 1877, 19:223.)

Heber C. Kimball: 38
What I the Lord have spoken, I have spoken

The Spirit of Prophecy foresees future events. God does not bring to pass a thing because you say it shall be so, but because he designed it should be so, and it is the future purposes of the Almighty that the Prophet foresees. That is the way I prophesy; but I have predicted things I did not foresee, and did not believe anybody else did, but I have said it, and it came to pass even more abundantly than I predicted; and that was with regard to the future situation of the people who first came into this valley. Nearly every man was dressed in skins, and we were all poor, destitute, and distressed, yet we all felt well. I said, "It will be but a little while, brethren, before you shall have food and raiment in abundance, and shall buy it cheaper than can be bought in the cities of the United States." I did not know there were any Gentiles coming here, I never thought of such a thing; but after I spoke it, I thought I must be mistaken this time. Brother [Charles C.] Rich remarked at the time, "I do not believe a word of it." And neither did I; but, to the astonishment and joy of the saints, it came to pass just as I had spoken it, only more abundantly. The Lord led me right, but I did not know it.

I have heard Joseph Smith say many times that he was much tempted about the revelations the Lord gave through him — it seemed to be impossible for them to be fulfilled. (*JD*, March 19, 1854, 3:111-12.)

Eldred G. Smith: 39

We were reminded . . . in our meeting in the temple . . . that the greatest testimony is that which comes and testifies of the Spirit. We cannot always trust what we see and what we hear, but we can always trust the prompting of the Spirit that comes to us, which declares to us that which is truth; and by that power we get our strength and testimony of the Gospel of Jesus Christ. . . . If there are members in the Church who are uncertain, who are lacking in that strength of a testimony, ask yourself and ye shall receive, knock and it shall be opened unto you. If you will put yourself in tune that your spirit shall be in tune with the Spirit of the Holy Ghost, then you shall receive a knowledge of the Gospel of Jesus Christ. [D&C 88:63-65; 11:12-17.] (*CR*, Oct.1956, p.76.)

Joseph F. Smith: 39

Men may deny truth, through a wilful desire to do it, or through ignorance on their part, and they may reject the truth; but no man that lives can say of a truth that God has not spoken from the heavens to men in this latter day as he spoke to ancient prophets and inspired men, and revealed unto them anciently, and also in our present time, his mind and will, and his law. Men say they do not believe it; but that does not make the truth of non-effect. Men may express their doubts about it; but the truth remains. Men may reject it; still the foundation of the truth is unshaken. [D&C 88:66.] Men may array themselves against it; they may fight it bitterly, as many have done from its incipiency; but the truth remains unshaken and undisturbed — the truth that God did speak to his servant Joseph Smith, and did reveal himself unto him; not only the Father, but the Son also. (*CR*, October 1909, pp. 2-3.)

SECTION 2

Words spoken by Moroni, the Angel, to Joseph Smith the Prophet, while in his father's house at Manchester, New York, on the evening of September 21, 1823. See History of the Church, vol. 1, page 12. Moroni was the last of a long line of historians who had made the record that is now before the world as the Book of Mormon. Compare Malachi 4:5,6. See also Sections 27:9 and 110:13-16.

1. Behold, I will reveal unto you the Priesthood, by the hand of Elijah the prophet, before the coming of the great and dreadful day of the Lord.

2. And he shall plant in the hearts of the children the promises made to the fathers, and the hearts of the children shall turn to their fathers.

3. If it were not so, the whole earth would be utterly wasted at his coming.

Joseph Smith: *Introduction*

I continued to pursue my common vocation in life until the twenty-first of September, one thousand eight hundred and twenty-three, all the time suffering severe persecution at the hands of all classes of men, both religious and irreligious, because I continued to affirm that I had seen a vision. . . .

While I was thus in the act of calling upon God, I discovered a light appearing in my room, which continued to increase until the room was lighter than at noonday, when immediately a personage appeared at my bedside, standing in the air, for his feet did not touch the floor. He had on a loose robe of most exquisite whiteness. It was a whiteness beyond anything earthly I had ever seen; nor do I believe that any earthly thing could be made to appear so exceedingly white and brilliant. His hands were naked, and his arms also, a little above the wrist; so, also, were his feet naked, as were his legs, a little above the ankles. His head and neck were also bare. I could discover that he had no other clothing on but his robe, as it was open, so that I could see into his bosom.

Not only was his robe exceedingly white, but his whole

person was glorious beyond description, and his countenance truly like lightning. The room was exceedingly light,
but not so very bright as immediately round his person.
When I first looked upon him, I was afraid; but the fear soon
left me.

He called me by name, and said unto me that he was a
messenger sent from the presence of God to me, and that his
name was Moroni; that God had a work for me to do. . . .

After telling me these things, he commenced quoting
the prophecies of the Old Testament. He first quoted part of
the third chapter of Malachi, and he quoted also the fourth
or last chapter of the same prophecy, though with a little
variation from the way it reads in our Bible. . . .

And again, he quoted the fifth verse thus: [Sec. 2:1,
quoted.]

He also quoted the next verse differently: [Sec. 2:1-2,
quoted.] (HC 1:9, 11, 12, September 21, 1823; Manchester,
New York.)

Joseph Fielding Smith: 1-3

The whole world ought to take notice of this prediction
[Mal. 4:5,6], but the world does not understand it. Surely the
signs of the times point to the fact that the great and dreadful
day is near, even at our doors. The fig tree figuratively, is
putting forth her leaves. The turmoil, trouble, the war and
bloodshed that we have seen, and which we still see, all
point to the fact that this day for the coming of the Son of
God is near. Therefore, Elijah the prophet is due to appear. I
am sure you agree with me that he has already appeared, for
we have it so recorded by the testimony of witnesses. [See
Setion 110.] It was on the third day of April, 1836, when he
came to the Kirtland Temple, to Joseph Smith and Oliver
Cowdery, and conferred upon them the keys of his priesthood and told them that he came in fulfillment of the
prophecy of Malachi, to turn the hearts of the fathers to the
children and the children to their fathers, lest the whole
earth be smitten with a curse. (CR, April 1948, p. 132.)

Joseph Smith: 1

Elijah was the last prophet that held the keys of the Priesthood, and who will, before the last dispensation, restore the authority and deliver the keys of the Priesthood, in order that all the ordinances may be attended to in righteousness. It is true that the Savior had authority and power to bestow this blessing; but the sons of Levi were too prejudiced. "And I will send Elijah the prophet before the great and terrible day of the Lord," etc. etc. [Mal. 4:5-6.] Why send Elijah? Because he holds the keys of the authority to administer in all the ordinances of the Priesthood; and without the authority is given, the ordinances could not be administered in righteousness. (HC 4:211, October 5, 1840.)

Joseph Fielding Smith: 1

Joseph Smith was ordained under the hands of Peter, James, and John, receiving the Melchizedek Priesthood, and he went forth and built the Church in this dispensation. All that he did was valid, all those ordinances were valid, but in order that the binding power should come which is recognized in the heavens, and by which we pass by the angels and the Gods to exaltation, had to come from Elijah, who held that power upon the face of the earth, for the Lord had given it to him, and so he came to Joseph Smith and Oliver Cowdery on the 3rd day of April, 1836, and bestowed upon them the keys of his priesthood. [Sec. 110:13-16.] (*Elijah the Prophet and His Mission,* 1936, p. 22.)

Joseph Smith: 1

In the days of Noah, God destroyed the world by a flood, and he has promised to destroy it by fire in the last days: but before it should take place Elijah should come first and turn the hearts of the fathers to the children, etc.

Now comes the point. What is this office and work of Elijah? It is one of the greatest and most important subjects that God has revealed. He should send Elijah to seal the children to the fathers, and the fathers to the children.

Now was this merely confirmed to the living, to settle difficulties with families on earth? By no means. It was a far greater work. Elijah! what would you do if you were here? Would you confine your work to the living alone? No, I would refer you to the Scriptures, where the subject is manifest: that is; without us, they could not be made perfect, nor we without them; the fathers without the children, nor the children without the fathers. [Heb. 11:40; D&C 128:18.]

I wish you to understand this subject, for it is important; and if you will receive it, this is the spirit of Elijah, that we redeem our dead, and connect ourselves with our fathers which are in heaven, and seal up our dead to come forth in the first resurrection; and here we want the power of Elijah to seal those who dwell on earth to those who dwell in heaven. This is the power of Elijah and the keys of the kingdom of Jehovah. (HC 6:251-52, 1844.)

Rudger Clawson: 1

As early as the year 1823, the Lord made use of this language. [Sec. 2:1, quoted.]

A dreadful day; a day of pestilence, of famine, of earthquake, of tempests, and a day of burning, designated here in very impressive language as "the great and dreadful day of the Lord!" When that day comes, the power of the Priesthood must be upon the earth to protect and deliver the people of God from destruction; for the righteous and those who keep the commandments of God, including those who are tithed, shall not be burned. [Sec. 64:23-24.] (CR, April 1902, p. 28.)

John A. Widtsoe: 2

In our pre-existent state, in the day of the great council, we made a certain agreement with the Almighty. The Lord proposed a plan, conceived by him. We accepted it. Since the plan is intended for all men, we become parties to the salvation of every person under that plan. We agreed, right then and there, to be not only saviors for ourselves, but measurably saviors for the whole human family. We went into a partnership with the Lord. The working out of the plan became then not merely the Father's work, and the Savior's work, but also our work. The least of us, the humblest, is in partnership with the Almighty in achieving the purpose of the eternal plan of salvation.

That places us in a very responsible attitude towards the human race. By the doctrine, with the Lord at the head, we become saviors on Mount Zion, all committed to the great plan of offering salvation to the untold numbers of spirits. To do this is the Lord's self-imposed duty, this great labor his highest glory. Likewise, it is man's duty, self-imposed, his pleasure and joy, his labor, and ultimately his glory.

There is no place for forgetting the other man, in the Gospel of the Lord Jesus Christ. There stands my brother, it was for him that the whole plan was made, for him the Church was organized, for him all these blessings were given — not for me alone. Oh, I stand there, too. The Church was made for me, the Gospel was given for me, all the blessings were given for me; but my brother is entitled to them just as much as I am. He and I together and all of us must unitedly work together to fulfill the great purposes of the Almighty Father. [Sec. 38:27.]

Under the Gospel, what is man's highest ideals? Under the Gospel it must be to become like the Father. [Sec. 76:54-60; 132:24; Moses 1:39.] If the Lord's concern is chiefly to bring happiness and joy, salvation, to the whole human family, we cannot become like the Father unless we too engage in that work. There is no chance for the narrow, selfish, introspective man in the kingdom of God. He may survive in the world of men; he may win fame, fortune and power before men, but he will not stand high before the Lord unless he learns to do the works of God, which always point toward the salvation of the whole human family. [Sec. 15:6; 18:10-16; 128:5, 15-18.] (*Utah Genealogical and Historical Magazine*, October 1934, p. 289.) [See HC 6:59-61.]

Joseph Fielding Smith: 2
The promises made to the fathers

The question is asked: "What is meant by the 'promises made to the fathers' in the instruction of Moroni to the Prophet Joseph Smith, as recorded in the second section of the Doctrine and Covenants?"

This expression has reference to certain promises made to those who died without a knowledge of the Gospel, and without the opportunity of receiving the sealing ordinances of the Priesthood in matters pertaining to their exaltation. According to these promises, the children in the latter days are to perform all such ordinances in behalf of the dead.

At various times during the history of the world the opportunity for mankind to receive the blessings of the Gospel has been denied them. For instance, during the time of the apostasy, following the ministry of our Savior and his apostles down to the time of the restoration, the opportunity for men to receive the remission of their sins by baptism and partake of other ordinances essential to exaltation was impossible, for the Church, with its authorized ministers, was not on the earth. It is true that similar conditions have existed at other and more remote periods of time. Even when the Priesthood has been on the earth and every opportunity given to men to repent and embrace the Gospel, many have died without that opportunity who, perhaps, would have done so had the privilege been presented to them. . . .

The Lord has said that his great work is to bring to pass the immortality and eternal life of man. [Moses 1:39.] This being true, then all men must have the opportunity of hearing the Gospel, either now or in the spirit world. Moreover, the Lord declared to Joseph Smith that "all who have died without a knowledge of the gospel who would have received it if they had been permitted to tarry, shall be heirs of the celestial kingdom." [See Sec. 76:67-70, Joseph Smith.] This is likewise true of all those who shall die henceforth without receiving it, who would receive it if the opportunity came. . . .

Some of these promises made to the fathers are found in the Scriptures. For instance, Isaiah said in reference to our

Savior: "I the Lord have called thee in righteousness, and will hold thine hand, and will keep thee, and give thee for a covenant of the people, for a light of the Gentiles to open the blind eyes, to bring out the prisoners from the prison, and them that sit in darkness out of the prison house." (42:6-7.)

Again he says: "The Spirit of the Lord is upon me; because the Lord hath appointed me to preach good tidings unto the meek; he hath sent me to bind up the broken-hearted, to proclaim liberty to the captives and the opening of the prison to them that are bound, to proclaim the acceptable year of the Lord, and the day of vengeance of our God; to comfort all that mourn." (61:1-2.)

It is generally understood by the Latter-day Saints that these references to the prisoners who are bound refer to those who are dead, who were to hear the Gospel and be redeemed. Further light is thrown on this by another reference by Isaiah: "And it shall come to pass in that day that the Lord shall punish the host of the high ones that are on high, and the kings of the earth upon the earth. And they shall be gathered together in the pit and shall be shut up in the prison, and after many days shall they be visited." (24:21-22.)

Another significant passage embodying this promise is found in the Pearl of Great Price in the words of the Lord to Enoch: "But behold, these which thine eyes are upon shall perish in the floods; and behold, I will shut them up; a prison have I prepared for them.

"And that which I have chosen hath plead before my face. Wherefore, he suffereth for their sins; inasmuch as they . . . shall be in torment." (Moses 7:38-39.) (*IE*, July 1922, 25:829-31.)

Joseph Smith: 3
If it were not so

The greatest responsibility in this world that God has laid upon us is to seek after our dead. The Apostle says, " . . . they without us cannot be made perfect" (Heb. 11:40); for it is necessary that the sealing power should be in our hands to seal our children and our dead for the fulness of the dispensation of times — a dispensation to meet the promises made by Jesus Christ before the foundation of the world for the salvation of man. [Titus 1:2.]

Now I will speak of them. I will meet Paul halfway. I say to you, Paul, you cannot be perfect without us. [Sec. 128:15,18.] It is necessary that those who are going before and those who come after us should have salvation in common with us; and thus hath God made it obligatory upon man. Hence, God said, "I will send you Elijah the prophet before the coming of the great and dreadful day of the Lord; and he shall turn the heart of the fathers to the children, and the heart of the children to their fathers, lest I come and smite the earth with a curse." (Malachi 4:5.) (*TPJS*, April 6, 1844, p. 356.)

SECTION 3

Revelation given to Joseph Smith the Prophet, at Harmony, Pennsylvania, July, 1828, relating to the loss of certain manuscripts of the first part of the Book of Mormon, which Joseph had reluctantly allowed to pass from his custody to that of Martin Harris, who had served for a brief period as scribe in the translation of the Book of Mormon. This revelation was given through the Urim and Thummim. See History of the Church, vol. 1, p. 21. Compare Section 10.

1. The works, and the designs, and the purposes of God cannot be frustrated, neither can they come to naught.

2. For God doth not walk in crooked paths, neither doth he turn to the right hand nor to the left, neither doth he vary from that which he hath said, therefore his paths are straight, and his course is one eternal round.

3. Remember, remember that it is not the work of God that is frustrated, but the work of men;

4. For although a man may have many revelations, and have power to do many mighty works, yet if he boasts in his own strength, and sets at naught the counsels of God, and follows after the dictates of his own will and carnal desires, he must fall and incur the vengeance of a just God upon him.

5. Behold, you have been entrusted with these things, but how strict were your commandments; and remember also the promises which were made to you, if you did not transgress them.

6. And behold, how oft you have transgressed the commandments and the laws of God, and have gone on in the persuasions of men.

7. For, behold, you should not have feared man more than God. Although men set at naught the counsels of God, and despise his words —

8. Yet you should have been faithful; and he would have extended his arm and supported you against all the fiery darts of the adversary; and he would have been with you in every time of trouble.

9. Behold, thou art Joseph, and thou wast chosen to do the work of the Lord, but because of transgression, if thou art not aware thou wilt fall.

10. But remember, God is merciful; therefore, repent of that which thou hast done which is contrary to the commandment which I gave you, and thou art still chosen, and art again called to the work;

11. Except thou do this, thou shalt be delivered up and become as other men, and have no more gift.

12. And when thou deliveredst up that which God had

given thee sight and power to translate, thou deliveredst up that which was sacred into the hands of a wicked man,

13. Who has set at naught the counsels of God, and has broken the most sacred promises which were made before God, and has depended upon his own judgment and boasted in his own wisdom.

14. And this is the reason that thou hast lost thy privileges for a season—

15. For thou hast suffered the counsel of thy director to be trampled upon from the beginning.

16. Nevertheless, my work shall go forth, for inasmuch as the knowledge of a Savior has come unto the world, through the testimony of the Jews, even so shall the knowledge of a Savior come unto my people—

17. And to the Nephites, and the Jacobites, and the Josephites, and the Zoramites, through the testimony of their fathers—

18. And this testimony shall come to the knowledge of the Lamanites, and the Lemuelites, and the Ishmaelites, who dwindled in unbelief because of the iniquity of their fathers, whom the Lord has suffered to destroy their brethren the Nephites, because of their iniquities and their abominations.

19. And for this very purpose are these plates preserved, which contain these records — that the promises of the Lord might be fulfilled, which he made to his people;

20. And that the Lamanites might come to the knowledge of their fathers, and that they might know the promises of the Lord, and that they may believe the gospel and rely upon the merits of Jesus Christ, and be glorified through faith in his name, and that through their repentance they might be saved. Amen.

Joseph Smith: *Introduction*

In the meantime, while Martin Harris was gone with the writings, I went to visit my father's family at Manchester. I continued there for a short season, and then returned to my place in Pennsylvania. Immediately after my return home, I was walking out a little distance, when, behold, the former heavenly messenger appeared and handed to me the Urim and Thummim again — for it had been taken from me in consequence of my having wearied the Lord in asking for the privilege of letting Martin Harris take the writings, which he lost by transgression — and I inquired of the Lord through it, and obtained the following: [Sec. 3, follows.] (HC 1:20-22; Harmony, Pennsylvania.)

Joseph Fielding Smith: 1
The works . . . and the purposes of God cannot be frustrated

Naturally, both Martin Harris and Joseph Smith passed through very severe mental torture following the loss of the manuscript. This was especially true of the Prophet. The Lord, knowing the end from the beginning, had provided for just this emergency and in a revelation given to the Prophet before the Lord took from him his gift, he was informed that the work and designs of the Almighty cannot be frustrated by puny man or by the devil. The Prophet was taught that even though a man may receive many revelations, if he sets himself up in his own strength or follows his carnal desires he will incur the displeasures, even the vengeance, of a just God. In his infinite wisdom our Father has provided for every problem or difficulty that may arise to stop or hinder the progress of his work. No power on earth or in hell can overthrow or defeat that which God has decreed. Every plan of the adversary will fail, for the Lord knows the secret thoughts of men, and sees the future with a vision clear and perfect, even as though it were in the past. [Sec. 38:21.] Jacob, son of Lehi, in his rejoicing declared: "O how great the holiness of our God! For he knoweth all things, and there is not anything save he knows it." (2 Nephi 9:20.) He knew that Satan would try to frustrate the coming forth of the Book of Mormon by the stealing and changing of the manuscript, and provided for it hundreds of years before the birth of Jesus Christ. Martin Harris without a doubt fell a prey to the enticings of Satan, in his constant pleading for the manuscript. Satan played upon his pride and he foolishly thought that by the showing of the manuscript his kindred could be convinced.

There is always danger when men boast in their own strength, or when they seek to satisfy their own desires. When those desires are contrary to the will of the Lord, and are still persisted in, they will without fail return in punishment upon their heads. (*CHMR*, 1947, 1:24-25.)

Abraham O. Woodruff: 1-4

I wish to read to you a few verses from Section 3 of the Book of Doctrine and Covenants: [Sec. 3:1-4, quoted.]

The Apostle Paul, in his day, said: "For we can do nothing against the truth, but for the truth." [2 Cor. 13:8.]

Are we not witnesses this day that this prediction has been fulfilled in the history of the Latter-day Saints? No weapon that has ever been formed against Zion has prospered. [Sec. 71:9-10.] The efforts of the evil one to destroy the work of the Lord have only tended to spread it abroad. The persecutions which have been heaped upon this people have been the means of cementing us together, drawing us more closely to God, and making us more united and powerful. It is the heritage of the saints of God to be misrepresented and persecuted by the insincere and the wicked; but their efforts have never blocked the progress of the work of our Eternal Father. On the contrary, the labors of our most bitter enemies have been among the main factors in spreading the work abroad. The Lord has turned the wrath of the wicked to his own glory. Had it not been for the persecution of the Latter-day Saints, the mustard seed would not have been cast abroad; but in the attempt to destroy the mustard stalk, to which the Savior compared the Gospel [Lk. 13:18-19], they have scattered the seed, and it has taken root wherever it has fallen.... I thank God that it is not his purposes which have failed, but the purposes of man. This should be an encouragement to every Latter-day Saint and a strong testimony that this is the work of God. It ought to be a testimony also to those who have sought to bring to naught the purposes of God. (*CR*, October 1901, pp. 1, 12.)

George Q. Cannon: 5-15

The work of translating the plates progressed through the two months from April until June; not steadily, for Martin [Harris] was much called away. But at the expiration of that time, on the 14th day of June, 1828, Martin had written one hundred and sixteen pages foolscap of the translation.

And at this hour came a test, bitter in its experiences and consequences to the Prophet of God.

A woman wrought a betrayal of the confidence reposed in Martin Harris and a temporary destruction of Joseph's power.

The wife of the scribe was desirous to see the writings dictated to her husband by Joseph: she importuned Martin until he, too, became anxious to have in his own possession the manuscript. Long before the 14th day of June, he began to solicit from the Prophet the privilege of taking the papers away that he might show them to curious and skeptical friends; and thereby be able to give convincing proof to doubting persons, of Joseph's divine mission.

A simple denial was not sufficient, and he insisted that Jehovah should be asked to thus favor him. Once, twice, in answer to his demands, the Prophet inquired; and each time the reply was that Martin Harris ought not be entrusted with the sacred manuscript. Even a third time Martin required that Joseph should solicit permission in his behalf; and on this occasion, which was near the 14th day of June, 1828, the word came that Joseph, at his own peril, might allow Harris to take possession of the manuscript and exhibit it to a few other persons who were designated by the Prophet in his supplication. But because of Joseph's wearying applications to God, the Urim and Thummim and seer-stone were taken from him. Accordingly the precious manuscript was entrusted to the keeping of Martin Harris; and he bound himself by a solemn oath to show it to only his wife, his brother Preserved Harris, his father and mother, and Mrs. Cobb, his wife's sister. After entering into his sacred covenant, Martin Harris departed from Harmony, carrying with him the inspired writings.

Then came about the punishment of Martin for his importunacy and of Joseph for his blindness. Wicked people, through the vanity and treachery of Martin's wife and his own weakness, gained sight of the precious manuscript and they contrived to steal it away from Harris, so that his eyes and the eyes of the Prophet never again beheld it.

For his disobedient pertinacity in voicing to the Lord the request of Martin Harris, Joseph had been deprived of the Urim and Thummim and seer-stone; but this was not his only punishment. The pages of the manuscript which contained the translation he had been inspired to make, and which thereby became the words of God, had been loaned to Martin Harris and been stolen; and now the plates themselves were taken from him by the angel of the record.

The sorrow and humiliation Joseph felt were beyond description. The Lord's rebukes for his conduct pierced him to the center. He humbled himself in prayer and repentance; and so true was his humility that the Lord accepted it as expiation and the treasures were restored to his keeping.

Martin Harris was also shamed and grieved; and he repented in anguish the violation of his trust. But, though a measure of confidence was restored to him, he was never again permitted to act as a scribe for the Prophet in the work of the translation.

While Joseph was mourning the loss of the manuscript, the Lord revealed to him many truths regarding the situation to which he had brought himself, and also warning him of the designs of wicked men who plotted to overthrow him and to put the name of God and his newly revealed record to shame in the land.

A rebuke was given at this time in words which Joseph always remembered. (*Life of Joseph Smith,* 1907, pp. 31-33.)

Anthony W. Ivins: 16-20

One of the great future accomplishments of this Church, and one which devolves upon us, is the preaching of the Gospel of the Redeemer to the scattered remnants of the House of Israel. I am a believer in the word of the Lord. I believe the things that are written in this book from which I read, the Doctrine and Covenants. [Sec. 4:1-2.] I believe the promises of God as they are contained here in this Book of Mormon . . . just as certain as the sun shines in yonder heaven, so will the remnant who have descended from the men who wrote it, be brought to a knowledge of the truth of the Gospel of the Redeemer, come into the Church and be numbered with the saints of God. The Lord has promised it, unconditionally; that is to say, unconditionally except as it depends upon their repentance, but that they will repent he has told us in the most definite manner, and there are millions of them around us. . . . These Lamanites are heirs to the promises, and God has said, without qualification, that he will give this land to them for an everlasting inheritance [3 Ne. 20:13-14]; that they shall be, with us, the builders of the new Jerusalem [3 Ne. 21:20-25]; the powers of heaven shall be among them, and they shall know the record of their fathers which has been brought to us through the instrumentality of the Prophet Joseph Smith. (CR, April 1915, p. 112.)

LeGrand Richards: 16-20

We learned that the prophets who lived among the people upon this land of America were instructed by the Lord to keep records; that the prophet Mormon, the father of Moroni, made an abridgment of all these records, from which the Book of Mormon was translated. The book bears the name of the great prophet, Mormon.

Mormon's introduction to his abridgment, taken from the introductory page of the Book of Mormon, is as follows:

Wherefore, it is an abridgment of the record of the people of Nephi, and also of the Lamanites — Written to the Lamanites, who are a remnant of the house of Israel; and also to Jew and Gentile — Written by way of commandment, and also by the spirit of prophecy and of revelation — Written and sealed up, and hid up unto the Lord, that they might not be destroyed — to come forth by the gift and power of God unto the interpretation thereof — Sealed by the hand of Moroni, and hid up unto the Lord, to come forth in due time by way of the Gentile — The interpretation thereof by the gift of God.

And an abridgment taken from the Book of Ether also, which is a record of the people of Jared, who were scattered at the time the Lord confounded the language of the people, when they were building a tower to get to heaven — Which is to show unto the remnant of the House of Israel what great things the Lord hath done for their fathers; and that they may know the covenants of the Lord, that they are not cast off forever — And also to the convincing of the Jew and Gentile that JESUS is the CHRIST, the ETERNAL GOD, manifesting himself unto all nations — And now, if there are faults they are the mistakes of men;

39

wherefore, condemn not the things of God, that ye may be found spotless at the judgment-seat of Christ.

From this it will be noted that one of the chief purposes for which this record has been preserved is for "the convincing of the Jew and Gentile that Jesus is the Christ, the Eternal God, manifesting himself unto all nations."

It is general knowledge that faith in Jesus Christ as the Son of God, the Redeemer of the world, is waning, both among clergy and laity. In February, 1934, the Northwestern University School of Education, Chicago, Illinois, sent a questionnaire to five hundred Protestant ministers, which revealed many modifications in religious beliefs. Of this number, twenty-six percent, or 130 of the five hundred ministers, were opposed to the Deity of Jesus. (*The Deseret News*, February 8, 1934.) If such be the result with the ministers, what can be expected from the laity? Such a condition would seem to indicate the great wisdom of God in providing a new witness for the divine mission of his Son, that he was in very deed "the Christ, the Eternal God, manifesting himself unto all nations." (*A Marvelous Work and a Wonder*, 1950, pp. 45-46.)

SECTION 4

Revelation given through Joseph Smith the Prophet, to his father, Joseph Smith, Sen., at Harmony, Pennsylvania, February, 1829. — Qualifications for the labors of the ministry are set forth.

1. Now behold, a marvelous work is about to come forth among the children of men.

2. Therefore, O ye that embark in the service of God, see that ye serve him with all your heart, might, mind and strength, that ye may stand blameless before God at the last day.

3. Therefore, if ye have desires to serve God ye are called to the work;

4. For behold the field is white already to harvest; and lo, he that thrusteth in his sickle with his might, the same layeth up in store that he perisheth not, but bringeth salvation to his soul;

5. And faith, hope, charity and love, with an eye single to the glory of God, qualify him for the work.

6. Remember faith, virtue, knowledge, temperance, patience, brotherly kindness, godliness, charity, humility, diligence.

7. Ask, and ye shall receive; knock, and it shall be opened unto you. Amen.

Joseph Fielding Smith: *Introduction*

He [Joseph Smith, Sr.] was the first person who received the Prophet's testimony after the appearance of the angel, and was always true to the mission of his son. He moved to Kirtland in 1831, where he was ordained patriarch and an assistant counselor to the Prophet in the Presidency of the High Priesthood, December 18, 1833. He served as a member of the first high council in 1834. During the persecutions in Kirtland, in 1837, he was made a prisoner by the apostate enemies of the Church, but gained his liberty and made his way to Far West in 1838. From here he was again driven by enemies under the exterminating order of the infamous Lilburn W. Boggs. In midwinter he made his way to Quincy, and later in the spring of 1839, to Commerce, where he made his home. He was six feet two inches tall, and well proportioned. His ordinary weight was about two hundred pounds. He was a very strong, active man, but the exposure he suffered during the expulsion from Missouri brought on consumption, from which he died. His funeral services were held September 15, 1840, Elder Robert B. Thompson delivering the discourse. (*Essentials in Church History*, 1967 ed., pp. 246-47.)

Heber J. Grant: 1
A marvelous work

This "marvelous work and a wonder" has come to pass and has spread all over the world where there has been religious liberty; and from every land and from every clime honest, faithful, God-fearing men and women have heard the sound of the true voice of the shepherd through his servants who have gone forth to proclaim the Gospel. And men of great influence have been gathered into this Church. Men like John Taylor, who presided over the Church, heard the Gospel in a foreign land; the parents of George Q. Cannon, and many other leaders in this Church, heard the sound of this Gospel and embraced it and gathered to Zion, and labored with all the power and ability that they possessed for the advancement of God's kingdom. Year by year this great and wonderful work has rolled on and we are becoming known as a God-fearing people, as a people with a destiny that is sure to be fulfilled. (CR, October 1929, p. 9.)

George Albert Smith: 1-7

One of the very first revelations that was given by our Heavenly Father, as contained in the Doctrine and Covenants, reads as follows: [Sec. 4:1-2, quoted.]

Now I do not understand that we are serving God with all our might if we forsake his children, or if we spend so much of our time selfishly building up ourselves, accumulating things of this life, and leaving his children in darkness, when we could bring them into the light. My understanding is that the most important mission that I have in this life is: first, to keep the commandments of God, as they have been taught to me; and next, to teach them to my

Father's children who do not understand them. It makes little difference when I go to the other side, whether I have been a man of wealth in this world or not, unless I have used that wealth to bless my fellow men. Though I be a wanderer in this world, and suffer for the necessities of life, if by reason of the knowledge that my Father has given me I devote myself to the instruction of his children, to planting faith in their hearts, to dissipating the errors that have come to them by tradition, I believe when I go to the other side that I will find a bank account that will be beyond compare with what I would have if I lived for the things of this earth alone. I read a portion of the Section 4 and I want to read that last verse again: [Sec. 4:2-3, quoted.]

It is not necessary for you to be called to go into the mission field in order to proclaim the truth. Begin on the man who lives next door by inspiring confidence in him, by inspiring love in him for you because of your righteousness, and your missionary work has already begun. [Sec. 4:4-7, quoted.] (CR, October 1916, pp. 50-51.)

Joseph Fielding Smith: 5-6

It is true, we are engaged in a warfare, and all of us should be valiant warriors in the cause in which we are engaged. Our first enemy we will find within ourselves. It is a good thing to overcome that enemy first, and bring ourselves into strict obedience to the principles of life and salvation which he has given to the world for the salvation of men. When we shall have conquered ourselves, it will be well for us to wage our war without, against false teachings, false doctrines, false customs, habits and ways, against error, unbelief, the follies of the world that are so prevalent, and against infidelity, and false science under the name of science, and every other thing that strikes at the foundation of the principles set forth in the doctrine of Christ for the redemption of man and the salvation of their souls. (CR, October 1914, pp. 128-29.)

George Teasdale: 5-6

Before this Church was organized the Lord gave instructions concerning those who should assist in this work, and what should qualify them for the work. Said he [Sec. 4:5-6, quoted]. We have understood the necessity of all these things from the beginning. We have been patient in affliction. When we have been smitten and driven, we have not retaliated; but we have prayed for our enemies, and have taken the Gospel to them, simply because we have learned to love God and our neighbor, according to his commandment. (CR, October 1901, p. 38.)

SECTION 5

Revelation given through Joseph Smith the Prophet, at Harmony, Pennsylvania, March, 1829. – Three witnesses to the Book of Mormon are promised, of whom Martin Harris is to be one if he shall prove himself worthy – Baptism is foreshadowed, but as no one had at this time been ordained to administer the ordinance, patient waiting is enjoined – Note that ordination followed, a few weeks later; see Section 13.

1. Behold, I say unto you, that as my servant Martin Harris has desired a witness at my hand, that you, my servant Joseph Smith, Jun., have got the plates of which you have testified and borne record that you have received of me;

2. And now, behold, this shall you say unto him — he who spake unto you, said unto you: I, the Lord, am God, and have given these things unto you, my servant Joseph Smith, Jun., and have commanded you that you should stand as a witness of these things;

3. And I have caused you that you should enter into a covenant with me, that you should not show them except to those persons to whom I commanded you; and you have no power over them except I grant it unto you.

4. And you have a gift to translate the plates; and this is the first gift that I bestowed upon you; and I have commanded that you should pretend to no other gift until my purpose is fulfilled in this; for I will grant unto you no other gift until it is finished.

5. Verily, I say unto you, that woe shall come unto the inhabitants of the earth if they will not hearken unto my words;

6. For hereafter you shall be ordained and go forth and deliver my words unto the children of men.

7. Behold, if they will not believe my words, they would not believe you, my servant Joseph, if it were possible that you should show them all these things which I have committed unto you.

8. Oh, this unbelieving and stiffnecked generation — mine anger is kindled against them.

9. Behold, verily I say unto you, I have reserved those things which I have entrusted unto you, my servant Joseph, for a wise purpose in me, and it shall be made known unto future generations;

10. But this generation shall have my word through you;

11. And in addition to your testimony, the testimony of three of my servants, whom I shall call and ordain, unto whom I will show these things, and they shall go forth with my words that are given through you.

12. Yea, they shall know of a surety that these things are true, for from heaven will I declare it unto them.

13. I will give them power that they may behold and view these things as they are;

14. And to none else will I grant this power, to receive this same testimony among this generation, in this the beginning of the rising up and the coming forth of my church out of the wilderness — clear as the moon, and fair as the sun, and terrible as an army with banners.

15. And the testimony of three witnesses will I send forth of my word.

16. And behold, whosoever believeth on my words, them will I visit with the manifestation of my Spirit; and they shall be born of me, even of water and of the Spirit —

17. And you must wait yet a little while, for ye are not yet ordained —

18. And their testimony shall also go forth unto the condemnation of this generation if they harden their hearts against them;

19. For a desolating scourge shall go forth among the inhabitants of the earth, and shall continue to be poured out from time to time, if they repent not, until the earth is empty, and the inhabitants thereof are consumed away and utterly destroyed by the brightness of my coming.

20. Behold, I tell you these things, even as I also told the people of the destruction of Jerusalem; and my word shall be verified at this time as it hath hitherto been verified.

21. And now I command you, my servant Joseph, to repent and walk more uprightly before me, and to yield to the persuasions of men no more;

22. And that you be firm in keeping the commandments wherewith I have commanded you; and if you do this, behold I grant unto you eternal life, even if you should be slain.

23. And now, again, I speak unto you, my servant Joseph, concerning the man that desires the witness —

24. Behold, I say unto him, he exalts himself and does not humble himself sufficiently before me; but if he will bow down before me, and humble himself in mighty prayer and faith, in the sincerity of his heart, then will I grant unto him a view of the things which he desires to see.

25. And then he shall say unto the people of this generation: Behold, I have seen the things which the Lord hath shown unto Joseph Smith, Jun., and I know of a surety that they are true, for I have seen them, for they have been shown unto me by the power of God and not of man.

26. And I the Lord command him, my servant Martin Harris, that he shall say no more unto them concerning these things, except he shall say: I have seen them, and they have been

shown unto me by the power of God; and these are the words which he shall say.

27. But if he deny this he will break the covenant which he has before covenanted with me, and behold, he is condemned.

28. And now, except he humble himself and acknowledge unto me the things that he has done which are wrong, and covenant with me that he will keep my commandments, and exercise faith in me, behold, I say unto him, he shall have no such views, for I will grant unto him no views of the things of which I have spoken.

29. And if this be the case, I command you, my servant Joseph, that you shall say unto him, that he shall do no more, nor trouble me any more concerning this matter.

30. And if this be the case, behold, I say unto thee Joseph, when thou hast translated a few more pages thou shalt stop for a season, even until I command thee again; then thou mayest translate again.

31. And except thou do this, behold, thou shalt have no more gift, and I will take away the things which I have entrusted with thee.

32. And now, because I foresee the lying in wait to destroy thee, yea, I foresee that if my servant Martin Harris humbleth not himself and receive a witness from my hand, that he will fall into transgression;

33. And there are many that lie in wait to destroy thee from off the face of the earth; and for this cause, that thy days may be prolonged, I have given unto thee these commandments.

34. Yea, for this cause I have said: Stop, and stand still until I command thee, and I will provide means whereby thou mayest accomplish the thing which I have commanded thee.

35. And if thou art faithful in keeping my commandments, thou shalt be lifted up at the last day. Amen.

Joseph Smith: *Introduction*

The following [Section 5] I applied for and obtained, at the request of . . . Martin Harris. (*HC* 1:28, March 1829; Harmony, Pennsylvania.)

Joseph Fielding Smith: 1-4

Having humbly repented of his folly which brought upon him the charge from the Lord of wickedness [Sec. 3:12;

10:1], Martin Harris again sought the Prophet Joseph Smith and pleaded for the privilege to become one of the three witnesses which were spoken of in the Book of Mormon (II Nephi 27:12-14). It was in the summer of 1828 when the manuscript was lost, and in March, 1829, when Martin again pleaded with the Prophet for this great privilege of being a witness. The Lord hearkened to his request and the Lord gave the revelation known as Section 5 in the Doctrine and Covenants. . . . The Lord commenced this wonderful revelation with an admonishment and stated that Joseph Smith had been called as a witness and had entered into a covenant with the Lord, that he would not show the record except to those persons to whom the Lord had commanded him. He was further informed that he had received the gift to translate the plates and that he should pretend to no other gift until this duty was fulfilled, for no other gift would be given him until this work was finished, after that he would be called on to bear witness to all the world. (*CHMR*, 1947, 1:35-36.)

John A. Widtsoe: 1
Martin Harris

Martin Harris (1783-1875), was the first of the witnesses to appear in the story of Joseph Smith. He was acquainted with the Smith family and, it is said, employed the boy Joseph on his farm. Martin Harris was a religiously-minded, prosperous farmer. He appears to have been a rather willful, but honest man, who wanted to be sure of everything he undertook. It was he who took the transcript of characters from the Book of Mormon plates to Professor Anthon for verification. He was one of the three witnesses who had most difficulty on the occasion when the plates were shown to them. He was not easily led. But so certain was he at last of the claims of Joseph Smith that he advanced $3,000 for the publication of the Book of Mormon. In a mistaken allegiance to Joseph Smith after the martyrdom he did not go westward with the Church. In his old age, however, he sought out the Church, bore to the members, in the valleys of the mountains, his oft-repeated testimony of the truth of Joseph

Smith's claims, and died a faithful member of the Church. (*Joseph Smith*, 1957, p. 53.)

Joseph Fielding Smith: 5-15

So said the Lord. [Sec. 5:5, quoted.] It was his purpose that the word to his ancient prophets as contained in the Book of Mormon would be proclaimed to all the world, but this was to be done in his own way. It seems apparent that some of those who believed the words of the Prophet, and perchance he partook somewhat of that same spirit, thought that it would be a great asset that would convince many of the truth of the Prophet's story, if the record of the Nephites could be placed on exhibition where all men could see them. The Lord has made it clear, in the Book of Mormon, that this was contrary to his will and in conflict with all of his dealings with the children of men. [2 Ne. 27:12-14, 23-25.] However, this thought must have been in Martin Harris' mind when he felt that even a view of the manuscript would be the means of convincing the members of his family, if they had the privilege of examining it. Evidently this matter had been discussed, for the Lord declared in this revelation: [Sec. 5:7-8, quoted.]

When we consider this declaration from the Lord we are reminded of the story of Lazarus and the rich man, as told in Luke. (16:19-31.) The story reads that the rich man, lifting his eyes in torment, pleaded with father Abraham to send Lazarus to dip his finger in water and cool his tongue. When he was informed that this could not be done, then he requested that Lazarus be sent back to earth to warn his five brothers and his father's house, that they might repent and not come to the same kind of torment. "Abraham saith unto him, They have Moses and the prophets; let them hear them. And he said, Nay, father Abraham: but if one went unto them from the dead they will repent. And he said unto him, If they hear not Moses and the prophets, neither will they be persuaded, though one rose from the dead."

The Lord has always sent his accredited witnesses to testify of his truth, and has declared that all who reject these witnesses shall be under condemnation. This revelation declared that this generation shall have the word of the Lord through Joseph Smith. There may be some who think that this is unreasonable, and the Lord should use some miraculous means to convert the world. Frequently when strangers . . . hear the story of the coming forth of the Book of Mormon, they ask if the plates are in some museum where they may be seen. Some of them with some scientific training, express themselves to the effect that if the scholars could see and examine the plates and learn to read them, they would bear witness to the truth of the Book of Mormon and the veracity of Joseph Smith and the whole world would then be converted. When they are informed that the angel took the plates again, they turn away in their skepticism, shaking their heads, but the Lord has said: "For my thoughts are not your thoughts neither are your ways my ways," saith the Lord. "For as the heavens are higher than the earth, so are my ways higher than your ways, and my thoughts than your thoughts." (Isa. 55:8-9) We have learned that people are not converted by miracles or by examining records. If the Lord had the plates where scholars could examine them, they would have scoffed at them just as much as they do today. People are converted by their hearts being penetrated by the Spirit of the Lord when they humbly hearken to the testimonies of the Lord's servants. The Jews witnessed the miracles of our Lord, but this did not prevent them from crying out against him and having him crucified. (CHMR, 1947, 1:36-37.)

Joseph Fielding Smith: 16-20

In giving the world the testimony of three witnesses in addition to Joseph Smith, the Lord fulfilled the law. We are called upon in this life to walk by faith, not by sight, not by the proclamation of heavenly messengers with the voice of thunder, but by the proclamation of accredited witnesses whom the Lord sends and by whom every word shall be established. [John 8:17.] The Lord made the promise that the testimony of the three should go forth with his words that were given through Joseph Smith, and this should be declared to all the world. These witnesses should know that these things are true and "from heaven will I declare it unto them," said the Lord. The testimony which they have given and which is recorded in each copy of the Book of Mormon in the most solemn language has gone forth to the four corners of the earth, in fulfillment of the promise made in the Book of Mormon. (See 2 Nephi 27:12-14.)

The effect of the testimony of the three witnesses is the power of salvation to all those who believe and accept the Gospel. On the other hand, it is the power of damnation to all those who, after having heard it, reject it. The Lord said in relation to the testimony of his servants: "Behold, I sent you out to testify and warn the people, and it becometh every man who hath been warned to warn his neighbor. Therefore, they are left without excuse, and their sins are upon their own heads." (D&C 88:81-82.) If the Lord will hold all those who have been warned under condemnation because they fail to warn neighbors, then what will he require of those who hear the testimony of his servants and reject it? Nephi warns the present generation that they should not reject his testimony and that of the other Nephite prophets, for they spoke as "the voice of one crying from the dust." Said he: "For what I seal on earth, shall be brought against you at the judgment bar; for thus hath the Lord commanded me, and I must obey." (2 Nephi 33:10-15.) Moroni also closed his record with a similar warning, declaring that "ye shall know that I lie not, for ye shall see me at the bar of God; and the Lord will say unto you: Did I not declare my words unto you, which were written by this man, like as one crying from the dead, yea, even as one speaking out of the dust?" [Moroni 10:27.]

Those who reject the solemn testimony of these three witnesses, or the testimony of others of the servants of the Lord, are guilty before the Lord and, according to his word, shall suffer condemnation.

It seems that quite generally mankind looks upon the word of the Lord as given by Isaiah and other prophets, in which they speak of the destruction of the wicked or the making of the earth empty, as figures of speech which are not to be taken literally. However, we have no reason to believe that the Lord means anything other than just what the words imply. The great and dreadful day of the Lord will come, and the wicked, according to his promise, shall be consumed. [Sec. 5:20, quoted.] (*CHMR*, 1947, 1:37-38.)

Orson Pratt: 16-18

The Lord has promised that if I will repent, if you will repent, if the people of the United States will repent, if the people of all the nations of the earth will repent, turn unto him and obey his commandments that they should receive the Holy Ghost. Will that give us a knowledge as clear, as definite, as pointed as could be revealed by the ministration of angels? Yes. . . .

We are living, then, in the great and last dispensation, in which God has provided a way that he might raise up scores of thousands of witnesses, a way that all might know as Peter did. Peter did not get his knowledge from seeing miracles wrought. He did not obtain his knowledge because some other man had received a knowledge. The Savior blessed him and said, "Blessed art thou, Simon Barjona, for flesh and blood hath not revealed it unto thee, but my Father which is in heaven." [Matt. 16:17.] The Lord had revealed this knowledge unto Peter, consequently Peter was constituted a witness. And so the Lord, by having given revelation from the heavens to scores of thousands of the Latter-day Saints, has made them witnesses of the divinity of this work. (*JD*, September 21, 1879, 21:175-76.)

Marion G. Romney: 19-20

Our whole world is in confusion. The wisdom of our wise men has proved inadequate to stay the rising crisis. With the means to unleash universal destruction in the hands of evil men, fear and apprehension ride with every breeze. In the past, situations similar to ours have generally terminated in destruction. It would seem that the judgments of God are about to be once more poured out upon the nations. [Mormon 8.]

The world situation being as it is, I feel impelled to emphasize the fact that . . . the Lord saw this one coming, and, in harmony with his universal pattern, sounded the warning and prescribed the means of escape. For although the pattern is universal so that the lesson may be clearly drawn from history, the Lord always warns the people of a new dispensation through prophets raised up unto them in their own day. This he has done for this generation through the great prophet of the restoration, Joseph Smith, Jr. Through him the Lord repeatedly declared that the world was ripening in iniquity and that unless men repented destruction would overtake them.

For example, in March, 1829, he said: [Sec. 5:19-20, quoted.]

You will note that this prediction, as were like predictions in the past, is conditional. "If they repent not," is the condition. For this generation, as for all others, the Lord has provided the means of escape. This means is now, and has always been, the Gospel of Jesus Christ. . . .

By spurning the warning and rejecting the means of escape, we shall most certainly bring upon ourselves the predicted destruction, for the words of Jesus, "Although . . . heaven and earth shall pass away; . . . my words shall not pass away" (Joseph Smith 1:35), are still immutable.

On the other hand, if men will hearken to and accept the means of escape, the Gospel of Jesus Christ as restored through the Prophet Joseph Smith, the rewards shall as certainly follow. Fears will give way to confidence; war clouds will fade; righteousness will come; peace will reign. Again there shall return to earth that glorious state of felicity which blessed the Nephites in the days of Jesus. [4 Nephi.] (CR, April 1958, pp. 128-29.)

Joseph Fielding Smith: 21-28

The wish of Martin Harris was granted on condition that he would humble himself and acknowledge the things that he had done which were wrong. He was commanded also that from this time henceforth he was to keep the commandments of the Lord. He was also to say to the world that the plates and such other things as should be shown he had seen by the gift and power of God, and his testimony was to be, "I know of a surety that they are true, for I have seen them, for they have been shown unto me by the power of God and not of man." More than this he was not to say. (*CHMR*, 1947, 1:38.)

John Taylor: 35

If I am doing right, I am preparing for thrones, principalities, and dominions, resolved by the help of God that no man shall rob me of my crown. With this view of the subject, all the outward circumstances of this life do not trouble me. (*JD*, June 17, 1860, 8:100.)

First Presidency (Heber J. Grant, Anthony W. Ivins, Charles W. Nibley): 35

Refrain from evil; do that which is good. Visit the sick, comfort those who are in sorrow, clothe the naked, feed the hungry, care for the widow and the fatherless. [Sec. 52:40.] Observe the laws of health which the Lord has revealed [Sec. 89], and keep yourselves unspotted from the sins of the world. [Sec. 59:9.] Pay your tithes and offerings, and the Lord will open the windows of heaven and pour out blessings until there shall not be room to contain them. [Sec. 119; Mal. 3:8-10.] Be obedient to the laws of God and the civil laws of the country in which you reside, and uphold and honor those who are chosen to administer them. [Sec. 58:21-22; 98:8-10; 134:6.] (*CR*, April 1930, p. 13.)

Mark E. Petersen: 35

All our lives we have been taught the doctrine that we must endure to the end if we expect to receive the blessings of salvation. [Sec. 14:7; 18:22; 50:5.] This requires continued devotion to our duty and devotion likewise to the high principles which the Lord has revealed to us in the Gospel of Christ.

The Church has had many outstanding examples of men and women who have been completely devoted to the cause, and have been willing to put God first in their lives and to mold their lives according to his desires. This is what is expected of us all. (*Your Faith and You*, 1953, pp. 98-99.)

Erastus Snow: 35

I understand that every son and daughter of Adam who hear the sound of the everlasting Gospel when it is proclaimed by a servant of God having authority, and who yield obedience to that Gospel and who retain that Holy Spirit and offer themselves in humility as candidates and receive baptism for the remission of sins, — such persons become candidates for celestial honors — for that inheritance which is eternal and fadeth not away, and eventually become prepared to enter into the glory and presence of the Father and the Son. This is the promise to the saints, if they continue faithful, and in all things abide the law of the Lord, and keep sacred and holy the covenants they made in baptism. [Sec. 76:50-70.] (JD, August 26, 1860, 8:218.)

SECTION 6

Revelation given to Joseph Smith the Prophet, and Oliver Cowdery, at Harmony, Pennsylvania, April, 1829. Oliver Cowdery began his labors as scribe, in the translation of the Book of Mormon, April 7, 1829. He had already received a divine manifestation attesting the truth of Joseph's testimony respecting the plates on which was engraved the Book of Mormon record. Joseph inquired of the Lord through the Urim and Thummim and received this response. See History of the Church, vol. 1, pp. 32-35. – Oliver's willingness to serve is commended; and both to him and to Joseph blessings of great import are promised.

1. A great and marvelous work is about to come forth unto the children of men.

2. Behold, I am God; give heed unto my word, which is quick and powerful, sharper than a two-edged sword, to the dividing asunder of both joints and marrow; therefore give heed unto my words.

3. Behold, the field is white already to harvest; therefore, whoso desireth to reap, let him thrust in his sickle with his might, and reap while the day lasts, that he may treasure up for his soul everlasting salvation in the kingdom of God.

4. Yea, whosoever will thrust in his sickle and reap, the same is called of God.

5. Therefore, if you will ask of me you shall receive; if you will knock it shall be opened unto you.

6. Now, as you have asked, behold, I say unto you, keep my commandments, and seek to bring forth and establish the cause of Zion;

7. Seek not for riches but for wisdom, and behold, the mysteries of God shall be unfolded unto you, and then shall you be made rich. Behold, he that hath eternal life is rich.

8. Verily, verily, I say unto you, even as you desire of me so it shall be unto you; and if you desire, you shall be the means of doing much good in this generation.

9. Say nothing but repentance unto this generation; keep my commandments, and assist to bring forth my work, according to my commandments, and you shall be blessed.

10. Behold thou hast a gift, and blessed art thou because of thy gift. Remember it is sacred and cometh from above —

11. And if thou wilt inquire, thou shalt know mysteries which are great and marvelous; therefore thou shalt exercise thy gift, that thou mayest find out mysteries, that thou mayest bring many to the knowledge of the truth, yea, convince them of the error of their ways.

12. Make not thy gift known unto any save it be those who are of thy faith. Trifle not with sacred things.

13. If thou wilt do good, yea, and hold out faithful to the end, thou shalt be saved in the kingdom of God, which is the greatest of all the gifts of God; for there is no gift greater than the gift of salvation.

14. Verily, verily, I say unto thee, blessed art thou for what thou hast done; for thou hast inquired of me, and behold, as often as thou hast inquired thou hast received instruction of my Spirit. If it had not been so, thou wouldst not have come to the place where thou art at this time.

15. Behold, thou knowest that thou hast inquired of me and I did enlighten thy mind; and now I tell thee these things that thou mayest know that thou hast been enlightened by the Spirit of truth;

16. Yea, I tell thee, that thou mayest know that there is none else save God that knowest thy thoughts and the intents of thy heart.

17. I tell thee these things as a witness unto thee — that the words or the work which thou hast been writing are true.

18. Therefore be diligent; stand by my servant Joseph, faithfully, in whatsoever difficult circumstances he may be for the word's sake.

19. Admonish him in his faults, and also receive admonition of him. Be patient; be sober; be temperate; have patience, faith, hope and charity.

20. Behold, thou art Oliver, and I have spoken unto thee because of thy desires; therefore treasure up these words in thy heart. Be faithful and diligent in keeping the commandments of God, and I will encircle thee in the arms of my love.

21. Behold, I am Jesus Christ, the Son of God. I am the same that came unto mine own, and mine own received me not. I am the light which shineth in darkness, and the darkness comprehendeth it not.

22. Verily, verily, I say unto you, if you desire a further witness, cast your mind upon the night that you cried unto me in your heart, that you might know concerning the truth of these things.

23. Did I not speak peace to your mind concerning the matter? What greater witness can you have than from God?

24. And now, behold, you have received a witness; for if I have told you things which no man knoweth have you not received a witness?

25. And, behold, I grant unto you a gift, if you desire of me, to translate, even as my servant Joseph.

26. Verily, verily, I say unto you, that there are records

which contain much of my gospel, which have been kept back because of the wickedness of the people;

27. And now I command you, that if you have good desires — a desire to lay up treasures for yourself in heaven — then shall you assist in bringing to light, with your gift, those parts of my scriptures which have been hidden because of iniquity.

28. And now, behold, I give unto you, and also unto my servant Joseph, the keys of this gift, which shall bring to light this ministry; and in the mouth of two or three witnesses shall every word be established.

29. Verily, verily, I say unto you, if they reject my words, and this part of my gospel and ministry, blessed are ye, for they can do no more unto you than unto me.

30. And even if they do unto you even as they have done unto me, blessed are ye, for you shall dwell with me in glory.

31. But if they reject not my words, which shall be established by the testimony which shall be given, blessed are they, and then shall ye have joy in the fruit of your labors.

32. Verily, verily, I say unto you, as I said unto my disciples, where two or three are gathered together in my name, as touching one thing, behold, there will I be in the midst of them — even so am I in the midst of you.

33. Fear not to do good, my sons, for whatsoever ye sow, that shall ye also reap; therefore, if ye sow good ye shall also reap good for your reward.

34. Therefore, fear not, little flock; do good; let earth and hell combine against you, for if ye are built upon my rock, they cannot prevail.

35. Behold, I do not condemn you; go your ways and sin no more; perform with soberness the work which I have commanded you.

36. Look unto me in every thought; doubt not, fear not.

37. Behold the wounds which pierced my side, and also the prints of the nails in my hands and feet; be faithful, keep my commandments, and ye shall inherit the kingdom of heaven. Amen.

Joseph Smith: *Introduction*

On the 5th day of April, 1829, Oliver Cowdery came to my house, until which time I had never seen him. He stated to me that, having been teaching school in the neighborhood where my father resided, and my father being one of those who sent to the school, he went to board for a season at his house, and while there the family related to him the circumstances of my having received the plates, and accordingly he had come to make inquiries of me. Two days after the arrival of Mr. Cowdery (being the 7th of April) I commenced to translate the Book of Mormon, and he began to write for me, which, having continued for some time, I inquired of the Lord through the Urim and Thummim, and obtained the following: [Section 6, follows.] (*HC* 1:32-33, April 1829; Harmony, Pennsylvania.)

John A. Widtsoe: 1

At least one prophecy of the Prophet Joseph Smith has been literally fulfilled. When he was not much more than a boy, in the early years of his manhood, before the Church was organized, the Lord said to him: [Sec. 6:1, quoted.]

Unknown, untaught, with no reputation, he should have been forgotten in the small hamlet, almost nameless, in the backwoods of a great state; but he dared to say that the work that he was doing, under God's instruction, was to become a marvel and a wonder in the world. We know . . . that whether it be friend or enemy who speaks of us, if he is a sober-thinking, honest man, he will declare that whatever in his opinion the foundations of this work may be — we know the foundations — it is a marvelous work and a wonder, none like it in the long history of the world. The truths set loose by the Prophet Joseph Smith have touched every man of faith throughout the whole civilized world, and measurably changed their beliefs for good. (*CR*, April 1946, pp. 21-22.)

George Teasdale: 5

It is easy to understand the principles of eternal life if we want to know them, because the Lord has said, "Ask, and ye shall receive; knock, and it shall be opened unto you; seek, and ye shall find." [Matt. 7:7.] (*CR*, October 1901, p. 38.)

Joseph Fielding Smith: 5

There is no reason in the world why any soul should not know where to find the truth. If he will only humble himself and seek in the spirit of humility and faith, going to the Lord just as the Prophet Joseph Smith went to the Lord to find the truth, he will find it. There's no doubt about it. There is no reason in the world, if men would only hearken to the whisperings of the Spirit of the Lord and seek as he would have them seek for the knowledge and understanding of the Gospel of Jesus Christ, for them not to find it, no reason, except the hardness of their hearts and their love of the world. "Knock, and it shall be opened unto you." This is my testimony. I know it is true. (CR, April 1951, p. 59.)

Joseph Smith: 6

We ought to have the building up of Zion as our greatest object. (HC 3:390, July 2, 1839.)

Joseph Fielding Smith: 6

In the early days of the Church the brethren came to the Prophet Joseph Smith asking what the Lord would have them do. The answer given to them was "to bring forth the cause of Zion." That is our work, to establish Zion, to build up the kingdom of God, to preach the Gospel to every creature in the world that not one soul may be overlooked where there is the possibility for us to present unto him the truth. (CR, April 1951, pp. 152-53.)

Anthon H. Lund: 7
Seek not for riches

The Lord, in one of his revelations given early in the Church, says: [Sec. 6:7, quoted]. The riches of eternal life we ought to seek, not the riches of the world. . . .We do not look upon wealth in itself as a curse. We believe that those who can handle means rightly can do much to bless their fellows. But he who is ruled by the love of money is tempted to commit sin. The love of money is the root of all evil. [1 Tim. 6:10.] There is hardly a commandment but is violated through this seeking for riches. (CR, April 1903, p. 24.)

Heber J. Grant: 7
Seek not for riches

The great criterion of success in the world is that men can make money, but I want to say to you Latter-day Saints that to do this is not true success. . . . What is the matter? Why, the appetite for money grows upon a man, increases and strengthens unless he is careful, just as much as the appetite for whiskey, and it gets possession of him, and he loves the money instead of loving it only for the good that he can do with it. He does not estimate properly the value of things. (CR, October 1911, p. 23-24.)

Brigham Young: 7
Seek not for riches

It is thought by many that the possession of gold and silver will produce for them happiness, and hence, thousands hunt the mountains for the precious metals; in this they are mistaken. The possession of wealth alone does not produce happiness, although it will produce comfort, when it can be exchanged for the essentials and luxuries of life. When wealth is obtained by purloining, or if any other unfair and dishonorable way, fear of detection and punishment robs the possessor of all human happiness. When wealth is honorably obtained by men, still the possession of it is embittered by the thought that death will soon strip them of it and others will possess it. What hopes have they in the future, after they get through with this sorrowful world? They know nothing about the future; they see nothing but death and hell. Solid comfort and unalloyed joy are unknown to them. When the faithful Latter-day Saints come to the end of their earthly existence, "we know that if our earthly house of this tabernacle were dissolved, we have a building of God, an house not made with hands, eternal in the heavens." [2 Cor. 5:1.] The faithful Latter-day Saint knows that the dissolution of this mortal house will introduce his immortal spirit to freedom from death and punishment, and to the enjoyment of the society of the spirits of just men made perfect. To a person who has such a glorious hope everything is bright and beautiful. If he has but little, he enjoys that little with a thankful heart to his Heavenly Father; if he possesses much, he is still thankful, not worshipping, or placing his heart upon the filthy lucre God has placed in his power to do good with. In poverty he feels blest and happy; in riches he feels blest and happy; for his hope is in God, and his wealth consists in eternal riches, having laid up treasures in heaven, where moth doth not destroy, nor rust corrode, nor thief break through nor steal. [Matt. 6:19.] (JD, December 11, 1864, 11:15-16.)

Orson F. Whitney: 7
Seek not for riches

What more eloquent preaching of the Gospel has there ever been, in this or any previous age, than the great gathering movement which has been going on since Joseph Smith lifted up the standard of the restored Gospel in this dispensation? There is no more eloquent preaching than when men and women will forsake their native land, their homes, their parents, their children, their material possessions — every earthly thing, and cross the stormy ocean, the heated plains, the frosty mountains, many of them laying down their lives, to be buried in lonely graves by the wayside; pulling hand carts, wading rivers, crossing deserts, climbing mountains, and settling in a barren waste — all for what? Was it for gold and silver, houses and lands, flocks and herds, and the betterment of their temporal condition? Was it for the honors of men and the applause of the world that they did these things? No, it was because they loved God and wanted to build up his kingdom. They had heard the voice of the Shepherd; they were his sheep, and a stranger they would not follow. [John 10:1-5.] Yet these people, our grandfathers and grandmothers, our parents, who came from Scandinavia, from Germany, from Switzerland, from England, Scotland, and Wales, from Australia and the islands of the sea, from Canada and the States of the Union, braving every hardship, facing every peril, laying their all upon the altar, coming out and fighting for God and his divine purpose — they are called by some "the offscourings of the earth," "the scum of creation!" Perhaps it is because they "came out on top!" (laughter.) But cream also rises, and if I were asked to characterize and describe the Latter-day Saints who have made such sacrifices, I would say they are the cream of God's creation — the heroes and heroines of modern times. There is no more eloquent preaching of the Gospel than is found in their toils and privations, in their struggles and achievements. (CR, April 1915, p. 101.)

Joseph Smith: 7
The mysteries of God shall be unfolded unto you

Many men will say, "I will never forsake you, but will stand by you at all times." But the moment you teach them some of the mysteries of the kingdom of God that are retained in the heavens and are to be revealed to the children of men when they are prepared for them, they will be the first to stone you and put you to death. (HC 5:424, June 11, 1843.)

Joseph Fielding Smith: 7
The mysteries of God shall be unfolded unto you

The Lord has promised to reveal his mysteries to those who serve him in faithfulness. . . . There are no mysteries pertaining to the Gospel, only as we, in our weakness, fail to comprehend Gospel truth. The Gospel is very simple, so that even children at the age of accountability may understand it. Without question, there are principles which in this life we cannot understand, but when the fulness comes we will see that all is plain and reasonable and within our comprehension. The "simple" principles of the Gospel, such as baptism, the atonement, are mysteries to those who do not have the guidance of the Spirit of the Lord. (CHMR, 1947, 1:40.)

Francis M. Lyman: 7
He that hath eternal life is rich

We will seek the riches of eternity here. We can take the riches of eternal life with us when we leave this sphere, but we cannot take the riches of this world. [Alma 39:14.] Yet the riches of this are convenient and necessary, and we cannot very well get along without them. But the riches of eternal life are lasting and permanent. They come from the good we accomplish, the righteousness we bring to pass, the purity to which we attain, the cleansing and purifying of our own hearts, that we may come as near being perfect in this life as our Father and his Son, Jesus Christ, are perfect. Why shall we not do right? What commandments of the Lord are there that we cannot observe? What requirements are there in this Church that we cannot comply with? The Lord wants us to have faith in him. Now, that is possible. He has the faith to bestow. He is the giver of it. Man cannot import it. It is the gift of God — a gift that he is anxious to bestow upon all his children. (CR, April 1899, pp. 38-39.)

John A. Widtsoe: 8
Even as you desire of me so it shall be unto you

If we want something for this Church and Kingdom, or if we want something for our individual lives, we must have a great, earnest, overpowering desire for that thing. We must reach out for it, with full faith in our Heavenly Father that the gift may be given us. Then it would seem as if the Lord himself cannot resist our petition. If our desire is strong enough, if our whole will is tempered and attuned to that which we desire, if our lives make us worthy of the desired gift, the Lord, by his own words, is bound to give us that which we desire, in his own time and in his own manner. (CR, April 1935, p. 82.)

Joseph Fielding Smith: 9
Say nothing but repentance

In the revelation to Oliver Cowdery, and to several others who came to ask what the Lord would have them do, the Lord said: "Say nothing but repentance unto this generation; keep my commandments, and assist to bring forth my work." We must not infer from this expression that those who went forth to preach were limited in their teachings so that all they could say was "repent from your sins," but in

teaching the principles of the Gospel they should do so with
the desire to teach repentance to the people and bring them
in humility to a realization of the need for remission of sins.
Even today in all of our preaching it should be with the desire
to bring people to repentance and faith in God. That was the
burden of John's message as he went forth to prepare the way
for the Lord: "Repent ye; for the kingdom of heaven is at
hand," he declared to the people, but he also taught them
the necessity of baptism and officiated in that ordinance for
all who repented of their sins. [Matt. 3:11.] (*CHMR*, 1947,
1:39-40.)

Joseph F. Smith: 13
If thou wilt do good

Now, so long as the Latter-day Saints are content to
obey the commandments of God, to appreciate the privileges
and blessings which they enjoy in the Church, and will use
their time, their talents, their substance, in honor to the
name of God, to build up Zion, and to establish truth and
righteousness in the earth, so long our Heavenly Father is
bound by his oath and covenant to protect them from every
opposing foe, and to help them to overcome every obstacle
that can possibly be arrayed against them or thrown in their
pathway; but the moment a community begin to be wrapt up
in themselves, become selfish, become engrossed in the
temporalities of life, and put their faith in riches, that moment the power of God begins to withdraw from them, and if
they repent not the Holy Spirit will depart from them entirely, and they will be left to themselves. That which was
given them will be taken away, they will lose that which they
had, for they will not be worthy of it. God is just as well as
merciful, and we need not expect favors at the hand of the
Almighty except as we merit them, at least in the honest
desire of our hearts, and the desire and intent will not always
avail unless our acts correspond. For we are engaged in a
literal work, a reality; and we must practice as well as profess.
We must be what God requires us to be, or else we are not his
people nor the Zion which he designed to gather together
and to build up in the latter days upon the earth. (*JD*, April
8, 1883, 24:176.)

James E. Talmage: 13
Thou shalt be saved in the kingdom of God

Our belief in the universal application of the atonement implies no supposition that all mankind will be saved with like endowments of glory and power. In the kingdom of God there are numerous degrees or gradations provided for those who are worthy of them; in the house of our Father there are many mansions, into which only those who are prepared are admitted. . . . [Sec. 98:18; 88:20-24.] There are some who have striven to obey all the divine commandments, who have accepted the testimony of Christ, obeyed "the laws and ordinances of the Gospel," and received the Holy Spirit; these are they who have overcome evil by Godly works and who are therefore entitled to the highest glory; these belong to the Church of the Firstborn, unto whom the Father has given all things; they are made kings and priests of the Most High, after the order of Melchizedek; they possess celestial bodies, "whose glory is that of the sun, even the glory of God, the highest of all, whose glory the sun of the firmament is written of as being typical" [Sec. 76:70]; they are admittd to the glorified company, crowned with exaltation in the Celestial Kingdom. (*AF*, 1950, pp. 91-92.)

Joseph Smith: 14-24

After we had received this revelation [Section 6], Oliver Cowdery stated to me that after he had gone to my father's to board, and after the family had communicated to him concerning my having obtained the plates, that one night after he had retired to bed he called upon the Lord to know if these things were so, and the Lord manifested to him that they were true, but he had kept the circumstances entirely secret, and had mentioned it to no one; so that after this revelation was given he knew that the work was true, because no being living knew of the thing alluded to in the revelation, but God and himself. (*HC* 1:35, April 1829.)

Orson Pratt: 14-24

"Elder Orson Pratt: Did you see the angel at this time?

"David Whitmer: Yes, he stood before us. Our testimony as recorded in the Book of Mormon is strictly and absolutely true, just as it is there written. Before I knew Joseph [Smith], I had heard about him and the plates from persons who declared they knew he had them, and swore they would get them from him. When Oliver Cowdery went to Pennsylvania, he promised to write me what he should learn about these matters, which he did. He wrote me that Joseph had told him his (Oliver's) secret thoughts, and all he had meditated about going to see him, which no man on earth knew, as he supposed, but himself, and so he stopped to write for Joseph. Soon after this, Joseph sent for me (D. Whitmer) to come to Harmony to get him and Oliver and bring them to my father's house. I did not know what to do, I was pressed with my work. I had some 20 acres to plow, so I concluded I would finish plowing and then go. I got up one morning to go to work as usual, and on going to the field, found between five and seven acres of my ground had been plowed during the night. I don't know who did it; but it was done just I would have done it myself, and the plow was left standing in the furrow. This enabled me to start sooner. When I arrived at Harmony, Joseph and Oliver were coming toward me, and met me some distance from the house. Oliver told me that Joseph had informed him when I started from home, where I had stopped the first night, how I read the sign at the tavern, where I stopped the next night, etc., and that I would be there that day before dinner, and this is why they had come out to meet me; all of which was exactly as Joseph had told Oliver, at which I was greatly astonished." (*Historical Record, Church Encyclopedia*, Book I, May 1887, 6:208-9.)

Orson Pratt: 26
There are records which contain much of my gospel

Then he [Nephi] saw in the latter days . . . that by the power of God the records of his people should come forth; and he saw that a Church of the saints should arise, and that it should spread itself upon all the face of the earth, among all the nations and kingdoms of the Gentiles; and he saw also that the great and abominable church that was among all the nations of the Gentiles, having dominion among all people and tongues, should gather together in multitudes among the nations of the earth and fight against the Lamb of God and against the Saints of the Most High and his covenant people. [1 Nephi 14:10-13.]

But what I wish to call your attention to at this time is one event which has been in a measure literally fulfilled. It is an event that no man, unless he were a prophet inspired by the Most High God, could have had a heart big enough to prophesy of with the least expectation of its fulfillment; and that is, the Church of the Lamb of God that was to be raised up after the coming forth of these records of the ancient Israelites should be among all nations and kingdoms of the Gentiles. [1 Nephi 14:14.]

This was uttered and printed before the Church of Latter-day Saints was in existence. How could a young man, inexperienced as Joseph Smith was, have had all this foreknowledge of future events, unless he was inspired of God? How did he know that any church believing in the Book of Mormon would arise? He was then in the act of translating these records; the Church had not yet an existence; and he was young, inexperienced, and ignorant as regards the education and wisdom of this world. How did he know that, after his manuscript was published, a church called the Church of the Lamb would arise and be built upon the fulness of the Gospel contained in the book? How did he know that, if it did arise, it would have one year's existence? What wisdom, education, or power could have given him this foreknowledge independent of the power of God? How could he know, if a church should arise, that it would have any influence beyond his own neighborhood? How did he know it would extend through the state of New York, where it was first raised? How could he know that it would extend over the United States, and much more, that it would go to all nations and kingdoms of the Gentiles? And how did he know that the dominions of this Church among all the nations and kingdoms of the Gentiles should be small, because of the wickedness of the great "mother of abominations"? How did he know that the "mother of harlots" among these Gentiles would gather together in great multitudes among all the nations and kingdoms of the earth to fight against the Saints of the Lamb of God? Common sense tells us that this would be taking a stretch far beyond what any false prophet dare take, with any hope of fulfillment. (JD, July 10, 1859, 7:182-83.)

John A. Widtsoe: 28
In the mouth of two or three witnesses

Oliver Cowdery, whose reputation for honesty has never been questioned, was with Joseph Smith when John the Baptist came to restore the authority of the Aaronic Priesthood, and when Peter, James and John appeared to restore the Melchizedek Priesthood, and also when the foundation-laying revelations from spiritual beings, given at the time of the dedication of the Kirtland Temple, were received. [Sec. 13; 27:12-13; 110.] Of all these joint experiences, Oliver Cowdery often bore testimony.

Sidney Rigdon, who was with Joseph Smith when the revelation called the Vision was received, bore testimony in diverse places to the glimpse at that time, with Joseph Smith, of heavenly personages, including the Lord himself. [Sec. 76:19-24.] (*Joseph Smith*, 1957, pp. 338-39.)

John A. Widtsoe: 32
There will I be in the midst of them

At times it has seemed to me that the spirit that has moved upon those who have spoken and listened in the small gatherings in the mission field has been even stronger and more powerful than we feel here at home. It often happens that, when far away from home, far from the sheltered protection of the temple, the tabernacle, and stakes of Zion, we draw more heavily upon the spiritual forces about us. (CR, April 1934, p. 113.)

Brigham Young: 33
If ye sow good ye shall also reap good

A man who wishes to receive light and knowledge, to increase in the faith of the Holy Ghost, and to grow in the knowledge of the truth as it is in Jesus Christ, will find that when he imparts knowledge to others he will also grow and increase. Be not miserly in your feelings, but get knowledge and understanding by freely imparting it to others, and be not like a man who selfishly hoards his gold; for that man will not thus increase upon the amount, but will become contracted in his views and feelings. So the man who will not impart freely of the knowledge he has received will become so contracted in his mind that he cannot receive truth when it is presented to him. Wherever you see an opportunity to do good, do it, for that is the way to increase and grow in the knowledge of the truth. [Sec. 58:26-28.] (JD, April 8, 1855, 2:267.)

L. Tom Perry: 33

"There is a law, irrevocably decreed in heaven before the foundations of this world, upon which all blessings are predicated—

"And when we obtain any blessing from God, it is by obedience to that law upon which it is predicated." (D&C 130:20-21.)

The Lord has clearly charted a course for us to obtain his blessings. He is bound by his divine law to bless us for our righteousness. The overwhelming question in each age is why each generation must test his law, when the Lord's performance from generation to generation has been absolutely consistent. Is this not the time to again reexamine our position? Is that which we are building in our personal lives, our families, our communities, and our nations firmly anchored to a foundation based on divine law? (CR, April 1976, p. 98.)

George Q. Cannon: 34

Every man and woman who has received the truth should live in such a manner before the Lord as to have the light of the Holy Spirit constantly beaming upon their minds. They should be in close communion through that Holy Spirit, with their God, so that if they had to stand alone in the midst of a gainsaying world they should be a living witness to the truth of the Gospel and the power of God manifested in these days, and that if the Priesthood from Zion were to be withdrawn from their midst, they could stand firm and unshaken, enjoying the light of revelation and having the consciousness that God was directing them in all their ways. (MS, January 3, 1863, 25:9.)

John A. Widtsoe: 34-37

I remember reading, when a boy, a helpful passage from the Doctrine and Covenants. Let me read it here in conclusion. As a lad I felt fear, sometimes of men, but more often of the dark outside forces. I often wondered if this persecuted people, after all, would be able to accomplish all that was pictured in its destiny. Then I found in my reading of the Doctrine and Covenants this passage which has been a joy and a help and a strength to me all my life, for the Lord said to his people in Harmony, Pennsylvania, before the Church was organized: [Sec. 6:34-37, quoted.]

What do we care for the slanderer or the liar; what do we care for the enemy who arises to defeat our holy purposes? We have the truth, the mightiest weapon God has given to his people, and we shall win, in the end, if we do the things that God requires us to do. (CR, October 1923, p. 27.)

Ezra Taft Benson: 36

In the Church we have no fear that any discovery of new truths will ever be in conflict with these standards — with any fundamental basic principle which we advocate in the Gospel. Truth is always consistent. This fact gives to us as members of the Church a feeling of great security, a feeling of peace, a feeling of assurance. We know beyond any question that the truths which we advocate, the truths of the Gospel restored to the earth through the Prophet Joseph, are in very deed the truths of heaven. These truths will always be consistent with the discovery of any new truths, whether discovered in the laboratory, through research of the scientist, or whether revealed from heaven through prophets of God. Time is always on the side of truth. (CR, April 1958, p. 60.)

Richard L. Evans: 36

Keep courage. Do not feel sorry for yourselves. Whatever you do, do not feel sorry for yourselves. You live in a great age of opportunity. I remember the words of one very sharp and shrewd observer who said, "Whenever I hear someone sigh and say that life is hard, I am tempted to ask 'compared to what'?" What are the alternatives? No one ever promised us it would be easy. It is a schooling; it is an opportunity; it is a learning period, and a wonderful one. Despite all the disappointments and difficulties, the great and ultimate rewards are beyond price.

Keep faith. "And, if you keep my commandments," the Lord God has said to us, "and endure to the end you shall have eternal life, which gift is the greatest of all the gifts of God." [D&C 14:7.] (CR, April 1961, p. 76.)

SECTION 7

Revelation given to Joseph Smith the Prophet, and Oliver Cowdery, at Harmony, Pennsylvania, April, 1829, when they inquired through the Urim and Thummim as to whether John, the beloved disciple, tarried in the flesh or had died. The revelation is the translated version of the record made on parchment by John and hidden up by himself. See History of the Church, vol. 1, pp. 35, 36.

1. And the Lord said unto me: John, my beloved, what desirest thou? For if you shall ask what you will, it shall be granted unto you.

2. And I said unto him: Lord, give unto me power over death, that I may live and bring souls unto thee.

3. And the Lord said unto me: Verily, verily, I say unto thee, because thou desirest this thou shalt tarry until I come in my glory, and shalt prophesy before nations, kindreds, tongues and people.

4. And for this cause the Lord said unto Peter: If I will that he tarry till I come, what is that to thee? For he desired of me that he might bring souls unto me, but thou desiredst that thou mightest speedily come unto me in my kingdom.

5. I say unto thee, Peter, this was a good desire; but my beloved has desired that he might do more, or a greater work yet among men than what he has before done.

6. Yea, he has undertaken a greater work; therefore I will make him as flaming fire and a ministering angel; he shall minister for those who shall be heirs of salvation who dwell on the earth.

7. And I will make thee to minister for him and for thy brother James; and unto you three I will give this power and the keys of this ministry until I come.

8. Verily I say unto you, ye shall both have according to your desires, for ye both joy in that which ye have desired.

Joseph Smith: *Introduction*

During the month of April I continued to translate, and he (Oliver Cowdery) to write, with little cessation, during which time we received several revelations. A difference of opinion arising between us about the account of John the Apostle, mentioned in the New Testament, as to whether he died or continued to live, we mutually agreed to settle it by the Urim and Thummim and the following is the word which we received: [Sec. 7:1-8, follows.] (*HC* 1:35-36, April 1829; Harmony, Pennsylvania.)

Joseph Fielding Smith: 1-8

From this revelation the conversation between our Lord and Peter recorded in the twenty-first chapter of John (verses 18-24), is clarified, and we know that John was blessed with the privilege of remaining on the earth until the second coming of Christ. This also explains the words of the Savior regarding some remaining until he should come to his kingdom. [Matt. 16:28.]

This desire made by John was a noble one, for he desired to live, not that he might lengthen out his life in mortality, for that of itself would not have been a blessing, but that he might bring souls unto Christ. Peter's desire was a very natural one — to come to the Lord as soon as his mission was finished on the earth. John desired, because of his love of mankind, that he might do a greater work by laboring in this mortal world until Christ should come the second time, in the clouds of glory.

When Jesus Christ visited the Nephites on this continent, he also chose twelve men and gave them authority similar to the authority of the Twelve at Jerusalem, that they might labor among their people in the Church and for the salvation of souls. Before he left them he granted their desires, as he had to Peter and John. Nine of the Twelve chose the same blessing that Peter did, but three of them "sorrowed in their hearts, for they durst not speak unto him the thing which they desired." "And he said unto them: Behold, I know your thoughts, and ye have desired the thing which John, my beloved, who was with me in my ministry, before that I was lifted up by the Jews, desired of me." (See 3 Nephi 28:6.)

"Therefore more blessed are ye, for ye shall never taste of death; but ye shall live to behold all the doings of the Father unto the children of men, even until all things shall be fulfilled according to the will of the Father, when I shall come in my glory with the powers of heaven." [3 Nephi 28:5-7.] (*CHMR*, 1947, 1:44.)

Joseph Smith: 6
As flaming fire and a ministering angel

Now the doctrine of translation is a power which belongs to this Priesthood. There are many things which belong to the powers of the Priesthood and the keys thereof, that have been kept hid from before the foundation of the world; they are hid from the wise and prudent to be revealed in the last times.

Many have supposed that the doctrine of translation was a doctrine whereby men were taken immediately into the presence of God, and into an eternal fulness, but this is a mistaken idea. Their place of habitation is that of the terrestrial order, and a place prepared for such characters he held in reserve to be ministering angels unto many planets, and who as yet have not entered into so great a fulness as those who are resurrected from the dead. "Others were tortured, not accepting deliverance, that they might obtain a better resurrection." (Heb. 11th chap., part of the 35th verse.)

Now it was evident that there was a better resurrection, or else God would not have revealed it unto Paul. Wherein then, can it be said a better resurrection. This distinction is made between the doctrine of the actual resurrection and translation: translation obtains deliverance from the tortures and sufferings of the body, but their existence will prolong as to the labors and toils of the ministry, before they can enter into so great a rest and glory. (*HC* 4:209-10, October 5, 1840.)

Translated bodies cannot enter into rest until they have undergone a change equivalent to death. Translated bodies are designed for future missions. (*HC* 4:425, October 3, 1841.)

Heber C. Kimball: 6
As flaming fire and a ministering angel

When the Prophet Joseph [Smith] had finished the

endowments of the First Presidency, the Twelve and the Presiding Bishops, the First Presidency proceeded to lay hands upon each one of them to seal and confirm the anointing; and at the close of each blessing the whole of the quorums responded to it with a loud shout of Hosanna! Hosanna! etc. [In the Kirtland Temple.]

While these things were being attended to, the beloved disciple John was seen in our midst by the Prophet Joseph, Oliver Cowdery and others. (*Life of Heber C. Kimball,* March 1836, pp. 91-92.)

Joseph Fielding Smith: 7
The keys of this ministry

The keys of the ministry which John says (Sec. 7:7) were given to Peter, James and himself, constituted the authority of Presidency of the Church in their dispensation. (See *DHC* 3:387; Matt. 17:1-9; D&C 81:1-2.) These keys were given at the transfiguration to these three Apostles, and they in turn gave them to Joseph Smith and Oliver Cowdery in this dispensation. (D&C 27:12-13; 128:20.) (*CHMR,* 1947, 1:45.)

SECTION 8

Revelation given through Joseph Smith the Prophet, to Oliver Cowdery, at Harmony, Pennsylvania, April, 1829. In the course of the translation of the Book of Mormon, Oliver, who continued to serve as scribe, writing at the prophet's dictation, desired to be endowed with the gift of translation. The Lord responded to his supplication by granting this revelation. − The spirit of revelation is defined and the gift of Aaron specified.

1. Oliver Cowdery, verily, verily, I say unto you, that assuredly as the Lord liveth, who is your God and your Redeemer, even so surely shall you receive a knowledge of whatsoever things you shall ask in faith, with an honest heart, believing that you shall receive a knowledge concerning the engravings of old records, which are ancient, which contain those parts of my scripture of which has been spoken by the manifestation of my Spirit.

2. Yea, behold, I will tell you in your mind and in your heart, by the Holy Ghost, which shall come upon you and which shall dwell in your heart.

3. Now, behold, this is the spirit of revelation; behold, this is the spirit by which Moses brought the children of Israel through the Red Sea on dry ground.

4. Therefore this is thy gift; apply unto it, and blessed art thou, for it shall deliver you out of the hands of your enemies, when, if it were not so, they would slay you and bring your soul to destruction.

5. Oh, remember these words, and keep my commandments. Remember, this is your gift.

6. Now this is not all thy gift; for you have another gift, which is the gift of Aaron; behold, it has told you many things;

7. Behold, there is no other power, save the power of God, that can cause this gift of Aaron to be with you.

8. Therefore, doubt not, for it is the gift of God; and you shall hold it in your hands, and do marvelous works; and no power shall be able to take it away out of your hands, for it is the work of God.

9. And, therefore, whatsoever you shall ask me to tell you by that means, that will I grant unto you, and you shall have knowledge concerning it.

10. Remember that without faith you can do nothing; therefore ask in faith. Trifle not with these things; do not ask for that which you ought not.

11. Ask that you may know the mysteries of God, and that you may translate and receive knowledge from all those ancient

records which have been hid up, that are sacred; and according to your faith shall it be done unto you.

12. Behold, it is I that have spoken it; and I am the same that spake unto you from the beginning. Amen.

Joseph Smith: *Introduction*

Whilst continuing the work of translation, during the month of April, Oliver Cowdery became exceedingly anxious to have the power to translate bestowed upon him, and in relation to this desire the following revelations were obtained: [Sections 8 and 9, follow.] (HC 1:36, April 1829; Harmony, Pennsylvania.)

Joseph Fielding Smith: 1-5

The Lord placed great emphasis on the necessity of holding sacred the gifts of God. Oliver had a gift (Sec. 8:3-4), even that of revelation, but he was admonished to receive it in humility and with a contrite spirit. All who receive gifts of the Spirit should do so with a humble spirit. The gifts are sacred and we should hold them so, and "trifle not with sacred things." [Sec. 6:12.] No doubt but Oliver Cowdery and Joseph Smith were impressed with this counsel, for it was only a short time before when Joseph Smith was punished, and Martin Harris lost the privilege of being associated in the work of translation because of trifling with sacred things. Oliver had learned of the punishment meted out to Martin Harris. [Sec. 3:12-13; 10:6-7; 19:20.] This admonition should be thoughtfully considered by every Elder of the Church, for trifling with the gifts may lead to dire consequences, even to loss of life, and at any event brings displeasure of God. His gifts are holy, sacred, and all who receive them should remember from whence they come and for what they are to be used. [Sec. 46:9-10.] (CHMR, 1947, 1:40.)

Joseph Smith: 2-3

The Spirit of Revelation is in connection with these blessings. A person may profit by noticing the first intimation of the spirit of revelation; for instance, when you feel pure intelligence flowing unto you, it may give you sudden strokes of ideas, so that by noticing it, you may find it fulfilled the same day or soon; (i.e.) those things that were presented into your minds by the Spirit of God [Sec. 85:6; Enos 10], will come to pass; and thus by learning the Spirit of God and understanding it, you may grow into the principle of revelation, until you become perfect in Christ Jesus. (HC 3:381, June 26, 1839.)

Heber J. Grant: 2-3

The Lord gives to many of us the still, small voice of revelation. [Sec. 85:6.] It comes as vividly and strongly as though it were with a great sound. It comes to each man, according to his needs and faithfulness, for guidance in matters that pertain to his own life. For the Church as a whole it comes to those who have been ordained to speak for the Church as a whole — and I say to you again, that it is the duty of the presidency of this Church to ask the people to do anything and everything that the inspiration of God tells them to do. We as Latter-day Saints, holding the Priesthood of God, should magnify it [Sec. 84:33-38], and we should respect the General Authorities of the Church; and as we respect them, God will respect us. [Sec. 124:84, 118.] (CR, April 1945, p. 9.)

Henry D. Moyle: 2-3

Where else in all the world are the true fruits of the inspiration of the Almighty to be found, inspiration that giveth the souls of men understanding? Throughout the history of the Church innumerable examples of spiritual guidance are found. One which I have cherished since childhood is an early experience of Wilford Woodruff.

While traveling in New England, on assignment by Brigham Young, President Woodruff drove his carriage into the yard of Brother Williams. Brother Orson Hyde drove a wagon by the side of his carriage. He had only been there a few minutes when the Spirit said to him, "Get up and move that carriage." When he told his wife that he had to move the carriage, she asked. "What for?" He answered, "I don't know."

That was all she asked on such occasions. When he told her that he did not know, that was enough. President Woodruff got up and moved his carriage four or five rods, and put the off fore wheel against the corner of the house. He then returned to bed. The same Spirit said, "Go and move your animals from the oak tree." They were two hundred yards from his carriage. He moved his horses and put them in a little hickory grove. Again he went to bed. In thirty minutes a whirlwind came up and broke that oak tree off within two feet of the ground. It swept over three or four fences and fell square in the dooryard, near Brother Orson Hyde's wagon, and right where the carriage had stood. What would have been the consequences if he had not listened to that Spirit? Why, President Woodruff, his wife, and children doubtless would have been killed.

That was the still, small voice to him — no thunder, no lightning, but the still small voice of the Spirit of God. It saved his life. It was the Spirit of revelation.

We can all afford to develop a sensitiveness to the promptings of the Spirit in all things pertaining to our physical as well as our spiritual well-being.

In speaking on this, Joseph Fielding Smith said, "The testimony of the Holy Ghost is Spirit speaking to spirit, and is not confined solely to the natural or physical sense." (CR, April 1957, pp. 33-34.)

George Q. Cannon: 2-3

I will read a portion of a revelation given through the Prophet Joseph Smith, previous to the organization of the Church, dated April 1829: [Sec. 8:1-3, quoted.]

The point I wish to call to your attention is contained in the second and third verses of this revelation. The Latter-day Saints are in many respects like other people who are not

Latter-day Saints. We are apt to entertain views which are not very correct, and which may be the result of our traditions and preconceived ideas. This is a peculiarity that pertains to mankind generally, that whenever they deal with the things of God, or speak about them, or contemplate them, and especially when they read the predictions made by the servants of God concerning future events, or events that may transpire right before their eyes, they are apt to get, sometimes, erroneous ideas, or, at least, exaggerated ideas, in relation to them. . . . How many of the Latter-day Saints are there who understand that this is the way in which Moses led the children of Israel so miraculously? How many are there who think that if we had a man like Moses among us, the people would be led differently and with greater manifestations of power than they are? How many are there who are dissatisfied with what God is doing at present, and are looking for someone to appear in the future who shall exhibit convincing and overwhelming manifestations of power? How many are there at the present time who are neglecting the precious and inestimable gift of revelation which God has bestowed upon his people, because it does not come to them in the way to suit their preconceived notions and ideas, or who are not suited with the way the Church has been and is led, because there is not that wonderful degree of power exhibited which they imagine should be? . . . The same Spirit of revelation that Moses had, concerning which God speaks through the Prophet Joseph Smith, has rested upon men that have held the keys of this kingdom, whether it was during President [Brigham] Young's life or at the present time — that same Spirit of revelation rests upon him who holds the presidency as senior apostle in the midst of the people of God. The apostles of this Church have all the authority, they have all the keys, and it is within the preview of their office and calling to have all the Spirit of revelation necessary to lead this people into the presence of the Lamb in the celestial kingdom of our God. . . .

But it is the truth, that the same Spirit of revelation that rested upon Moses, and which enabled him to lead the children of Israel through the Red Sea [Ex. 14:26-31; Heb. 11:29], rests upon the servants of God in the midst of this people, and you will find it so to your entire satisfaction if you will listen to their counsels and be guided by them. (JD, November 1879, 21:264, 268, 270, 271.)

Joseph Fielding Smith: 6-12

At this time the Lord seemed perfectly willing that Oliver Cowdery as well as Joseph Smith should engage in this labor of translating the plates, and he gave in some detail what qualifications are necessary for the reception of knowledge by revelation and also the procedure necessary in translating ancient records. Oliver was informed that this power could not be received except by the exercise of faith with an honest heart, and by this faith, knowledge of the ancient records and their engravings should be made known. The Lord said: "Behold, I will tell you in your mind and in your heart, by the Holy Ghost, which shall come upon you and which shall dwell in your heart." [Sec. 8:2.] This is the Spirit of revelation. (CHMR, 1947, 1:46.)

Joseph Fielding Smith: 6
The gift of Aaron

There was another gift bestowed upon Oliver Cowdery, and that was the gift of Aaron. Like Aaron with his rod in his hand going before Moses as a spokesman, so Oliver Cowdery was to go before Joseph Smith. Whatever he should ask the Lord by power of this gift should be granted if asked in faith and in wisdom. Oliver was blessed with the great honor of holding the keys of this dispensation with Joseph Smith, and like Aaron [Ex. 4:10-17], did become a spokesman on numerous occasions. It was Oliver who delivered the first public discourse in this dispensation. (CHMR, 1947, 1:48.

J. Reuben Clark, Jr.: 10
Without faith you can do nothing

As I think about faith, this principle of power, I am obliged to believe that it is an intelligent force. Of what kind, I do not know. But it is superior to and overrules all other forces of which we know. It is the principle, the force, by which the dead are restored to life.

I do not believe that the Lord, that God permits any man to have faith that would overrule his purposes. In that connection, I call to your attention the fact that the Savior himself pled that his crucifixion might be turned aside. Yet, on one occasion he said, when he asked that the hour might be passed on, " . . . but for this cause came I unto this hour." [John 12:27.] The Son of God was not given the necessary faith at the time to enable him to turn aside the purposes reached by himself and the Father before and still remembered the Father. . . .

You brethren . . . have had this great power given unto us, this power of faith. What are we doing about it? Can you, can we, do the mighty things that the Savior did? Yes. They have been done by the members of the Church who had the faith and righteousness so to do. Think of what is within your power if you but live the Gospel, if you but live so that you may invoke the power which is within you. (CR, April 1960, p. 21.)

SECTION 9

Revelation given through Joseph Smith the Prophet, to Oliver Cowdery, at Harmony, Pennsylvania, April, 1829. Oliver is admonished to patience, and is urged to be content to write, for the time being, at the dictation of the translator, rather than to attempt to translate. — It is not sufficient for one merely to ask for a divine gift, without prayerful thought and study — Oliver loses such small measure of the gift of translation as he had temporarily possessed.

1. Behold, I say unto you, my son, that because you did not translate according to that which you desired of me, and did commence again to write for my servant, Joseph Smith, Jun., even so I would that ye should continue until you have finished this record, which I have entrusted to him.

2. And then, behold, other records have I, that I will give unto you power that you may assist to translate.

3. Be patient, my son, for it is wisdom in me, and it is not expedient that you should translate at this present time.

4. Behold, the work which you are called to do is to write for my servant Joseph.

5. And, behold, it is because that you did not continue as you commenced, when you began to translate, that I have taken away this privilege from you.

6. Do not murmur, my son, for it is wisdom in me that I have dealt with you after this manner.

7. Behold, you have not understood; you have supposed that I would give it unto you, when you took no thought save it was to ask me.

8. But, behold, I say unto you, that you must study it out in your mind; then you must ask me if it be right, and if it is right I will cause that your bosom shall burn within you; therefore, you shall feel that it is right.

9. But if it be not right you shall have no such feelings, but you shall have a stupor of thought that shall cause you to forget the thing which is wrong; therefore, you cannot write that which is sacred save it be given you from me.

10. Now, if you had known this you could have translated; nevertheless, it is not expedient that you should translate now.

11. Behold, it was expedient when you commenced; but you feared, and the time is past, and it is not expedient now;

12. For, do you not behold that I have given unto my servant Joseph sufficient strength, whereby it is made up? And neither of you have I condemned.

13. Do this thing which I have commanded you, and you shall prosper. Be faithful, and yield to no temptation.

14. Stand fast in the work wherewith I have called you, and a hair of your head shall not be lost, and you shall be lifted up at the last day. Amen.

Joseph Fielding Smith: 1-12

With a glad heart Oliver took over the work of translating, and the Prophet Joseph was ready to act as scribe. The attempt was a failure; it seems that Oliver Cowdery thought that it would be an easy matter with the aid of the Urim and Thummim to understand the engravings and give their equivalent meaning in the English language, without taking thought or studying it out in his mind. He therefore failed to comprehend the instructions the Lord had given him, notwithstanding the Lord told him he should have the gift of revelation.

It seems probable that Oliver Cowdery desired to translate out of curiosity, and the Lord taught him his place by showing him that translating was not the easy thing he had thought it to be. In a subsequent revelation (Sec. 9), the explanation was made that Oliver's failure came because he did not continue as he commenced, and the task being a difficult one, his faith deserted him. The lesson he learned was very necessary, for he was shown that his place was to act as scribe for Joseph Smith and that it was the latter who was called and appointed by command of the Lord to do the translating. There must have been some impatience in having to sit and act as scribe, but when he failed to master the gift of translating, he was then willing to accept the will of the Lord, who said to him: [Sec. 9:3-9, quoted.]

A similar privilege is given to any member of the Church who seeks knowledge of the spirit of prayer and faith. The Lord will cause the feeling of security and truth to take hold of the individual and burn within the bosom, and there will be overwhelming feeling that the thing is right. . . .

The Lord told him that he was to continue as scribe until the translation of the Book of Mormon was completed, and that there were other ancient records to come forth, and that he might have the privilege of translating these at some future day if he would remain faithful. We learn from the Book of Mormon that there are many records and that at some time when the people are prepared by faith to receive them that they shall also be translated and published for the knowledge and salvation of the faithful. (2 Nephi 27:7-8; 3 Nephi 26:6-11; Ether 3:22-28 and 4:5-7.)

Later there came into the hands of the Prophet other records which had to be translated, such as the Book of Abraham, but these records of ancient inhabitants on this American continent were not translated. It is possible that some of them might have been translated had the people received the Book of Mormon with full purpose of heart and had been faithful to its teachings. This was the promise the Lord made through Mormon. He said he would try the faith of the people and if they were willing to accept the lesser things (i.e., the Book of Mormon), then he would make known to them the greater things. That we have failed in this is very apparent, we have not accepted the revelations in the Book of Mormon, neither in the Doctrine and Covenants with that faith and willingness to know the will of the Lord which would entitle us to receive this greater information. Oliver Cowdery was a party to this failure by turning away from the Church for a number of years when it needed his service. He therefore lost his privilege to translate through his own disobedience, and the people have lost the privilege of receiving the "greater things" spoken of by the Lord to Mormon (3 Nephi 26:8-11) until the day shall come when they are willing to be obedient in all things and will exercise faith such as was had by the brother of Jared. It should be remembered that such faith has rarely been seen on the earth. It appears, therefore, that we must wait until the reign of unrighteousness is at an end before the Lord will give to the people these writings, containing "a revelation from God, from the beginning of the world to the ending thereof." [2 Nephi 27:7.] (CHMR, 1947, 1:46-49.)

Brigham Young: 2
Other records

When Joseph got the plates, the angel instructed him to carry them back to the hill Cumorah, which he did. Oliver says that when Joseph and Oliver went there, the hill opened, and they walked into a cave, in which there was a large and spacious room. He says he did not think, at the time, whether they had the light of the sun or artificial light; but that it was just as light as day. They laid the plates on a table; it was a large table that stood in the room. Under this table there was a pile of plates as much as two feet high, and there were altogether in this room more plates than probably many wagon loads; they were piled up in the corners and along the walls. The first time they went there the sword of Laban hung upon the wall; but when they went again it had been taken down and laid upon the table across the gold plates; it was unsheathed, and on it was written these words: "This sword will never be sheathed again until the kingdoms of the world become the kingdom of our God and his Christ." I tell you this as coming not only from Oliver Cowdery, but others who were familiar with it, and who understood it just as well as we understand coming to this meeting, enjoying the day, and by and by we separate and go away, forgetting most of what is said, but remembering some things. (*JD*, June 17, 1877, 19:38.)

Lorenzo Snow: 8-9

It is impossible to advance in the principles of truth, to increase in heavenly knowledge, except we exercise our reasoning faculties and exert ourselves in a proper manner. We have an instance recorded in the Doctrine and Covenants of a misunderstanding on the part of Oliver Cowdery, touching this principle. The Lord promised him the gift to translate ancient records. Like many of us today, he had misconceptions in regard to the exercise of this gift. He thought all that was necessary for him to do, inasmuch as this gift had been promised him of God, was to allow his mind to wait in idleness without effort, until it should operate spontaneously. But when those records were placed before him, there was no knowledge communicated, they still remained sealed, as it were, for no power to translate came upon him.

Although the gift to translate had been conferred, he could not prosecute the work, simply because he failed to exert himself before God with the view of developing the gift within him; and he became greatly disappointed, and the Lord, in his goodness and mercy, informed him of his mistake, using the following language. [Sec. 9:7-8, quoted.]

So in regard to us, respecting the things which we are undertaking, if we expect to improve, to advance in the work immediately before us, and finally to obtain possession of those gifts and glories, coming up to that condition of exaltation we anticipate, we must take thought and reflect, we must exert ourselves, and that to the utmost of our ability. (JD, April 5, 1877, 18:371-72.)

Melvin J. Ballard: 8-9

There is a key given in the ninth section of the book of Doctrine and Covenants, which would be very profitable for the Latter-day Saints to follow even now. You remember the circumstance of Oliver Cowdery translating portions of the Book of Mormon, and then all became darkness to him and he could not proceed. He inquired of the Lord to know why it was, and the answer came that he had taken no thought save it was to ask the Lord, and left the burden of responsibility there. [Sec. 9:8-9, quoted.]

You do not know what to do today to solve your financial problems, what to plant, whether to buy or sell cattle, sheep or other things. It is your privilege to study it out; counsel together with the best wisdom and judgment the Lord shall give you, reach your conclusions, and then go to the Lord with it, tell him what you have planned to do. If the thing you have planned to do is for your good and your blessing, and you are determined to serve the Lord, pay your tithes and your offerings and keep his commandments, I promise that he will fulfil that promise upon your head, and your bosom shall burn within by the whisperings of the Spirit that it is right. But if it is not right, you shall have no such feelings, but you shall have a stupor of thought, and your heart will be turned away from that thing.

I know of nothing today that the Latter-day Saints need more than the guidance of the Holy Spirit in the solution of the problems of life. (CR, April 1931, pp. 37-38.)

Brigham Young: 13-14

We have only the privilege to do right. There is not an iota in the revelations, from Adam down to the present day, but what requires strict obedience. They who cannot abide a celestial law — the law that God has revealed for the sanctification of his people to prepare them to enter into the presence of the Father and the Son, should try and abide a lesser law, but they must expect a lower glory, a secondary glory. (JD, January 2, 1870, 13:92.)

SECTION 10

Revelation given to Joseph Smith the Prophet, at Harmony, Pennsylvania, in the summer of 1828. – Herein the Lord informs Joseph of alterations made by wicked men in the 116 manuscript pages of the Book of Mormon, which had been lost from the possession of Martin Harris, to whom the sheets had been temporarily entrusted. Compare Section 3. See History of the Church, vol. 1, pp. 21, 23. The evil design was to await the expected re-translation of the matter covered by the stolen pages, and then to discredit the translator by showing the discrepancies created by the alterations. That this wicked purpose had been conceived by the evil one, and was known to the Lord even while Mormon, the ancient Nephite historian, was making his abridgment of the accumulated plates is shown in the Book of Mormon. See The Words of Mormon 3-7.

1. Now, behold, I say unto you, that because you delivered up those writings which you had power given unto you to translate by the means of the Urim and Thummim, into the hands of a wicked man, you have lost them.

2. And you also lost your gift at the same time, and your mind became darkened.

3. Nevertheless, it is now restored unto you again; therefore see that you are faithful and continue on unto the finishing of the remainder of the work of translation as you have begun.

4. Do not run faster or labor more than you have strength and means provided to enable you to translate; but be diligent unto the end.

5. Pray always, that you may come off conquerer; yea, that you may conquer Satan, and that you may escape the hands of the servants of Satan that do uphold his work.

6. Behold, they have sought to destroy you; yea, even the man in whom you have trusted has sought to destroy you.

7. And for this cause I said that he is a wicked man, for he has sought to take away the things wherewith you have been entrusted; and he has also sought to destroy your gift.

8. And because you have delivered the writing into his hands, behold, wicked men have taken them from you.

9. Therefore, you have delivered them up, yea, that which was sacred, unto wickedness.

10. And, behold, Satan hath put it into their hearts to alter the words which you have caused to be written, or which you have translated, which have gone out of your hands.

11. And behold, I say unto you, that because they have altered the words, they read contrary from that which you translated and caused to be written;

12. And, on this wise, the devil has sought to lay a cunning plan, that he may destroy this work;

13. For he hath put into their hearts to do this, that by lying they may say they have caught you in the words which you have pretended to translate.

14. Verily, I say unto you, that I will not suffer that Satan shall accomplish his evil design in this thing.

15. For behold, he has put it into their hearts to get thee to tempt the Lord thy God, in asking to translate it over again.

16. And then, behold, they say and think in their hearts — We will see if God has given him power to translate; if so, he will also give him power again;

17. And if God giveth him power again, or if he translates again, or, in other words, if he bringeth forth the same words, behold, we have the same with us, and we have altered them;

18. Therefore they will not agree, and we will say that he has lied in his words, and that he has no gift, and that he has no power;

19. Therefore we will destroy him, and also the work; and we will do this that we may not be ashamed in the end, and that we may get glory of the world.

20. Verily, verily, I say unto you, that Satan has great hold upon their hearts; he stirreth them up to iniquity against that which is good;

21. And their hearts are corrupt, and full of wickedness and abominations; and they love darkness rather than light, because their deeds are evil; therefore they will not ask of me.

22. Satan stirreth them up, that he may lead their souls to destruction.

23. And thus he has laid a cunning plan, thinking to destroy the work of God; but I will require this at their hands, and it shall turn to their shame and condemnation in the day of judgment.

24. Yea, he stirreth up their hearts to anger against this work.

25. Yea, he saith unto them: Deceive and lie in wait to catch, that ye may destroy; behold, this is no harm. And thus he flattereth them, and telleth them that it is no sin to lie that they may catch a man in a lie, that they may destroy him.

26. And thus he flattereth them, and leadeth them along until he draggeth their souls down to hell; and thus he causeth them to catch themselves in their own snare.

27. And thus he goeth up and down, to and fro in the earth, seeking to destroy the souls of men.

28. Verily, verily, I say unto you, wo be unto him that lieth to deceive because he supposeth that another lieth to deceive, for such are not exempt from the justice of God.

29. Now, behold, they have altered these words, because Satan saith unto them: He hath deceived you — and thus he flattereth them away to do iniquity, to get thee to tempt the Lord thy God.

30. Behold, I say unto you, that you shall not translate again those words which have gone forth out of your hands;

31. For, behold, they shall not accomplish their evil designs in lying against those words. For, behold, if you should bring forth the same words they will say that you have lied and that you have pretended to translate, but that you have contradicted yourself.

32. And, behold, they will publish this, and Satan will harden the hearts of the people and stir them up to anger against you, that they will not believe my words.

33. Thus Satan thinketh to overpower your testimony in this generation, that the work may not come forth in this generation.

34. But behold, here is wisdom, and because I show unto you wisdom, and give you commandments concerning these things, what you shall do, show it not unto the world until you have accomplished the work of translation.

35. Marvel not that I said unto you: Here is wisdom, show it not unto the world — for I said, show it not unto the world, that you may be preserved.

36. Behold, I do not say that you shall not show it unto the righteous;

37. But as you cannot always judge the righteous, or as you cannot always tell the wicked from the righteous, therefore I say unto you, hold your peace until I shall see fit to make all things known unto the world concerning the matter.

38. And now, verily I say unto you, that an account of those things that you have written, which have gone out of your hands, is engraven upon the plates of Nephi;

39. Yea, and you remember it was said in those writings that a more particular account was given of these things upon the plates of Nephi.

40. And now, because the account which is engraven upon the plates of Nephi is more particular concerning the things which, in my wisdom, I would bring to the knowledge of the people in this account —

41. Therefore, you shall translate the engravings which are on the plates of Nephi, down even till you come to the reign of king Benjamin, or until you come to that which you have translated, which you have retained;

42. And behold, you shall publish it as the record of Nephi; and thus I will confound those who have altered my words.

43. I will not suffer that they shall destroy my work; yea, I will show unto them that my wisdom is greater than the cunning of the devil.

44. Behold, they have only got a part, or an abridgment of the account of Nephi.

45. Behold, there are many things engraven upon the plates of Nephi which do throw greater views upon my gospel; therefore, it is wisdom in me that you should translate this first part of the engravings of Nephi, and send forth in this work.

46. And, behold, all the remainder of this work does contain all those parts of my gospel which my holy prophets, yea, and also my disciples, desired in their prayers should come forth unto this people.

47. And I said unto them, that it should be granted unto them according to their faith in their prayers;

48. Yea, and this was their faith — that my gospel, which I gave unto them that they might preach in their days, might come unto their brethren the Lamanites, and also all that had become Lamanites because of their dissensions.

49. Now, this is not all — their faith in their prayers was that this gospel should be made known also, if it were possible that other nations should possess this land;

50. And thus they did leave a blessing upon this land in their prayers, that whosoever should believe in this gospel in this land might have eternal life;

51. Yea, that it might be free unto all of whatsoever nation, kindred, tongue, or people they may be.

52. And now, behold, according to their faith in their prayers will I bring this part of my gospel to the knowledge of my people. Behold, I do not bring it to destroy that which they have received, but to build it up.

53. And for this cause have I said: If this generation harden not their hearts, I will establish my church among them.

54. Now I do not say this to destroy my church, but I say this to build up my church;

55. Therefore, whosoever belongeth to my church need not fear, for such shall inherit the kingdom of heaven.

56. But it is they who do not fear me, neither keep my commandments but build up churches unto themselves to get gain, yea, and all those that do wickedly and build up the kingdom of the devil — yea, verily, verily, I say unto you, that it is they that I will disturb, and cause to tremble and shake to the center.

57. Behold, I am Jesus Christ, the Son of God. I came unto mine own, and mine own received me not.

58. I am the light which shineth in darkness, and the darkness comprehendeth it not.

59. I am he who said — Other sheep have I which are not of this fold — unto my disciples, and many there were that understood me not.

60. And I will show unto this people that I had other sheep, and that they were a branch of the house of Jacob;

61. And I will bring to light their marvelous works, which they did in my name;

62. Yea, and I will also bring to light my gospel which was ministered unto them, and, behold, they shall not deny that which you have received, but they shall build it up, and shall bring to light the true points of my doctrine, yea, and the only doctrine which is in me.

63. And this I do that I may establish my gospel, that there may not be so much contention; yea, Satan doth stir up the hearts of the people to contention concerning the points of my doctrine; and in these things they do err, for they do wrest the scriptures and do not understand them.

64. Therefore, I will unfold unto them this great mystery;

65. For, behold, I will gather them as a hen gathereth her chickens under her wings, if they will not harden their hearts;

66. Yea, if they will come, they may, and partake of the waters of life freely.

67. Behold, this is my doctrine — whosoever repenteth and cometh unto me, the same is my church.

68. Whosoever declareth more or less than this, the same is not of me, but is against me; therefore he is not of my church.

69. And now, behold, whosoever is of my church, and endureth of my church to the end, him will I establish upon my rock, and the gates of hell shall not prevail against them.

70. And now, remember the words of him who is the life and light of the world, your Redeemer, your Lord and your God. Amen.

Joseph Smith: *Introduction*

After I had obtained the above revelation [Section 3], both the plates and the Urim and Thummim were taken from me again; but in a few days they were returned to me, when I inquired of the Lord, and the Lord said thus unto me: [Section 10, follows.] (HC 1:21-23, Summer, 1828; Harmony, Pennsylvania.)

Rudger Clawson: 5

To show the importance of prayer I remind you . . . that in this world there are two great powers, and these two powers are at warfare. There is the power of good and the power of evil. They do not harmonize, they do not mix. Like oil and water, they will not mix. On one hand, there is the power of good striving with every man and woman; on the other hand, there is the power of evil striving with every man and woman. Their prospects, their record, and all their future will depend upon which of these two great powers control them.

I firmly believe that if it were not for the faith and prayers of this people, which are ascending continually to heaven, Satan certainly would have power over us, and perhaps in many instances we would be overcome and destroyed. . . . We must bear in mind this great conflict that is going on between good and evil. Everything that is good, every power and principle that leads to good, is from God; and every influence that enticeth man to do evil is from Satan, the father of lies. [Alma 5:40.] Thus we may judge between the good and the evil. [Moroni 7:15-17.] (CR, April 1904, p. 44.)

Joseph F. Smith: 5
Pray always

It is not such a difficult thing to learn how to pray. It is not the words we use particularly that constitute prayer. Prayer does not consist of words altogether. True, faithful, earnest prayer consists more in the feeling that rises from the heart and from the inward desire of our spirits to supplicate the Lord in humility and in faith, that we may receive his blessings. It matters not how simple the words may be, if our desires are genuine and we come before the Lord with a broken heart and a contrite spirit to ask him for that which we need. . . .

Do not learn to pray with your lips only. Do not learn a prayer by heart, and say it every morning and evening. That is something I dislike very much. It is true that a great many people fall into the rut of saying over a ceremonious prayer.

They begin at a certain point, and they touch at all the points along the road until they get to the winding-up scene; and when they have done, I do not know whether the prayer has ascended beyond the ceiling of the room or not. (CR, October 1899, pp. 69, 71-72.)

Joseph Fielding Smith: 6-45

In section ten, the Lord revealed to Joseph Smith the plan of his enemies into whose hands the [Book of Mormon] manuscript had fallen. In their hate of the truth, for "their hearts are corrupt, and full of wickedness and abominations," the Lord said, they felt that they were justified in destroying Joseph Smith and the work of the Lord even by resorting to wilful and malicious lying. (Sec. 10:25-26, quoted.]

How often this is the case. Today Satan is raging in the hearts of the children of men, and he has stirred them up to anger against that which is good. (2 Nephi 28:20.) From the very beginning he tried to stop or destroy this work, and no effort is left undone to bring to pass the destruction of the Church of Jesus Christ from within as well as from attacks without. Therefore all members of the Church should be constantly on their guard and prayerfully obedient to all covenants and commandments given them in the word of the Lord. We are commanded to "beware concerning ourselves, to give diligent heed to the words of eternal life. For you shall live by every word that proceedeth forth from the mouth of God." (D&C 84:43.) Never before in the history of the world has Satan raged more determinedly in the hearts of the people than he is doing today.

The Prophet Nephi kept a record of the sacred history of his people on what he was pleased to call the small plates which he had made. The historians who followed him continued that history down to the reign of King Benjamin, when the plates of this record were full. When Mormon was making his abridgment the Lord inspired him to attach these "small plates" to his abridgment. He did not know why, only that the Spirit whispered to him to do so. [Words of Mormon

3-7.] The Lord, who knows the end from the beginning, thus prepared for the loss of the abridged record which was given to Martin Harris. Mormon therefore had a double account of the early history of his people from the time of the call of Lehi from Jerusalem down to the end of the writings of Amaleki, the last to write on the small plates of Nephi. The Lord, thus knowing that the manuscript covering this period of history would be stolen in the manner described, provided the better record to take the place of the abridgment. He denied Joseph Smith the privilege of translating the abridgment the second time, and thus prevented him from falling into the trap set by his enemies, but commanded him to translate the small plates giving the full account as kept by the early prophets and scribes. (CHMR, 1947, 1:28-29.)

Orson F. Whitney: 20-21

All men will not receive the Gospel. Some hate the truth, and turn from it instinctively. A man who is wallowing in sensuality, giving himself up to the gratification of his base appetites and desires, he does not love the person who comes to him and warns him to stop these evil practices; he hates him — hates him for the message that he bears, for he wants to be let alone to continue his wallowing in the mire. Such men will not receive the truth — unless God puts his Spirit in their hearts; for, after all, men are not converted by preaching, nor by anything else than the Spirit of the Lord. Some people hate the truth, and love darkness rather than light, "because their deeds are evil." (CR, April 1915, pp. 101-2.)

Brigham Young: 24
He stirreth up their hearts to anger against this work

The devil . . . offers resistance to the progress of the spirit of the Gospel by arousing the wicked, who are under his influence, to hate, and persecute, and annoy in every possible way, the true followers of the Lord Jesus. (JD, June 3, 1866, 11:236.)

Marvin J. Ashton: 26
And thus he flattereth them

Satan and his forces were never more strongly arrayed than today. He is cunning. He is successful. One of the most subtle and effective tools he is using among us today is the convincing of some that they have arrived, they have reached their destination, they have earned a rest, they aren't needed anymore, they are out of danger, they are beyond temptation, and they can take pride in their accomplishments. (CR, April 1972, p. 61.)

Anthony W. Ivins: 26
He . . . leadeth them along until he draggeth their souls down to hell

From the time of his fall, Lucifer has sought to establish and maintain dominion over the earth and those who dwell upon it, and with few exceptions, and then for brief periods only, he has been successful. . . .

Knowing that his dominion over the people of the earth is to be broken, and that certain defeat awaits him, he arrays himself in the livery of Christ, and masquerading as his representative, in the words of Shakespeare, wins the hearts of men by honest trifles which are true, while he betrays them, and leads them away to deepest consequences. (CR, April 1934, p. 98.)

Joseph Fielding Smith: 46-53

The Lord makes known that the Nephite prophets in prayer earnestly sought that their writings should be preserved to come forth and to speak as from the dead, to bear witness to the remnant of Lehi, and also the Jews and Gentiles, that God had revealed to them the fulness of the Gospel. Their anxiety was that in these last days men might be brought to repentance and faith in God through the testimony given many centuries before to these Nephites prophets. In fact, we learn from the Book of Mormon that this is the main object of the Book of Mormon as stated in many of its passages. [1 Nephi ch. 13.] (CHMR, 1947, 1:29.)

Joseph Fielding Smith: 55-56

I desire to read a little from one of the revelations given to the Prophet Joseph Smith: [Sec. 10:55-56, quoted.]

Now there are those who declare more or less than this. They will not repent of their sins. They will not accept Jesus as the Redeemer of the world. They will not believe that he spoke the truth when he declared unto the people that he was the Son of God, and that he came to fulfill the mission that was given to him of his Father, to redeem the world from remaining in the bondage of sin, and cannot be redeemed, because they will not receive the principles by which salvation comes. [Sec. 84:49-53.] There are many of this class that go around the country stirring up the hearts of the people against the truth, declaring that these principles and ordinances that are declared in the scriptures to be essential to salvation. They are destroying the faith of the people wherever it is possible. But we should be strong in the faith; each one of us should be filled with a determination to serve the Lord and keep his commandments, for we have received the light which shineth in darkness that comes from the Lord. We are not walking in darkness, but in the light of truth as it has been revealed. There is no occasion for the members of the Church to go astray, to disregard the principles of the Gospel, for they are so plain and have been set forth in such clearness, that none need stumble or be in doubt concerning them. It is necessary that we should keep them in mind constantly, living worthily before the Lord, that we may receive his blessings. (CR, October 1913, pp. 71-72.)

Joseph Fielding Smith: 57-70

The Lord declares that only those who keep his commandments are of his Church. [Sec. 10:69, quoted.] Frequently throughout the scriptures mankind is warned that it is he who endureth to the end that shall be saved in the kingdom of God. [Mark 13:13; D&C 14:7; 1 Nephi 22:31.] There are those who profess his name who think that because he is merciful they can procrastinate their repentance to the end; they can forsake his commandments and then, not-withstanding their unfaithfulness, the time will come when they shall be forgiven and fully entitled to all the blessings and to share them with those who have endured the faith to the end. There is no such promise anywhere in the Scriptures. We all may read with profit Alma 34:32-35.

The Lord has always been willing to bless and extend his mercy to those who are willing to humble themselves and accept his commandments: "If this generation harden not their hearts, I will establish my church among them." [Sec. 10:53.] It is just as true today as it was two thousand years ago, that men love darkness rather than the light, because their deeds are evil. The very sound of the Gospel causes a spirit of resentment, often anger, in the hearts of the wicked. The principles of the Gospel, all of which are glorious and uplifting and which any person can readily discover to be worthy of all acceptance, seem to create a spirit of hate and antagonism in the bosoms of those who oppose the truth and whose deeds are evil. Although the Jews saw Jesus heal the sick, raise the dead, give sight to the blind and perform all kinds of merciful deeds, yet they hated him and his good deeds because they caused them to hate him the more. The Lord knew very well that the people of this generation, with the exception of the few, would turn away from his truth so that he could not establish branches of his Church among them, in any great numbers. [Sec. 45:28-29.] (CHMR, 1947, 1:30-31.)

Joseph F. Smith: 57
I am Jesus Christ, the Son of God

I accept Jesus of Nazareth as the only begotten Son of God in the flesh. This is a great principle, though it seems hard for some people to understand it — those who believe in the foolish notion that God is a *"vapor,"* if you please, ether, electricity, *"energy"* or anything else you might call him or it, and that he fills the immensity of space, is everywhere present at the same time, etc., etc. It is difficult indeed for those who believe this foolish doctrine to believe that Christ could be the Son of God; that God, being only spirit, or "energy," as defined by a certain learned preacher, could beget a son in his "likeness" and "image" and the Son also be in the likeness and image of mortal man. [Gen. 1:26-27.] The apostles of Jesus Christ, his witnesses, declared it [John 3:16; 1 John 4:9], and he himself has declared it by his own voice in the day in which we live [Sec. 29:42, 46; 49:5; 76:23], but it is hard to get people to understand how that nondescript creation of man's ignorance called "God" by the sectarian world, which fills the immensity of space and is everywhere present at the same time, can beget a Son in the form of himself and at the same time in the form of man. (CR, April 1917, pp. 7-8.)

LeGrand Richards: 59
Other sheep have I which are not of this fold

Jesus enlightens us . . . on this subject:

And other sheep I have, which are not of this fold: them also I must bring, and they shall hear my voice; and there shall be one fold, and one shepherd. (John 10:16.)

A writer on the life of Christ has indicated that he would find no excuse for this passage of scripture, since he knew of no other sheep except those to whom Jesus ministered. Some have explained that it must have been the Gentiles, but Jesus indicated: " . . . I am not sent but unto the lost sheep of the house of Israel." (Matt. 15:24.)

It should be noted that Jesus did not minister unto the Gentiles, although he did send his Apostles unto them after his crucifixion. [Matt. 28:19-20.]

After Jesus had been crucified and had ascended unto his Father, he visited his "other sheep" in America, known as the Nephites, and there chose twelve disciples and organized his Church, as he had done among the Jews, an account of which is given in some detail in Third Nephi of the Book of Mormon. [3 Nephi 15:11-24.] (*A Marvelous Work and a Wonder*, 1950, pp. 51-52.)

Mark E. Petersen: 63
They do wrest the scriptures and do not understand them

One of the reasons people apostatize from this Church is that they have failed to heed the warning of the scriptures against listening to false teachers who raise their voices in our midst. [Sec. 45:5-6; 2 Nephi 28:20-31.] In spite of the fact that these warnings of the scriptures are crystal clear, many of our people fail to heed them.

How do these false teachers lead people astray? They do so by attacking the fundamental doctrines of the Church. [Sec. 52:9, 14-20, 36.] They attack the teachings of the Authorities. They seek to develop doctrinal disputes among the people to undermine their faith, and they lead people to apostasy when they do such things as that. Very often false teachers who have come among us endeavor to justify their position by claiming to have received some revelation or dream directing them, they say, in the paths which they tread. . . .

So, Latter-day Saints, beware of false teachers, when men come among you and begin to preach doctrines unto you which tend to destroy your confidence in the holy scriptures. . . . When you have persons come to you teaching doctrines of this kind, remember also the words of the Savior when he said:

. . . neither shall there be disputations among you concerning the points of my doctrine, . . . for verily, verily, I say unto you, that he that hath the spirit of contention is not of me, but is of the devil, who is the father of contention and he stirreth up the hearts of men. (3 Nephi 11:28-29.)

Remember, too, the Savior told the Prophet Joseph Smith that it is Satan who "doth stir up the hearts of the people to contention concerning the points of doctrine," and that when individuals put themselves in the hands of Satan in doing these things "they do err, for they do wrest the scriptures and do not understand them."

So if you really desire to avoid deceptions, if you really desire to do that which is right and proper, then you take advantage of the safeguard that the Lord has given you in the organization of this Church. And you remember that if you will follow the teachings of your inspired prophets, seers, and revelators, of your apostles, of your pastors and teachers, your bishops, and your stake presidents, you won't need to wonder whether or not such and such a doctrine is a deception, whether it is false or whether it is true, because those authorized servants of the Lord will lead you into paths of righteousness, and they will keep you on the right track.

Salvation comes not by being tossed about by every wind of doctrine, but by learning the truth as it is taught by the inspired, authorized leaders of the Church, and then having learned the truth, by living up to it and enduring in faithfulness unto the very end. [Sec. 53:7.] (CR, October 1945, pp. 88-92.)

Abraham O. Woodruff: 68
Whosoever declareth more or less than this . . . is not of me

There is no need of this people being called together to change the Articles of their Faith, or their creed, for that which they have received is not of man, but from God. It must be very humiliating indeed to a religionist when he thinks upon the fact that his religious sect is forced to call its representatives together from time to time for the purpose of revising its creed, for the reason that the age has outgrown it; that scientific and other discoveries have brought to light certain truths that prove the creeds of fifty or a hundred years ago to be incorrect.

I thank God that this is not the case with Mormonism, and that there has never been, nor will there ever be, any change in the creed or principles of the system upon which the faith of this people is founded. And this is a grand difference between the work of man and the work of God. [Sec. 88:66-67; 93:24-25.] That which is of man must be modified and changed to meet the demands of various ages in which mankind live, but that which is of God will endure, as the Gospel of Jesus Christ, as revealed through the Prophet Joseph Smith, has endured the scrutiny of critics, the discoveries and the light of science in our day and time. (CR, October 1901, p. 53.)

Mark E. Petersen: 69-70

Why endure to the end? Why is it so important to our salvation? Can we not be faithful part of the time and stray a bit, and yet get our salvation? Why does he limit the application to "whosoever is of my church, and endureth of my church to the end"?

To answer these questions we must ask and answer one more: What is the purpose of our existence?

We are the children of God, actually his offspring. He is our Father. We are not mere creatures of the Almighty, but rather we are his sons and daughters. We are of the divine race. We are in this life to prove ourselves, and develop within us Godlike traits of character. We must become Christlike in our souls in order to come into his presence . . .

The Gospel is the plan. The commandments are the detailed instructions. By living them we achieve our goal. But where does "enduring to the end" come in?

Steadfastness is part of good character. If we are not steadfast, we are not strong. If we are not steadfast, we waver, we are undecided, unpredictable; we stumble and fall; we lack the "backbone" to achieve; we are weaklings; we cannot make up our mind; we never overcome.

There is nothing Christlike in weakness, neither in disobedience. We are commanded to "overcome." What is it that we are to overcome? Weakness, indecision, turning back, failure, sin. We are to fight a battle and win. The victory and all the effort leading up to it, build character. Do we build character in being wishy-washy? Do we build character in only partial performance?

To become like him we must be strong. We must not bow to temptation. We must not be idle. Only in labor is there true excellence. But we must follow the right road to perfection. We must adopt the correct instructions. That is why he emphasized that he is the door to the sheepfold, that the way to life is straight and narrow. There is only one way.

Hence he taught: [Sec. 10:69, quoted.] In his Church, and only in his Church, is the way of salvation. By following that path — to the very end — we gain salvation. [Sec. 53:7; 66:12; 76:5.] (*Your Faith and You*, 1953, pp. 288-89.)

SECTION 11

Revelation given through Joseph Smith the Prophet, to his brother, Hyrum Smith, at Harmony, Pennsylvania, May, 1829. This revelation was received through the Urim and Thummim in answer to Joseph's supplication and inquiry. – The coming forth of a great and marvelous work proclaimed – Hyrum restrained from preaching for the time being, he not being yet baptized and ordained – He is assured of the gift of God awaiting his preparation to receive – The organization of the Church foreshadowed – Hyrum admonished to learn the word of God before attempting to proclaim it – Warned against denying the spirit of revelation and prophecy.

1. A great and marvelous work is about to come forth among the children of men.

2. Behold, I am God; give heed to my word, which is quick and powerful, sharper than a two-edged sword, to the dividing asunder of both joints and marrow; therefore give heed unto my word.

3. Behold, the field is white already to harvest; therefore, whoso desireth to reap let him thrust in his sickle with his might, and reap while the day lasts, that he may treasure up for his soul everlasting salvation in the kingdom of God.

4. Yea, whosoever will thrust in his sickle and reap, the same is called of God.

5. Therefore, if you will ask of me you shall receive; if you will knock it shall be opened unto you.

6. Now, as you have asked, behold, I say unto you, keep my commandments, and seek to bring forth and establish the cause of Zion.

7. Seek not for riches but for wisdom; and, behold, the mysteries of God shall be unfolded unto you, and then shall you be made rich. Behold, he that hath eternal life is rich.

8. Verily, verily, I say unto you, even as you desire of me so it shall be done unto you; and, if you desire, you shall be the means of doing much good in this generation.

9. Say nothing but repentance unto this generation. Keep my commandments, and assist to bring forth my work, according to my commandments, and you shall be blessed.

10. Behold, thou hast a gift, or thou shalt have a gift if thou wilt desire of me in faith, with an honest heart, believing in the power of Jesus Christ, or in my power which speaketh unto thee;

11. For, behold, it is I that speak; behold, I am the light which shineth in darkness, and by my power I give these words unto thee.

12. And now, verily, verily, I say unto thee, put your trust in

that Spirit which leadeth to do good — yea, to do justly, to walk humbly, to judge righteously; and this is my Spirit.

13. Verily, verily, I say unto you, I will impart unto you of my Spirit, which shall enlighten your mind, which shall fill your soul with joy;

14. And then shall ye know, or by this shall you know, all things whatsoever you desire of me, which are pertaining unto things of righteousness, in faith believing in me that you shall receive.

15. Behold, I command you that you need not suppose that you are called to preach until you are called.

16. Wait a little longer, until you shall have my word, my rock, my church, and my gospel, that you may know of a surety my doctrine.

17. And then, behold, according to your desires, yea, even according to your faith shall it be done unto you.

18. Keep my commandments; hold your peace; appeal unto my Spirit;

19. Yea, cleave unto me with all your heart, that you may assist in bringing to light those things of which has been spoken — yea, the translation of my work; be patient until you shall accomplish it.

20. Behold, this is your work, to keep my commandments, yea, with all your might, mind and strength.

21. Seek not to declare my word, but first seek to obtain my word, and then shall your tongue be loosed; then, if you desire, you shall have my Spirit and my word, yea, the power of God unto the convincing of men.

22. But now hold your peace; study my word which hath gone forth among the children of men, and also study my word which shall come forth among the children of men, or that which is now translating, yea, until you have obtained all which I shall grant unto the children of men in this generation, and then shall all things be added thereto.

23. Behold thou art Hyrum, my son; seek the kingdom of God, and all things shall be added according to that which is just.

24. Build upon my rock, which is my gospel;

25. Deny not the spirit of revelation, nor the spirit of prophecy, for wo unto him that denieth these things;

26. Therefore, treasure up in your heart until the time which is in my wisdom that you shall go forth.

27. Behold, I speak unto all who have good desires, and have thrust in their sickle to reap.

28. Behold, I am Jesus Christ, the Son of God. I am the life and the light of the world.

29. I am the same who came unto mine own and mine own received me not;

30. But verily, verily, I say unto you, that as many as receive me, to them will I give power to become the sons of God, even to them that believe on my name. Amen.

Joseph Smith: Introduction

Not many days afterwards [Samuel H. Smith was baptized], my brother Hyrum Smith came to us to inquire concerning these things ["what the Lord was about to do for the children of men"], when at his earnest request, I inquired of the Lord through the Urim and Thummim, and received for him the following: [Section 11, follows.] (HC 1:44-45, May 1829, Harmony, Pennsylvania.)

Joseph Fielding Smith: 1-9

From the days of the Prophet's first vision he [Hyrum Smith] had manifested faith in the testimony of his younger brother. When he arrived he asked the Prophet to inquire of the Lord by Urim and Thummim what the Lord would have him do. The answer is the interesting and profitable revelation known as Section Eleven. Like others who had inquired, the Lord repeated to him that a "great and marvelous work" was about to come forth among the children of men. [Sec. 11:2, quoted.] This expression is also found in Hebrews. (4:12.)

The truth of this may seem difficult to realize, but when the "still small voice" of the Lord speaks to men it is overwhelming. We have the story of Elijah, who withstood the great wind when the Lord passed by, that rent the mountains, likewise the earthquake which shook the earth, and then fire, but the Lord was not in the fire and then the Lord spoke by the "still small voice." Then Elijah wrapped his face in his mantle, for the fear of the Lord came upon him. [1 Kings 19:9-14.] When the Lord comes he will speak, and the rocks will be rent, the mountains will be laid low and the valleys exalted and men will try to hide themselves from his presence. They will not be able to stand the piercing of the "still small voice," unless the Spirit of the Lord is upon them. [Sec. 133:40-51.]

"The field is white." Frequently the Lord refers to the world as a field that has turned white ready for the harvest. When the Elders went forth in the beginning, they found it so and by thousands converts came into the Church. Today it is a time of gleaning in all the nations where the Gospel has been preached. All of the brethren who sought counsel of the Lord were invited to thrust in their sickle with their might and reap, "while the day lasts," for there was promised a time of darkness in which there could be no work. Hyrum Smith was taught not to seek for riches, but for wisdom. It would be natural for Hyrum Smith and his brothers to seek for riches, for they had come up through poverty, trial and hatred. Now the Lord declared that riches are not important, but wisdom is, for they would bring forth the mysteries of God and these will make one rich, rewarding eternal life, which is the greatest gift of God. "He that hath eternal life is rich." Yet how slow are we to seek it in the face of the great promise from the Lord?

Hyrum Smith, like others of that day, was commanded to "cry nothing but repentance unto this generation." This was the cry of John the Baptist. [Matt 3:7-11; Mark 1:4.] When the Lord calls upon his servants to cry nothing but repentance, he does not mean that they may not cry baptism, and call upon the people to obey the commandments of the Lord, but he wishes that all they say and do be in the spirit of bringing the people to repentance. Any missionary who fails to do this in his ministry is derelict in his duty. (CHMR, 1947, 1:51-52.)

Heber J. Grant: 1-9

Remember, all you Latter-day Saints, this saying: "Behold, I speak unto all who have good desires and have thrust in their sickle to reap." [Sec. 11:27.] Remember that this revelation (Section 11) calls upon us to seek, not for riches, but for wisdom, "and behold, the mysteries of God shall be unfolded unto you." I do not think I ever read in my life a revelation that made a more profound impression upon me that did this, and I believe that all Latter-day Saints who will read it with a prayerful heart, seeking to God for the light of his Holy Spirit, will have their minds lit up, and the same inspiration that must have come to our beloved patriarch at the time the revelation was given to him, will come to them. (MS, February 12, 1894, 56:102.)

First Presidency (Brigham Young, Heber C. Kimball, Willard Richards): 7
Seek not for riches

Gold is good in its place — it is good in the hands of good men to do good with, but in the hands of a wicked man it often proves a curse instead of a blessing. Gold is a good servant, but a miserable, blind, and helpless god, and at last will have to be purified by fire, with all its followers. (MS, August 15, 1850, 12:241-46.)

Wilford Woodruff: 7
Seek not for riches but for wisdom

As for gold and silver, they are of very little account compared with eternal life. When we die we must leave the riches of this world behind. We were born naked and we will go out of the world in the same condition. We cannot take with us houses, gold, silver, or any of this world's goods. [Alma 39:14.] We will even leave our tabernacles for somebody to bury. Our spirits must appear in the presence of God, and there receive our reward for the deeds done in the body. [Alma 40:11-14.] (JD, June 1880, 21:127.)

Joseph Smith: 7
The mysteries of God shall be unfolded unto you

We are called to hold the keys of the mysteries of those things that have been kept hid from the foundation of the world until now. Some have tasted a little of these things, many of which are to be poured down from heaven upon the heads of babes; yea, upon the weak, obscure and despised ones of the earth. [Sec. 128:18.] Therefore we beseech of you, brethren, that you bear with those who do not feel themselves more worthy than yourselves, while we exhort one another to a reformation with one and all, both old and young . . . let honesty, and sobriety, and candor, and solemnity, and virtue, and pureness, and meekenss, and simplicity crown our heads in every place; and, in fine, become as little children, without malice, guile or hypocrisy. (*HC* 3:296, March 25, 1839.)

Joseph Fielding Smith: 10-14

The Lord declared that Hyrum Smith had a gift. The great gift which he possessed was that of a tender, sympathetic heart, a merciful spirit. The Lord on a later occasion said: "Blessed is my servant Hyrum Smith; for I, the Lord, love him because of the integrity of his heart, and because he loveth that which is right before me, saith the Lord." (D&C 124:15.) This great gift was manifest in his jealous watchcare over the Prophet lest some harm come to him. (*CHMR*, 1947, 1:52.)

Lorenzo Snow: 12-14

There is a way by which persons can keep their consciences clear before God and man, and that is to preserve within them the Spirit of God, which is the spirit of revelation to every man and woman. It will reveal to them, even in the simplest of matters, what they shall do, by making suggestions to them. We should try to learn the nature of this spirit, that we may understand its suggestions, and then we will always be able to do right. This is the grand privilege of every Latter-day Saint. We know that it is our right to have the manifestations of the spirit every day of our lives. . . . The spirit is in every man and every woman so that they need not walk in the darkness at all, and it is not always necessary for them to come to the President of the Church, or to the Twelve, or to the Elders of Israel, to get counsel; they have it within them, there is a friend that knows just exactly what to say to them. From the time we receive the Gospel, go down into the waters of baptism, and have hands laid upon us afterwards for the gift of the Holy Ghost, we have a friend, if we do not drive it from us by doing wrong. That friend is the Holy Spirit, the Holy Ghost, which partakes of the things of God and shows them unto us. This is a grand means that the Lord has provided for us, that we may know the light, and not be groveling continually in the dark. [Sec. 88:66-68.] (CR, April 1899, p. 52.)

Francis M. Lyman: 12-14

No man can be a successful Latter-day Saint without the Spirit of the Lord. No man can hope to enjoy the Spirit of the Lord unless he keep the commandments of the Lord and preserve himself in all purity and righteousness; for the Spirit of the Lord will not dwell in unholy tabernacles. . . . Therefore, every Latter-day Saint is competent to sit in judgment upon himself, and to know whether he is in favor of the Lord or under condemnation. The Lord has ordered that every man should judge for himself, in his own heart, in regard to all the duties of life. As a man thinks, so he is. As a man decides in his own heart, so he does. If we judge correctly and under the light and inspiration of the Lord, we will always do right. [Moro. 7:15-19.] So far as we today are doing wrong, it is because we have judged wrongfully, whether it is in regard to what would be considered important matters or concerning the minor matters of life; for we never do anything without thinking and deciding and exercising our will and judgment. . . .

It is not sufficient for the Latter-day Saints to have good professions and to have really entered into the Church of Christ; but it is necessary that they should continue faithful every day, in all matters doing the will of God. The Lord has revealed to us his will, so that no one need be at a loss to know what to do and how to do it; for if there be not enough already revealed, or should we not be where we can refer to the revealed will at all times, we are entitled to the presence and inspiration of the Spirit of the Lord to inform us what to do. If we have not that Spirit, we are not in the line of our duty as Latter-day Saints; we are not serving the Lord and keeping his commandments as perfectly as we can do. (MS, March 5, 1894, 56:145-46.)

Marriner W. Merrill: 12-13

In our secret places we should sit in judgment upon ourselves and ask ourselves such questions: How has been my course today; has it been approved of the Lord? We may know by the whisperings of the Holy Spirit whether or nor out course has been approved by the Lord; and if we feel condemned, then we may know that there is something wrong with us. (CR, April 1899, p. 17.)

LeGrand Richards: 13

I will impart unto you of my Spirit . . . which shall fill your soul with joy

In Washington just recently, while holding a missionary meeting, a young mother of two children, a new convert to the Church, was asked to say a few words, and when she stood up, she said:

"The missionaries promised me if I would read the Book of Mormon and ask God the Eternal Father, that he would manifest the truth of it unto me by the power of the Holy Ghost. [Moroni 10:3-5.] I did that. I got down on my knees, and then I read that book, and my whole soul was illuminated, and I knew that the book is divine."

This is another tangible evidence that Joseph Smith was a prophet of God and one that the world has not yet been able to account for except as the Prophet Joseph declared. (CR, April 1958, p. 43.)

Charles W. Penrose: 15

God's house is a house of order and not a house of confusion, and he will not accept an offering or an ordinance, or an appointment that he has not established and authorized by his word, which is his law, through those that hold the keys; and there is . . . but one man at a time on the earth that holds the keys of that sealing power. [Sec. 132:7-8.] Now . . . while we look upon the world as stepping out of the proper line of conduct in performing ordinances to administer which they have not been appointed, let us be careful that we do not step out of the narrow way and go into by and forbidden paths. (CR, October 1910, pp. 63-64.)

Brigham Young: 17

Live for the blessings you desire, and you will obtain them, if you do not suffer selfishness, pride, or the least alienation from the path of true virtue and holiness to creep into your hearts. (JD, April 25, 1860, 8:54-55.)

Charles W. Penrose: 18
Appeal unto my Spirit

And this is a certainty: If with our whole heart we seek God, God will draw near to us and we will find him, not expecting, of course, that we will behold him, visibly, that he will come down to everybody and appear in his personality, but by the power of his divine spirit. He will draw near to us and we will draw near to him, and every Latter-day Saint who has really been born of the Spirit as well as of the water, understands something of this. [Sec. 88:62-68.] I don't know of any joy or pleasure, any sensation that is delightful, to be compared with beholding the visions of eternity by the power of the Holy Ghost, and to have the soul lifted up above sublunary things and all earthly and material matters, to draw near to God or Heavenly Father . . . and those who seek the Lord and try to serve him with all their heart and mind and strength, will be able to draw near unto him. (CR, October 1915, pp. 38-39.)

Heber J. Grant: 20

I am thoroughly convinced that all the Lord wants of you and me or of any other man or woman in the Church is for us to perform our full duty and keep the commandments of God. (CR, April 1944, p. 10.)

Brigham Young: 21
You shall have my Spirit and my word

Let one go forth who is careful to logically prove all he says by numerous quotations from the revelations, and let another travel with him who can say, by the power of the Holy Ghost, Thus saith the Lord, and tell what the people should believe — what they should do — how they should live, and teach them to yield to the principles of salvation — though he may tremble under a sense of his weakness, cleaving to the Lord for strength, as such men generally do, you will invariably find that the man who testifies by the power of the Holy Ghost will convince and gather many more of the honest and upright than will the merely logical reasoner. (*JD*, April 25, 1860, 8:53-54.)

Joseph Fielding Smith: 23-25

He [Hyrum Smith] was not to deny the Spirit of Revelation. This is good counsel for all of us today. There are some members of the Church who seemingly complain because the Lord is not giving revelations to be placed in the Doctrine and Covenants as in the beginning, and they ask why revelation has ceased in the Church. Usually it is the case that these critics are not faithfully keeping the commandments the Lord has already given and their eyes are blind to the fact that revelation and the guidance of the Lord is being meted out to the Church constantly. No one with the spirit of discernment can fail to see that the hand of the Lord has guided this people from the beginning and this guidance is manifest today as in other times to all who are humble and have a contrite spirit. (See Jacob 4:8.) The great commandment to us all is to seek first the kingdom of God. If we would pay heed to this commandment there could come peace to the Church today as it came to Enoch and his city. [Moses 7:18-21.] If we are not seeking his kingdom first of all, then we are worthy of condemnation and retarding our progress towards the Kingdom of God. (*CHMR*, 1947, p. 53.)

Harold B. Lee: 25

Just as the Prophet Joseph was called, so have been called Brigham Young, and everyone who has presided in the Presidency of this Church, down to President [Heber J.] Grant, President [J. Reuben] Clark, and President [David O.] McKay, who today occupy the high place as the mouthpieces of God in directing this people.

We as a people seem to be willing to accept many of the ancient prophecies as having been literally fulfilled, but when we see prophecies fulfilled in our own day we are prone to question and to express some doubts. As the Master said, "... A prophet is not without honour, but in his own country, ..." (Mark 6:4), and he might have added, "Save in his own time...."

The voice of the Lord was declared back in 1894, in October of that year, by that man whom we sustained then as the prophet, seer, and revelator unto this Church. He said:

"So far as temporal matters are concerned, we must go to work to provide for ourselves. The day will come, as we have all been told, that we shall see the necessity of making our own shoes and our own clothing, and providing our own foodstuffs, and uniting together to carry out the purposes of the Lord. We will be preserved in the mountains of Israel in the days of God's judgments. I therefore say unto you, my brethren and sisters, prepare for that which is to come." (Wilford Woodruff — Weber Stake, October 8, 1894.)

The voice of the Lord was again heard in 1936, when again we were told by our leaders that there should be a production of all the things needed by those who would otherwise be unable to provide for themselves. For seven years the Church has been schooled in the methods of production and distribution. Storehouses have been established — eighty-six of them today — grain elevators have been erected and yet in the face of all that anxious, feverish activity that has been directed by the Presidency of this Church, there have been contrary voices, there have been contrary philosophies of spending ourselves into prosperity; we have had a subversive economic program; we have had subsidies and controls of every kind that seemed to work at cross purposes with that which the prophets of the Lord were guiding us to do.

The spirit of all this welfare activity throughout the Church and the meaning of all this preparation seemed to have found expression in a dedication prayer offered by one of the Presidency of the Church in August 1940, when the elevator down on Welfare Square was dedicated. Here was a statement from that beautiful and inspired dedicatory prayer:

"May this be an edifice of service, a contribution of love, and as such we dedicate it to thee and ask thy blessings to attend all who may have contributed to its erection, and all who may contribute to keeping of these bins filled with the wheat *which is considered necessary to be preserved preparatory for the judgments that await the nations of the earth.*" (David O. McKay, August 1940.)

Then came 1937. The voice of the Lord again spoke through his mouthpiece from this place to Israel. Individuals were told to go beyond Welfare production, putting storage in their own places sufficient for a needed supply. Oh, there were some who sat back in that day, just like the scorners who sat in the house of Lehi's dreams, and pointed fingers of scorn at the Latter-day Saints who heeded that call, and came to a point after the declaration of war when all such were dubbed as hoarders, and were accused of being unpatriotic to the great urge that was being made of this great American nation. But shortly after that finger of scorn was pointed and those epithets were thus hurled, we had a letter from a state consumer officer in connection with the O.P.A. office who asked the Church to stimulate its membership to produce and to store, to do the very thing that for five and six years the Church had actually been doing under the direction and by the counsel of the leadership of this Church.

Again there came counsel in 1942, a change was made.

"We renew our counsel," said the leaders of the Church, "and repeat our instructions: Let every Latter-day Saint that has land, produce some valuable essential foodstuff thereon and preserve it; or, if we cannot produce an essential foodstuff, let him produce some other kind and exchange it for an essential foodstuff; let them who have no land of their own, and who have knowledge of farming and gardening, try to rent some, either by themselves or with others, and produce foodstuff thereon, and preserve it. Let those who have land produce enough extra to help their less fortunate brethren." (Message of First Presidency, April 1942.)

It was as though they knew fully a year before the present rationing program was inaugurated that there had to be a change from the previous activity if we would be sustained in this time. . . .

On January 17, 1942, a letter was sent out to all the Church urging and instructing that they discontinue stake meetings; to restrict the travel by stake board members, to cut down on other activities where otherwise they would not be able to conserve. And when you remember that all this happened from eight months to nearly a year before the tire and gas rationing took place, you may well understand if you will only take thought that there again was the voice of the Lord to this people, trying to prepare them for the conservation program that within a year was forced upon them. No one at this time could surely foresee that the countries that had been producing certain essential commodities were to be overrun and we thereby be forced into a shortage.

Yes, you remember when the missionaries were taken out of Europe a few years ago, there were many who sat in the scorners' seats who said: "Why, that is silly. During the last world war we did not have all the missionaries taken out." But those who thus spoke forgot that Brigham Young had voiced the word of the Lord some years ago when he said:

"Do you think there is calamity abroad now among the people? . . . All we have yet heard, and all we have experienced is scarcely a preface to the sermon that is going to be preached."

Now, mark you this:

When the testimony of the Elders ceases to be given and the Lord says to them, "Come home; I will now preach my own sermons to the nations of the earth," all you now know can scarcely be called a preface to the sermon that will be preached with fire and sword, tempests, earthquake, hail, rain, thunders and lightnings, and fearful destruction. [Sec. 29:14-21; 43:21-29; 45:26-45; 63:32-35; 88:87-94.]

And it is a matter of record that hardly had the last missionary been called home until all hell seemed to break loose in Europe, in veritable fulfillment of the prophecy that had been given. When likewise the missionaries were called from the island missions of the sea we heard the same clamor, criticizing these brethren because they were doing things that seemed to some members of the Church to be not necessary, and yet we see the great wisdom displayed in what already has been done. (CR, April 1942, pp. 124-28.)

Anthony W. Ivins: 25

I thank the Lord for the written word which we have that is contained in the scriptures; that he has sent prophets into every dispensation of the world. From the time that this earth was created and mankind began to inhabit it the Lord has been very near to his children. He has always guided them or sought to guide them in the right way. He has revealed himself to them through his servants. Prophecy does not come to us simply that we may know that which is to transpire. The Lord sends inspired men to outline to us the future in order that, having that knowledge, we may be brought to repentance; that we may avoid, by repentance, the inevitable judgments which come to men because of their wickedness, that we may become partakers of the blessings which are vouchsafed to all those who repent and serve the Lord. This is the purpose of prophecy, this is the spirit of prophecy, and the prophets have always been with God's children from the beginning of time, and they are with them today to warn and admonish them and to point out to them the way in which they should walk. A prophet is not only one who foretells events that are to come, but one who, inspired of the Lord, instructs people in that which they ought to do in the day of their own probation, that they may be brought back into the presence of the Lord. (CR, October 1914, p. 92.)

Brigham Young: 28
I am Jesus Christ, the Son of God

The errand of Jesus to earth was to bring his brethren and sisters back into the presence of the Father; he has done his part of the work, and it remains for us to do ours. There is not one thing that the Lord could do for the salvation of the human family that he has neglected to do; and it remains for the children of men to receive the truth or reject it; all that can be accomplished for their salvation, independent of them, has been accomplished in and by the Savior. . . . "Jesus paid the debt; he atoned for the original sin; he came and suffered and died on the cross." (*JD*, July 18, 1869, 13:59.)

First Presidency (Joseph F. Smith, Anthon H. Lund, Charles W. Penrose): 30
As many as receive me . . . I give power to become the sons of God

Salvation is attainable only through compliance with the laws and ordinances of the Gospel; and all who are thus saved become sons and daughters unto God in a distinctive sense. In a revelation given through Joseph Smith the Prophet to Emma Smith, the Lord Jesus addressed the woman as "My daughter," and said: "for verily I say unto you, all those who receive my gospel are sons and daughters in my kingdom." (D&C 25:1.) In many instances the Lord had addressed men as his sons. (e.g. D&C 9:1; 34:3; 121:7.)

That by obedience to the Gospel men may become sons of God, both as sons of Jesus Christ, and, through him, as sons of his Father, is set forth in many revelations given in the current dispensation. Thus we read in an utterance of the Lord Jesus to Hyrum Smith in 1829: [D&C 11:28-30, quoted.] To Orson Pratt the Lord spoke through Joseph the Seer, in 1830: [D&C 34:1-3, quoted.] In 1830 the Lord thus addressed Joseph Smith and Sidney Rigdon: [D&C 35:1-2, quoted.] Consider also the following given in 1831: [D&C 39:1-4, quoted .] In a revelation given through Joseph Smith in March, 1831, we read: [D&C 45:7-8, quoted.] (*AF*, 1950, pp. 468-69.)

SECTION 12

Revelation given through Joseph Smith the Prophet, to Joseph Knight, Sen., at Harmony, Pennsylvania, May, 1829. Joseph Knight believed the declarations of Joseph Smith, concerning his possession of the Book of Mormon plates, and the work of translation then in progress, and had given material assistance to the translator and his scribe. See History of the Church, vol. 1, p. 47. – Great and marvelous character of the Lord's work – Personal participation in the bringing forth and establishment of the cause of Zion open to all who have earnest desires and who possess the requisite qualifications.

1. A great and marvelous work is about to come forth among the children of men.

2. Behold, I am God; give heed to my word, which is quick and powerful, sharper than a two-edged sword, to the dividing asunder of both joints and marrow; therefore, give heed unto my word.

3. Behold, the field is white already to harvest; therefore, whoso desireth to reap let him thrust in his sickle with his might, and reap while the day lasts, that he may treasure up for his soul everlasting salvation in the kingdom of God.

4. Yea, whosoever will thrust in his sickle and reap, the same is called of God.

5. Therefore, if you will ask of me you shall receive; if you will knock it shall be opened unto you.

6. Now, as you have asked, behold, I say unto you, keep my commandments, and seek to bring forth and establish the cause of Zion.

7. Behold, I speak unto you, and also to all those who have desires to bring forth and establish this work;

8. And no one can assist in this work except he shall be humble and full of love, having faith, hope, and charity, being temperate in all things, whatsoever shall be entrusted to his care.

9. Behold, I am the light and the life of the world, that speak these words, therefore give heed with your might, and then you are called. Amen.

Joseph Smith: *Introduction*

About the same time an old gentleman came to visit us of whose name I wish to make honorable mention — Mr. Joseph Knight, Sen., of Colesville, Broome County, New

York, who, having heard of the manner in which we were occupying our time, very kindly and considerately brought us a quantity of provisions, in order that we might not be interrupted in the work of translation (of the Book of Mormon plates) by the want of such necessities of life; and I would just mention here, as in duty bound, that he several times brought us supplies, a distance of at least thirty miles, which enabled us to continue the work when otherwise we must have relinquished it for a season. Being very anxious to know his duty as to this work, I inquired of the Lord for him, and obtained the following: [Section 12 follows.] (HC 1:47-48, May 1829; Harmony, Pennsylvania.)

George Teasdale: 1-9

Just think of it! that we should live to fulfil that, and to be associated with this "marvelous work and a wonder." Then there are so many opportunities given unto us to assist in this work. There is plenty of room for all, male and female, who desire to labor for the glory of God. But the Lord has said that those who assist in this work should be full of love, having faith, hope and charity, being temperate in all things, trusting in the Lord, and doing good. (CR, April 1901, pp. 36-37.)

John A. Widtsoe: 6

The question as to individual responsibility for the welfare of the Church was asked in the early days of members of the Church. Several of the men who labored with the Prophet Joseph Smith came to him in those early days and said: "What shall we do?" They might have said: "What shall we do to be saved?" The Lord in every instance gave an answer. We have a series of short revelations in the Doctrine and Covenants, which are the answers to that question. I find in every one a significant statement, worded almost identically in all of these revelations, to Hyrum Smith, David Whitmer, Oliver Cowdery, and others of less fame in the Church: "Keep my commandments, and seek to bring forth and establish the cause of Zion." [Sec. 6:6; 11:6; 14:6.] That is our business, the business of the Latter-day Saints.

From one point of view, it is selfish enough, perhaps, to keep the commandments that I may be blessed, but it is something even greater to keep the commandments that Zion may be established. As the foundation of his great cause, the Lord gave the law of sacrifice. [Moses 5:5-8.] Unless we give of ourselves we cannot build Zion, or any-thing else worthy of the great cause that the Lord has given us. The law of sacrifice, from the day of Adam to the present day, in one form or another, is the basic principle of life among the communities of Saints. [Sec. 64:23; 97:8; 101:35-40; 117:12-14.]

So we need, in this Church and Kingdom, for our own and the world's welfare, a group of men and women in their individual lives who shall be as a light to the nations, and rally standards for the world to follow. [Sec. 45:9; 115:4-5.] Such a people must be different from the world as it now is. There is no opportunity for Latter-day Saints to say we shall be as the world is, unless the world has the same aim that we have. We are here to build Zion to Almighty God, for the blessing of all the world. In that aim we are unique and different from all other peoples. We must respect that obli-gation, and not be afraid of it. We cannot walk as other men, or talk as other men, or do as other men, for we have a different destiny, obligation, and responsibility placed upon us, and we must fit ourselves for that great destiny and obligation. (CR, April 1940, p. 36.)

Anthon H. Lund: 6
Keep my commandments . . . and establish the cause of Zion

The Lord has asked us to do certain things. We will find that they are for our own good. These commandments have been given by a kind Father to his children. He has seen our conditions and our circumstances, and what he has ordained has been calculated for our greatest benefit. When such is the case, we should all feel that we want to keep his com-mandments. We want to benefit ourselves. In fact, this feeling is so strong with us that often we forget what is righteousness, on account of our selfishness. But if we will work truly for our own benefit, then we will keep the laws upon the earth, and we will listen to the counsels which he gives us through his servants. If we do this, the greatest amount of happiness will be ours and we will be able to do our share towards carrying out God's purposes on the earth. (CR, October 1897, p. 3.)

Joseph Smith: 8
Full of love

It is a time-honored adage that love begets love. Let us pour forth love — show forth our kindness unto all mankind, and the Lord will reward us with everlasting increase; cast our bread upon the waters and we shall receive it after many days, increased to a hundredfold. . . .

I do not dwell upon your faults, and you shall not upon mine. Charity which is love, covereth a multitude of sins [1 Pet. 4:8], and I have often covered up all the faults among you; but the prettiest thing is to have no faults at all. We should cultivate a meek, quiet and peaceable spirit. (HC 5:517, July 23, 1843.)

Delbert L. Stapley: 8
Having faith

I desire . . . to challenge each of you to have faith in God; know that he lives, that he is the Father of our spirits, that we are created in the image of his person, that we possess like traits, qualities, and powers, that we are in very deed his children, that he loves us and has made glorious preparation in his many mansions for our eternal well-being.

Have faith in life and its purpose; know that God has provided and planned it for our joy and happiness. Live each day wisely and fruitfully.

Have faith in Christ, our Lord, as the Son of God, the Only Begotten of the Father in the flesh, who is full of grace and truth.

Have faith that Jesus is the Author of peace and salvation to the people of the world.

Have faith in his Gospel plan of salvation, exaltation, and glory.

Have faith in his matchless love in giving his life as an atoning sacrifice to ransom the souls of men from the grave.

Have faith that he is our Redeemer, Savior, and God; that there is no other name under heaven given among men whereby we must be saved.

Have faith in his earthly ministry and divine teachings which lead to joy and happiness in life.

Have faith in his resurrection and ascension to glory and that he now sits on the right hand of God the Father.

Have faith that by his resurrection he broke the bands of death, and that resurrection of the body applies to all mankind.

Have faith in the First Vision of this dispensation. . . .

Have faith that God the Father and his Son, Jesus Christ, personally appeared to the boy Joseph Smith, and revealed themselves to him.

Have faith in Joseph Smith as a true Prophet of God, called to usher in this, the Dispensation of the Fulness of Times.

Have faith in the Church and Kingdom of God established by our Lord through Joseph Smith.

Have faith in continued revelation. Have faith in all that God has revealed. Have faith that he will yet reveal many great and important things concerning his work and kingdom.

Have faith in priesthood authority, knowing that the Lord has said, "For he that receiveth my servants, receiveth me." (D&C 84:36.)

Have faith in the power of God and the gift of healing and miracles.

Have faith in the Bible as the word of God, as far as it is translated correctly.

Have faith in the Book of Mormon and its inspiring message of truth and faith.

Have faith in the Doctrine and Covenants and in its doctrines and teachings which apply to our day and time.

Have faith in the Pearl of Great Price and its valuable information and teachings by two chosen prophets of God —

Abraham, the father of the faithful, and Moses, the great law-giver.

Have faith in your heritage as descendants of Abraham, that you belong to the house of Israel and are children and heirs of promise.

Have faith in our beloved President, David O. McKay, who is not only the President of the Church, but is also prophet, seer, and revelator to the Church and the world today.

Have faith to pray for and sustain him in his high calling and position.

Have faith to be humble and believe and not doubt.

Have faith to receive and obey the truths, principles, and ordinances of the Gospel of Christ.

Have faith to set aside your own views and personal desires to do God's will with confidence and good works.

Have faith in the value of service and be willing to devote your time, talents, and gifts to the building of the kingdom and to the blessing of people.

Have faith to be honest, true, chaste, benevolent, virtuous, and in doing good to all men.

Have faith that God will bless and reward the faithful who love him and serve him in righteousness and in truth unto the end.

Have faith . . . to do these things, walking always in obedience to the commandments, doing those things that will please the Lord and lead you back into his presence. (CR, April 1960, pp. 74-75.)

SECTION 13

Ordination of Joseph Smith and Oliver Cowdery to the Aaronic Priesthood, at Harmony, Pennsylvania, May 15, 1829, under the hands of an Angel, who announced himself as John, the same that is called John the Baptist in the New Testament. The angelic visitant averred that he was acting under the direction of Peter, James, and John, the ancient Apostles, who held the keys of the higher Priesthood, which was called the Priesthood of Melchizedek. The promise was given to Joseph and Oliver that in due time the Priesthood of Melchizedek would be conferred upon them. See History of the Church, vol. 1, p. 39. Compare Section 27:7, 8, 12.

Upon you my fellow servants, in the name of Messiah I confer the Priesthood of Aaron, which holds the keys of the ministering of angels, and of the gospel of repentance, and of baptism by immersion for the remission of sins; and this shall never be taken again from the earth, until the sons of Levi do offer again an offering unto the Lord in righteousness.

Joseph Smith: Introduction

On the 5th of April, 1829, Oliver Cowdery came to my house, until which time I had never seen him. . . . Two days after the arrival of Mr. Cowdery (being the 7th of April), I commenced to translate the Book of Mormon, and he began to write for me. . . .

We still continued the work of translation, when in the ensuing month (May, 1829), we on a certain day went into the woods to pray and inquire of the Lord respecting baptism for the remission of sins, that we found mentioned in the translation of the plates. While we were thus employed, praying and calling upon the Lord, a messenger from heaven descended in a cloud of light, and having laid his hands upon us, he ordained us, saying: [Section 13, quoted.]

He said this Aaronic Priesthood had not the power of laying on hands for the gift of the Holy Ghost, but that this should be conferred on us hereafter; and he commanded us to go and be baptized, and gave us instructions that I should baptize Oliver Cowdery, and afterwards that he should baptize me. Accordingly we went and were baptized. I baptized him first, and afterwards he baptized me, after which I laid my hands upon his head and ordained him to the Aaronic Priesthood, and afterwards he laid his hands on me and ordained me to the same Priesthood—for so we were commanded.

The messenger who visited us on this occasion, and conferred this Priesthood upon us, said that his name was John, the same that is called John the Baptist in the New Testament [Lk. 3:1-17; 7:24-35], and that he acted under the direction of Peter, James and John, who held the keys of the Priesthood of Melchizedek, which Priesthood he said would in due time be conferred on us, and that I should be called the first Elder of the Church and he (Oliver Cowdery) the second. It was on the 15th day of May, 1829, that we were ordained under the hand of this messenger and baptized.

Immediately on our coming up out of the water after we had been baptized we experienced great and glorious blessings from our Heavenly Father. No sooner had I baptized Oliver Cowdery, than the Holy Ghost fell upon us and he stood up and prophesied concerning the rise of this Church, and many other things connected with the Church, and this generation of the children of men. We were filled with the Holy Ghost, and rejoiced in the God of our salvation. (HC 1:32-33, 39-42, April-May, 1829; Harmony, Pennsylvania.)

Oliver Cowdery: *Introduction*

Near this time of the setting of the sun, Sabbath evening, April 5th, 1829, my natural eyes for the first time beheld this brother [Joseph Smith]. He then resided in Harmony, Susquehanna County, Pennsylvania. On Monday, the 6th, I assisted him in arranging some business of a temporal nature, and on Tuesday, the 7th, commenced to write the Book of Mormon. These were days never to be forgotten—to sit under the sound of a voice dictated by the inspiration of heaven, awakened by the utmost gratitude of this bosom! Day after day I continued, uninterrupted, to write from his mouth, as he translated with the Urim and Thummim, or as the Nephites would have said, "Interpreters," the history or record called "The Book of Mormon." . . .

No men, in their sober senses, could translate and write the directions given to the Nephites from the mouth of the Savior, of the precise manner in which men should build up his Church, and especially when corruption had spread an uncertainty over all forms and systems practiced among men, without desiring a privilege of showing the willingness of the heart by being buried in the liquid grave, to answer a "good conscience by the resurrection of Jesus Christ."

After writing the account given of the Savior's ministry to the remnant of the seed of Jacob, upon this continent, it was easy to be seen, as the people said would be, that darkness covered the earth and gross darkness the minds of the people. On reflecting further it was easy to be seen that amid the great strife and noise concerning religion, none had authority from God to administer the ordinances of the gospel. For the question might be asked, have men authority to administer in. the name of Christ, who deny revelations? when his testimony is no less than the spirit of prophecy? and his religion based, built, and sustained by immediate revelations in all ages of the world when he has had a people on the earth? If these facts were buried, and carefully concealed by men whose craft would have been in danger if once permitted to shine in the faces of men, they were no longer to us; and we only waited for the commandment to be given "Arise and be baptized."

This was not long desired before it was realized. The Lord, who is rich in mercy, and ever willing to answer the consistent prayer of the humble, after we had called upon him in a fervent manner, aside from the abodes of men, condescended to manifest to us his will. On a sudden, as from the midst of eternity, the voice of the Redeemer spake to us. While the veil was parted and the angel of God came down clothed with glory and delivered the anxiously looked-for message, and the keys of the gospel of repentance. What joy!

what wonder! what amazement! While the world was racked and distracted—while millions were groping as the blind for the wall, and while all men were resting upon uncertainty, as a general mass, our eyes beheld, our ears heard, as in the "blaze of day"; yes, more — above the glitter of the May sunbeam, which shed its brilliancy over the face of nature! Then his voice, though mild, pierced to the centre, and his words, "I am thy fellow-servant," dispelled every fear. We listened, we gazed, we admired! 'Twas the voice of an angel from glory,'twas a message from the Most High! And as we heard we rejoiced, while his love enkindled upon our souls, and we were wrapt in the vision of the Almighty! Where was room for doubt? Nowhere; uncertainty had fled, doubt had sunk no more to rise, while fiction and deception had fled forever!

But, dear brother, think further, think for a moment what joy filled our hearts and with what surprise we must have bowed, (for who would not have bowed the knee for such a blessing?) when we received under his hand the Holy Priesthood as he said, "Upon you, my fellow servants, in the name of the Messiah, I confer this Priesthood and this authority, which shall remain upon earth, that the sons of Levi may yet offer an offering unto the Lord in righteousness!"

I shall not attempt to paint to you the feelings of this heart, nor the majestic beauty and glory which surrounded us on this occasion; but you will believe me when I say, that earth, nor men, with the eloquence of time, cannot begin to clothe language in as interesting and sublime a manner as this holy personage. No; nor has this earth power to give the joy, to bestow the peace, or comprehend the wisdom which was contained in each sentence as they were delivered by the power of the Holy Spirit! Man may deceive his fellow-men, deception may follow deception, and the children of the wicked one may have power to seduce the foolish and untaught; till naught but fiction feeds the many, and the fruit of falsehood carries in its current the giddy to the grave; but one touch with the finger of his love, yes, one ray of glory from the upper world, or one word from the mouth of the Savior, from the bosom of eternity, strikes it all into insignificance, and blots it forever from the mind. The assurance that we were in the presence of an angel! the certainty that we heard the voice of Jesus, and the truth unsullied as it flowed from a pure personage, dictated by the will of God, is to me past description, and I shall ever look upon this expression of the Savior's goodness with wonder and thanksgiving while I am permitted to tarry; and in those mansions where perfection dwells and sin never comes, I hope to adore in that day which shall never cease. (MS, January 1843, 3:153-54, quoting from a letter to W. W. Phelps, September 7, 1834.)

Joseph Smith: *Introduction*

The question arose from the saying of Jesus, "Among those that are born of women there is not a greater prophet than John the Baptist; but he that is least in the kingdom of God is greater than he." [Luke 7:28.] How is it that John was considered one of the greatest of prophets? His miracles could not have constituted his greatness.

First, he was entrusted with a divine mission of preparing the way before the face of the Lord. Whoever had such a trust committed to him before or since? No man.

Secondly, he was entrusted with the important mission, and it was required at his hands, to baptize the Son of man. Whoever had the honor of doing that? Whoever had so great a privilege and glory? . . .

Thirdly, John, at that time, was the only legal administrator in the affairs of the kingdom there was then on the earth, and holding the keys of power. . . . (HC 5:260-61, January 29, 1843.)

Orson Pratt:
My fellow servants

Perhaps you may inquire here: Was John without a tabernacle? Was he a spirit or was he a personage of tabernacle, of flesh and bones? We all know that he was beheaded before the crucifixion of Christ; and if you wish to know the condition of John when he came to Joseph and Oliver, read the appendix to the Book of Doctrine and Covenants, and you will find that Abraham, Isaac, Jacob, Joseph and many others who are named there, among whom was John the Baptist, were with Christ in his resurrection; that is, they came forth in the first resurrection, at the time that Jesus received his body. [Sec. 133:55.] About that period the graves of the Saints were opened and many of them came forth. [Matt. 27:52-53.] John was amongst them; and he held, legally, the power, keys and Priesthood bestowed upon the lineage of his father, Aaron.

What did John do when he appeared to brothers Joseph Smith and Oliver Cowdery? He did not go forth into the water to baptize them, as he did anciently in Jordan, but he gave the authority to them to baptize—he laid his hands upon their heads and ordained them. Thus the hands of an immortal being—a man sent from heaven—were laid upon their heads! They were ordained to that same Priesthood that John himself held, with the promise and prediction that that Priesthood should not be taken from the earth while the earth should stand. (JD, December 19, 1869, 13:67.)

LeGrand Richards:
The Priesthood of Aaron

From the visit of John the Baptist, we learn these great truths:

1. That one must be ordained to the necessary priesthood by one having authority before he can administer the ordinances of the Gospel.
2. That the Aaronic Priesthood holds the keys of:
   a. The ministering of angels.
   b. The Gospel of repentance.
   c. Baptism by immersion for the remission of sins.
3. That this Priesthood shall never be taken again from the earth until "the sons of Levi do offer again an offering unto the Lord in righteousness."
4. That while the Aaronic Priesthood is divine authority from God, its administration is limited; it "had not the power of laying on hands for the gift of the

Holy Ghost"; that in conferring this Priesthood upon Joseph Smith and Oliver Cowdery, John the Baptist acted under the direction of Peter, James, and John, who held the keys of the Priesthood of Melchizedek, which should thereafter be conferred upon them. (*A Marvelous Work and a Wonder*, 1950, p. 73.)

Parley P. Pratt:
The keys of the ministering of angels

Whenever the keys of Priesthood, or, in other words, the keys of the science of Theology, are enjoyed by man on the earth, those thus privileged are entitled to the ministering of angels, whose business with men on the earth is to restore the keys of the Apostleship when lost; to ordain men to the apostleship when there has been no Apostolic succession; to commit the keys of a new dispensation; to reveal the mysteries of history, the facts of present or past times, and to unfold the events of a future time. They can also be present without being visible to mortals. (*Key to the Science of Theology*, 1943, p. 112.)

Charles W. Penrose:
The sons of Levi

Now as to the "sons of Levi," spoken of by John the Baptist in his ordination of Joseph Smith and Oliver Cowdery. (D&C 13.) They are, or will be, descendants of Levi, holding the Priesthood of Aaron, who will make the offerings predicted by the prophets to be presented to the Lord in latter days in Zion and in Jerusalem. (See Malachi 3:2-4; D&C 124:38, and 128:24.) In Zion, men chosen of the Lord for the special work mentioned will be persons sanctified by the spirit unto "the renewing of their bodies." (D&C 84:32-34.) At Jerusalem they will be Levites by lineal descent, offering the sacrifices that will be required after the restoration spoken of in Zechariah 14:16-21, and many others of the prophets of old concerning "the restitution of all things." (Acts 3:19-21.) (*IE*, August 1912, 15:952.)

Joseph Smith:

An offering unto the Lord in righteousness

Thus we behold the keys of this Priesthood consisted in obtaining the voice of Jehovah that He talked with him (Noah) in a familiar and friendly manner; that He continued to him the keys, the covenants, the power and the glory with which he blessed Adam at the beginning; and the offering of sacrifice, which also shall be continued at the last time; for all the ordinances and duties that ever have been required by the Priesthood, under the directions and commandments of the Almighty in any of the dispensations, shall all be had in the last dispensation, therefore all things had under the authority of the Priesthood at any former period, shall be had again, bringing to pass the restoration spoken of by the mouth of all the Holy Prophets; then shall the sons of Levi offer an acceptable offering to the Lord. "And he shall sit as a refiner and purifier of silver: and he shall purify the sons of Levi, and purge them as gold and silver, that they may offer unto the Lord. . . ." (See Malachi 3:3)

It will be necessary here to make a few observations on the doctrine set forth in the above quotation, and it is generally supposed that sacrifice was entirely done away when the Great Sacrifice (i.e., the sacrifice of the Lord Jesus) was offered up, and that there will be no necessity for the ordinance of sacrifice in future: but those who assert this are certainly not acquainted with the duties, privileges and authority of the priesthood, or with the Prophets.

The offering of sacrifice has ever been connected and forms a part of the duties of the Priesthood. It began with the Priesthood, and will be continued until after the coming of Christ, from generation to generation. We frequently have mention made of the offering of sacrifice by the servants of the Most High in ancient days, prior to the law of Moses [Moses 5:5-8]; which ordinances will be continued when the Priesthood is restored with all its authority, power and blessings. . . .

It is a very prevalent opinion that the sacrifices which were offered were entirely consumed. This was not the case;

if you read Leviticus, second chapter, second and third verses, you will observe that the priests took a part as a memorial and offered it up before the Lord, while the remainder was kept for the maintenance of the priests; so that the offerings and sacrifices are not all consumed upon the altar—but the blood is sprinkled, and the fat and certain other portions are consumed. [Lev. 4.]

These sacrifices, as well as every ordinance belonging to the Priesthood, will, when the Temple of the Lord shall be built, and the sons of Levi be purified, be fully restored and attended to in all their powers, ramifications, and blessings. [Sec. 84:4-5, 31; 124:39.] This ever did and ever will exist when the powers of the Melchisedic Priesthood are sufficiently manifest; else how can the restitution of all things spoken of by the Prophets be brought to pass? [Acts 3:19-21.] It is not to be understood that the law of Moses will be established again with all its rites and variety of ceremonies; this has never been spoken of by the Prophets [3 Nephi 9:19-20; 15:3-9]; but those things which existed prior to Moses' day, namely, sacrifice, will be continued.

It may be asked by some, what necessity for sacrifice, since the Great Sacrifice was offered? In answer to which, if repentance, baptism, and faith existed prior to the days of Christ [Moses 6:62-68; 7:23-24; Gal. 3:8; 1 Cor. 10:1-4], what necessity for them since that time? (HC 4:210-12, October 5, 1840.)

Joseph Fielding Smith:
The sons of Levi . . . an offering . . . in righteousness

What kind of offering will the sons of Levi make to fulfil the words of Malachi and John? (Mal. 3:1-4; D&C 13; 124:39; 128:24.) Logically such a sacrifice as they were authorized to make in the days of their former ministry when they were first called. (Ezek. 43:18-27; 44:9-27.) Will such a sacrifice be offered in the temple? Eventually not in any temple as they are constructed for work of salvation and exaltation today. It should be remembered that the great temple, which is yet to be built in the city of Zion, will not be one edifice, but twelve. Some of these temples will be for the lesser priesthood. [*History of the Church*, vol. 1, pp. 357-59.]

When those temples are built, it is very likely that provision will be made for some ceremonies and ordinances which may be performed by the Aaronic Priesthood and a place provided where the sons of Levi may offer their offering in righteousness. This will have to be the case because all things are to be restored. There were ordinances performed in ancient Israel in the tabernacle when in the wilderness, and after it was established at Shiloh in the land of Canaan, and later in the temple built by Solomon. The Lord has informed us that this was the case and has said that in those edifices ordinances for the people were performed. [D&C 124:28-29.]

These temples that we now have, however, the Lord commanded to be built for the purpose of giving to the saints the blessings which belong to their exaltation, blessings which are to prepare those who receive them to "enter into his rest, . . . which rest is the fulness of his glory," and these ordinances have to be performed by authority of the Melchizedek Priesthood, which the sons of Levi did not hold. [D&C 84:24.]

. . . Now in the nature of things, the law of sacrifice will have to be restored, or all things which were decreed by the Lord would not be restored. It will be necessary, therefore, for the sons of Levi, who offered the blood sacrifices anciently in Israel, to offer such a sacrifice again to round out and complete this ordinance in this dispensation. Sacrifice by the shedding of blood was instituted in the days of Adam and of necessity will have to be restored. [Moses 5:5-8]

The sacrifice of animals will be done to complete the restoration when the temple spoken of is built; at the beginning of the millennium, or in the restoration, blood sacrifices will be performed long enough to complete the fulness of the restoration in this dispensation. Afterwards sacrifice will be of some other character. [3 Nephi 9:10-20.] (*Doctrines of Salvation*, 1956, 3:93-94.)

SECTION 14

Revelation given through Joseph Smith the Prophet, to David Whitmer, at Fayette, New York, June, 1829. The Whitmer family had become greatly interested in the translating of the Book of Mormon. Joseph changed his residence to the Whitmer home, where he dwelt until the work of translation was carried to completion and the copyright on the forthcoming book secured. Each of the three sons, having received a testimony as to the genuineness of the work, became deeply concerned over the matter of his individual duty; and the Prophet inquired of the Lord respecting the matter. This revelation and the two next following (Sections 15 and 16) were given in answer, through the Urim and Thummim. See History of the Church, vol. 1, p. 48. David Whitmer later became one of the Three Witnesses to the Book of Mormon. – Conditions of attaining eternal life specified – The Lord's purpose of bringing the fulness of his Gospel from the gentiles to the house of Israel – David Whitmer informed of his call to assist in the latter-day work – His reward, conditioned by his faithfulness, is promised.

1. A great and marvelous work is about to come forth unto the children of men.

2. Behold, I am God; give heed to my word, which is quick and powerful, sharper than a two-edged sword, to the dividing asunder of both joints and marrow; therefore give heed unto my word.

3. Behold, the field is white already to harvest; therefore, whoso desireth to reap let him thrust in his sickle with his might, and reap while the day lasts, that he may treasure up for his soul everlasting salvation in the kingdom of God.

4. Yea, whosoever will thrust in his sickle and reap, the same is called of God.

5. Therefore, if you will ask of me you shall receive; if you will knock it shall be opened unto you.

6. Seek to bring forth and establish my Zion. Keep my commandments in all things.

7. And, if you keep my commandments and endure to the end you shall have eternal life, which gift is the greatest of all the gifts of God.

8. And it shall come to pass, that if you shall ask the Father in my name, in faith believing, you shall receive the Holy Ghost, which giveth utterance, that you may stand as a witness of the things of which you shall both hear and see, and also that you may declare repentance unto this generation.

9. Behold, I am Jesus Christ, the Son of the living God, who created the heavens and the earth, a light which cannot be hid in darkness;

10. Wherefore, I must bring forth the fulness of my gospel from the Gentiles unto the house of Israel.

11. And behold, thou art David, and thou art called to assist; which thing if ye do, and are faithful, ye shall be blessed both spiritually and temporally, and great shall be your reward. Amen.

Joseph Smith: *Introduction*

Shortly after commencing to translate, I became acquainted with Mr. Peter Whitmer, of Fayette, Seneca County, New York, and also with some of his family. In the beginning of the month of June, his son, David Whitmer, came to the place where we were residing, and brought with him a two-horse wagon, for the purpose of having us accompany him to his father's place, and there remain until we should finish the work. [See Sec. 6:14-24, Orson Pratt commentary.] It was arranged that we should have our board free of charge, and the assistance of one of his brothers to write for me, and also his own assistance when convenient. Having much need of such timely aid in an undertaking so arduous, and being informed that the people in the neighborhood of the Whitmers were anxiously awaiting the opportunity to inquire into these things, we accepted the invitation, and accompanied Mr. Whitmer to his father's house, and there resided until the translation was finished and the copyright secured. Upon our arrival, we found Mr. Whitmer's family very anxious concerning the work, and very friendly toward ourselves. They continued so, boarded and lodged us according to arrangements; and John Whitmer, in particular, assisted us very much in writing during the remainder of the work.

In the meantime, David, John and Peter Whitmer, Jun., became our zealous friends and assistants in the work; and being anxious to know their respective duties, and having desired with much earnestness that I should inquire of the Lord concerning them, I did so, through the means of the Urim and Thummim, and obtained for them in succession the following revelations: [Sections 14, 15, and 16 follow.] (HC 1:48-49, June 1829; Fayette, New York.)

John A. Widtsoe:
A great and marvelous work

Not only in numbers have we become a "marvelous work and a wonder" in a little less than one hundred years; but in a greater and a larger sense have we become a marvelous people, for we have impressed our thought upon the whole world. The world does not believe today as it did ninety years ago. A few days ago I picked up a recent number of a great magazine, and my feelings were roused within me and my testimony increased when I found one of the writers declaring to the readers of the magazine that "God cannot look upon sin with the least degree of tolerance," borrowed almost word for word from section one of the Doctrine and Covenants [v.31]. In such a way have the doctrines taught by the despised Latter-day Saints been appropriated by the nations of the earth; and whether the people of the earth accept the inspiration of Joseph Smith, nevertheless, in fact the whole current of human thought has been changed by the doctrines of this people. That is perhaps the greatest achievement of "Mormonism" during the last ninety years, unless it be the achievement to secure a body of people numbering hundreds of thousands who almost always see eye to eye, who understand as with one mind, who feel as with one heart, who worship God alike, and who in that united worship and action find a tremendous advantage in life. Do you know of a happier people? I find happiness wherever I go, for Latter-day Saints understand the truth. They have seen the beginning and they know the end of the designs of God with respect to his children. They do not grope in darkness. Who cares if we are few in comparison with the 1,500 millions of people on the face of the earth? We are as yeast in the dough, and will yet ferment the whole earth. (CR, October 1921, p.109.)

Anthon H. Lund: 6
Seek to bring forth and establish my Zion

The Prophet Nephi, in speaking of Zion, gives us characteristics that should be found in the Zion of the latter days. [2 Nephi 26:29-31.] Among them was that there should not be priestcraft; and he defines priestcraft as preaching for gain and for influence among the people. This the Lord forbids. He says that the people should work for Zion. That should be the object of their coming together, the one aim and purpose of their lives—to work for Zion, and not to make anything else the object of their lives. If they make money their object he says they shall perish. How often have we seen this fulfilled! Those who have forgotten why the Lord called them from their homes and gathered them here, and who have made money their sole object, have perished spiritually; they have lost the faith which was once so strong in their breasts that they were able to leave everything that was dear unto them and gather here. We want to take this lesson to heart. We want to be laborers in Zion, and work for the cause of Zion, and not for other objects—that is, not to make them the only objects of our lives. (CR, October 1897, pp. 2-3.)

Brigham Young: 6
Seek to bring forth and establish my Zion

You hear brethren talk of coming to Zion to enjoy the blessings of this land; but do you not see that it is the shortsightedness of men which causes their disappointment when they arrive here. They read in the Bible, in the Book of Mormon, and Book of Doctrine and Covenants, about Zion, and what is to be . . . before they came here they were the ones to help to build up Zion. They gathered here with the spirit of Zion resting upon them, then expecting to find Zion in its glory, whereas their own doctrine should teach them that they are coming here to make Zion.

We can make Zion, or we can make Babylon, just as we please. We can make just what we please of this place. The people can make Zion: they can make a heaven within themselves. When people gather here, they should come with a determination to make Zion within themselves, with the resolution that "I will carry myself full of the Spirit of Zion wherever I go; and this is the way in which I will control evil spirits; for I mean that my spirit shall have control over evil," and do you not see that such a course will make Zion? (JD, July 5, 1857, 5:4.)

Joseph F. Smith: 7
Keep my commandments and endure to the end

We have entered into the bond of that new and everlasting covenant agreeing that we would obey the commandments of God in all things whatsoever he shall command us. This is an everlasting covenant even unto the end of our days, and when is the end of our days? We may think it has reference to the end of our mortal lives, that a time will come after we have finished this probation when we can live without obedience to the commandments of God. This is a great error. We shall never see the day in time nor eternity when it will not be obligatory, and when it will not be a pleasure as well as a duty for us, as his children, to obey all the commandments of the Lord throughout the endless ages of eternity. It is upon this principle that we keep in touch with God, and remain in harmony with his purposes. It is only in this way that we can consummate our mission, and obtain our crown and the gift of eternal lives, which is the greatest gift of God. Can you imagine any other way? (CR, April 1898, p. 68.)

Orson F. Whitney: 7
Eternal life . . . is the greatest of all the gifts of God

God's greatest gift is eternal life, but that pertains to Eternity. The greatest blessing that our Heavenly Father can bestow upon us in time, or while we are here, is the power to lay hold upon eternal life. The everlasting Gospel, through obedience to its every requirement, and the gift of the Holy Ghost, gives this power. It not only saves—it exalts men to

where God and Christ dwell in the fulness of celestial glory.
[Sec. 76:54-62.] (CR, October 1929, p. 30.)

Joseph Fielding Smith: 8-11

In the revelation given to David Whitmer (Sec. 14), the Lord made him the promise that if he would keep the commandments and endure to the end, he should have eternal life, moreover he was commanded to assist in bringing forth the Lord's work and that the time would come when he would be a witness "of the things of which you shall both hear and see, and also that you may declare repentance unto this generation." This promise was based upon his faithfulness, and David was faithful and sincerely in earnest in his devotion to the Church and Joseph Smith when that witness came and for several years afterwards. There was one incident of significance that occurred when the Angel Moroni presented the plates before the three witnesses. The record states: "In his hands he held the plates which we had been praying for these to have a view of. He turned over the leaves one by one, so that we could see them, and discern the engravings thereon distinctly. He then addressed himself to David Whitmer, and said, 'David, blessed is the Lord, and he that keepeth his commandments,' when immediately afterwards, we heard a voice from out of the bright light above us, saying, 'These plates have been revealed by the power of God, and they have been translated by the power of God.' " (HC 1:54.) (CHMR, 1947, 1:63.)

Orson Pratt: 8

You may stand as a witness

As I have already mentioned, one more witness remains who saw that angel and the plates. Who is it? David Whitmer, a younger man than Martin Harris, probably some seventy years of age, I do not recollect his age exactly. Where does he live? In the western part of Missouri. Does he still hold fast to his testimony? He does. Many of the Elders of this Church, in going to and fro among the nations, have called upon him from time to time, and they all bear the same testimony—that Mr. David Whitmer still, in the most solemn manner, declares that he saw the angel and that he saw the plates in his hands. But he is not here with us; he has not gathered up with the people of God. That, however, does not prove that his testimony is not true, by no means. (JD, July 18, 1875, 18:161.)

Wilford Woodruff: 10
From the Gentiles unto the house of Israel

Sometimes our neighbors and friends think hard of us because we call them Gentiles; but, bless your souls, we are all Gentiles. The Latter-day Saints are all Gentiles in a national capacity. The Gospel came to us among the Gentiles. We are not Jews, and the Gentile nations have got to hear the Gospel first. The whole Christian world have got to hear the Gospel, and when they reject it, the law will be bound and the testimony sealed, and it will turn to the house of Israel. Up to the present day we have been called to preach the Gospel to the Gentiles, and we have had to do it. For the last time we have been warning the world, and we have been engaged in that work for forty-five years. (JD, September 12, 1875, 18:112.)

John A. Widtsoe: 11

Perhaps the event of that troubled year [1838] which gave keenest sorrow was the loss of Oliver Cowdery and David Whitmer from the membership roll of the Church—two of the three original witnesses of the Book of Mormon, men of high esteem in the Church. Oliver Cowdery was excommunicated, and for many years remained outside the Church, rather than to confess his error and repent. David Whitmer withdrew from the Church rather than to face trial upon the charges made against him. The absence from the councils of the Church of these fine men who had been so gloriously blessed by heaven was grieved by the whole Church membership.

Though these men were no longer members of the Church, yet they always maintained the truth of their tes-

timony as found in the Book of Mormon, and their belief in
the divinity of the revelations given to Joseph Smith the
Prophet. Moreover, Oliver Cowdery, after some years,
humbly entered the waters of baptism again [Oct. 1848] and
was on his way to plead with David Whitmer to return to the
Church, when death overtook him. [Mar. 3, 1850.] Both
affirmed with their last breath the truth of their testimony
regarding the Lord's latter-day work. Their knowledge of the
truth of the restored Gospel did not leave them.

Naturally the question arises: How could these men,
both of whom had seen the angelic guardian of the plates
from which the Book of Mormon was translated and the
plates themselves, and one of whom in addition had been
privileged to have converse with heavenly beings, John the
Baptist, Peter, James and John—how could such men so
conduct themselves as to endanger their Church membership or be content to remain ouside the Church? They had
knowledge, beyond that of other men, of the reality and
divinity of the events which led to the organization of The
Church of Jesus Christ of Latter-day Saints.

The answer to the question is simple, well understood
by all. These brethren did not use their knowledge in conformity with the order of the Church as set forth in the
revelations of the Lord. That is, they entered forbidden
paths; they did not obey the commandments of God. The
practices of their lives did not correspond with their knowledge. (CR, April 1938, p. 49.)

SECTION 15

Revelation given through Joseph Smith the Prophet, to John Whitmer, at Fayette, New York, June, 1829. See heading to Section 14. John Whitmer later became one of the Eight Witnesses to the Book of Mormon. – The message is intimately and impressively personal, in that the Lord tells of what was known only to John Whitmer and himself – The recipient blessed for his worthy desire – The thing of greatest worth to him.

1. Hearken, my servant John, and listen to the words of Jesus Christ, your Lord and your Redeemer.

2. For behold, I speak unto you with sharpness and with power, for mine arm is over all the earth.

3. And I will tell you that which no man knoweth save me and thee alone—

4. For many times you have desired of me to know that which would be of the most worth unto you.

5. Behold, blessed are you for this thing, and for speaking my words which I have given you according to my commandments.

6. And now, behold, I say unto you, that the thing which will be of the most worth unto you will be to declare repentance unto this people, that you may bring souls unto me, that you may rest with them in the kingdom of my Father. Amen.

Joseph Fielding Smith: *Introduction*

John [Whitmer] displayed his eagerness to be of assistance and did some writing for the Prophet at that time [June 1829]. With his brothers, he desired earnestly to know what message the Lord had for him, and due to his solicitation the Lord gave him a revelation (Sec. 15) through the Urim and Thummim. . . .

Peter Whitmer, Jr., became one of the eight witnesses of the Book of Mormon. He was the fifth son of Peter Whitmer and was born September 27, 1809. With other members of the Whitmer family, he became very friendly with the Prophet and assisted him when the Prophet was translating the Book of Mormon. He also desired the word of the Lord in relation to his responsibilities and received the revelation by Urim and Thummim known as section sixteen. [June 1829; Fayette, New York.] (CHMR, 1947, 1:64.)

Rudger Clawson: 1-6

The matters that are brought to our attention in these words of revelation [Sec. 15] are most glorious for contemplation. Cast your minds back to the early days of this Church, and there stood this man John Whitmer, recently come into the Church of Christ. Various occupations in which he might engage were before him. He had the opportunity to labor upon the farm, to engage in merchandising, to follow mining, to study the profession of medicine or law, or to adopt one of the many other occupations in which men employ themselves. The question he asked himself at that time was, What would be the most worth to him? . . . I say, these opportunities were before him, because the country was before him, and this country is full of opportunities, which are within the reach of all. . . . He stood there in this situation, not having been trained long in the Gospel of Christ, and I say to you — for it is on record here — that a voice came to that man from the eternal worlds, and that voice set at rest in him every doubt, every dubiety, every fearful anticipation. At a critical time in his life, when he must choose which way to go, that voice said unto him that which would be of most worth unto him was to declare repentance unto the people and bring souls unto Christ. The message was of such importance that it came to him with "sharpness and with power." It was the voice of Jesus Christ. (CR, April 1902, p. 7.)

SECTION 16

*Revelation given through Joseph Smith the Prophet, to Peter
Whitmer, Jun., at Fayette, New York, June, 1829. See heading to
Section 14. Peter Whitmer, Jun., later became one of the Eight
Witnesses to the Book of Mormon.*

1. Hearken, my servant Peter, and listen to the words of
Jesus Christ, your Lord and your Redeemer.

2. For behold, I speak unto you with sharpness and with
power, for mine arm is over all the earth.

3. And I will tell you that which no man knoweth save me
and thee alone—

4. For many times you have desired of me to know that
which would be of the most worth unto you.

5. Behold, blessed are you for this thing, and for speaking my
words which I have given unto you according to my
commandments.

6. And now, behold, I say unto you, that the thing which
will be of the most worth unto you will be to declare repentance
unto this people, that you may bring souls unto me, that you may
rest with them in the kingdom of my Father. Amen.

John A. Widtsoe: 1-6

The Doctrine and Covenants is a compilation of the
revelations received by Joseph Smith to individuals and for
the guidance of the Church. From the first years of the work
the Prophet kept every scrap of paper pertaining to the
progress of the work, in fact, this care of things that must
have seemed trivial is one of the evidences of the sincerity of
the man. For example, when John and Peter Whitmer asked
for help, he received for each of them a revelation, substan-
tially the same: [Sections 15 and 16, quoted.]

This simple revelation is directed to the individual and
at first sign it has no permanent value for the Church. Yet as
a revelation from God it was preserved and published. An
insincere man could have eliminated this and other similar
revelations as of little consequence. Not so with Joseph. The

Lord has spoken. The words were part of the building of the kingdom of God, and the same advice would be useful to many men then and now. [Sec. 93:49.] (*Joseph Smith*, 1951, pp. 251-52.)

Charles W. Penrose: 1

God is made manifest sometimes by his own voice through the appointed channels; sometimes through the ministration of angels authorized to speak for him; sometimes by the voice of Jesus Christ, our Redeemer, through whom revelations contained in the Doctrine and Covenants have come to us and always by the inspiration of the Holy Ghost, the witness for the Father and the Son, and it is the privilege of every member of the Church to receive and be inspired by the divine influence. (CR, October 1912, p. 60.)

Joseph Smith: 6

After all that has been said, the greatest and most important duty is to preach the Gospel. (*HC* 2:478, April 6, 1837.)

Abraham H. Cannon: 6
Declare repentance unto this people

It is the duty of the Latter-day Saints to preach to the world the Gospel of the Son of God, to chide them for their sins, to reprove them for their iniquities, to encourage them in everything that is good and ennobling, but to be fearless in the defense and proclamation of the truth, for truth will be sustained. (MS, July 18, 1895, 57:452-53.)

David O. McKay: 6
Declare repentance unto this people

Today, in the midst of the world's perplexity, there should be no question in the mind of the true Latter-day Saint as to what his mission is. The answer is as clear as the noonday sun in a cloudless sky.

In the year 1830 there was given to the people of this land and of the world a divine plan whereby individuals can find security and peace of mind and live in harmonious accord with their fellow beings. In all men's theories and experiments since history began, human intelligence has never devised a system which, when applied to the needs of humanity, can even appproach this plan in effectiveness.

In simple words, this is the word which we should preach and live—the Gospel plan of salvation.

First: Preach and live, in season and out of season, belief in God the Eternal Father, in his Son Jesus Christ, and in the Holy Ghost.

Second: Proclaim that fundamental in this Gospel plan is the sacredness of the individual, that God's work and glory is "to bring to pass the immortality and eternal life of man." (Moses 1:39.)

Under this concept, it is a great imposition, if not indeed a crime, for any government or any other organization to deny a man the right to speak, to worship and to work.

Third: Preach and live the belief that governments were instituted of God for the benefit of the state. Preach that ". . . no government can exist in peace," and I quote from the Doctrine and Covenants, "except such laws are framed and held inviolate as will secure to each individual the free exercise of conscience, the right and control of property, and the protection of life." (D&C 134:2.)

Fourth: Preach and live the sacredness of family ties—the perpetuation of the family as the cornerstone of society. . . .

Fifth: Proclaim that God's Beloved Son, the Redeemer and Savior of mankind, stands at the head of his Church that bears his name—that he guides and inspires those who are authorized to represent him here on earth—authorized by the Priesthood when heavenly messengers bestowed upon the Prophet Joseph Smith and others associated with his divine authority.

Sixth: Preach and live that the responsibility of declaring this plan of life, this way of life, this plan of salvation, rests upon the entire membership of the Church, but most particularly upon those who have been ordained to the

Priesthood and who have been called as leaders and servants of the people. (*IE*, November 1956, 59:781-82.)

Orson F. Whitney: 6
Declare repentance unto this people

The obligation of saving souls rests upon every man and woman in this Church—if not with equal weight, at least proportionately, according to their strength, their time, their opportunities, their abilities; and they cannot get out from under this responsibility on the plea that it belongs only to such and such persons. Did not the Lord say, through Joseph the Seer, at the beginning of this work, "Behold, it is a day of warning, and not a day of many words. . . . it becometh every man who hath been warned to warn his neighbor"? [Sec. 63:58, 88:81.] (CR, October 1913, p. 99.)

SECTION 17

Revelation given through Joseph Smith the Prophet, to Oliver Cowdery, David Whitmer and Martin Harris, at Fayette, New York, June, 1829, prior to their viewing the engraved plates that contained the Book of Mormon record. Joseph and his scribe, Oliver Cowdery, had learned from the translation of certain passages on the Book of Mormon plates that three special witnesses would be designated. See Ether 5:2-4; also 2 Nephi 11:3, and 27:12. Oliver Cowdery, David Whitmer and Martin Harris were moved upon by an inspired desire to be the three special witnesses. The Prophet inquired of the Lord, and this revelation was given in answer, through the Urim and Thummim. See History of the Church, vol. 1, p. 52. – The three conditionally promised that they shall be permitted to view not only the plates but also other sacred relics of Book of Mormon record – Only by faith like unto that of the prophets of old can they be thus privileged – They to testify of what they shall see – Joseph Smith's solemn avowals to be supported – The Lord declares that as he lives the translation is true.

1. Behold, I say unto you, that you must rely upon my word, which if you do with full purpose of heart, you shall have a view of the plates, and also of the breastplate, the sword of Laban, the Urim and Thummim, which were given to the brother of Jared upon the mount, when he talked with the Lord face to face, and the miraculous directors which were given to Lehi while in the wilderness, on the borders of the Red Sea.

2. And it is by your faith that you shall obtain a view of them, even by that faith which was had by the prophets of old.

3. And after that you have obtained faith, and have seen them with your eyes, you shall testify of them, by the power of God;

4. And this you shall do that my servant Joseph Smith, Jun., may not be destroyed, that I may bring about my righteous purposes unto the children of men in this work.

5. And ye shall testify that you have seen them, even as my servant Joseph Smith, Jun., has seen them; for it is by my power that he has seen them, and it is because he had faith.

6. And he has translated the book, even that part which I have commanded him, and as your Lord and your God liveth it is true.

7. Wherefore, you have received the same power, and the same faith, and the same gift like unto him;

8. And if you do these last commandments of mine, which I have given you, the gates of hell shall not prevail against you; for my grace is sufficient for you, and you shall be lifted up at the last day.

9. And I, Jesus Christ, your Lord and your God, have spoken it unto you, that I might bring about my righteous purposes unto the children of men. Amen.

John A. Widtsoe: *Introduction*

In March, 1829, [Fayette, New York] the Lord declared to Joseph that three men should have the privilege of seeing the plates and bearing witness to their existence. (D&C Sec. 5; *History of the Church*, vol. 1, p. 52.) A similar prediction was found also in the Book of Mormon itself. (2 Nephi 11:3; Ether 5:3.) Oliver Cowdery, David Whitmer, and Martin Harris were later designated as these witnesses. In full conformity with the prediction, in June 1829, when the translation of the plates was approaching the end, this promise was realized. [Sec. 17 was received by Joseph Smith at Fayette, New York, June 1829.]

Joseph and his three friends at the Peter Whitmer, Sr., home in Fayette, Seneca County, New York, went into the nearby woods one day, and there engaged in earnest prayer that the plates might by shown to them by Moroni. (*History of the Church*, vol. 1, pp. 52-59.) To this they testified in a written and published statement. This event is related by Joseph Smith in his history, and published while the witnesses were living.

Sometime later, divine permission was given to show these plates to eight other men. (*Ibid.*, vol. 1, p. 57.) To have more witnesses was making the assurance of the reality of the plates doubly sure. The corroboration of the testimony of the three men, by the eight under different conditions, and at different times, certifies immeasurably to the truth of the events. The men, Christian Whitmer, Jacob Whitmer, Peter Whitmer, Jr., John Whitmer, Hiram Page, Joseph Smith, Sr., Hyrum Smith, and Samuel H. Smith unitedly signed a testimony in which they describe the plates and the engravings on them, and further declare that they actually handled and "hefted" the plates. There are no generalities in these testimonies; they are specific. (*Joseph Smith*, 1951, pp. 46-47.)

Joseph Fielding Smith: 1-9

When Nephi was writing of the coming forth of the record of the Nephites, he stated that witnesses should be called to testify of it before the world. These words are as follows:

> Wherefore, at that day when the book shall be delivered unto the man of whom I have spoken, the book shall be hid from the eyes of the world, that the eyes of none shall behold it save it be that three witnesses shall behold it, by the power of God, besides him to whom the book shall be delivered; and they shall testify to the truth of the book and the things therein.
>
> And there is none other which shall view it, save it be a few according to the will of God, to bear testimony of his word unto the children of men; for the Lord God hath said that the words of the faithful should speak as if it were from the dead.
>
> Wherefore, the Lord God will proceed to bring forth the words of the book; and in the mouth of as many witnesses as seemeth him good will he establish his word; and wo be unto him that rejecteth the word of God! (2 Nephi 27:12-14.)

Joseph Smith in his youth, when he was translating the Book of Mormon, surely was not acquainted with the law of God in relation to witnesses. The law had been established in the beginning, and was reiterated by Moses to Israel, that in the mouth of two or three witnesses should all things be established. [Deut. 17:6.] When the Jews accused Christ of standing alone with no one to testify with him, he, reading their thoughts, called attention to their law and said he did not stand alone, but he and his Father fulfilled the law as witnesses of his mission. (John 8:14-18.) Here are his words:

> Jesus answered and said unto them, Though I bear record of myself, yet my record is true: for I know whence I came, and whither I go; but ye cannot tell whence I come, and whither I go.
>
> Ye judge after the flesh; I judge no man.
>
> And yet if I judge, my judgment is true; for I am not alone, but I and the Father that sent me.

It is also written in your law, that the testimony of two men is true. I am one that bear witness of myself, and the Father that sent me beareth witness of me.

In preparing witnesses for the Book of Mormon, and the restoration of the Church with its keys of power, the Lord provided for the necessary witnesses, according to his divine purposes to fulfil the law and to place that testimony before the people of the world with binding force. Therefore Nephi could well say "Wo be unto him that rejecteth the word of God." . . . Moreover, the purpose of this testimony was that Joseph Smith might not be destroyed; in other words, had Joseph Smith stood alone without these witnesses, he could not have fulfilled the law, and his testimony would have fallen to the ground and he and his work would have been destroyed; . . . but this testimony buoyed him up and makes his story binding on all who hear it.

The Urim and Thummim shown to the witnesses and which Joseph Smith received were prepared by the Lord for the purpose of translating these sacred records. They were given to the brother of Jared on the mount and he sealed them up with the writings which he made of the visions of the Lord, so that at a later day they were to be used to bring to light his record of the Jaredite people. [Ether 3:23, 28.] These "stones" were in the possession of King Mosiah and by him were used in translating the Jaredite record. [Moses 28:11-19.] they were later hidden up by Moroni with the abridgment of Nephite history, with the other articles mentioned in section seventeen. (*CHMR*, 1947, 1:40-42.)

Orson Pratt and Joseph F. Smith: 1

"On Saturday morning, Sept. 7 [1878], we met Mr. David Whitmer (at Richmond, Ray Co., Mo.), the last remaining one of the three witnesses of the Book of Mormon. . . .

"Elder O. Pratt to David Whitmer: 'Do you remember what time you saw the plates?'

"D. Whitmer: It was in June, 1829, the latter part of the month, and the eight witnesses saw them, I think, the next day or the day after (i.e., one or two days after). Joseph showed them the plates himself, but the angel showed us (the three witnesses) the plates, as I suppose to fulfill the words of the book itself. Martin Harris was not with us at this time; he obtained a view of them afterwards (the same day). Joseph, Oliver, and myself were together when I saw them. We not only saw the plates of the Book of Mormon, but also the brass plates, the plates of the Book of Ether, the plates containing the records of the wickedness and secret combinations of the people of the world down to the time of their being engraved, and many other plates. The fact is, it was just as though Joseph, Oliver and I were sitting just here on a log, when we were overshadowed by a light. It was not the light of the sun, nor like that of a fire, but more glorious and beautiful. It extended away round us, I cannot tell how far, but in the midst of this light about as far off as he sits (pointing to John C. Whitmer, sitting a few feet from him), there appeared as it were a table with many records or plates upon it, besides the plates of the Book of Mormon, also the sword of Laban, the directors (i.e., the ball which Lehi had) and the interpreters. I saw them just as plain as I see this bed (striking the bed beside him with his hand), and I heard the voice of the Lord, as distinctly as I ever heard anything in my life, declaring that the records of the plates of the Book of Mormon were translated by the gift and power of God." (*Historical Record, Church Encyclopedia*, Book I, May 1887, 207-8.)

John A. Widtsoe: 9
That I might bring about my righteous purposes

Three men, and later eight men, declared in two formal, signed testimonies that they saw and handled the plates from which the Book of Mormon was translated.

The great importance of these statements in establishing faith in the divine mission of Joseph Smith the Prophet, has been recognized by all students of the restored gospel. To Latter-day Saints these affidavits, published in every authorized edition of the Book of Mormon, have been and are a source of faith.

Unbelievers in the divine origin of the Book of Mormon have been forced, on the other hand, to stand, baffled and perplexed before the testimonies of these witnesses.

The evidences for the truth of the witnesses are convincing. They cannot be denied. Here are some of these proofs:

1. *It was prophetically foretold that three witnesses should see the plates and bear witness of their experience.*

It is a remarkable fact that this prophecy was received by the Prophet in March, 1829, before the Book of Mormon had been translated. It reads in part as follows: ". . . in addition to your testimony, the testimony of three of my servants, whom I shall call and ordain, unto whom I will show these things, and they shall go forth with my words that are given through you. Yea, they shall know of a surety that these things are true, for from heaven will I declare it unto them. I will give them power that they may behold and view these things as they are." (D&C 5:11-13.)

The united testimony of the three witnesses is a literal fulfillment of this prophecy. It cannot be explained away, for the prophecy and its fulfillment actually occurred. It leads directly to the divine purpose to which the Prophet said he was called.

2. *The events which led to the testimonies of the witnesses are described in circumstantial detail.*

Soon after the announcement the three men who became the first group of witnesses—Oliver Cowdery, David Whitmer, and Martin Harris—asked that they may be selected to see the plates. While very different in temperament, they were alike in having minds of their own and doubts of their own. They wanted to make sure for themselves that Joseph's story was true.

About two months later, in June 1829, the plates were shown to the three witnesses. . . .

True, the record of this event was written by Joseph Smith, but the witnesses were still living, and could have corrected any errors in the account. This they did not do.

A detailed account of any event is always an evidence of its truth. Deceivers are careful to deal in few details and many generalities. The whole event occurred in full daylight. All of them were vigorous young men in good health.

3. *Eight witnesses corroborated the testimony of the three witnesses.*

As if to make assurance doubly sure, the plates were later shown to eight other men. Whether all eight saw the plates at the same time is not known. However, the men, Christian Whitmer, Jacob Whitmer, Peter Whitmer, Jr., John Whitmer, Hiram Page, Joseph Smith, Sen., Hyrum Smith, and Samuel H. Smith, unitedly signed the testimony in which they described the plates and the engravings on them, and further declared that they actually handled, and "hefted" the plates.

Such corroboration of the testimony of the three, under different conditions, and at different times, certifies immeasurably to the truth of the events.

4. *The witnesses remained true to their testimonies to the end of their days.*

Some of the witnesses left the Church, others were excommunicated, but their testimonies for the truth of the Book of Mormon remained unchanged.

Of the three witnesses, Oliver Cowdery and David Whitmer were excommunicated. Martin Harris drifted away. Cowdery, of undisputed high intelligence, and Harris, holding stubbornly to his views, both returned and were again baptized into the Church. Whitmer, hugging old grievances and remaining unaffiliated with the Church, bore frequent testimony to the truth of the translation of the Book of Mormon from the Nephite record. Oliver Cowdery practiced law. Several times, before the courts, his integrity was impugned because of his acceptance of the Book of Mormon. Each time he bore powerful testimony to the truth of the Nephite record. Wherever he went, he was looked upon as a man of honor. He died with his testimony upon his lips.

David Whitmer remained in Richmond, Missouri, to the end of his life. He lived to be a very old man. Many persons called on him to ask about his testimony to the Book of Mormon. Orson Pratt, Joseph F. Smith, James H. Moyle, and C. C. Richards were among these visitors. To each and all he reaffirmed his testimony. He died with his testimony upon his lips.

Martin Harris, after various misadventures, remained for many years in the East near the Kirtland Temple. Visitors there would quiz him about his belief in the Book of Mormon. Among them were Edward Stevenson and W. H. Homer. His answer was invariable, that he was as certain of his testimony as he was of the sun in the high heavens. He finally settled, in his old age, in Clarkston, Utah. He died with his testimony upon his lips.

The lives of the eight witnesses tell the same story. One of the witnesses, John Whitmer, was excommunicated from the Church. Two, Jacob Whitmer and Hiram Page, withdrew from the Church. The other five, Christian Whitmer, Peter Whitmer, Jr., Joseph Smith, Sen., Hyrum Smith, and Samuel H. Smith, remained faithful, useful members of the Church during their whole lives.

All of the eight witnesses, whether in or out of the Church, maintained to their last breath that they saw and handled the plates from which the Book of Mormon was translated.

5. *The explanation by the witnesses alone is acceptable.*

The facts connected with the Book of Mormon witnesses are so unanswerable that they have been disconcerting stumbling blocks to unbelievers. Unfriendly critics have usually tried to draw attention away from them, as being of little significance.

More honest unbelievers have attempted two explanations, and two only.

The first suggestion is that the witnesses were dishonest, and in collusion with the Prophet. That is, the whole story of seeing the plates was invented, and had no basis in fact. . . . If their testimonies had been untrue, one or the other would have revealed his perfidy. Many opportunities were given them. Oliver Cowdery, David Whitmer, and John Whitmer were excommunicated from the Church, improperly, as they thought. They then soured upon the Prophet and the Church. That would have given them a chance to declare the whole thing a fraud. Instead they remained true to their testimony. . . .

The second explanation, conceived in desperation by those who will not believe the truth, has been that Joseph Smith was endowed with great hypnotic power, which enabled him to make the eleven witnesses think they saw things which did not exist. This explanation is much like the drowning man clutching at a straw.

This far-fetched explanation asks us to believe that eleven very dissimilar men, all of them questioning the claims of the Prophet, could be made to see, hear, and touch, alike, figments of nothingness. It is an absurd request to make of intelligent people. The testimonies of the witnesses rest upon three senses: seeing, hearing, touching. Even the confirmed believer in hypnotism would hardly dare cover so big a territory. Moreover, though it is conceded that the Prophet had a magnetic personality, there is nothing in his well-documented life to credit him with such, or any, hypnotic power.

The more the witnesses are studied, the more certain the student becomes that their testimonies are true and irrefutable.

They were honest men, clear-headed, hard-headed, not easily influenced. They had seen and handled the Nephite plates. They had heard a voice from heaven, declaring the work to be true. They could do nothing else than to bear witness to their glorious experience. The testimonies of the witnesses to the Book of Mormon is an unanswerable proof of the divine mission of Joseph Smith the Prophet. (*Gospel Interpretations*, 1947, pp. 133-38.)

SECTION 18

Revelation to Joseph Smith the Prophet, Oliver Cowdery and David Whitmer, given at Fayette, New York, June, 1829: Making known the calling of Twelve Apostles in these last days; and also containing instructions relative to building up the Church of Christ according to the fulness of the Gospel. When the Aaronic Priesthood was conferred, the bestowal of the Melchizedek Priesthood was promised. See heading to Section 13. In response to fervent supplication for greater knowledge on the matter the Lord gave this revelation. See History of the Church, vol. 1, pp. 60-64. – Diligence enjoined – Oliver Cowdery and David Whitmer called with the calling of Paul the Apostle of old – The value of souls emphasized – The great joy attending conversion of souls to the Gospel of Christ – The calling of twelve to assist in the ministry foreshadowed – The Twelve, here called disciples but later named Apostles, to be chosen from among those who desire to take upon them the name of Christ with full purpose of heart – Oliver Cowdery and David Whitmer commissioned to search out the Twelve.

1. Now, behold, because of the thing which you, my servant Oliver Cowdery, have desired to know of me, I give unto you these words:

2. Behold, I have manifested unto you, by my Spirit in many instances, that the things which you have written are true; wherefore you know that they are true.

3. And if you know that they are true, behold, I give unto you a commandment, that you rely upon the things which are written;

4. For in them are all things written concerning the foundation of my church, my gospel, and my rock.

5. Wherefore, if you shall build up my church, upon the foundation of my gospel and my rock, the gates of hell shall not prevail against you.

6. Behold, the world is ripening in iniquity; and it must needs be that the children of men are stirred up unto repentance, both the Gentiles and also the house of Israel.

7. Wherefore, as thou hast been baptized by the hands of my servant Joseph Smith, Jun., according to that which I have commanded him, he hath fulfilled the thing which I commanded him.

8. And now, marvel not that I have called him unto mine own purpose, which purpose is known in me; wherefore, if he shall be diligent in keeping my commandments he shall be blessed unto eternal life; and his name is Joseph.

9. And now, Oliver Cowdery, I speak unto you, and also

unto David Whitmer, by the way of commandment; for, behold, I command all men everywhere to repent, and I speak unto you, even as unto Paul mine apostle, for you are called even with that same calling with which he was called.

10. Remember the worth of souls is great in the sight of God;

11. For, behold, the Lord your Redeemer suffered death in the flesh; wherefore he suffered the pain of all men, that all men might repent and come unto him.

12. And he hath risen again from the dead, that he might bring all men unto him, on conditions of repentance.

13. And how great is his joy in the soul that repenteth!

14. Wherefore, you are called to cry repentance unto this people.

15. And if it so be that you should labor all your days in crying repentance unto this people, and bring, save it be one soul unto me, how great shall be your joy with him in the kingdom of my Father!

16. And now, if your joy will be great with one soul that you have brought unto me into the kingdom of my Father, how great will be your joy if you should bring many souls unto me!

17. Behold, you have my gospel before you, and my rock, and my salvation.

18. Ask the Father in my name, in faith believing that you shall receive, and you shall have the Holy Ghost, which manifesteth all things which are expedient unto the children of men.

19. And if you have not faith, hope, and charity, you can do nothing.

20. Contend against no church, save it be the church of the devil.

21. Take upon you the name of Christ, and speak the truth in soberness.

22. And as many as repent and are baptized in my name, which is Jesus Christ, and endure to the end, the same shall be saved.

23. Behold, Jesus Christ is the name which is given of the Father, and there is none other name given whereby man can be saved;

24. Wherefore, all men must take upon them the name which is given of the Father, for in that name shall they be called at the last day;

25. Wherefore, if they know not the name by which they are called, they cannot have place in the kingdom of my Father.

26. And now, behold, there are others who are called to declare my gospel, both unto Gentile and unto Jew;

27. Yea, even twelve; and the Twelve shall be my disciples, and they shall take upon them my name; and the Twelve are they who shall desire to take upon them my name with full purpose of heart.

28. And if they desire to take upon them my name with full purpose of heart, they are called to go into all the world to preach my gospel unto every creature.

29. And they are they who are ordained of me to baptize in my name, according to that which is written;

30. And you have that which is written before you; wherefore, you must perform it according to the words which are written.

31. And now I speak unto you, the Twelve — Behold, my grace is sufficient for you; you must walk uprightly before me and sin not.

32. And, behold, you are they who are ordained of me to ordain priests and teachers; to declare my gospel, according to the power of the Holy Ghost which is in you, and according to the callings and gifts of God unto men;

33. And I, Jesus Christ, your Lord and your God, have spoken it.

34. These words are not of men nor of man, but of me; wherefore, you shall testify they are of me and not of man;

35. For it is my voice which speaketh them unto you; for they are given by my Spirit unto you, and by my power you can read them one to another; and save it were by my power you could not have them;

36. Wherefore, you can testify that you have heard my voice, and know my words.

37. And now, behold, I give unto you, Oliver Cowdery, and also unto David Whitmer, that you shall search out the Twelve, who shall have the desires of which I have spoken;

38. And by their desires and their works you shall know them.

39. And when you have found them you shall show these things unto them.

40. And you shall fall down and worship the Father in my name.

41. And you must preach unto the world, saying: You must repent and be baptized, in the name of Jesus Christ;

42. For all men must repent and be baptized, and not only men, but women, and children who have arrived at the years of accountability.

43. And now, after that you have received this, you must keep my commandments in all things;

44. And by your hands I will work a marvelous work among the children of men, unto the convincing of many of their sins, that they may come unto repentance, and that they may come unto the kingdom of my Father.

45. Wherefore, the blessings which I give unto you are above all things.

46. And after that you have received this, if you keep not my commandments you cannot be saved in the kingdom of my Father.

47. Behold, I, Jesus Christ, your Lord and your God, and your Redeemer, by the power of my Spirit have spoken it. Amen.

Joseph Smith: *Introduction*

We now became anxious to have that promise realized to us, which the angel that conferred upon us the Aaronic Priesthood had given us [Sec. 13], viz., that provided we continued faithful, we should also have the Melchizedek Priesthood, which holds the authority of the laying on of hands for the gift of the Holy Ghost. We had for some time made this matter a subject of humble prayer, more particularly to seek of the Lord what we now so earnestly desired; and here, to our unspeakable satisfaction, did we realize the truth of the Savior's promise — "Ask, and it shall be given you; seek, and ye shall find; knock, and it shall be opened unto you" — for we had not long been engaged in solemn and fervent prayer, when the word of the Lord came unto us in the chamber [of old Father Whitmer in Fayette, Seneca County (Sec. 128:21)], commanding us that I should ordain Oliver Cowdery to be an Elder in the Church of Jesus Christ; and that he also should ordain me to the same office; and then to ordain others, as it should be made known unto us from time to time. We were, however, commanded to defer this our ordination until such times as it should be practicable to have our brethren, who had been and who should be baptized, assembled together, when we must have by vote whether they were willing to accept us as spiritual teachers or not; when also we were commanded to bless bread and break it with them, and to take wine, bless it, and drink it with them; afterward proceed to ordain each other according to commandment; then call out such men as the Spirit should dictate, and ordain them; and then attend to the laying of hands for the gift of the Holy Ghost, upon all those whom we had previously baptized, doing all things in the name of the Lord. The following commandment will further illustrate the nature of our calling to this Priesthood, as well as that of others who were yet to be sought after. [Section 18.] (HC 1:60-62, June 1829; Fayette, New York.)

Joseph Fielding Smith: 1-8

Before the Church could be organized it was essential that there be revealed such matters as pertained to the organization of the Church. This was done between the time the witnesses viewed the plates of the ancient record and the sixth of April, 1830. The first of these (D&C Sec. 18) was given to Joseph Smith, Oliver Cowdery and David Whitmer, at Fayette. It made known the calling of the Twelve Apostles who should be chosen in this dispensation, although it was about six years before they were called. It gave instructions "relative to the building up of the Church of Christ according to the fulness of the Gospel." It was also stated that the Book of Mormon contained "all things written concerning the foundation" of the Church and the Gospel. The Church, when organized, should be built upon the foundation of the Gospel and "the gates of hell shall not prevail" against it. Moreover, it was declared that "the world is ripened in iniquity, and it must needs be that the children of men are stirred up unto repentance, both the Gentiles and also the house of Israel." (Essentials in Church History, 1950, pp. 84-85.)

Joseph Smith: 2
The things which you have written are true

I told the brethren that the Book of Mormon was the most correct of any book on earth, and the keystone of our religion, and a man would get nearer to God by abiding by its precepts than by any other book. (HC 4:461, November 28, 1841.)

Hyrum M. Smith: 2-5

All of us may have a knowledge that this is the one and only religion in all the wide world of which it can be said, "All they have is true." Yet how gladly we would extend it to everyone else! How gladly we would give to others that which we have received, and how assiduously are we working for the salvation of man, as is evidenced by the hundreds upon hundreds of Elders sent forth to proclaim repentance and salvation to the world! (CR, April 1902, p. 21.)

Daniel H. Wells: 5
The gates of hell shall not prevail against you

If we are faithful we shall increase in the things of God. The devil can claim no right to the blessings of the Lord; for those things belong to the saints; therefore let us do all we can for the building up of the kingdom of God, and he will furnish us all we need, for all belongs to him. No part of the human family belongs to the devil, unless they sell themselves to him. But the Lord cannot consistently bless us, unless he knows that we will serve him and make a good use of what he bestows. (JD, March 22, 1857, 5:43-44.)

David O. McKay: 6
The world

Now, what do we mean by the world? It is sometimes used as an indefinite term. I take it that the world refers to the inhabitants who are alienated from the saints of God. They are aliens to the Church, and it is the spirit of this alienation that we should keep ourselves free from. (CR, October 1911, p. 58.)

First Presidency (Brigham Young, Heber C. Kimball, Jedediah M. Grant): 6
It must needs be that . . . men are stirred up unto repentance

To all the honest in heart throughout the world, both of high and low degree, we say "repent, and be baptized for the remission of your sins" [Sec. 18:41-42], obey the ordinances of the Gospel through the administrations of the servants of the living God, for the judgments of the Almighty are upon you, flee therefore from the sinks of iniquity and corruption, lest the fiery indignation of the Lord also consume you with the wicked, of whom he has decreed that he will empty the earth. [Sec. 5:18-20.] (MS, August 11, 1855, 17:504.)

Hyrum G. Smith: 6
Both the Gentiles and also the house of Israel

We have also a number in the Church who, so far as we are able to judge and learn, did not originally belong to the house of Israel at all. Then you say, where do they get their blessings? What is their lineage? Well, I explain that in this way: When you adopt a child that is born in the world I share my blessings with that child, as he shares his blessings with me. In my household I am responsible, he partakes at the same "table" the same blessings. By the law of adoption that child receives his right through the law of adoption. Through our faithfulness, we are all adopted into the fold of Christ. We are his and his blessings are upon us, through our faithfulness in obeying the laws of his Gospel. And so, if other people outside the house of Israel have faith and obedience enough to come into the Church they will receive the same lineage as the house or tribe that adopted them, just the same as the adopted child receives the blessings of the family that adopted him. (CR, April 1929, p. 124.)

Rudger Clawson: 10-16

And how are we to determine the value of souls? This matter has been determined for us also by revelation: [Sec. 18:16, quoted.] The souls of men are so precious in the sight of God that he gave to the world his Only Begotten Son, that by the shedding of his blood he might draw all men unto him. That is why the great Prophet of this dispensation, Joseph Smith, and these others, John Whitmer, Oliver Cowdery, David Whitmer, and the rest, were called to bring souls unto Christ. And if one of these men should labor all his days, and bring save it be but one soul unto Christ, and that one should be his wife, what great joy he would have with his wife in heaven. Then if he should labor all his days and bring unto

Christ the souls of his wife and his children, and none else perchance, how great would be his joy in heaven with his wife and children. (CR, April 1901, pp. 7-8.)

David O. McKay: 10
The worth of souls

And now . . . let me emphasize that *the noblest aim in life is to strive to live to make other lives better and happier. The most worthy calling in life is that in which man can serve best his fellow man.* . . .

Such is the divine message given to the Prophet Joseph Smith in these words: "Remember the worth of souls is great in the sight of God." (D&C 18:10.) Such is the philosophy expressed by the Redeemer in the seemingly paradoxical statement "Whosoever will lose his life for my sake will find it." (Matthew 16:25.)

The meaning of this becomes clear in the light of another passage which says: "Inasmuch as ye have done it unto one of the least of these my brethren, ye have done it unto me." (Matthew 25:40.)

To no other group of men in all the world is given a better opportunity to engage in the noblest calling in life than that which is afforded the Elders of The Church of Jesus Christ of Latter-day Saints. To establish salvation and peace to the extent of their individual efforts, their lives are dedicated. To make the world a better or a safer or a fitter place for men, their talents and means are consecrated. (CR, April 1961, p. 131.)

Charles W. Penrose: 12
And he hath risen again from the dead

In the fifth chapter of the gospel according to St. John, Jesus speaks very clearly on matters that may seem mysterious to some people. You know there are some of our brethren who have thought that Jesus, in his first estate, as we call it, or in his former state, was a resurrected being. I do not know where they get the idea from, but it is likely from this that he was called God by John the Revelator and by a great number of writers in the Book of Mormon and in the Doctrine and

Covenants and in other revelations. "He was in the beginning with God, and was God" [Sec. 93:21]; and he could not be a god, they say, unless he had a body, and passed through mortality and had been resurrected. What scripture did they find to suggest that notion? I don't know of any revelation that declares it. I don't know of any that intimates at all that he could not be God unless he had passed through a mortal probation and had been tried and tempted and had suffered; that he could not be God beforehand; but we are told that in the beginning he was with God, and he says that the Father had shown him all things that he himself doeth. That is in the fifth chapter of the gospel according to St. John. (CR, April 1916, p. 20.)

Abraham H. Cannon: 12
On conditions of repentance

Then we want them [men] to be filled with the spirit of repentance, which follows faith, and which is the natural result of faith in God; for if men are filled with faith in the Father and in the Son, they will naturally desire to place themselves in a condition to be fit associates for such holy beings, and they will look back upon their past lives with sorrow — with a sorrow which will prompt them to be more righteous, more God-fearing, more upright, in the future. Then repentance of sin will come upon them; not repentance as the murderer possesses; not such as men feel who are called to account in the flesh for their crimes, and who, when the penalty is paid, go back to their iniquities, and only fail to sin because the opportunity to do so is lacking; but a repentance that prompts men to make restitution, so far as it is possible for them to do so, for the sins which they have committed, and to restore four-fold, if necessary, in order to obtain pardon for the wrong done; but a repentance which will keep before our minds continually the view of our own sinfulness, our own weaknesses, and fill us with a desire to avoid the sins and weaknesses of the past. This is the repentance which worketh salvation to the souls of men, and prepares them to receive any ordinance, however humiliating it may be considered. (MS, July 18, 1895, 57:453.)

David O. McKay: 15
If... you should labor all your days

Many of us fail to realize the value and potent possibilities of this great branch of Church activity [missionary work].

1. As an example of voluntary service in the cause of the Master, it is unexcelled.
2. As an incentive to clean living among youth, as a contributing factor to character building, its influence is immeasurable.
3. As an educative force and uplifting influence upon our communities, its effect is clearly manifest.
4. As a contributing factor to a better understanding among nations, and to the establishing of international friendship, it wields a significant influence.
5. As it is the purpose of the Almighty to save the individual, not to make him a mere cog in the machinery of the state, the missionary service works most harmoniously in the consummation of this eternal plan! (CR, October 1949, p. 117.)

Lorenzo Snow: 16
How great will be your joy

We send missionaries among the children of men. . . . There are things about a mission which are not altogether agreeable to our young Elders. They realize that they have to sacrifice the pleasures of home, and they understand that they are going among people who will not always feel gratified at what they have to say to them; yet, on the other hand, they feel that they have the seeds of life in their possession, and that if they can find an honest man or woman, the Spirit of the Lord will operate upon their hearts and they will perchance receive this glorious message which they have to deliver. This affords them pleasure and satisfaction. (CR, April 1902, pp. 2-3.)

Joseph Fielding Smith: 17-19

If members of the Church would place more confidence in the word of the Lord and less confidence in the theories of men, they would be better off. I will give you a key for your guidance. Any doctrine, whether it comes in the name of religion, science, philosophy, or whatever it may be, that is in conflict with the revelations of the Lord that have been accepted by the Church as coming from the Lord, will fail. It may appear to be very plausible; it may be put before you in such a way that you cannot answer it; it may appear to be established by evidence that cannot be controverted, but all you need do is to bide your time. Time will level all things. You will find that every doctrine, theory, principle, no matter how great it may appear, no matter how universally it may be believed, if it is not in accord with the word of the Lord, it will perish. Nor is it necessary for us to try to stretch the word of the Lord to make it conform to these theories and teachings. The word of the Lord shall not pass away unfulfilled. . . . The theories of men change from day to day . . . but the word of the Lord will endure forever. (*Utah Genealogical and Historical Magazine*, October 1930, pp. 155-56.)

Stephen L Richards: 19
And if you have not faith

Why is it so difficult to accept things on faith? I think I can suggest an answer. It is because we are so conceited. Men of the world are in the world only because they adopt the philosophy of the world, which is the philosophy of self-sufficiency. It is not a humble philosophy — it is highly egotistical. It makes men themselves the arbiters of all things. They look to no higher source than themselves for the solution of all questions.

Such a philosophy is diametrically opposed to the philosophy of Christ, which is that of faith. When men adopt his philosophy they are humble — they acknowledge an intelligence far superior to their own and they seek guidance and wisdom from that source. When they adopt the philosophy of faith, they come out of the world, for the world, as a term in theology, is not a place but a condition or state of mind and feeling. It requires courage to come out of the world and adopt the philosophy of faith. Sometimes it subjects one to ridicule and to contempt of friends which are harder for most men to endure than physical pain; but because a thing is hard to do or hard to believe is no assurance that it is not right.

I am one, however, who believes that it is not so hard for most people to have faith and accept spiritual realities if they will but let their minds and their native inclinations pursue their natural bent. I think that altogether too often we permit thinking complexes and sophisticated reasoning to warp our intuitive judgment and entrammel the spontaneous feelings and emotions of our souls. So, when I prescribe that acceptance of Christ as a condition of orthodoxy, I mean an acceptance without reservation — a whole-souled intelligent, joyous acceptance of him that proclaims him Lord, Savior, Redeemer and Mediator with the Father and lays claim on his mercy, his grace and his love for all the finer things we know in life. What hope — what peace and satisfaction such a full acceptance of the Christ brings to the heart of man, only those who have received a testimony of Jesus will ever know. (CR, April 1935, pp. 30-31.)

Joseph Smith: 20-21

The Elders would go forth, and each must stand for himself... to go in all meekness, in sobriety, and preach Jesus Christ and him crucified; not to contend with others on account of their faith, or systems of religion, but pursue a steady course. This I delivered by way of commandment; and all who observe it not will pull down persecution upon their heads, while those who do, shall always be filled with the Holy Ghost; this I pronounced as a prophecy, and sealed with hosanna and amen. (HC 2:431, March 30, 1836.)

James E. Talmage: 20-21

We are ofttimes charged with being very exclusive, and we admit the charge; we are exclusive, but in a rational sense. How can we solemnly testify that this is the Church of Jesus Christ and then ascribe that same high title to other organizations that have been formed not under the direction of Jesus Christ, but according to man's thoughts and plans? Some people say that we are illiberal because we do not admit that all other churches are what they profess to be, when their profession is based on facts.

Now when we say that the Lord is not pleased with those churches, we do not mean that he is not pleased with the members thereof. We hold that God is no respecter of persons, but, on the contrary, that he will acknowledge good in any soul, no matter whether that person belongs to a church or not. But the Lord is not pleased with those churches that have been constructed by men and then labeled with his name. He is not pleased with those doctrines that are being taught as being his doctrines when they are only the effusion of men's brains, undirected by inspiration and utterly lacking in revelation.

He has expressed himself with regard to the churches that are built by man and has said they shall be overthrown. Indeed he has applied strong terms to some of those churches, or to church organizations in general, that have been brought into being by men. Read his words to John the Revelator. See what he means by the synagogue of Satan to which some of the people belonged. [Rev. 2:9; 3:9.] Read what he has said about the great and abominable church, the mother of abominations. [Rev. 17.] The church as such may be wholly corrupt because of the false claims that are being made for it, and yet within that church as members there may be people who are doing their best. They have been deceived. As to the degree of culpability that will be charged up to them for their having become subjects of deception, we may not be able to judge.

But I do not understand that when the Lord states that those churches shall be overthrown — I mean the church of the devil, using his expression, and those that are making false claims, and shall be thrown into the fire, as he says [Rev. 18] — I do not understand that all members of those churches are to meet destruction, physically or otherwise. He is speaking there of the church collectively, and he is not pleased with it; but individually he may be well pleased with many of his sons and daughters who have been under an environment that has led them into those churches which are not of God. (CR, October 1928, p. 120.)

George F. Richards: 21

Talk about Christianity in the world! If you can find a people who have not rejected Jesus Christ as the Son of God in the flesh, the Messiah, the Savior and Redeemer of the world, then we will not question their right to be called Christians; but, we do not acknowledge those as Christians, those who deny him in part or whole of what he is. I understand that many, if not most, of the preachers of today, professed Christians, reject Jesus Christ as the Savior and Redeemer of the world, accepting him only as a great philosopher or wise teacher. They have rejected the chief cornerstone of Christianity, and have undermined and rendered powerless for salvation their professed Christianity. Not so with the Latter-day Saints. We realize that there is no virtue for salvation and exaltation outside of the atoning blood of Jesus Christ, our Savior. There is no other name under heaven by which man may obtain salvation. [Sec. 29:17; 38:4; 45:4; 76:69; Alma 34:8-17.] The whole plan of salvation is founded upon revelation and Jesus Christ; rejecting these there is no foundation left upon which to build nor to stand. The ordinances of the Gospel have virtue in them by reason of the atoning blood of Jesus Christ, and without it there would be no virtue in them for salvation. [Moses 6:57-63.] (CR, April 1916, pp. 53-54.)

James E. Talmage: 23-25

I rejoice in the testimony of the Savior that he is verily the Christ and we proclaim him as such. Great interest is manifest at this time in the work and ministry of Jesus Christ, not only among the Latter-day Saints but in the world in general; and he has been analyzed and measured and written about from many different angles. There are volumes of recent publications dealing with the Christ of literature, the Christ of history, the Christ of reason, the Christ of experience. Never lived a man of whom more has been said or sung; and there is none to whom is devoted a greater share of the world's literature. But the tendency is to view him from this angle or that and not to look with direct vision. I am thankful that the Church to which I belong preaches Christ and him crucified, and resurrected, the Christ that ascended into heaven, the Christ that was the offspring in the flesh, as well as in the spirit, of the very eternal Father, the Christ who is the Savior and Redeemer of mankind, beside whom there is none, beside whose name there is no name under haven whereby mankind may be saved. (CR, April 1916, p. 131.)

Hugh B. Brown: 23-25

As to the actuality of the resurrection of Christ, his divinity, his universal Godhood, let us hear his own declaration and read the testimony of a multitude of people on the American Continent, to whom he appeared just after his crucifixion.

This scripture may be new to many of you, but in America, as in Jerusalem, there were holy men of God who spake as they were moved by the Holy Ghost. You will remember reading in Luke's account of the crucifixion:

"And it was about the sixth hour, and there was a darkness over all the earth until the ninth hour.

"And the sun was darkened, and the veil of the temple was rent in the midst." (Luke 23:44-45.) And in Matthew: "And behold, the veil of the temple was rent in twain from the top to the bottom; and the earth did quake, and the rocks rent;

"And the graves were opened; and many bodies of the Saints which slept arose." (Matt. 27:51-52.)

Now this thick darkness, which covered the earth, and the convulsions of the earth at the time of the crucifixion, extended to America. Here the darkness lasted three days, and it was so thick upon all the face of the land that the people could feel the vapor of darkness, and they could make no light.

At the end of the period of darkness and upheaval, they who survived were assembled near the temple. There they heard a voice as if it came out of heaven. They did not understand it at first, but afterwards understood when the voice said:

"Behold my beloved Son, in whom I am well pleased, in

whom I have glorified my name — hear ye him." [3 Nephi 11:7, verses 8-11 also quoted.] . . .

And thus we have the testimony of eyewitnesses from two continents that Jesus is the Christ. We add our testimony not only that he did live, but that he still lives. This fact is the greatest hope of this divided and imperiled world, for if the Christ still lives then the anti-Christ will be defeated. There can be no peace in a godless world.

But our testimony would not be complete if we did not reaffirm our faith in the second coming of Christ, in the millennium which is to come, when he will reign as King of kings, and Lord of lords. That this climatic event is not far distant is indicated by the signs of the times, by wars and rumors of wars, by the satanic schemes of evil men who would enslave not only the bodies but also the minds of all who dare refuse to subscribe to the idealogies invented by the anti-Christ. [Sec. 133.] (CR, October 1960, pp. 93-94.)

Joseph Fielding Smith: 26-36

After the opening of the Dispensation of the Fulness of Times the Lord made it known that the organization of the primitive Church of Jesus Christ was to be restored. As early as June, 1829, before the Church was organized, a revelation came calling the witnesses of the Book of Mormon to choose the twelve who should constitute the council of the apostles. In this revelation the Lord gave this instruction to the future twelve: [Sec. 18:26-36, quoted.]

It was nearly six years after this revelation that the apostles were chosen. After the return of Zion's Camp from Missouri to Kirtland the Prophet Joseph Smith called together all the brethren who went forth on that journey. From these men who had been willing to risk their lives in the service of the Lord, the three witnesses, who were set apart to choose out of the twelve, made the selection of the apostles. This was on the 14th day of February, 1835, and the men were chosen in the following order: (1) Lyman E. Johnson, (2) Brigham Young, (3) Heber C. Kimball, (4) Orson Hyde, (5) David W. Patten, (6) Luke S. Johnson, (7) William E. McLellin, (8) John F. Boynton, (9) Orson Pratt, (10) William Smith, (11) Thomas B. Marsh, (12) Parley P. Pratt. Lyman E. Johnson, Brigham Young and Heber C. Kimball were then called forward, ordained and instructed in that order, after which the meeting adjourned. The following day, February 15th, the ordinations continued. William E. McLellin, John F. Boynton, and William Smith were also each ordained, after which the congregation adjourned. Some of the brethren were absent on this occasion. On February 21, 1835, Parley P. Pratt was ordained. Elders Thomas B. Marsh and Orson Pratt being away on missions, it was not until near the end of April when they were ordained. Elder Marsh returned to Kirtland on April 25th and Elder Orson Pratt returned on the following day.

After the twelve had all been selected and ordained they were organized according to age in the council. Thomas B. Marsh, the oldest, became the senior and the first man ordained. Lyman E. Johnson, the junior. There have been in the Council of Twelve since the beginning of this dispensation fifty-eight apostles to this date. (*IE*, April 1935, 38:212.)

George Teasdale: 28-29

Every conference where the Twelve Apostles have been they have borne their testimony that they know Joseph Smith was a true Prophet sent of God. How do they know it? Because they have accepted the doctrine of the Savior, taught by his authority. We bear testimony that the authority of God is restored to the earth. . . . The word of the Lord is unto all people. Repent and be baptized and obey the Gospel, worship the living and the true God, and you shall have a living witness that he lives, and that Jesus is the Christ. (*CR*, April 1901, p. 35.)

George Q. Cannon: 37-40

Under the hands of the Prophet, the three witnesses of the Book of Mormon, Oliver Cowdery, David Whitmer and Martin Harris, were blessed by the direction of the Holy Spirit to choose the Twelve Apostles of the Church. (*Life of Joseph Smith*, 1907, p. 177.)

James E. Talmage: 41-42

The righteous Nephite, King Benjamin, toward the close of a forceful address, which he offered on the occasion of his yielding up the authority of kingship to his son, admonished the people most earnestly to retain the remission of sins which they had received through their baptism, to make it perpetual. And Alma, prophet, high priest, and chief judge, rejoiced when he found that a great part of his people had verily retained the remission of their sins. I refer you to the Book of Mormon, Mosiah, chapter four, verse twenty-six, for the second. Neither you nor I will waste time by reading it again nor in pondering upon the principle embodied therein, the retention of the blessing or remission of sins. . . .

That the Lord can pronounce and change, that he can give and recall, is attested by scripture after scripture. [Sec. 58:30-33.] There comes to my mind the parable of the unmerciful servant, in which we find that though one was forgiven, the forgiveness was revoked because he forfeited his right to it. He did not retain it, he did not keep it. Not to take time here to read it in full, I commend the parable to you for perusal. You will find it recorded in the eighteenth chapter of Matthew, beginning with the twenty-third verse. . . .

The act of baptism does not simply blot out the sins of the past and enable us to begin with a new start, but it provides that if we have submitted to baptism worthily, we are entitled to remission of sins, that is, if we try to do our best, so as to be worthy of that boon.

It is not required nor is it allowed that we shall be baptized over and over again with the thought of wiping out our sins up to date; but it is ordained of God, having been baptized, after manifesting true faith and sincere repentance, if we shall live to be worthy of the remission of sins through continued repentance, through our unfailing efforts to overcome through our course of good works, doing unto our neighbors as we would have them do unto us, and in short, through our continued compliance with the commandments of God, we shall have our sins remitted, if they be not so heinous as to be unforgivable. [Sec. 76:30-49.] (CR, April 1922, pp. 110-12.)

Orson F. Whitney: 42

Little children too young to have sinned, and therefore without need of repentance, are exempt from baptism, and it is a sin to baptize them, involving as it does the vain use of a sacred ordinance. (Moroni 8:8-10, 19, 22.) Redeemed by the blood of Christ from the foundation of the world, their innocence and purity are typical of the saved condition of men and women, who must become like them before entering the kingdom of heaven. [Sec. 29:46-47; 74:6.] As children advance in years, however, they become accountable, and then must yield obedience to the requirements of the Gospel. (Moses 6:55.) Eight years is the recognized age of accountability in the Church of Christ. [Sec. 68:25-27.] (*Saturday Night Thoughts*, 1921, pp. 245-46.)

Joseph Smith: 42

"Do you believe in the baptism of infants?" asks the Presbyterian. No. "Why?" Because it is nowhere written in the Bible. Circumcision is not baptism, neither was baptism instituted in the place of circumcision. Baptism is for remission of sins. [Luke 3:3; Acts 2:38; 22:16.] Children have no sins. [Matt. 18:1-6.] Jesus blessed them and said, "Do what you have seen me do." Children are all made alive in Christ, and those of riper years through faith and repentance. (*HC* 5:499, July 9, 1843.)

Orson F. Whitney: 43-47

At Far West, in April, 1838, Presidents Oliver Cowdery and David Whitmer were excommunicated from the Church. The charges sustained against the former were for urging vexatious lawsuits against the brethren, slandering President Joseph Smith, contempt of the Church in not attending meetings, leaving his calling in which God had appointed him by revelation, for the sake of filthy lucre, and turning to the practice of law, disgracing the Church by being connected in the bogus business, dishonesty, and finally for "leaving or forsaking the cause of God, and returning to the beggarly elements of the world, and neglecting his high and holy calling, according to his profession."

President Whitmer was charged with not observing the Word of Wisdom, neglecting meetings and possessing the same spirit as the dissenters, writing letters to the dissenters in Kirtland, unfavorable to the cause of God and the character of his Prophet, neglecting the duties of his calling and separating himself from the Church and signing himself President of the Church of Christ, after being cut off from the Presidency, in an insulting letter to the High Council. (*Life of Heber C. Kimball*, 1945, p. 185.)

George A. Smith: 43-47

Oliver Cowdery, previous to his apostasy, said to President Joseph Smith: "If I should leave the Church, it would break up." Joseph said to Oliver—"What, who are you? The Lord is not dependent upon you, the work will roll forth do what you will." Oliver left the Church, and was gone about ten years; then he came back again, to a branch of the Church in meeting on Mosquito Creek, in Pottawattamie County, Iowa. The body of the Church had come off here to the West, but there was still remaining there a branch of about fifteen hundred or two thousand people, and when he came there he bore his testimony to the truth of the Book of Mormon and the divine mission of the Twelve Apostles, and asked to be received into the Church again, and said that he had never seen in all his life so large a congregation of saints as the one then assembled. We loved to hear brother Oliver testify, we were pleased with his witness, but when he passed off and went among our enemies he was forgotten, and the work rolled steadily along step by step, so that, ten years after, when he came back to an outside branch, he expressed his astonishment at seeing such a vast body of saints. Some men in their hours of darkness may feel—I have heard of men feeling so—that the work is about done, that the enemies of the saints have become so powerful, and bring such vast wealth and energy to bear against them that we are all going to be crushed out pretty soon. I will say to such brethren, it is very bad policy for you, because you think the old ship Zion is going to sink, to jump overboard, for if you jump overboard you are gone anyhow, and the old ship Zion will ride triumphantly through all the storms, and everybody who proves unworthy to remain on board her and jumps overboard will repent of it when it is too late, as many have done already. (JD, October 6, 1874, 17:199-200.)

SECTION 19

A commandment of God, and not of man, revealed through Joseph Smith the Prophet, to Martin Harris, at Manchester, New York, March, 1830, by him who is Eternal. – Christ affirms his omnipotence – Declares that punishment and suffering are inevitable consequences of unrepented sins – Explains the signification of endless torment and eternal damnation – Reaffirms the actuality of his own suffering in the flesh – Emphasizes the necessity of prayer – gives specific commandment to Martin Harris.

1. I am Alpha and Omega, Christ the Lord; yea, even I am he, the beginning and the end, the Redeemer of the world.

2. I, having accomplished and finished the will of him whose I am, even the Father, concerning me — having done this that I might subdue all things unto myself—

3. Retaining all power, even to the destroying of Satan and his works at the end of the world, and the last great day of judgment, which I shall pass upon the inhabitants thereof, judging every man according to his works and the deeds which he hath done.

4. And surely every man must repent or suffer, for I, God, am endless.

5. Wherefore, I revoke not the judgments which I shall pass, but woes shall go forth, weeping, wailing and gnashing of teeth, yea, to those who are found on my left hand.

6. Nevertheless, it is not written that there shall be no end to this torment, but it is written *endless torment.*

7. Again, it is written *eternal damnation;* wherefore it is more express than other scriptures, that it might work upon the hearts of the children of men, altogether for my name's glory.

8. Wherefore, I will explain unto you this mystery, for it is meet unto you to know even as mine apostles.

9. I speak unto you that are chosen in this thing, even as one, that you may enter into my rest.

10. For, behold, the mystery of godliness, how great is it! For, behold, I am endless, and the punishment which is given from my hand is endless punishment, for Endless is my name. Wherefore—

11. Eternal punishment is God's punishment.

12. Endless punishment is God's punishment.

13. Wherefore, I command you to repent, and keep the commandments which you have received by the hand of my servant Joseph Smith, Jun., in my name;

14. And it is by my almighty power that you have received them;

15. Therefore I command you to repent — repent, lest I smite you by the rod of my mouth, and by my wrath, and by my anger, and your sufferings be sore — how sore you know not, how exquisite you know not, yea, how hard to bear you know not.

16. For behold, I, God, have suffered these things for all, that they might not suffer if they would repent;

17. But if they would not repent they must suffer even as I;

18. Which suffering caused myself, even God, the greatest of all, to tremble because of pain, and to bleed at every pore, and to suffer both body and spirit — and would that I might not drink the bitter cup, and shrink—

19. Nevertheless, glory be to the Father, and I partook and finished my preparations unto the children of men.

20. Wherefore, I command you again to repent, lest I humble you with my almighty power; and that you confess your sins, lest you suffer these punishments of which I have spoken, of which in the smallest, yea, even in the least degree you have tasted at the time I withdrew my Spirit.

21. And I command you that you preach naught but repentance, and show not these things unto the world until it is wisdom in me.

22. For they cannot bear meat now, but milk they must receive; wherefore, they must not know these things, lest they perish.

23. Learn of me, and listen to my words; walk in the meekness of my Spirit, and you shall have peace in me.

24. I am Jesus Christ; I came by the will of the Father, and I do his will.

25. And again, I command thee that thou shalt not covet thy neighbor's wife; nor seek thy neighbor's life.

26. And again, I command thee that thou shalt not covet thine own property, but impart it freely to the printing of the Book of Mormon, which contains the truth and the word of God—

27. Which is my word to the Gentile, that soon it may go to the Jew, of whom the Lamanites are a remnant, that they may believe the gospel, and look not for a Messiah to come who has already come.

28. And again, I command thee that thou shalt pray vocally as well as in thy heart; yea, before the world as well as in secret, in public as well as in private.

29. And thou shalt declare glad tidings, yea, publish it upon the mountains, and upon every high place, and among every people that thou shalt be permitted to see.

30. And thou shalt do it with all humility, trusting in me, reviling not against revilers.

31. And of tenets thou shalt not talk, but thou shalt declare repentance and faith on the Savior, and remission of sins by baptism, and by fire, yea, even the Holy Ghost.

32. Behold, this is a great and the last commandment which I shall give unto you concerning this matter; for this shall suffice for thy daily walk, even unto the end of thy life.

33. And misery thou shalt receive if thou wilt slight these counsels, yea, even the destruction of thyself and property.

34. Impart a portion of thy property, yea, even part of thy lands, and all save the support of thy family.

35. Pay the debt thou hast contracted with the printer. Release thyself from bondage.

36. Leave thy house and home, except when thou shalt desire to see thy family;

37. And speak freely to all; yea, preach, exhort, declare the truth, even with a loud voice, with a sound of rejoicing, crying—Hosanna, hosanna, blessed be the name of the Lord God!

38. Pray always, and I will pour out my Spirit upon you, and great shall be your blessing—yea, even more than if you should obtain treasures of earth and corruptibleness to the extent thereof.

39. Behold, canst thou read this without rejoicing and lifting up thy heart for gladness?

40. Or canst thou run about longer as a blind guide?

41. Or canst thou be humble and meek, and conduct thyself wisely before me? Yea, come unto me thy Savior. Amen.

Joseph Fielding Smith: *Introduction*

This revelation was given some time in March, 1830 [Manchester, New York]. It would seem that Martin Harris had come to Joseph Smith seeking further assurance in relation to his standing before the Lord, being sorely troubled in his spirit because of his transgression. He had already been granted the privilege on his earnest solicitation of being one of the three witnesses, and that wonderful vision had been given. [Sections 5 and 17.] Perhaps out of this came much serious reflection and he sought further light. However, there is no indication in the *History of the Church* as to the reason why the revelation was given and the exact day is unknown when it was given. It was without question a revelation of great comfort to Martin, and it is one of the great revelations given in this dispensation; there are few of greater import than this. The doctrine of the atonement of the Lord, as directly applying to the individual, and his exposition of "eternal punishment," as here set forth, give to the members of the Church light which was not previously known. (CHMR, 1948, pp. 80-81.)

Charles W. Penrose: 1-3

Thanks be to God the eternal Father! Hallelujah, praise his holy name for the gift of his Son, Jesus Christ, for the redemption of mankind from the transgression of Adam, who is our earthly head. He is our Father in that sense, the father of all the race. . . . But our Father whom we worship is the Great Eloheim, who sits on high, who is working, through his Son Jesus Christ, for our redemption, and he is the Savior, after all, of all that are saved. Through and by his Son Jesus Christ are we redeemed from our own sins and also from the sin of our first parents, the transgression of Adam and Eve in the garden. He who knew no sin offered himself as a sacrifice for those who had sinned, and that reaches right back to Adam. . . .

What a glorious kingdom there will be, when sin is banished, when darkness is dispersed, when false governments will perish; when the true kingdom of God shall be set up, and Jesus Christ as King of Kings and Lord of Lords shall reign over all the earth. (CR, April 1920, pp. 33-34.)

Orson Pratt: 3
Judging every man according to his works

There is a certain degree of judgment rendered upon every man and every woman as soon as they have passed the ordeals of this present probation. When they lay their bodies down their spirits return into the presence of God, when a degree of judgment and sentence is immediately passed. Hence we read in the Book of Mormon, that the spirits of all men, as soon as they depart from this mortal body, return home again to that God who gave them life, and then shall it come to pass that the spirits of the righteous shall enter into a state of rest, peace and happiness, called Paradise, where they shall rest from all their labors. And then shall it come to pass that the spirits of the wicked—for behold they have no part or portion of the spirit of the Lord—shall depart into outer darkness, where there is weeping, and wailing and gnashing of teeth; and in these two states or conditions the children of men shall be placed until the time of the resurrection. [Alma 40:11-14.]

Then again there will be a judgment after the resurrection, that will not be the final judgment, that is the judgment of the twelve tribes of Israel, spoken of by our Savior, which will take place when he and the Twelve return again to the earth. That judgment will be exercised more directly on the whole house of Israel that have loved the Lord and kept his commandments. [Sec. 29:12.]

Here then are the various times of judgment, and various conditions and circumstances of the children of men in the spiritual state, judged before the resurrection, assigned to happiness or misery as the case may be, and in the judgment of the first resurrection certain rewards, glory, power, exaltation, happiness, and eternal life will be conferred upon those who are not favored with coming forth on the morning of the first resurrection, namely, those who have disobeyed the Gospel. To all such the voice of the angel will be—"Let sinners stay and sleep until I call again" [Sec. 43:18], their sins having been sufficiently judged beforehand, that they are not counted worthy of a resurrection among the just and the righteous ones of the earth. This agrees with another passage recorded in the Book of Covenants, that at the sound of the third trump then come the spirits of men that are under condemnation. [Sec. 88:100-101.] These are the last of the dead, and they live not again till the thousand years are ended, neither again until the end of the earth. Why? Because a certain measure of judgment is pronounced upon them even then. (JD, October 11, 1874, 17:184-85.)

LeGrand Richards: 3
Judging every man according to . . . the deeds which he hath done

All men are to receive "according to their works" (see Rev. 20:12), which requires that suitable places shall be prepared for the souls of all men. Hence the statement of Jesus: "In my Father's house are many mansions." (See John 14:2.) The Gospel of Jesus Christ provides a plan whereby man cannot only be saved, but can also be exalted in the celestial kingdom. "In the day when God shall judge the secrets of men by Jesus Christ according to my gospel." (Rom. 2:16.) (*A Marvelous Work and a Wonder*, 1950, p. 237.)

George Q. Cannon: 5-12

Contemplate the condition of the world when this Gospel was restored! What was known about heaven? What was known about hell? There are two places, one of bliss, the other place of torment. How much terror was entertained by the people at large concerning this place of torment. To have to think that this was endless; to think how the hearts of mothers were wrung with anguish at the death of their wayward children, of their loved ones, when they were told by men who assumed authority and to whom they had been taught to look with respect, that they were eternally damned—sent to a place of torment worlds without end! Is it any wonder that men wished they had never been born? They did not know what to do. Suicide brought no relief; they could not get deliverance from the inexorable consequences of living, because their souls were indestructible. They could not hope to escape from the justice of God, go where they might. And this feeling of hopelessness and misery filled thousands of bosoms, millions, I may say. But what did this Gospel do? It brought light from God, the author of our being. Instead of thinking it was a bad condition to be born, it produced a feeling of gladness in the hearts of men and women that they ever had been born; because when they saw the justice of God, that they would get rewarded according to the deeds done in the body, all fear vanished, for they would be dealt with by a just and merciful God and not a tyrant, such as the world described the Lord to be.

Think of the glad tidings of salvation that have come to us through the revelations that God has given to this Church respecting the dead and their future fate. Before, the popular idea was that unnumbered millions of heathens who had died in ignorance of the Gospel had been sent to this endless place of torment; that they were sent to hell without any hope of deliverance through the endless ages of eternity. The feeling of those who would dare think upon this subject, when such thoughts were presented to them, was only to hate, as a monster, the God who would do such things. What could be more monstrous than to send innocent people to hell for not being that which they knew nothing of? No wonder that men revolted at the thought. No wonder that men defied the Almighty under such misconceptions. The Gospel has brought to us revelation concerning this. We see our God in all his beauty, in all his grandeur, clothed with all those attributes that call forth our highest admiration and worship. We can worship him in spirit and in truth. (CR, April 1899, p. 19.)

Brigham Young: 6
It is not written that there shall be no end to this torment

A gentleman asked the Prophet Joseph once if he believed that all other sects and parties would be damned excepting the Mormons. Joseph Smith's reply was, "Yes, sir, and most of the Mormons too, unless they repent." We believe that all will be damned who do not receive the gospel of Jesus Christ; but we do not believe that they will go into a lake which burns with brimstone and fire, and suffer unnamed and unheard-of torments, inflicted by cruel and malicious devils to all eternity.

The sectarian doctrine of final rewards and punishments is as strange to me as their bodiless, partless, and passionless God. Every man will receive according to the deeds done in the body, whether they be good or bad. [Sec.

76:110-11.] All men, excepting those who sin against the Holy Ghost, who shed innocent blood or who consent thereto, will be saved in some kingdom [Sec. 76:40-45; 88:29-32]; for in my father's house, says Jesus, are many mansions. [John 14:2.] Where is John Wesley's abode in the other world? He is not where the Father and the Son live, but he is gone into what is called hades, or paradise, or the spirit-world. He did not receive the gospel as preached by Jesus Christ and His apostles; it was not then upon the earth. The power of the Holy Priesthood was not then among men; but I suppose that Mr. Wesley lived according to the best light he had, and tried to improve upon it all the days of his life. Where is the departed spirit of that celebrated reformer? It occupies a better place than ever entered his heart to conceive of when he was in the flesh. (JD, June 18, 1865, 11:125-26.)

James E. Talmage: 11
Eternal punishment is God's punishment

During this hundred years many other great truths not known before, have been declared to the people, and one of the greatest is that to hell there is an exit as well as an entrance. [Sec. 76:81-85; Matt. 5:25-26.] Hell is no place to which a vindictive Judge sends prisoners to suffer and to be punished principally for his glory; but it is a place prepared for the teaching, the disciplining of those who failed to learn here upon the earth what they should have learned. True, we read of everlasting punishment, unending suffering, eternal damnation. [Matt. 18:8; 25:41, 46; Rev. 14:10-11.] That is a direful expression, but in his mercy the Lord has made plain what those words mean. "Eternal punishment," he says, "is God's punishment, for he is eternal; and that condition or state or possibility will ever exist for the sinner who deserves and really needs such condemnation; but this does not mean that the individual sufferer or sinner is to be kept in hell longer than is necessary to bring him to a fitness for something better. When he reaches that stage the prison doors will open and there will be rejoicing among the hosts who welcome him into a better state. The Lord has not abated in the least what he said in earlier dispensations concerning the operation of his law and his Gospel, but he had made clear unto us his goodness and mercy through it all, for it is his glory and his work to bring about the immortality and eternal life of man. [Moses 1:39.] (CR, April 1930, p. 97.)

Reed Smoot: 13
I command you to repent

There is another thing with our young people, as well as the people generally, that I desire to call your attention to and that is procrastination — putting off till tomorrow what we ought to do today, and thinking that we will live our religion a little better next year. The old saying that to travel by the road of by-and-by will reach the home of never, is just as true today as it ever was. Let us live our religion today. Let us do the duty of today. . . . Let us do everything required of us today, and not put it off for some future time. (CR, October 1900.)

Joseph Smith: 15

There is no pain so awful as that of suspense. This is the punishment of the wicked; their doubt, anxiety and suspense cause weeping, wailing and gnashing of teeth. (HC 5:340, April 8, 1843.)

Joseph Fielding Smith: 16-19

We cannot comprehend the great suffering that the Lord had to take upon himself to bring to pass this redemption from death and from sin. He spent a few years upon the earth, and during that short sojourn he suffered the abuse of men. They stoned him; they spat upon him; they cursed him; they ridiculed him; they accused him of almost every crime they could think of, and finally they took him and crucified him upon a cross.

We get into the habit of thinking, I suppose, that his great suffering was when he was nailed to the cross by his hands and his feet and was left there to suffer until he died. As excruciating as this pain was, that was not the greatest suffering that he had to undergo, for in some way which I cannot understand, but which I accept on faith, and which you must accept on faith, he carried on his back the burden of the sins of the whole world. It is hard enough for me to carry my own sins. How is it with you? And yet he had to carry the sins of the whole world, as our Savior and the Redeemer of a fallen world, and so great was his suffering before he went to the cross, we are informed that blood oozed from the pores of his body, and he prayed to his Father that the cup might pass if possible, but not being possible, he was willing to drink.

And here is what he has said to the Church: [Sec. 19:16-19, quoted.]

Now, when he said that if we do not repent we will have to suffer, even as he did, he had no reference to being nailed to a cross, but it was the torment of mind, of spirit, that he had reference to, before he ever got to the cross, and if men will not repent, they will have to suffer even as he suffered.

Now . . . briefly, he did all this for us, the Son of God, and he did it, as I have read to you, because his Father commanded him and because his Father so loved the world that he wanted to save the world from its sins. (CR, October 1947, pp. 147-48.)

Charles W. Penrose: 17
If they would not repent they must suffer

Alma states here [Alma 40:14-26] that he was very much troubled concerning the doctrine of the condition of people after they passed away from this life. He wanted to know something of the condition of man between death and the resurrection, and he says an angel of God made known to him that there is a space between death and the resurrection, that the spirits of wicked are in a state of unrest, having a knowledge of all their wickedness, and a remembrance of all their transgressions; that they are in a state of fear, looking for the wrath and indignation of God, not knowing what their punishment will be; while on the other hand, the spirits of the righteous enter into a state of rest. They have a perfect knowledge of all that God has done for them, and all their acts of righteousness, and they await in peace for the time when their bodies shall be brought forth from the dust to stand in the presence of their God to receive their crown. (JD, August 1880, 21:223.)

John Taylor: 18-19

The suffering of the Son of God was not simply the suffering of personal death; for in assuming the position that he did in making an atonement for the sins of the world he bore the weight, the responsibility, and the burden of the sins of all men, which, to us, is incomprehensible. As stated, "The Lord, your Redeemer, suffered death in the flesh; wherefore he suffered the pains of all men"; and Isaiah says: "Surely he hath borne our griefs, and carried our sorrows," also, "The Lord hath laid on him the iniquity of us all," and again, "He hath poured out his soul unto death, and he was numbered with the transgressors; and he bore the sin of many" [Isa. 53:4, 6, 12]; or, as it is written in the Second Book of Nephi: "For behold, he suffereth the pains of all men, yea, the pains of every living creature, both men, women, and children, who belong to the family of Adam" [9:21]; whilst in Mosiah it is declared: "He shall suffer temptations, and pain of body, hunger, thirst, and fatigue, even more than man can suffer, except it be unto death; for behold, blood cometh from every pore, so great shall be his anguish for the wickedness and the abominations of his people." [Mosiah 3:7.]

Groaning beneath this concentrated load, this intense, incomprehensible pressure, this terrible exaction of Divine justice, from which feeble humanity shrank, and through the agony thus experienced sweating great drops of blood, he was led to exclaim, "Father, if it be possible, let this cup pass from me." He had struggled against the powers of darkness that had been let loose upon him there; placed below all things, his mind surcharged with agony and pain, lonely and apparently helpless and forsaken, in his agony the blood oozed from his pores. Thus rejected by his own, attacked by the powers of darkness, and seemingly forsaken by his God, on the cross he bowed beneath the accumulated load, and cried out in anguish, "My God, why hast thou forsaken me?" "It is finished!" "Father, into thy hands I commend my spirit." [Matt. 27:46; John 19:30; Luke 23:46.] As a God, he descended below all things, and made himself subject to man in man's fallen condition; as a man, he grappled with all the circumstances incident to his sufferings in the world. Anointed, indeed, with the oil of gladness above his fellows, he struggled with and overcame the powers of men and devils, of earth and hell combined; and aided by this superior power of the Godhead, he vanquished death, hell and the grave, and arose triumphant as the Son of God, the very eternal Father, the Messiah, the Prince of Peace, the Redeemer, the Savior of the world; having finished and completed the work pertaining to the atonement, which his Father had given him to do as the Son of God and the Son of Man. As the Son of Man, he endured all that it was possible for flesh and blood to endure; as the Son of God, he triumphed over all, and forever ascended to the right hand of God, to further carry out the designs of Jehovah pertaining to the world and to the human family. (*Mediation and Atonement*, 1950, pp. 146-48.)

First Presidency (Brigham Young, Heber C. Kimball, Jedediah M. Grant): 23
Listen to my words

Finally, brethren, give heed unto the whisperings of the Spirit of the Lord, your God. Be ye filled with the Holy Ghost; let your peace flow like unto a river, without let or hindrance; be merciful and kind to the stranger, and forbearing to each other; be faithful to keep your covenants, and abide the trial of your faith. [Sec. 97:8.] Be humble before the Lord your God and keep his commandments, and the veil of the covering will be filled with joy and rejoicing from day to day, as ye see the time approaching, and witness the steppings of Almighty God amid the mighty tread of earth's millions hastening to destroy each other [Sec. 63:32-33]; put down iniquity, wickedness, and bring forth Zion, the peace of Jerusalem, and the universal triumph and reign of truth and righteousness upon the whole earth. (MS, July 8, 1854, 16:429-30.)

Spencer W. Kimball: 23
You shall have peace in me

Peace, joy, satisfaction, happiness, growth, contentment, all come with the righteous living of the commandments of God. The one who delights in all of the worldly luxuries of today, at the expense of spirituality, is living but for the moment. His day is coming; retribution is sure. (CR, April 1952, pp. 23-24.)

Richard L. Evans: 25
I command thee

I have a great respect for all men and their beliefs, but think it not a strange thing that in a kingdom, the kingdom of God, there should be specific requirements and commandments, and a way that God has given for our realizing the highest happiness and peace and progress. (CR, April 1961, p. 77.)

George Albert Smith: 25

Thou shalt not covet thy neighbour's house, thou shalt not covet thy neighbour's wife, nor his manservant, nor his maidservant, nor his ass, nor any thing that is thy neighbour's. [Ex. 20:17]

Do you believe that the Lord said that? Do you believe that he meant what he said? If we only understood how near we are to the judgment day there are men and women in the various communities of this world who would now be on their knees in sack-cloth and ashes; but they think that time's so far off that they procrastinate the day of repentance. [Sec. 45:26-27.] (CR, October 1935, p. 121.)

John A. Widtsoe: 26

On February 28, 1828, Martin Harris, a prosperous farmer of Palmyra, friendly to Joseph, took one of these transcripts [copy of characters from the gold plates] to New York City. There two eminent students of ancient languages, Doctors Anthon and Mitchell, examined them. In later years both of these men acknowledged that the characters were presented to them. Martin Harris declared that the "experts" said the characters were a mixture of ancient alphabets. However, when they learned how the characters had been obtained and that part of the "book" or plates were sealed, they repudiated their first positive statement. Egyptology was in its early infancy at that time. The visit and the statements of the two men were sufficient, however, to induce Harris to become a scribe for the Prophet, and later, when the Book of Mormon was to be published, to mortgage his farm for $3,000 with which to pay the printer. (*Joseph Smith*, 1951, p. 39.)

Orson F. Whitney: 27
The Gentile

The name Gentile is not with us a term of reproach. It comes from Gentilis, meaning of a nation, a family or a people not of Israel—that is all. "Mormon" is a nickname for Latter-day Saints, but "gentile" is not a nickname. It simply means, with us, one who does not belong to the Church. They are wiser than we are in material things—the things of earth and time. But when it comes to spiritual things—the things of heaven and eternity, we can teach them. We need their wealth and worldly wisdom, their wonderful skill in managing and manipulating temporalities. And they need the Gospel and the Priesthood. They need us, for we hold in our hands the key to their eternal salvation. (CR, April 1928, pp. 59-60.)

Joseph Fielding Smith: 27
The Jew, of whom the Lamanites are a remnant

It is true that Lehi and his family were descendants of Joseph through the lineage of Manasseh (Alma 10:3), and Ishmael was a descendant of Ephraim, according to the statement of the Prophet Joseph Smith. That the Nephites were descendants of Joseph is in fulfilment of the blessings given to Joseph by his father Israel. The Nephites were of the Jews, not so much by descent as by citizenship, although in the long descent from Jacob, it would be possible of some mixing of the tribes by intermarriage.

It should be remembered that in the days of Rehoboam, son of Solomon, ten of the twelve tribes of Israel revolted and were known as the kingdom of Israel from that time on until they were carried away into Assyria. The other two tribes of Judah and Benjamin remained loyal to Rehoboam and were known as the kingdoms of Judah. Lehi was a citizen of Jerusalem, in the kingdom of Judah. Presumably his family had lived there for several generations, and all the inhabitants of the kingdom of Judah, no matter which tribe they had descended through, were known as Jews. The condition is comparable to conditions today. For example: Many members of the Church have been gathered out of England, Germany, the Scandinavian countries, and other foreign lands. Coming to this country they have to take out citizenship papers, and then they and their descendants are known as Americans, being citizens of this country. There is also a comparable example in the case of Paul the apostle. When he was arrested on complaint of the Jews, the chief captain mistook him for an Egyptian who had created a rebellion, and Paul said to the captain, " . . . I am a man which am a Jew of Tarsus, a city in Cilicia, a citizen of no mean city: and, I beseech thee, suffer me to speak unto the people." When the privilege was granted, Paul spoke to the angry Jews and said: "I am verily a man which as a Jew, born in Tarsus, a city in Cilicia, yet brought up in this city at the feet of Gamaliel, and taught according to the perfect manner of the law of the fathers, and was zealous toward God, as ye are all this day." (Acts 21:37-39; 22:3.) In writing his epistles to the Roman saints and also to the saints of Philippi, Paul said: " . . . For I also am an Israelite, of the seed of Abraham of the tribe of Benjamin." (Romans 11:1 and Philippians 3:5.)

Not only in the Book of Mormon are the descendants of Lehi called Jews, but also in the Doctrine and Covenants. In section 19, verse 27, this is found: [Sec. 19:27, quoted.] Again, in giving instructions to the Elders who had journeyed from Kirtland to Missouri, the Lord revealed the place for the building of the temple and gave instruction for the purchase of land "lying westward, even unto the line running directly between Jew and Gentile." (Sec. 57:4.) This line westward was the dividing line between the whites and Indians. (*IE*, October 1955, 58:702.)

Wilford Woodruff: 28

You should enter your secret closets, and call upon the name of the Lord. Many of you have learned to pray; then fail not to let your prayers ascend up into the ears of the God of Sabaoth [hosts]; and he will hear you. I think sometimes that we do not fully comprehend the power that we have with God in knowing how to approach him acceptably. All that these men holding the Priesthood, and all that our sisters need do, is to live near to God, and call upon him, pouring out their soul's desire in behalf of Israel, and their power will be felt, and their confidence in God will be strengthened. But the blessings of heaven can only be obtained and controlled upon the principles of righteousness. I have heard the Prophet Joseph pray when the power of God rested down upon him, and all who heard him felt it; and I have seen his prayers answered in a marvelous manner almost immediately. Governor Reynolds of Missouri on one occasion employed men to try and kidnap Joseph, and they almost accomplished their designs, but Joseph had some Gentile friends as well as his brethren, through whom he was rescued, and was taken to Nauvoo and released under a writ of habeas corpus. But the governor continued to harass him with writs and was determined to destroy Joseph. Joseph and the Twelve went before God in prayer. Joseph, kneeling before the Lord, offered up prayer and asked God to deliver him from the power of that man. Among other things, he told the Lord that he was innocent before him, and that his heart was heavy under the persecutions he endured. In about forty-eight hours from that time word reached Joseph that Reynolds had blown his brains out. Before perpetrating the deed he left a note on his desk stating that, as his services were not appreciated by the people of the State, he took that course to end his days. (*JD*, January 27, 1883, 24:55.)

George Teasdale: 28

I was inducted into the Kingdom of God by prayer, and I

have been sustained by the Almighty Father by prayer ever since that day. I do not pray for form's sake. I pray because I earnestly desire to have the fellowship of the Holy Ghost. I cannot understand how anybody can pray for form's sake, although I have almost been led to believe that we do so on a great many times and occasions, and I will give you my reasons for so thinking. What is the idea, after singing, of one of the brethren standing up here to open this meeting by prayer? Is he not our spokesman, the mouthpiece, and should we not, while he utters the sentences, have those sentences pass through our minds in a prayer as a congregation, and when he has finished it, endorse the same by saying "amen." What is the meaning of amen? So be it. Well, I noticed today that there were few "amens." Why is this? Did we not endorse the prayer? Did we not sanction it? I should think if we did we would naturally say "amen"—so let it be. . . . What is the meaning of prayer? Why, it is to earnestly ask something that we require with all our hearts. All who are in fellowship of the Holy Ghost will ask God for his Spirit to be in their hearts in all their business relations even, that they might not soil their hands, but keep them clean and their hearts pure, and that they might merit his approbation. The Lord Jesus Christ encouraged his disciples to pray—to pray without ceasing. [1 Thess. 5:17.] (*JD*, January 11, 1885, 26:50-51.)

Anthon H. Lund: 30
Reviling not against revilers

Some there are who think we are afraid to meet anyone in debate. Not so. It is much harder for our young brethren to keep from debating than it is to engage in it; for they feel that they have the truth, and they are not afraid to meet anyone in defense of principles in which they believe. But we have only one object in view in going out amongst the nations, and that is to follow the Master's instructions—to go out and teach men. That is our work. We do not go out to win battles as debaters; but we go out to teach men that which we have received, and which we know is true. If men are not willing to receive it, that is their own concern, not ours. [Sec.

43:15-16.] When our Elders show the world the beauty of the principles of the Gospel as revealed to us, it is for men to say whether they will receive them or not. The Elders do their duty, and leave the result to the Lord. Those who seek to debate with our Elders and thirst for the honor of beating them in argument, do not want to be taught; they simply want contention. Paul tells us to avoid contention. He said: "But if any man seem to be contentious, we have no such custom, neither the churches of God." [1 Cor. 11:16.] So we say, contention is not our custom, and we advise our missionaries not to contend, but simply go out and teach the principles of the Gospel. (CR, October 1902, pp. 80-81.)

Francis M. Lyman: 31

We all remember that expression of the Apostle Paul, in regard to the principle of faith, that I have thought has unwittingly deluded the Christian people generally in the world, for he declared that "*without* faith it is impossible to please [God.]" [Heb. 11:6.] Naturally, it has been taken that *with* faith the Lord may be pleased, and that too with faith alone. But we have come to understand that faith, genuine living faith, produces the very important principle of repentance, and that without repentance it is not possible to please God. Without baptism for the remission of sins it is not possible to please him. Without the gift of the Holy Ghost it is not possible to please him. [Sec. 20:41; 35:6.] But, with these great and superior, and primary principles in the Gospel in life and salvation, we have discovered and have proven in our lives that men may be saved. (CR, October 1911, pp. 30-31.)

Lorenzo Snow: 31
By fire, yea, even the Holy Ghost

I had no sooner opened my lips in an effort to pray than I heard a sound, just above my head, like the rustling of silken robes, and immediately the Spirit of God descended upon me, completely enveloping my whole person, filling me, from the crown of my head to the soles of my feet, and O, the joy and happiness I felt! No language can describe the almost instantaneous transition from a dense cloud of mental and spiritual darkness into a refulgence of light and knowledge, as it was at that time imparted to my understanding. I then received a perfect knowledge that God lives, that Jesus Christ is the Son of God, and of the restoration of the Holy Priesthood, and the fulness of the Gospel. It was a complete baptism—a tangible immersion in the heavenly principle or element (the gift of) the Holy Ghost; and even more real and physical in its effects upon every part of my system than the immersion by water; dispelling forever, so long as reason and memory last, all possibility of doubt or fear in relation to the fact handed down to us historically, that the "babe of Bethlehem" is truly the Son of God; also the fact that he is now being revealed to the children of men, and communicating knowledge, the same as in the apostolic times. I was perfectly satisfied, as well as I might be, for my expectations were repeated, and continued to be for several successive nights. The sweet remembrance of those glorious experiences, from that time to the present, bring them fresh before me, imparting an inspiring influence which pervades my whole being, and I trust will to the close of my earthly existence. (IE, June 1919, 22:645-55.)

Joseph Fielding Smith: 32
This is a great and the last commandment . . . I shall give unto you

In this revelation [Sec. 19] Martin is again admonished and called on to repent, and the dire consequences of his failure to repent are pointed out to him. It is evident that Martin Harris came to the Prophet seeking the favor of the Lord and in response to his pleading this revelation was given. The Lord also warns him that he need not ask for favor again, for this is to be the last, and a great commandment unto him. (CHMR, 1947, 1:81.)

Rudger Clawson: 38

It is astonishing the amount of scripture and revelation that has been given upon the subject of prayer, touching its importance, its far-reaching character, and its necessity to the children of men, especially to the children of God. I am reminded of a passage which occurs in a revelation given to Martin Harris in March, 1830. The Lord said unto him: [Sec. 19:28, 38, quoted.]

How impressive are those few simple words in regard to prayer! How far-reaching! They center into a man's life and comprehend his whole existence, at least from the years of his accountability until he passes into the grave. He must pray under all circumstances. Prayer is not reserved for the Sabbath day or for any particular occasion. It is not only to be used at the general conferences of the Church, but the spirit of prayer must be in our hearts unceasingly. We must pray in our families, we must pray in secret; we must pray in our hearts. The spirit of prayer must be with us when we retire at night and when we arise in the morning. It must be upon us when we leave our homes or in the valleys, or wherever we are. We are told in the words which I have quoted that if the spirit is upon us the Lord will bless us, and the blessings which will come in answer to prayer will be of more importance to us than treasures of earth. We know something of the treasures of earth; we realize the value and the desirability of earthly things. We know how they are sought after, and what great sacrifices are made for them. But how much better it is to enjoy the full measure of the Spirit of God which is promised. (CR, April 1904, pp. 42-43.)

Reed Smoot: 38
Pray always

Many people say: What does prayer do? What good does it accomplish? Let us reflect; let us refer to the Bible, and see what prayer did for God's people in the past. As I recall it now, prayer has divided seas, and has rolled back flowing rivers; it has caused living streams of water to burst forth from solid rock; it has muzzled lions and has rendered vipers and poisons harmless; it has arrested the sun in its rapid race, and has stopped the course of the moon; it has burst open iron gates, and has recalled souls from eternity; it has called legions of angels down from the heavens. Prayer has bridled the vicious passions of men; it has routed and destroyed armies of proud, daring atheists. Prayer has brought one man from the bottom of the ocean, and carried another, in a chariot of fire, to heaven. I can imagine the scoffer and unbeliever saying: "Oh, this is ancient history. These are Bible stories; tell us what prayer has done on modern individuals; tell us what prayer has done touching the things of this life; something that prayer has done in this age of the world, and let the dark ages take care of themselves." Well, I know a people who can say that through the power of prayer there have been accomplished as great things in this day as were ever done in former ages. It was through prayer that the Father and the Son appeared to Joseph Smith; through prayer that the great plan of salvation was revealed unto him. It is through prayer that this people have been directed from the foundation of this Church to the present time. It was through prayer that the pioneers were protected and guided across the trackless plains of the western wilderness, and brought safely to the tops of these mountains. It has been through prayer that God has blessed the earth in these valleys and made it produce abundantly, of fruits, vegetables, grains, and nearly every other requisite for the sustaining of his people in comfort. It seems to me that if we look into our own lives, and see what prayer has done for each and every one of us, we will find countless blessings that have come to us through prayer.

But we must so live that we are worthy of the blessings asked for. I do not believe that a people steeped in sin, or a man corrupt in heart, can receive the full blessings of the eternal Father, for they do not place themselves in a position to receive them. A man must repent of his sins; he must have faith that God is the Giver of all good; he must believe that God actually exists before he can feel that his prayer will be answered. [Sec. 88:63-65.] (CR, October 1908, p. 77.)

David O. McKay: 38
Great shall be your blessing

If our young people will . . . approach the Lord, there are at least four great blessings which will come to them here and now.

The first is *Gratitude*. Their souls will be filled with thanksgiving for what God has done for them. They will find themselves rich in favors bestowed. The young man who closes the door behind him, who draws the curtains, and there in silence pleads with God for help, should first pour out his soul in gratitude for health, for friends, for loved ones, for the gospel, for the manifestations of God's existence. He should first count his many blessings and name them one by one.

The second blessing of prayer is *Guidance*. I cannot conceive of a young man's going astray who will kneel down by his bedside in the morning and pray to God to help him keep himself unspotted from the sins of the world. I think that a young girl will not go far wrong who will kneel down in the morning and pray that she might be kept pure and spotless during the coming day. I cannot think that a Latter-day Saint will hold enmity in his heart or feelings of envy and malice toward any of his fellow men. Guidance: Yes, God will be there to guide and direct him who will seek him in faith with all his might and with all his soul.

The third blessing is *Confidence*. All over this land there are thousands and tens of thousands of students who are struggling to get an education. In the Church, let us teach these students that if they want to succeed in their lessons they would seek their God; that the greatest Teacher known to the world stands near to guide them. Once the student feels that he can approach the Lord through prayer, he will receive confidence that he can get his lessons, that he can write his speech, that he can stand up before his fellow students and deliver his message without fear of failure. Confidence comes through sincere prayer.

Finally, he will get *Inspiration*. It is not imagination, if we approach God sincerely seeking light and guidance from him, our minds will be enlightened and our souls thrilled by his Spirit. Washington sought it; Lincoln received it; Joseph Smith knew it; and the testimony, the evidence of the Prophet Joseph's inspiration is manifest to all who will but open their eyes to see and their hearts to understand. (CR, April 1961, pp. 7-8.)

SECTION 20

Revelation on Church Organization and Government, given through Joseph Smith the Prophet, April, 1830. Preceding his record of this revelation the Prophet wrote: We obtained of him [Jesus Christ] the following, by the spirit of prophecy and revelation; which not only gave us much information, but also pointed out to us the precise day upon which, according to his will and commandment, we should proceed to organize his Church once more here upon the earth. – The Lord again attests the genuineness of the Book of Mormon – He gives commandment respecting baptism – Defines the functions of the several offices in the Priesthood – Specifies the duties of members – Prescribes the mode of baptism, and of administering the sacrament of bread and wine – Directs the keeping of records of Church membership.

1. The rise of the Church of Christ in these last days, being one thousand eight hundred and thirty years since the coming of our Lord and Savior Jesus Christ in the flesh, it being regularly organized and established agreeable to the laws of our country, by the will and commandments of God, in the fourth month, and on the sixth day of the month which is called April—

2. Which commandments were given to Joseph Smith, Jun., who was called of God, and ordained an apostle of Jesus Christ, to be the first elder of this church;

3. And to Oliver Cowdery, who was also called of God, an apostle of Jesus Christ, to be the second elder of this church, and ordained under his hand;

4. And this according to the grace of our Lord and Savior Jesus Christ, to whom be all glory, both now and forever. Amen.

5. After it was truly manifested unto this first elder that he had received a remission of his sins, he was entangled again in the vanities of the world;

6. But after repenting, and humbling himself sincerely, through faith, God ministered unto him by an holy angel, whose countenance was as lightning, and whose garments were pure and white above all other whiteness;

7. And gave unto him commandments which inspired him;

8. And gave him power from on high, by the means which were before prepared, to translate the Book of Mormon;

9. Which contains a record of a fallen people, and the fulness of the gospel of Jesus Christ to the Gentiles and to the Jews also;

10. Which was given by inspiration, and is confirmed to others by the ministering of angels, and is declared unto the world by them—

11. Proving to the world that the holy scriptures are true, and that God does inspire men and call them to his holy work in this age and generation, as well as in generations of old;

12. Thereby showing that he is the same God yesterday, today, and forever. Amen.

13. Therefore, having so great witnesses, by them shall the world be judged, even as many as shall hereafter come to a knowledge of this work.

14. And those who receive it in faith, and work righteousness, shall receive a crown of eternal life;

15. But those who harden their hearts in unbelief, and reject it, it shall turn to their own condemnation—

16. For the Lord God has spoken it; and we, the elders of the church, have heard and bear witness to the words of the glorious Majesty on high, to whom be glory forever and ever. Amen.

17. By these things we know that there is a God in heaven, who is infinite and eternal, from everlasting to everlasting the same unchangeable God, the framer of heaven and earth, and all things which are in them;

18. And that he created man, male and female, after his own image and in his own likeness, created he them;

19. And gave unto them commandments that they should love and serve him, the only living and true God, and that he should be the only being whom they should worship.

20. But by the transgression of these holy laws man became sensual and devilish, and became fallen man.

21. Wherefore, the Almighty God gave his Only Begotten Son, as it is written in those scriptures which have been given of him.

22. He suffered temptations but gave no heed unto them.

23. He was crucified, died, and rose again the third day;

24. And ascended into heaven, to sit down on the right hand of the Father, to reign with almighty power according to the will of the Father;

25. That as many as would believe and be baptized in his holy name, and endure in faith to the end, should be saved—

26. Not only those who believed after he came in the meridian of time, in the flesh, but all those from the beginning, even as many as were before he came, who believed in the words of the holy prophets, who spake as they were inspired by the gift of the Holy Ghost, who truly testified of him in all things, should have eternal life,

27. As well as those who should come after, who should believe in the gifts and callings of God by the Holy Ghost, which beareth record of the Father and of the Son;

28. Which Father, Son, and Holy Ghost are one God, infinite and eternal, without end. Amen.

29. And we know that all men must repent and believe on the name of Jesus Christ, and worship the Father in his name, and endure in faith on his name to the end, or they cannot be saved in the kingdom of God.

30. And we know that justification through the grace of our Lord and Savior Jesus Christ is just and true;

31. And we know also, that sanctification through the grace of our Lord and Savior Jesus Christ is just and true, to all those who love and serve God with all their mights, minds, and strength.

32. But there is a possibility that man may fall from grace and depart from the living God;

33. Therefore let the church take heed and pray always, lest they fall into temptation;

34. Yea, and even let those who are sanctified take heed also.

35. And we know that these things are true and according to the revelations of John, neither adding to, nor diminishing from the prophecy of his book, the holy scriptures, or the revelations of God which shall come hereafter by the gift and power of the Holy Ghost, the voice of God, or the ministering of angels.

36. And the Lord God has spoken it; and honor, power and glory be rendered to his holy name, both now and ever. Amen.

37. *And again, by way of commandment to the church concerning the manner of baptism* — All those who humble themselves before God, and desire to be baptized, and come forth with broken hearts and contrite spirits, and witness before the church that they have truly repented of all their sins, and are willing to take upon them the name of Jesus Christ, having a determination to serve him to the end, and truly manifest by their works that they have received of the Spirit of Christ unto the remission of their sins, shall be received by baptism into his church.

38. *The duty of the elders, priests, teachers, deacons, and members of the church of Christ* — An apostle is an elder, and it is his calling to baptize;

39. And to ordain other elders, priests, teachers, and deacons;

40. And to administer bread and wine — the emblems of the flesh and blood of Christ—

41. And to confirm those who are baptized into the church, by the laying on of hands for the baptism of fire and the Holy Ghost, according to the scriptures;

42. And to teach, expound, exhort, baptize, and watch over the church;

43. And to confirm the church by the laying on of the hands, and the giving of the Holy Ghost;

44. And to take the lead of all meetings.

45. The elders are to conduct the meetings as they are led by the Holy Ghost, according to the commandments and revelations of God.

46. The priest's duty is to preach, teach, expound, exhort, and baptize, and administer the sacrament,

47. And visit the house of each member, and exhort them to pray vocally and in secret and attend to all family duties.

48. And he may also ordain other priests, teachers, and deacons.

49. And he is to take the lead of meetings when there is no elder present;

50. But when there is an elder present, he is only to preach, teach, expound, exhort, and baptize,

51. And visit the house of each member, exhorting them to pray vocally and in secret and attend to all family duties.

52. In all these duties the priest is to assist the elder if occasion requires.

53. The teacher's duty is to watch over the church always, and be with and strengthen them;

54. And see that there is no iniquity in the church, neither hardness with each other, neither lying, backbiting, nor evil speaking;

55. And see that the church meet together often, and also see that all the members do their duty.

56. And he is to take the lead of meetings in the absence of the elder or priest—

57. And is to be assisted always, in all his duties in the church, by the deacons, if occasion requires.

58. But neither teachers nor deacons have authority to baptize, administer the sacrament, or lay on hands;

59. They are, however, to warn, expound, exhort, and teach, and invite all to come unto Christ.

60. Every elder, priest, teacher, or deacon is to be ordained according to the gifts and callings of God unto him; and he is to be ordained by the power of the Holy Ghost, which is in the one who ordains him.

61. The several elders composing this church of Christ are to meet in conference once in three months, or from time to time as said conferences shall direct or appoint;

62. And said conferences are to do whatever church business

is necessary to be done at the time.

63. The elders are to receive their licenses from other elders, by vote of the church to which they belong, or from the conferences.

64. Each priest, teacher, or deacon, who is ordained by a priest, may take a certificate from him at the time, which certificate, when presented to an elder, shall entitle him to a license, which shall authorize him to perform the duties of his calling, or he may receive it from a conference.

65. No person is to be ordained to any office in this church, where there is a regularly organized branch of the same, without the vote of that church;

66. But the presiding elders, traveling bishops, high councilors, high priests, and elders, may have the privilege of ordaining, where there is no branch of the church that a vote may be called.

67. Every president of the high priesthood (or presiding elder), bishop, high councilor, and high priest, is to be ordained by the direction of a high council or general conference.

68. *The duty of the members after they are received by baptism.* —The elders or priests are to have a sufficient time to expound all things concerning the church of Christ to their understanding, previous to their partaking of the sacrament and being confirmed by the laying on of the hands of the elders, so that all things may be done in order.

69. And the members shall manifest before the church, and also before the elders, by a godly walk and conversation, that they are worthy of it, that there may be works and faith agreeable to the holy scriptures—walking in holiness before the Lord.

70. Every member of the church of Christ having children is to bring them unto the elders before the church, who are to lay their hands upon them in the name of Jesus Christ, and bless them in his name.

71. No one can be received into the church of Christ unless he has arrived unto the years of accountability before God, and is capable of repentance.

72. Baptism is to be administered in the following manner unto all those who repent—

73. The person who is called of God and has authority from Jesus Christ to baptize, shall go down into the water with the person who has presented himself or herself for baptism, and shall say, calling him or her by name: Having been commissioned of Jesus Christ, I baptize you in the name of the Father, and of the Son, and of the Holy Ghost. Amen.

74. Then shall he immerse him or her in the water, and come forth again out of the water.

75. It is expedient that the church meet together often to partake of bread and wine in the remembrance of the Lord Jesus;

76. And the elder or priest shall administer it; and after this manner shall he administer it—he shall kneel with the church and call upon the Father in solemn prayer, saying:

77. O God, the Eternal Father, we ask thee in the name of thy Son, Jesus Christ, to bless and sanctify this bread to the souls of all those who partake of it, that they may eat in remembrance of the body of thy Son, and witness unto thee, O God, the Eternal Father, that they are willing to take upon them the name of thy Son, and always remember him and keep his commandments which he has given them; that they may always have his Spirit to be with them. Amen.

78. The manner of administering the wine—he shall take the cup also, and say:

79. O God, the Eternal Father, we ask thee in the name of thy Son, Jesus Christ, to bless and sanctify this wine to the souls of all those who drink of it, that they may do it in remembrance of the blood of thy Son, which was shed for them; that they may witness unto thee, O God, the Eternal Father, that they do always remember him, that they may have his Spirit to be with them. Amen.

80. Any member of the church of Christ transgressing, or being overtaken in a fault, shall be dealt with as the scriptures direct.

81. It shall be the duty of the several churches, composing the church of Christ, to send one or more of their teachers to attend the several conferences held by the elders of the church,

82. With a list of the names of the several members uniting themselves with the church since the last conference; or send by the hand of some priest; so that a regular list of all the names of the whole church may be kept in a book by one of the elders, whomsoever the other elders shall appoint from time to time;

83. And also, if any have been expelled from the church, so that their names may be blotted out of the general church record of names.

84. All members removing from the church where they reside, if going to a church where they are not known, may take a letter certifying that they are regular members and in good standing, which certificate may be signed by any elder or priest if the member receiving the letter is personally acquainted with the elder or priest, or it may be signed by the teachers or deacons of the church.

Joseph Smith: *Introduction*

In this manner [by giving revelations, as Section 18] did the Lord continue to give us instructions from time to time, concerning the duties which now devolved upon us; and among many other things of the kind, we obtained of him the following, by the spirit of prophecy and revelation; which not only gave us much information, but also pointed out to us the precise day upon which, according to his will and commandment, we should proceed to organize his Church once more here upon the earth: [Section 20, quoted.] (*HC* 1:64, April 1830.)

George Q. Cannon: 1-4

The Church of Jesus Christ of Latter-day Saints was organized on the 6th day of April, in the year of our Lord one thousand eight hundred and thirty, in Fayette, Seneca County, in the State of New York. Six persons were the original members: Joseph Smith the Prophet, Oliver Cowdery, Hyrum Smith, Peter Whitmer, Jun., Samuel H. Smith, and David Whitmer. Each of the men had already been baptized by direct authority from heaven. The organization was made on the day and after the pattern dictated by God in a revelation given to Joseph Smith. The Church was called after the name of Jesus Christ; because he so ordered. Jesus accepted the Church, declared it to be his own and empowered it to minister on earth in his name.

The sacrament, under inspiration from Jesus Christ, was administered to all who had thus taken upon them his name. . . .

As Joseph had not been permitted to officiate in baptism, or to confer the Aaronic Priesthood, until John had visited him and transmitted that authority from heaven, so after even this blessing had become his own, he was unable to seal the gift of the Holy Ghost, or to ordain an Elder until after Peter, James and John had endowed him with the Priesthood after the holy order of Melchizedek. And even after both these holy orders of Priesthood were given to him, and he had ordained Oliver unto them; even after he had beheld in vision the establishment of the work of righteousness, he knew not how nor when the organization of the Church should be accomplished. It was necessary that God should define the mode and the principle of organization and should direct each step to be taken in this establishment of his kingdom; and it was not until he did this that Joseph knew in what manner to obtain the restoration of the power which belongs to the body of the saints in Christ.

Joseph proceeded carefully, and exactly according to the instruction of the Almighty, and he laid the foundation of a work which will endure as long as earth shall last. (*Life of Joseph Smith*, 1907, pp. 52-54.)

Charles W. Nibley: 1

A wonderful day, the sixth day of April! Many notable things have occurred on it. The organization of the Church for one great and notable thing. The Prophet Joseph recites in his own story that it was early in the spring of 1820, one hundred and ten years ago, when he went into the woods to pray. I like to think of that also as being on the sixth day of April. We have no definite knowledge of it, but I believe it in my heart and in my soul.... I believe with all my heart and soul that the sixth day of April was the birthday of the Lord Jesus, our Savior and Redeemer.... More likely was it in the spring of the year than on the twenty-fifth day of December, which is celebrated as the birthday of the Savior; yet we go on celebrating that day, and it is all right to do so, inasmuch as that is the day the world generally accepts. But I repeat, it is my individual opinion, firmly fixed in my mind, that the sixth day of April is the birthday of the Savior of the world. I further like to believe that the resurrection of the Redeemer, which marked his triumph over death and the grave, also occurred on the sixth of April, though I have no definite proof.

Another notable event that occurred on this day is part of the history of this glorious country of ours—the United States of America. The Lord says in the revelations given through the Prophet Joseph Smith that he raised up wise men for the very purpose of framing the Constitution, which guarantees liberty to all. [Sec. 101:80.] It was born on the sixth of April. It had previously been adopted by the Constitutional Convention and submitted to the various States for ratification. While it was intended that the returns should all be in by the fourth of March, it was not until the sixth day of April that the electoral votes of the different States were counted by the Senate and House then in session. And on the sixth day of April, George Washington was declared to be the President of the United States. So the nation had its real birth at that time. (CR, April 1930, pp. 26-27.)

Joseph Smith: 1

The day was spent in a very agreeable manner in giving and receiving knowledge which appertained to this last kingdom—it being just 1,800 years since the Savior laid down his life that men might have everlasting life, and only three years since the Church had come out of the wilderness, preparatory for the last dispensation. (HC 1:337, April 6, 1833.)

Stephen L Richards: 1

The objectives of the Church are to bear witness to the divinity of the Lord Jesus Christ; to teach all men the principles of his Gospel; and to convert and persuade them to follow in his ways and keep the commandments of God, that they may thus advance the Kingdom of God in the earth to bring brotherhood and peace to men and nations, and even exaltation for themselves.

To achieve this objective The Church of Jesus Christ of Latter-day Saints builds and maintains churches, temples, educational institutions for all ages, recreational buildings and facilities, and projects designed to teach and encourage vocational and industrial preparation for self-reliant living. It teaches loyalty to country and fosters good citizenship in all communities where it is established. (CR, October 1956, pp. 40-41.)

James E. Talmage: 1
The coming of our Lord and Savior Jesus Christ in the flesh

The time of Messiah's birth is a subject upon which specialists in theology and history, and those who are designated in literature "the learned," fail to agree. Numerous lines of investigation have been followed, only to reach divergent conclusions, both as to the year and as to the month and day within the year at which the "Christian era" in reality began. . . .

Without attempting to analyze the mass of calculation data relating to this subject, we accept the Dionysian basis as correct with respect to the year, which to us is B.C. 1, and, as shall be shown, in an early month of that year. In support of this belief we cite the inspired record known as the "Revelation on Church Government, given through Joseph the Prophet, in April, 1830," which opens with these words: "The rise of the Church of Christ in these last days, being one thousand eight hundred and thirty years since the coming of our Lord and Savior Jesus Christ in the flesh."

Another evidence of the correctness of our commonly accepted chronology is furnished by the Book of Mormon record. Therein we read that "in the commencement of the first year of the reign of Zedekiah, king of Judah," the word of the Lord came to Lehi at Jerusalem, directing him to take his family and depart into the wilderness. [1 Nephi 1:4; 2:2-4.] In the early stages of their journey toward the sea, Lehi prophesied, as had been shown him of the Lord, concerning the impending destruction of Jerusalem and the captivity of the Jews. Furthermore, he predicted the eventual return of the people of Judah from their exile in Babylon, and the birth of the Messiah, which latter event he definitely declared would take place six hundred years from the time he and his people had left Jerusalem. [1 Nephi 10:4.] This specification of time was repeated by later prophecy [1 Nephi 19:8; 2 Nephi 25:19]; and the signs of the actual fulfilment are recorded as having been realized "six hundred years from the time that Lehi left Jerusalem." [3 Nephi 1:1.] These scriptures fix the time of the beginning of Zedekiah's reign as six hundred years before the birth of Christ. According to the commonly accepted reckoning, Zedekiah was made king in the year 597 B.C. This shows a discrepancy of about three years between the commonly accepted date of Zedekiah's inauguration as king and that given in the Book of Mormon statement; and, as already seen, there is a difference of between three and four years between the Dionysian reckoning and the nearest approach to an agreement among scholars concerning the beginning of the current era. Book of Mormon chronology therefore sustains in general the correctness of the common or Dionysian system.

As to the season of the year in which Christ was born, there is among the learned as great a diversity of opinion as that relating to the year itself. It is claimed by many biblical scholars that December 25th, the day celebrated in Christendom as Christmas, cannot be the correct date. We believe April 6th to be the birthday of Jesus Christ, as indicated in a revelation of the present dispensation already cited [Sec. 20:1; 21:3], in which that day is made without qualification the completion of the one thousand eight hundred and thirtieth year since the coming of the Lord in the flesh. This acceptance is admittedly based on faith in modern revelation, and in no wise is set forth as the result of chronological research or analysis. We believe that Jesus Christ was born in Bethlehem of Judea, April 6, B.C. 1. (*Jesus the Christ*, 1916, pp. 102-4.)

Anthon H. Lund: 1-4

Now the Church was organized [April 1830], but not all the officers of the Church as we have them today, for the simple reason they did not have enough members in the Church to make a complete organization. Ten months after the Church was organized, Edward Partridge was ordained a Bishop to the Church, and in June following the first High Priests were ordained. In December, 1833, Joseph Smith, Senior, was ordained a Patriarch, and two months later the first High Council was organized. The Quorum of Twelve

Apostles was organized. [Feb. 1835.] All the offices in the Priesthood were now established and men were ordained to fill them.

In regard to Church government I will state that during the first thirteen months all Church business was done by conferences of Elders presided over by Joseph Smith and Oliver Cowdery. Several of the leading brethren were now ordained High Priests who afterwards formed the presiding quorum of the Church. In March, 1832, Joseph was called by revelation to be President of the Church, and a month later he was sustained as President of the High Priests' quorum. Next spring, March 18, 1833, the First Presidency was organized and sustained, consisting of three High Priests; Joseph Smith, President; Sidney Rigdon, First Counselor, and Frederick G. Williams, Second Counselor.

Some may ask, was not this a kind of evolution of Church government from that directed by elders to the present form, during which time the leaders gradually added offices in the Melchizedek Priesthood according to their own notions, and as an afterthought added patriarchs, apostles, and seventies? The answer is that this was not the case. Already in June, 1829, before the Church was organized, the Lord told Joseph Smith that Oliver Cowdery and David Whitmer should seek out the twelve, and their mission was defined. [Sec. 18:26:40.] In a revelation given on the same day the organization took place the Lord says: "Behold, there shall be a record kept among you, and in it thou shall be called a seer, a translator, a prophet, an apostle of Jesus Christ." [Sec. 21:1.] The preceding section (20) of the Book of Doctrine and Covenants, called a revelation on Church government, explains the duties of the different officers of the Church, and the rules laid down there are still followed and considered the law of the Church. This shows that the plan of the organization of the Church was definitely given to the Church at the beginning and that it did not have its origin and development in the ideas of men. We rejoice in knowing that it was God-given. (CR, April 1917, pp. 14-15.)

Orson F. Whitney: 1-4

What! — exclaims one. After these men had communed with heavenly beings and received from them commandments for their guidance; after receiving divine authority to preach the gospel, administer the ordinances, and establish once more on earth the long absent Church of Christ! After all this must they go before the people and ask their consent to organize them and preside over them as a religious body? Yes, that was precisely the situation. Notwithstanding all those glorious manifestations, they were not yet fully qualified to hold the high positions unto which they had been divinely called. One element was lacking—the consent of the people. Until that consent was given, there could be no church with these people as its members and those men as its presiding authorities. [Sec. 26:2.] The Great Ruler of all never did and never will force upon any of his people, in branch, ward, stake or Church capacity, a presiding officer whom they are not willing to accept and uphold.

Happily for all concerned, the brethren associated with Joseph and Oliver on that memorable sixth of April of the year 1830, did sanction their ordinations, did "decide by vote" to accept them as their "spiritual teachers."

But suppose it had been otherwise. Suppose the brethren in question had their hands against instead of for them. What would have been the result? Would such action have taken from Joseph and Oliver their Priesthood or their gifts and powers as seers, prophets and revelators of the Most High? No. Any more than it would have blotted out the fact that Joseph had seen God, and that he and Oliver had communed with angels sent from heaven to ordain them. Their brethren had not given them the Priesthood, had not made them prophets and seers, and they would remained such regardless of any adverse action on the part of their associates. The Gospel, the Priesthood, the keys to the Kingdom of Heaven are not within the gift of the membership of the Church. They are bestowed by the Head of the Church, Jesus Christ, in person or by proxy, and without his consent no power on earth or under the earth could take them away.

But if the vote had been unfavorable, this would have resulted: The brethren and sisters who were waiting to be admitted into the Church would have closed the door in their own faces, would have cut themselves off from a most precious privilege, would have deprived themselves of the inestimable benefits flowing from the exercise of the gifts and powers possessed by the men divinely commissioned to inaugurate this great Latter-day work; and they could have gone elsewhere, and under divine direction, have organized the Church of Christ among any people worthy to constitute its membership and willing that these men should be their leaders. But the vote was in their favor, thank the Lord! and we who are here today are among the beneficiaries of that act of faith and humility. (CR, October 1930, pp. 46-47.)

Joseph Smith: 5
This first elder . . . was entangled again in the vanities of the world

During the space of time which intervened between the time I had the vision and the year eighteen hundred and twenty-three—having been forbidden to join any of the religious sects of the day, and being of very tender years, and persecuted by those who ought to have been my friends, and to have treated me kindly, and if they supposed me to be deluded to have endeavored in a proper and affectionate manner to have reclaimed me,—I was left to all kinds of temptations; and mingling with all kinds of society, I frequently fell into many foolish errors, and displayed the weakness of youth and the foibles of human nature; which, I am sorry to say, led me into divers temptations, offensive in the sight of God. In making this confession, no one need suppose me guilty of any great or malignant sins. A disposition to commit such was never in my nature. But I was guilty of levity, and sometimes associated with jovial company, etc., not consistent with that character which ought to be maintained by one who was called of God as I had been. But this will not seem very strange to any one who recollects my youth, and is acquainted with my native cheery temperament. (HC 1:910, 1820-23.)

I was born (according to the record of the same kept by my parents) in the town of Sharon, Windsor county, Vermont, on the 23rd of December, 1805. At the age of ten my father's family removed to Palmyra, New York, where, in the vicinity of which, I lived, or, made it my place of residence, until I was twenty-one; the latter part in the town of Manchester.

During this time, as is common to most, or all youths, I fell into many vices and follies; but as my accusers are, and have been forward to accuse me of being guilty of gross and outrageous violations of the peace and good order of the community, I take the occasion to remark that, though as I have said above, "as is common to most, or all youths, I fell into many vices and follies," I have not, neither can it be sustained, in truth, been guilty of wronging or injuring any man or society of men; and those imperfections to which I allude, and for which I have often had occasion to lament, were a light, and too often, vain mind, exhibiting a foolish and trifling conversation.

This being all, and the worst, that my accusers can substantiate against my moral character, I wish to add that it is not without a deep feeling of regret that I am thus called upon in answer to my own conscience, to fulfil a duty I owe to myself, as well as to the cause of truth, in making this public confession of my former uncircumspect walk, and trifling conversation and more particularly, as I often acted in violation of those holy precepts which I knew came from God. But as the "Articles and Covenants," of this Church are plain upon this particular point, I do not deem it important to proceed further. I only add, that I do not, nor never have, pretended to be any other than a man "subject to passion," and liable, without the assisting grace of the Savior, to deviate from that perfect path in which all men are commanded to walk. (HC 1:10, 1823.)

Heber J. Grant: 6-12

Like Paul, Joseph Smith, during the three years intervening after his vision, steadfastly maintained that in vision he had seen the Father and the Son, and had heard the voice of the Lord.

On the evening of September 21, 1823, he had retired

as usual to his bedroom for the night, a night fraught with events of which he had not dreamed, events of supreme importance to him and to the people of the world. He says:

> While I was thus in the act of calling upon God, I discovered a light appearing in my room, which continued to increase until the room was lighter than at noonday, when immediately a personage appeared at my bedside, standing in the air, for his feet did not touch the floor.
>
> He had on a loose robe of most exquisite whiteness. It was a whiteness beyond anything earthly I had ever seen; nor do I believe that any earthly thing could be made to appear so exceedingly white and brilliant. His hands were naked, and his arms also, a little above the wrist; so, also, were his feet naked, as were his legs, a little above the ankles. His head and neck were also bare. I could discover that he had no other clothing on but this robe, as it was open, so that I could see into his bosom.
>
> Not only was his robe exceedingly white, but his whole person was glorious beyond description, and his countenance truly like lightning. The room was exceedingly light, but not so very bright as immediately around his person. When I first looked upon him I was afraid; but the fear soon left me.
>
> He called me by name, and said unto me that he was a messenger sent from the presence of God to me, and that his name was Moroni; that God had a work for me to do; and that my name should be had for good and evil among all nations, kindreds, and tongues, or that it should be both good and evil spoken of among all people. [Joseph Smith 2:30-33.]

This messenger revealed to Joseph Smith that there was a book deposited written upon gold plates, giving an account of the ancient inhabitants of America and the source from whence they came, and that the plates would later be delivered into his hands to be translated and published to the world.

On the twenty-third day of September, 1827, the plates containing the record of the Book of Mormon were delivered to Joseph Smith who, by the gift and power of God, translated the characters which were engraven upon them.

The Book of Mormon does not in any degree conflict with or take the place of the Holy Bible, but is the strongest corroborative evidence in existence of the divine origin of that sacred record. It has been before the world for more than a century, during which time no statement contained in it, whether it refers to the civil history or the religion of the people who kept the record, has been proved to be untrue. (CR, April 1930, pp. 9-10.)

Oliver Cowdery: 7-12

Friends and Brethren, My name is Cowdery, Oliver Cowdery. In the early history of this Church I stood identified with her, and one of her councils. . . .

I wrote, with my own pen, the entire Book of Mormon (save a few pages) as it fell from the lips of the Prophet Joseph Smith, as he translated it by the gift and power of God, by the means of the Urim and Thummim, or, as it is called by that book, "holy interpreters." I beheld with my eyes, and handled with my hands, the gold plates from which it was transcribed. I also saw with my eyes and handled with my hands the "holy interpreters." That book is true. Sidney Rigdon did not write it; Mr. Spaulding did not write it; I wrote it myself as it fell from the lips of the Prophet. It contains the Everlasting Gospel, and came forth to the children of men in fulfillment of the revelations of John, where he says he saw an angel come with the Everlasting Gospel to preach to every nation, kindred, tongue and people. [Rev. 14:6-7.] It contains principles of salvation; and if you, my hearers, will walk by its light and obey its precepts, you will be saved with an everlasting salvation in the kingdom of God on high. Brother [Orson] Hyde has just said that it is very important that we keep and walk in the true channel, in order to avoid the sand-bars. This is true. The channel is here. The Holy Priesthood is here. (MS, January 28, 1865, 27:57-58.)

Charles W. Penrose: 9
Which contains a record of . . . the fulness of the gospel

We are told that the Book of Mormon contains the fulness of the gospel, that those who like to get up a dispute, say that the Book of Mormon does not contain any reference to the work of salvation for the dead, and there are many other things pertaining to the gospel that are not developed in that book, and yet we are told that book contains "the fulness of the everlasting gospel." Well, what is the fulness of the gospel? You read carefully the revelation in regard to the three glories, section 76, in the Doctrine and Covenants, and you find there defined what the gospel is. [Sec. 76:40-43.] There God, the Eternal Father, and Jesus Christ, his Son, and the Holy Ghost, are held up as the three persons in the Trinity—the one God, the Father, the Word and the Holy Ghost, all three being united and being one God. When people believe in that doctrine and obey the ordinances which are spoken of in the same list of principles [Sec. 20:17-28], you get the fulness of the gospel for this reason: If you really believe so as to have faith in our Eternal Father and in his Son, Jesus Christ, the Redeemer, and will hear him, you will learn all about what is needed to be done for the salvation of the living and the redemption of the dead.

When people believe and repent and are baptized by Divine authority and the Holy Ghost is conferred upon them as a gift, they receive the everlasting gospel . . . and when the Holy Ghost as a gift is conferred upon people, young or old, as an "abiding witness," as a continuous gift, as a revealing spirit, they have the beginning, and I would not say the end, but they have the substance of the gospel of Jesus Christ. They have that which will bring salvation, for the gift of the Holy Ghost is such that it will highly enliven everyone who receives it. (CR, April 1922, pp. 27-28.)

Anthony W. Ivins: 11
Proving to the world that the holy scriptures are true

This book [Book of Mormon] is the strongest corroborative evidence to the divinity of the things contained in the Bible, that there is in the world. It is the strongest evidence of the divinity of the mission of the Redeemer of the world, that can be found, the Bible alone excepted. It contains the fulness of the everlasting gospel, in simplicity, easy to be understood, as it was taught to the people by the Redeemer who established his Church among the Nephites. [3 Nephi 11:26.] The code of morals which it teaches is beyond criticism, and if adhered to would redeem the world from the condition of moral degeneracy which now prevails.

It teaches ethics in civil government which, if adhered to, would solve the perplexing political questions which bewilder the world today, would remove the burdens of taxation from the backs of the struggling masses, and bring peace to the earth and fraternity among all mankind. It declares the redemption of the remnant of Judah, the gathering of the Ten Tribes, the restoration of scattered Israel, and the fulfilment of the words of the prophets, both ancient and modern. While it strongly denounces wickedness, it holds out great hope to the righteous, and forgiveness and redemption to the repentant sinner; it unfolds the hitherto unknown past, and outlines to us events of the great future upon the threshold of which we stand. It has been before the world for nearly one hundred years, during which period it has been subjected to the criticisms of the learned and to the ridicule of the ignorant. Not one line in it, not one doctrine which it teaches, not one truth which it sets forth, has been found to be out of harmony with the word of the Lord, as contained in the Bible, and as it has come to us through his inspired servants—a thing which can be said of no other book in the world. (CR, April 1921, pp. 20-21.)

Joseph F. Smith: 13-16

Then look at the testimony of his disciples; they say they heard with their ears, they witnessed what they have declared to the world, and their testimony stands unimpeached to this day, and, in addition to this, we have the testimony of Joseph the Prophet.... Joseph the Prophet comes to us in this dispensation and declares that the heavens were opened to him and to his associates, and he saw and heard, and he declares as the last witness, who has seen and heard and knows, that Jesus is the Christ and the Redeemer of the world, even he who was born of Mary, crucified and rose again from the dead, and visited the inhabitants of this continent, as well as the inhabitants of the old continent as we call it, who also bear witness of him. (CR, October 1913, p. 9.)

Orson Pratt: 13

Were there any others who saw these plates [of the Book of Mormon]? Yes. How many? Eight; all of whom are dead except one, John Whitmer, who is still living. They saw and handled the plates, and saw the engravings upon them, and they testify of the same to all people to whom the work should be sent. How many does this make? Three witnesses, eight witnesses and the translator, twelve who saw and bare record of the original. Now I ask everyone in this house, Saints and strangers, have you as many witnesses that have seen the original of any one book of the Bible, the Old and New Testament? Have you one witness even that has seen the original from which any one of those books was transcribed? No, not one. You have the transcription of scribes from generation to generation; you have the translation from these manuscripts handed down from generation to generation, and transcribed one copy after another, until they have passed through, perhaps, thousands of copies, before the art of printing was known. But you believe the Bible, do you not? Replies one—"oh yes, we believe that, but as to the Book of Mormon we doubt very much about that."

Well, now, let me ask, is there anything inconsistent in a people receiving the testimony of twelve witnesses who saw and handled the original of the Book of Mormon, when they, at the same time, believe in the Bible, the original of which was never seen or handled by any man of this generation? In other words, which of the two is most consistent to believe in? The Latter-day Saints believe in both, because we know the Bible is true, for the Book of Mormon testifies of it [1 Ne. 13:38-42], and we have obtained a testimony of the divinity of the Book of Mormon; and hence, as that book speaks of the Bible, we know that the Bible is true. When the people, mentioned in the Book of Mormon left Jerusalem, and came to the land of America, they brought the books of the Old Testament with them from the history of the creation to the prophecies and truthfulness of the Old Testament scriptures. [1 Nephi 3:11-19.] Hence we, as Latter-day

Saints, know one book to be true just as well as we do the other. (JD, July 18, 1875, 18:162-63.)

James E. Talmage: 13-16

It [Mormonism] has taught me that the God I worship is the personification of love, but not that maudlin love that ofttimes blinds our eyes to facts and leads us to inconsistent actions. Not one whit of the ancient gospel has been abated, but new meaning has been shown through the words of his prophets in these latter times, down to this very day. The ancient edict stands, as voiced by the Lord Christ to the eleven immediately before the departure of the Savior: "He that believeth and is baptized shall be saved; but he that believeth not shall be damned." (Mark 16:16.) That last word is an awful one. If we do not understand its true import, it is terrifying, and that very affirmation, declaration, law, has been restated in this day and age; but thanks to the Lord of Hosts, he has given us to understand what he means by damnation. It is no less real than it ever was, but men have not always understood it aright. What is it to be damned? Does it mean that all who come under that sentence shall be cast into hell, there to dwell forever and forever? The light of the century, given by the Lord, declares the falsity of that construction.

Salvation is graded ever upward until it culminates in the glorious conditions of exaltation. Though the term salvation is used in scripture in a general way, and we must learn to discriminate between salvation and exaltation as we read, so damnation is graded; else what did the Lord mean as recorded in the twelfth chaper of Mark, when he spoke of those who used their power and position to oppress and to work evil; when he said of such: "These shall receive greater damnation"? Well, if there be a greater damnation there are lesser degrees of damnation and the term is used in the same sense of deprivation and forfeiture. That man enters into a degree of damnation who has forfeited his opportunities and therefore has rendered himself incapable of the advancement that would otherwise be possible.

The Lord has told us of places prepared for those entitled to salvation. He has told us that those who will keep all the laws and commandments of God can come where he is and shall be heirs of celestial glory and power. And he has told us of lesser degrees unto which others who have failed to rise to the occasion of laying hold on the blessing of eternal life, in its fulness, shall come; and concerning the last of these kingdoms of glories, known to us as the Telestial, the Lord has said that it excels all that the human mind can conceive in glory, and yet the one in the Telestial Kingdom is condemned so far as his actions have rendered him incapable of attaining to the higher glories and blessings which mean power and advancement. [Sec. 76:50-112.] (CR, April 1930, pp. 95-96.)

John A. Widtsoe: 17

One dominating doctrine runs through the books of the Bible and the Book of Mormon: There is one God, the Father of mankind, who reveals as may be necessary the laws by obedience to which men may win happiness in life. Whether in direct statement, in figure of speech, or in historical narrative, this doctrine is the concern of the writers of the scriptures. Indeed, the Bible and the Book of Mormon contain the most complete exposition existing of God's law for human conduct and destiny. It is this message for the moral guidance of humanity, coming from the Lord, that makes the Bible the "Book of Books" and the Book of Mormon a witness for the Bible. (*The Articles of Faith in Everyday Life*, 1949, p. 59.)

J. Reuben Clark, Jr.: 18-27

Adam became mortal; spiritual death came to him; and mortal death came to him. This was the first great crisis in the history of mankind. Indeed, it may be said to have produced mankind.

In order for him to get back to the place whence he began, it was necessary that there should be an atonement for this disobedience.

Quite obviously, Adam could not retrace his steps; he could not un-eat. He was mortal. No matter how good any of his children might be, they, also mortal, had no more power than had he. So, to pay for the disobedience, it took a Being conceived by the Infinite, not subject to death as were Adam's posterity; someone to whom death was subject; someone born of woman but yet divine. He alone could make the sacrifice which would enable us to have our bodies and our spirits reunited in due time of the Lord, and then go back to the Father, thus reunited; and finally, body and spirit together, we might go on through all the eternities.

Jesus of Nazareth was the one who was chosen before the world was, the Only Begotten of the Father, to come to earth to perform this service, to conquer mortal death which would atone for the Fall, that the spirit of man could recover his body, so reuniting them.

(Note: Speaking to the multitude in Jerusalem, Jesus said: "Therefore doth my Father love me, because I lay down my life, that I might take it again.

("No man taketh it from me, but I lay it down of myself. I have power to take it again. This commandment have I received of my Father." [John 10:17-18.])

That is the reason why, however good any man, son of Adam, may have been, he could not do the things, make the atonement that would bring us back into the presence of our Heavenly Father. [Alma 34:10-15.]

As John was baptizing in the Jordan, he saw Jesus approaching and exclaimed: " . . . Behold the Lamb of God, which taketh away the sin of the world." (John 1:29.) The record does not say sins.

We frequently are told and understand that not alone did Christ atone for that "original sin," so-called, but that he atoned for our sins, generally. As I understand it, so far as the resurrection is concerned, the overcoming of mortal death, he did atone for our sins. That is to say, no matter what we do here on earth, even though we commit the unpardonable sin, yet the atonement of Christ will for that purpose and to that end atone for our sins, and so will bring about our resurrection. [Sec. 88:29-32; Alma 11:42-45.] But after the resurrection, then we have to be judged according to the deeds of the flesh, good or bad. On the judgment day we will receive our rewards or punishments; we must pay for our own sins. [Sec. 76:110-11.]

It is our mission, perhaps the most fundamental purpose of our work, to bear constant testimony of Jesus Christ. We must never permit to enter into our thoughts, and certainly not into our teachings, the idea that he was merely a great teacher, a great philosopher, the builder of a great system of ethics. It is our duty, day after day, year in and year out, always to declare that Jesus of Nazareth was the Christ who brought redemption to the world and to all the inhabitants thereof. (CR, October 1955, pp. 23-24.)

Joseph Fielding Smith: 27-28

It is perfectly true, as recorded in the Pearl of Great Price and in the Bible, that to us there is but one God. [Moses 1:6; Mark 12:32.] Correctly interpreted, God in this sense means Godhead, for it is composed of Father, Son, and Holy Spirit. This Godhead presides over us, and to us, the inhabitants of this world, they constitute the only God, or Godhead. There is none other besides them. [1 Cor. 8:5-6.] To them we are amenable and subject to their authority, and there is no other Godhead unto whom we are subject. However, as the Prophet has shown, there can be, and are, other Gods. [*Teachings of the Prophet Joseph Smith*, pp. 369-74. See also John 10:34-36; Ps. 82:6.] (*Answers to Gospel Questions*, 1958, 2:142.)

Charles W. Penrose: 28

The Holy Ghost is a personage of spirit, as we are told in the 130th section of the Doctrine and Covenants; the Father is a person with a body of flesh and bones, and the Son also, (he is now, undoubtedly), and the Holy Ghost is a personage of spirit. Now that Holy Ghost, a personage of spirit, is also called God. Take the 20th section of the Doctrine and Covenants. In the laying of the very foundation of the organization of the Church it is declared most distinctly that "The Father, Son and Holy Ghost, are one God." Just as in the presidency of a stake or of a quorum or of the Church there are three distinct persons, the Father and the Son and the Holy Ghost, as one Deity. (CR, April 1916, pp. 20-21.)

Joseph Fielding Smith: 29-34

We read here, in this admonition and commandment, that he [man] is to endure to the end. It is essential that we endure to the end. In the revelation that was given to the Church, this same revelation at the time the Church was organized, the Lord said this: [Sec. 20:29, quoted.]

Now I believe the Lord meant what he said. . . .

Baptism is not merely a door into the kingdom, which entitles us to enter, bringing with us a trail of sins unrepented of. It is not that at all. We must not enter that door until our hearts are humble, our spirits contrite, and we give the assurance that we will serve the Lord in faithfulness and righteousness to the end. [Sec. 20:30, quoted.]

That is, if we come into this Church with a broken heart and a contrite spirit, with a determination to forsake all our sins and live faithfully to the end, then we are justified, and the sanctification of the blood of Jesus Christ is efficacious, and we receive the blessings. [Sec. 20:31, quoted.]

Again here we are involved: it is our duty, as members of the Church to serve the Lord our God with all our mights, with all our minds, with all our strength, and as it is stated in another revelation, with all our hearts. [Sec. 59:5.] That is our duty — not to serve him half-heartedly, not to accept a portion of the commandments only, not to receive only those things which appeal to us, and refuse to accept those principles which do not apeal to us. We should be converted in full to the Gospel of Jesus Christ. [Sec. 20:32-33, quoted.]

Not only the Church collectively, but you and me; let us take heed. Never in the history of the world, that is, in the history of the Church, have there been so many temptations, so many pitfalls, so many dangers, to lure away the members of the Church from the path of duty and from righteousness, as we find today. Every day of our lives we come in contact with these temptations, these dangers. We should continue in the spirit of prayer and faith, remembering that there is this possibility that we may turn from the grace of the living

God, and fall unless we continue in that humility, in the exercise of faith and obedience to every principle of truth. (CR, October 1941, pp. 93-94.)

Brigham Young: 31
Sanctification through the grace of our Lord

I will put my own definition to the term sanctification, and say it consists in overcoming every sin and bringing all into subjection to the law of Christ. God has placed in us a pure spirit; when this reigns predominant, without let or hindrance, and triumphs over the flesh and rules and governs and controls as the Lord controls the heavens and the earth, this I call the blessing of sanctification. Will sin be perfectly destroyed? No, it will not, for it is not so designed in the economy of heaven.

Do not suppose that we shall ever in the flesh be free from temptations to sin. Some suppose that they can in the flesh be sanctifed body and spirit and become so pure that they will never again feel the effects of the power of the adversary of truth. Were it possible for a person to attain to this degree of perfection in the flesh, he could not die, neither remain in a world where sin predominates. Sin has entered into the world, and death by sin. [Rom. 5:12.] I think we shall more or less feel the effects of sin so long as we live, and finally have to pass the ordeals of death. . . .We should so live as to make the world and all its natural blessings subservient to our reasonable wants and holy desires. (JD, May 24,1863, 10:173.)

Francis M. Lyman: 32
But there is a possibility that man may fall

I am brought to believe that it is possible for men to repent and then to unrepent, and to fail to keep their repentance good; and I believe that the victory is in the retaining our repentance and making it good, so that the spirit of the Lord may dwell richly with us. . . . I believe that my heart should be as tender today as it ever was. I cannot afford to be haughty and high-minded. [Sec.38:39.] (CR, October 1897, p. 16.)

Francis M. Lyman: 37

I must be contrite in spirit and my heart broken and tender, for the Lord has prescribed that all those who humble themselves before God and desire to be baptized should come forth with broken hearts and contrite spirits, and witness before the Church that they have truly repented of their sins and are willing to take upon them the name of Jesus Christ, having a determination to serve him to the end. He says: "All who truly manifest by their works that they have received of the Spirit of Christ unto the remission of their sins shall be received by baptism into this church." I take it that this requirement is necessary to entitle them to receive the Holy Ghost. I believe that it is necessary also that that repentance and that broken heart and that contrite spirit and those good works before the Church should be continued, and manifested to the end of life, if we would have the blessing of eternal life. [Sec. 18:22; 50:5.] (CR, October 1897, p. 16.)

Joseph Fielding Smith: 37
Broken hearts

Mark you, the Lord says before a man comes into the Church he must have a desire, he must come with a broken heart and contrite spirit.

What is a broken heart? One that is humble, one that is touched by the Spirit of the Lord, and which is willing to abide in all the covenants and the obligations which the Gospel entails. . . .

Every baptized person who has fully repented, who comes into the Church with a broken heart and a contrite spirit, has made a covenant to continue with that broken heart, with that contrite spirit, which means a repentant spirit. He makes a covenant that he will do that. (CR, October 1941, p. 93.)

Rudger Clawson: 38-60

The duty of the Elder is to be a standing minister in Zion, to administer in spiritual things, to administer the

sacrament, to baptize, to lay on hands for the reception of
the Holy Ghost, to take the lead of all meetings when no
higher authority is present, and to conduct them under the
influence and power of the Holy Ghost. No Elder or High
Priest is to conduct meetings in this Church by any other
spirit than the Spirit of God. Heaven-delegated authority to
man! The duty of the Bishop is to preside over the Lesser
Priesthood and the quorums thereof. The duty of the Priest is
to preach, teach and expound the scriptures, to baptize, to
administer the sacrament, to visit the homes of the people,
to pray with them vocally, and to teach them all family
duties. The duty of the Teacher is to watch over the Church,
to be with the Church constantly, and strengthen it, to see
that iniquity doth not abound, to see that there is no evil-
speaking, or backbiting, and to preach, teach, exhort, and
expound; and he is to be assisted in his duties by the Deacon;
but the Teacher and the Deacon have no authority to baptize, or administer the sacrament. They do have the authority, however, to preach the Gospel, to show forth a good
example, to warn the people and invite all to come unto
Christ. There is not confusion in all this that I have told you.
Every duty is well expressed and clearly defined in the revelations. (CR, April 1902, p. 29.)

Ezra Taft Benson: 39

Our boys twelve years of age, if worthy, receive the
Holy Priesthood by the laying on of hands, and our young
men are hardly more than boys when at nineteen they
receive the Holy Melchizedek Priesthood, the authority to
officiate in the most sacred ordinances known to man. This
Priesthood will, if they are worthy, entitle them eventually
to a place in the Celestial kingdom of God. I have been
amazed at the great number of men and boys in the Church
who hold this great authority and who have in their hands
this great blessing, if they will only take advantage of it. . . .
(CR, October 1948, p. 99.)

Joseph Smith: 41

Baptism is a sign to God, to angels, and to heaven that

we do the will of God, and there is no other way beneath the heavens whereby God hath ordained for man to come to him to be saved, and enter into the Kingdom of God, except faith in Jesus Christ, repentance, and baptism for the remission of sins, and any other course is in vain; then you have the promise of the gift of the Holy Ghost. (HC 4:444, March 20, 1842.)

Joseph Smith: 42

"Do you believe in the baptism of infants?" asks the Presbyterian. No. "Why?" Because it is nowhere written in the Bible. Circumcision is not baptism, neither was baptism instituted in the place of circumcision. Baptism is for remission of sins. Children have no sins. Jesus blessed them and said, "Do what you have seen me do." [John 14:12.] Children are all made alive in Christ and those of riper years through faith and repentance. [Sec. 68:25-27; 33:11-13.] (HC 5:499, July 9, 1843.)

Heber J. Grant: 47

One of the requirements made of the Latter-day Saints is that they shall be faithful in attending to their prayers, both their secret and family prayers. [Sec. 46:7; 68:33.] The object that our Heavenly Father has in requiring this is that we may be in communication with him, and that we may have a channel open between us and the heavens whereby we can bring down upon ourselves blessings from above. No individual who is humble and prayerful before God and supplicates him every day for the light and inspiration of his Holy Spirit will ever become lifted up in the pride of his heart, or feel that the intelligence and the wisdom that he possesses are all-sufficient for him. (CR, April 1944, p. 11.)

Stephen L Richards: 45-60

Our young men missionaries are ministers of religion. I grant you that they do not always look as other ministers look. They may be disappointing to some in formality and grace of expression. Many of them may not have attained the scholastic standing reached by most of the profession. What is the missionary's training for the ministry?

First, he is usually reared in a home presided over by a man of the Priesthood, who, in certain aspects at least, may be looked on as a man of the ministry. The functions of the ministry are carried forward in large measure in the future missionary's home. Prayer, blessings, scriptural and religious learning are features of his early environment. He is accorded the opportunity of participation. He prays, he sings, he reads, he studies, and in adolescent years, joins in sacred religious ordinances.

Second, in the religious educational program of the Church, he become identified with the organizations of the Church. His mother may bring him to Sunday School as a baby; he toddles into the infant classes; and from then on he is taught, and he learns the literature of the Church and the way of the Lord.

Third, he is integrated into a spiritual society. His recreation, which not infrequently brings the contacts which enable him to choose his life's partner, is supervised and directed under religious auspices, whose constant endeavor is to clarify and define the ultimate goals of life. In the atmosphere of such spirituality, his spirit nature is nurtured and developed. His liberal participation in all such institutions and exercises is calculated for the development of that spirituality. What, may I ask, is more essential to a ministerial calling?

Fourth, there then comes to the adolescent youth training and experience without counterpart in any other institutions of which I am aware. He enters the quorums of the Priesthood. At the age of twelve he is first ordained and inducted into a group of approximately his own age. He is taught the history of the Priesthood, and he is made to understand that the power conferred upon him even though a mere youth, derives from the authentic power given by the Lord Jesus Christ through his servants to those selected to receive the Priesthood in this dispensation of time, and from whom it has come in direct and authentic succession to this boy. He has respect for this calling, and he seeks to discharge his duties as a youthful holder of the Priesthood of the Lord. Is that training for a minister in the Gospel of Christ? Is there anything taught in the seminaries of ecclesiastical learning more important as a groundwork for ministerial service than actual participation in the functions and offices of the Priesthood?

Well, this young man continues through the various gradations of the Priesthood, always being given and assuming larger participation in the functions of the Church and the blessing of the people.

Fifth, much of the education of the young man, not only in the Sunday School, the other auxiliary organizations, and the Priesthood quorum, but also in his academic training, is directed toward acquisition of theological learning and capacity to live and expound the principles of the Gospel. Church schools, institutes, and seminaries are available to him in this preparation.

If he avails himself of all these privileges, I say he is prepared for missionary service and for ordination and setting apart to go forth as an ambassador and minister of the Lord Jesus Christ in teaching this Gospel to the people and performing ministerial services among them. (CR, October 1955, pp. 97-98.)

Joseph Smith: 46-47

From a retrospect of the requirements of the servants of God to preach the Gospel, if a Priest understands his duty, his calling, and ministry, and preaches by the Holy Ghost, his enjoyment is as great as if he were one of the Presidency; and his services are necessary in the body, as are also those of Teachers and Deacons. (HC 2:478, April 6, 1837.)

Hyrum M. Smith: 53-55

Now, there is a certain preparation that should be had on the part of a teacher prior to his entering into the homes of the saints to instruct them in their family and religious duties. In the first place, he should be duly ordained to the Holy Priesthood, and called and set apart to labor among the people. Now, authority is not all that is necessary in order to be a successful teacher. He must have knowledge also, for except he have knowledge of the things of God, how can he impart instruction unto the Latter-day Saints? Therefore, the brother holding the Priesthood and designated as a teacher among the people, should have a knowledge of the truth. He should be well familiar with the doctrines of life and salvation. He should be a student of the Scripture. He should understand the word of the Lord, and be familiar with his commandments. And when he has this knowledge, then he should have a desire in his heart to impart of this knowledge unto the people, and to see that the people are instructed in the Gospel, and are obedient thereto. Before a teacher attempts to go into the homes of the people on a special visit, he should make his going a matter of prayer before the Lord.

Now let the teachers go forth and do their duty, and accomplish the strengthening of the Church, and the increasing of faith among the people and stir up the saints to greater diligence in the performing of the duties and obligations of their membership in the Church. (CR, October 1911, pp. 40-41.)

Joseph Fielding Smith: 60

At this same time [1877] a correspondent of the *Juvenile Instructor* asked why boys were ordained to the Priesthood, when in the days of Paul, only married men were chosen. President George Q. Cannon answered:

"With our Elders even in these days it is a very common thing to ordain, while in the world, very young men to any office. Mature men are frequently ordained as Deacons and to act as such. But the circumstances which surround us here in Zion are entirely different from those which surrounded the saints in the days of Paul, and of which he wrote. [1 Tim. 3:12.] There is no impropriety whatever in young men, even early, as at the age of twelve or fourteen years, acting as Deacons. They receive a training that is very valuable to them, and we know of many who have been and are greatly benefited to act in this position, meeting with the Deacons' quorums and receiving such instructions as are proper to be imparted to them in this capacity. . . ."

Other meetings were held in other wards throughout the Church in the summer of 1877, where brethren of the Council of the Twelve and others admonished the boys holding the Priesthood to be faithful in the discharge of their duties. These minutes indicate that there had been a universal movement throughout the Church to have the boys twelve years of age and upward organized in quorums of deacons, teachers and priests. Previous to this time the ordination of boys of twelve was not the universal practice, although such had been the practice in certain places. (*IE*, January 1957, 60:383.)

Alonzo A. Hinckley: 60

I have cherished the belief that it was not just a "happened so" that the Lord said that a clean, wholesome boy of twelve years of age should be permitted to receive the priesthood. I believe that it is natural to him at that period of his life to feel that he would like to be up and about his Father's business. [Luke 2:42, 49.]

I think, bishops — and I speak with some degree of understanding, because I have labored in such council — I think, presidents of stakes, I think, fathers, and I think, mothers, there is no higher ideal that could be pointed to a son than: "Watch the day, make your preparation, be ready to speak, have a spirit like a Samuel, and when the Lord calls, say: 'Lord, speak; thy servant heareth'." [See 1 Sam. 3:9.]

I know that the Lord wants us to have our boys, at twelve, in groups of twelve, presided over by sweet, clean, wholesome boys of their age. I know that he wants to have our boys, in groups of twenty-four, under presidencies of their own group, watching over the Church, to see that there is no iniquity, evil-speaking, or backbiting in the Church.

It seems so fitting to me to think that the Lord has made provision that the young men eighteen and nineteen years of age shall sit at the feet of the bishop and be instructed, with him as president; that he shall be taught, and that he shall go into the house of the saints; that he shall preach, teach, exhort, and expound the scripture; that ninety-six men, older, maturer, and receiving the Holy Melchizedek Priesthood, shall stand next to the presidency of the stake and be a standing ministry of the stake; . . .So beautiful, so perfect, so complete, is the Lord's way! [Sec. 107:85-89.] (CR, April 1935, pp. 74-75.)

Erastus Snow: 61-63

The Lord in his revelation to the Prophet Joseph, forty-seven years ago, required the Elders to meet together in conference once in three months or from time to time as appointed, for the purpose of transacting necessary business connected with the work, and for giving and receiving instructions in relation to the duties of the Priesthood. This commandment has been published in the book of Doctrine and Covenants, and is a standing revelation which has not been generally observed. We have had General Conferences of all the people — Priesthood and laymen — twice a year since our settlement in these valleys, which only a small portion of the people and a few of the General Authorities of the Church have been able to attend. We have had occasional conferences in some places in the Territory, and in various places abroad. It is time now that Stakes of Zion are organized, to hold our conferences with more regularity and in their order, for the saints to come together to be instructed, that reports may be heard from the various Wards, and the Elders enter into counsel and learn their duties. (JD, October 13, 1877, 19:130.)

John Taylor: 62

We have met together on the present occasion to attend our annual conference. The object of our meeting is not altogether for religious purposes, but to consult upon all matters for the interest of the Church and Kingdom of God upon the earth. . . . It is also usual to discuss the principles and doctrines that we believe in, and to attend to any business that may have to be presented from the different parts of this Territory, and from all parts of the earth; and we try to build up the people in their most holy faith. We meet also to consult upon the best course for us to pursue with regard to temporal things as well as spiritual things. For as we possess bodies as well as spirits, and have to live by eating, drinking, and wearing, it becomes necessary that temporal matters should be considered and discussed in our conferences, and that we should deliberate upon all things that are calculated to benefit, bless, and exalt the saints of God, whether they refer to our spiritual affairs or to our avocations and duties in life, as husbands and wives, as parents and children, as masters and servants; whether they refer to the policy we should pursue in our commercial relations, to protecting ourselves against the incursions of savages, or to any other matter affecting us as human beings composing part of the body politic of this nation or as citizens of the world. The idea of strictly religious feelings with us, and nothing else, is out of the question; yet we do everything in the fear of God. Our religion is more comprehensive than that of the world; it does not prompt its votaries with the desire to "sit and sing themselves away to everlasting bliss," but it embraces all the interests of humanity in every conceivable phase, and every truth in the world comes within its scope. [Sec. 29:34-35.] (JD, April 6, 1867, 11:353-54.)

Joseph F. Smith: 65-67

No man can preside in this Church in any capacity without the consent of the people. [Sec. 26:2.] The Lord has placed upon us the responsibility of sustaining by vote those who are called to various positions of responsibility. No man, should the people decide to the contrary, could preside over any body of Latter-day Saints, as they are assembled in conference or other capacity, by the uplifted hand, to sustain or to reject; and I take it that no man has the right to raise his hand in opposition, or with contrary vote, unless he has a reason for doing so that would be valid if presented before those who stand at the head. In other words, I have no right to raise my hand in opposition to a man who is appointed to any position in this Church simply because I may not like him, or because of some personal disagreement or feeling I may have, but only on the grounds that he is guilty of wrongdoing, of transgression of the laws of the Church which would disqualify him for the position which he is called to hold. This is my understanding of it. (CR, June 1919, p. 92.)

John Taylor: 65

What is meant by sustaining a person? Do we understand it? It is a very simple thing to me; I do not know how it is with you. For instance, if a man be a teacher, and I vote that I will sustain him in his position, when he visits me in an official capacity I will welcome him and treat him with consideration, kindness and respect, and if I need counsel I will ask it at his hand, and I will do everything I can to sustain him. That would be proper and a principle of righteousness, and I would not say anything derogatory to his character. If that is not correct I have it yet to learn. And then, if anybody in my presence were to whisper something about him disparaging to his reputation, I would say, "Look here! Are you a saint?" Yes. Did you hold up your hand to sustain him? Yes. Then why do you not do it? Now, I would call an action of that kind sustaining him. If any man make an attack upon his reputation — for all men's reputations are of importance to them — I would defend him in some such way. When we vote for men in the solemn way in which we do, shall we abide by our covenants? or shall we violate them? If we violate them we become covenant-breakers. We break our faith before God and our brethren, in regard to the acts of men whom we have covenanted to sustain. But supposing he should do something wrong, supposing he should be found lying or cheating, or defrauding somebody; or stealing or anything else, or even become impure in his habits, would you still sustain him? It would be my duty then to talk with him as I would with anybody else, and tell him that I had understood that things were thus and so, and that under these circumstances I could not sustain him; and if I found that I had been misinformed I would withdraw my charge; but if not, it would then be my duty to see that justice was administered to him, that he was brought before the proper tribunal to answer for the things he had done; and in the absence of that I would have no business to talk about him. (JD, March 1, 1880, 21:207-8.)

John Taylor: 66
Traveling bishops

We quote from some of the first revelations given to the Prophet Joseph Smith upon this subject. [Sec. 20:67, 77, quoted]. . . . It may be observed that traveling bishops are here referred to. These were given for the regulation of the newly organized branches or churches. (*Items on Priesthood*, 1899, p. 15.)

Marion G. Romney: 67

I believe that when the Presidency of this Church nominates a person for an office, it is not a personal nomination. I have that confidence in the Presidency and that testimony of the divinity of this Church. I believe that the Lord Jesus Christ reveals to them through the Spirit of the Holy Ghost the men they should name to office, and I believe that same Spirit will inspire and direct the presidents of stakes and the bishops of wards and the heads of other organizations in this Church, if they will live for such inspiration, so that when they name people for office they will name them under the inspiration of the Holy Ghost. (CR, October 1947, pp. 39-40.)

Joseph Fielding Smith: 68
The duty of the members after they are received by baptism

Now, when people come into this Church they should, by all means, subscribe to the regulations which the Lord himself has laid down by commandment. But does that mean that after we are in the Church, after we have confessed our sins and have forsaken them, that we can return to them after membership has been secured? That would not be consistent. Woe unto all those who are disobedient after they have made the preparation which is expressed in this commandment [2 Nephi 9:27] which I have read to you — woe unto them. (CR, October 1941, p. 93.)

David O. McKay: 68
Partaking of the sacrament

There are three things fundamentally important associated with the administration of the sacrament. The first is self-discernment. It is introspection. "This do in remembrance of me," but we should partake worthily, each one examining himself with respect to his worthiness.

Secondly, there is a covenant made; a covenant even more than a promise. . . . A covenant, a promise, should be as sacred as life. That principle is involved every Sunday when we partake of the sacrament.

Thirdly, there is another blessing, and that is a sense of close relationship with the Lord. There is an opportunity to commune with oneself and to commune with the Lord. . . . We are not prepared to meet him if we bring into that room our thoughts regarding our business affairs, and especially if we bring into the house of worship feelings of hatred toward our neighbor, or enmity and jealousy towards the Authorities of the Church. Most certainly no individual can hope to come into communion with the Father if that individual entertains any such feelings. (CR, April 1946, p. 112.)

John Taylor in behalf of the Council of the Twelve: 70

We have nothing to say against a father blessing his children, the genius of the Priesthood being primarily patriarchal, with God himself, the great Father of us all, at the head. Indeed, we claim that every man holding the Melchizedek Priesthood is a patriarch in his own home, with the right to bless all his children and grandchildren, even all the fruits of his loins, nor do we object to the father taking his babe on the eighth day and giving it a father's blessing. But we do not think that this privilege, whether exercised or unimproved, should interfere with our obedience to that law of the Lord wherein it is stated [New edition Doctrine and Covenants, sec. 20, verse 70, page 117, quoted.] Outside of the all-important fact that this is a direct command of Jehovah, and as such should be studiously complied with without hesitancy or objection, we think quite a number of excellent reasons can be adduced to prove that this command is attended with beneficial results to babe and to parents, who, by bringing their child before the Church, manifest their faith in the sight of their brethren and sisters, in God's word and to his promises, as well as their thankfulness to him for increasing their posterity and for the safe delivery of his handmaiden. The child is also benefited by the united faith and responsive prayers of the assembled saints, which faith seals the "more sure word of prophecy" pronounced upon the head of the child, as it also gives more abundant power to the officiating High Priest or Elder to manifest the good pleasure of the Lord with regard to it. And again, the blessing is thus given in the presence of the Church recorder, and there is much less likelihood of the record being omitted or errors entering therein than there would be should the rite be attended to at home. In this, as in all other things, the path of revelation is the path of safety. (MS, April 15, 1878, 40:235-36.)

Joseph Smith: 71

The doctrine of baptizing children, or sprinkling them, or they must welter in hell, is a doctrine not true, not supported in Holy Writ, and is not consistent with the character of God. All children are redeemed by the blood of Jesus Christ, and the moment that children leave this world, they are taken to the bosom of Abraham. [Sec. 29:46-47; 74:6.] The only difference between the old and young dying is, one lives longer in heaven and eternal light and glory than the other, and is freed a little sooner from this miserable, wicked world. Notwithstanding all this glory, we for a moment lose sight of it, and mourn the loss, but we do not mourn as those without hope. (HC 4:554, March 20, 1842.)

Sylvester Q. Cannon: 71

The correct training of children is of fundamental importance to the child and to the happiness and peace of the parents. From its infancy up every child is entitled to the love and spiritual care which it deserves and which will establish it in faith and confidence in the Lord and in his purposes. As every boy and girl approaches eight years of age, they should be taught clearly and lovingly the atonement of the Savior for us all, and the first principles of the Gospel. This spiritual development should be carefully and wisely continued. [Sec. 68:25-29.] Every young person should be encouraged to take part in the various Church activities. They should learn the value of prayer and of faith and the blessings which follow. It is a splendid practice for families to discuss Gospel principles and the application of the same in the lives of family members. They should be encouraged to read the standard Church works and to discuss incidents in ancient scripture and in Church history. They should learn the importance of gaining a spiritual testimony of the divinity of the Gospel restoration, and realize that such testimonies come through living the Gospel principles and observing the commandments of the Lord. (CR, April 1939, p. 85.)

Orson F. Whitney: 74
Then shall he immerse him or her in the water

That immersion was the form of ordinance introduced by John the Baptist, submitted to by the Savior, and perpetuated by his Apostles, is a plain and reasonable inference from the teachings of the New Testament. Jesus, when about to be baptized, must have gone down into the water; for after baptism, he "went up straightway out of the water." (Matt. 3:16.) When Philip baptized the Eunuch, "they went down both into the water." (Acts 8:38.) John baptized in Aenon, near to Salim, because there was much water there" (John 3:23) — another proof presumptive of immersion, the only mode requiring "much water" for its performance.

If this had not been the proper form, Paul would not have compared baptism to burial and resurrection (Rom. 6:3-5; Col. 2:12) nor would he have recognized as baptism the passage of the Israelites through the Red Sea. (1 Cor. 10:1, 2.) Note also his words to the Corinthians relative to vicarious baptism and in support of resurrection, a doctrine that some of them denied: "Else what shall they do which are baptized for the dead, if the dead rise not at all? Why are they then baptized for the dead?" (*Ibid.*, 15:29.) In other words, why use the symbol of the resurrection if there be no resurrection — if the symbol does not symbolize? (*Saturday Night Thoughts*, 1921, 251-53.)

David O. McKay: 75-79

"It is expedient that the Church meet together often." We meet in the house of God not as mere acquaintances suspicious of one another, but as brethren in the brotherhood of Christ. We meet in the presence of him who has said, "Love one another. . . ."

Do we always stop to think, on that sacred Sabbath day when we meet together to partake of the sacrament, that we witness, promise, obligate ourselves, in the presence of God, that we will do certain things? Note them. I have time merely to mention them.

The first: That we are willing to take upon ourselves the name of the Son. In so doing we choose him as our leader and our ideal; and he is the one perfect character in all the world. It is a glorious thing to be a member of the Church of Christ and to be called a Christian in the true sense of the term; and we promise that we should like to be that, that we are willing to do it.

Secondly, that we will always remember him. Not just on Sunday, but on Monday, in our daily acts, in our self-control. [D&C 59:10-11.] When our brother hurts us are we going to try to master our feelings and not retaliate in the same spirit of anger? When a brother treats us with contempt, are we going to try to return kindness? That's the spirit of the Christ and that's what we are promised, — that we will do our best to achieve these high standards of Christianity, true Christian principles.

The third: We promise to "keep the commandments which he has given." Tithing, fast offerings, the Word of Wisdom, kindness, forgiveness, love. The obligation of a member of the Church of Christ is great, but it is as glorious as it is great, because obedience to these principles gives life eternal life. On the other hand, the man who seeks to live by violating the principles is deceived by the adversary and goes the way to death. (CR, October 1929, pp. 10-11, 14.)

Melvin J. Ballard: 75

I realize that each time we partake of these emblems we manifest before the Father that we do remember his Son, and by the act of partaking of the bread and the cup, we make a solemn covenant that we do take upon us the name of our Redeemer, and that we do, further, make a pledge and an agreement by that act that we keep his commandments. . . .

It is just as necessary for our spiritual body that we should partake of this sacrament, and by it obtain spiritual food for our souls. If we were given our physical food only on stated occasions and at specified places we would all be there. . . .

How can we have spiritual hunger? Who is there among us that does not wound his spirit by word, thought, or deed, from Sabbath to Sabbath? We do things for which we are sorry, and desire to be forgiven, or we have erred against someone and given injury. If there is a feeling in our hearts that we are sorry for what we have done; if there is a feeling in our souls that we would like to be forgiven, then the method to obtain forgiveness is not through rebaptism . . . but it is to repent of our sins, to go to those against whom we have sinned or transgressed and obtain their forgiveness, and then repair to the sacrament table, where, if we have sincerely repented and put ourselves in proper condition, we shall be forgiven, and spiritual healing will come to our souls. [Sec. 46:4.] . . .

There is a feature of this pledge to which I should like to call your attention. We not only desire our boys and girls, our brothers and sisters, to come to the sacrament table and eat of these emblems, but we want them to eat worthily, for you have already heard quoted the scripture [3 Nephi 18:28-29] that, if we eat and drink unworthily, we eat and drink damnation to our own souls. Here is what the Lord said: [Sec. 20:68-69, quoted.] . . .

There may be some instances where the Elders of the Church would say, properly, to one who, in transgression, stretches forth his hands to partake of the emblems: You should not do this until you have made restitution; but ordinarily we will be our own judges. If we are properly instructed, we know that it is not our privilege to partake of the emblems of the flesh and blood of the Lord in sin, in transgression, or having injured and holding feelings against our brethren and sisters. No man goes away from this Church and becomes an apostate in a week, nor in a month. It is a slow process. The one thing that would make for the safety of every man and woman would be to appear at the sacrament table every Sabbath day. We would not get very far away in one week, not so far away that, by the process of self-investigation, we could not rectify the wrongs we may have done. If we should refrain from partaking of the sacrament, condemned by ourselves as unworthy to receive these emblems, we could not endure that long, and we would soon, I am sure, have the spirit of repentance. The road to the sacrament table is the path of safety for Latter-day Saints. (*IE*, October 1919, pp. 1025-28.)

Joseph Fielding Smith: 75

All little children virtually belong to the Church until they are eight years of age. Should they die before that age, they would enter the celestial kingdom. [Sec. 29:46-47; 74:6.] The Savior said: "Of such is the kingdom of heaven." (Matt. 19:14.) Then why should they be deprived of the sacrament?

Non-members cannot comply with the covenants embodied in the blessings of the sacrament and, therefore, should not partake of it. They are old enough to reason and should understand that the sacrament, so far as adults are concerned, is for those who have repented of their sins in the waters of baptism.

It would be proper in a meeting to say, "The sacrament will now be administered to the members of the Church," in cases where there are non-members present; otherwise nothing need be said of this nature. *If non-members are present and partake of the sacrament, we would not do anything to prevent it, for evidently they would take it in good faith, notwithstanding the nature of the covenant.*

The Lord has said that we should not permit anyone to partake of the sacrament unworthily. This means, as I understand it, anyone in the Church who has been in transgression of some kind and who has not repented. It would also apply to the apostate. (*Doctrines of Salvation*, 1944, 2:350.)

Anthon H. Lund: 77-79

There has been considerable difference of opinion in regard to his meaning of the phrase, "This is my body," when he said to his disciples, "Take, eat, this is my body," and also when he gave to them the cup and said, "Drink ye all of it, for this is my blood of the new testament, which is shed for many for the remission of sins." [Matt. 26:26-29.] A great number of Christian sects and denominations claim that this did not signify that the bread and wine were emblems, but that we partake really of his flesh and blood, in the administration of the sacrament. Transubstantiation means that the bread changes by the blessing into his flesh, and the wine into his blood. This is not our opinion. We believe that the bread and wine are simply emblems of his body and blood. If we could imagine ourselves in that sacred room where he and his disciples were having the last evening together, where they partook of the paschal meal, and where he instituted this holy ordinance, we should see him standing in the full vigor of health and the blood circulating in his veins. It was not his blood in the cup, for he calls it at the very same time, "this fruit of the vine." It was wine he gave unto them, but it represented his blood that was to be shed for the remission of sins. . . .

We do not partake of the sacrament for the remission of sins, as they do in many of the different churches. We believe that baptism was instituted for the remission of sins, and that, having received the Spirit of God, if we humbly repent of what wrongs we have done, and earnestly seek the Lord's forgiveness, that forgiveness may come to us. (*CR*, October 1916, pp. 12-14.)

Joseph Fielding Smith: 80-84

The matter of record keeping is one of the most important duties devolving on the Church. In the early days of the Church, because of lack of experience, this duty was neglected, therefore many important historical events were not recorded. Even today it is difficult to impress upon clerks in stakes, wards and missions the importance of proper record keeping. There has, however, been a vast improvement in recent years. The Church today endeavors to keep a record of each individual member and files that record in the archives where it may be preserved. On the day of the organization of the Church the Lord impressed the small body of members with the importance of record keeping, and this duty the Church has endeavored to perform truthfully ever since. In 1835 the Prophet Joseph Smith deplored the lack of records because of inexperience and in some instances neglect, on the part of those appointed to keep the record. He said this in a charge to the Twelve, February 27, 1835, shortly after they were chosen. [HC 2:198-199.] . . .

If a man values his membership in the Church he will guard with the most jealous care his standing in the ward or branch to which he belongs. One of the most deporable things with which we have to contend is the fact that members of the Church will move from one ward or branch to another, and fail to keep in touch with the local organization of the Church. Sometimes this is done because such members desire to hide and avoid being handled for their standing. Others do this evil thing because they are afraid they will be called upon to attend to Church duties; others out of pure neglect. Membership in the Church is our very valued possession and treasure. Why? Because without it we are deprived, not only of the fellowship of the Church but of all its blessings, and a continued course of aloofness will in time place us outside the pale of the Church entirely. (CHMR, 1947, 1:96-97, 99.)

Joseph F. Smith: 80-83

Drunkards, whoremongers, liars, thieves, those that betray the confidence of their fellowmen, those who are unworthy of credence, unworthy of love and confidence — all such, when their character becomes known, are disfellowshipped from the Church, and are not permitted to have a standing in it, if we know it. It is true that there are none of us but have our imperfections and shortcomings. Perfection dwells not with mortal man. We all have our weaknesses. But when a man abandons the truth, virtue, his love for the Gospel and for the people of God, and becomes an open, avowed enemy, it becomes the duty of the Church, and the Church would be recreant to its duty if it did not sever him from communion, cut him off, and let him go where he pleases. We would do wrong if we hung on to and tried to nurture such evil creatures in our midst, no matter what the relationship may be that exists between us and them. Therefore, I say again, the Church of Jesus Christ stands for virtue, honor, truth, purity of life, and good will to all mankind. It stands for God the Eternal Father, and for Jesus Christ, whom the Father sent into the world, and whom to know is life eternal. This is what the Church stands for, and it cannot tolerate abomination, crime and wickedness on the part of those who may claim to have some connection with it. We must sever ourselves from them, and let them go. Not that we want to hurt them. We do not want to hurt anybody. We never have, and we do not intend to hurt anybody. But we do not intend to be hurt by those who are seeking our destruction, if we can help it. It is our right to protect ourselves. [Sec. 64:10-14.] (CR, April 1906, pp. 7-8.)

SECTION 21

Revelation given to Joseph Smith the Prophet, at Fayette, New York, April 6, 1830. This revelation was given at the organization of the Church of Jesus Christ of Latter-day Saints, on the date named, in the home of Peter Whitmer, Sen. Six men, who had previously been baptized, participated. By unanimous vote these expressed their desire and determination to organize, according to the commandment of God; see Section 20. They also voted to accept and sustain Joseph Smith, Jun., and Oliver Cowdery as the presiding officers of the Church. With the laying on of hands, Joseph then ordained Oliver an Elder of the Church of Jesus Christ of Latter-day Saints; and Oliver similarly ordained Joseph. After administration of the sacrament, Joseph and Oliver laid hands upon the participants individually, for the bestowal of the Holy Ghost, and for the confirmation of each as a member of the Church. See History of the Church, vol. 1, p. 75. – Church records – The Lord manifests acceptance of the Church, and recognition of the presiding officers.

1. Behold, there shall be a record kept among you; and in it thou shalt be called a seer, a translator, a prophet, an apostle of Jesus Christ, an elder of the church through the will of God the Father, and the grace of your Lord Jesus Christ,

2. Being inspired of the Holy Ghost to lay the foundation thereof, and to build it up unto the most holy faith.

3. Which church was organized and established in the year of your Lord eighteen hundred and thirty, in the fourth month, and on the sixth day of the month which is called April.

4. Wherefore, meaning the church, thou shalt give heed unto all his words and commandments which he shall give unto you as he receiveth them, walking in all holiness before me;

5. For his word ye shall receive, as if from mine own mouth, in all patience and faith.

6. For by doing these things the gates of hell shall not prevail against you; yea, and the Lord God will disperse the powers of darkness from before you, and cause the heavens to shake for your good, and his name's glory.

7. For thus saith the Lord God: Him have I inspired to move the cause of Zion in mighty power for good, and his diligence I know, and his prayers I have heard.

8. Yea, his weeping for Zion I have seen, and I will cause that he shall mourn for her no longer; for his days of rejoicing are come unto the remission of his sins, and the manifestations of my blessings upon his works.

9. For, behold, I will bless all those who labor in my vineyard with a mighty blessing, and they shall believe on his

words, which are given him through me by the Comforter, which manifesteth that Jesus was crucified by sinful men for the sins of the world, yea, for the remission of sins unto the contrite heart.

10. Wherefore it behooveth me that he should be ordained by you, Oliver Cowdery mine apostle;

11. This being an ordinance unto you, that you are an elder under his hand, he being the first unto you, that you might be an elder unto this church of Christ, bearing my name —

12. And the first preacher of this church unto the church, and before the world, yea, before the Gentiles; yea, and thus saith the Lord God, lo, lo! to the Jews also. Amen.

Joseph Smith: *Introduction*

Whilst the Book of Mormon was in the hands of the printer, we still continued to bear testimony and give information, as far as we had opportunity; and also make known to our brethren that we had received a commandment to organize the Church; and accordingly we met together for that purpose, at the house of Mr. Peter Whitmer, Sen., (being six in number) on Tuesday, the sixth day of April, A.D. one thousand eight hundred and thirty. Having opened the meeting by solemn prayer to our Heavenly Father, we proceeded, according to previous commandment, to call on our brethren to know whether they accepted us as their teachers in the things of the Kingdom of God, and whether they were satisfied that we should proceed and be organized as a Church according to said commandment which we had received. To these several propositions they consented by a unanimous vote. I then laid my hands upon Oliver Cowdery, and ordained him an Elder of the "Church of Jesus Christ of Latter-day Saints"; after which, he ordained me also to the office of an Elder of said Church. We then took bread, blessed it, and brake it with them; also wine, blessed it, and drank it with them. We then laid our hands on each individual member of the Church present, that they might receive the gift of the Holy Ghost, and be confirmed members of the Church of Christ. The Holy Ghost was poured out upon us to a very great degree — some prophesied, whilst we all praised the Lord, and rejoiced exceedingly. Whilst yet together, I received the following commandment: [Section 21, follows.] (*HC* 1:74-78, April 6, 1830; Fayette, New York.)

Rudger Clawson: 1-8

These words [Sec.21:1-12] were the words of Jehovah, delivered to the Prophet Joseph Smith upon the day that the Church was organized. The Church was very weak in numbers then, but strong in spirit. In this revelation the Lord intimates that he was about to move the cause of Zion in mighty power, and talked to the Prophet as if it were an accomplished fact. He desired, it seems, that his people, though few in number, should be impressed with the fact that a Prophet, Seer and Revelator stood at the head; for he instructed that a record to this effect should be kept. He also desired to impress the people with the great truth that this Church should be built up, not by the power of man, but by the power of the Holy Ghost; that no man, though he might be a Prophet or an Apostle, should take the honor unto himself of building up the Church of Christ, but that the honor and the glory must be given to God. Did not the Lord say to the Prophet Daniel that in the latter days the God of heaven would set up his kingdom, and it should be as a stone cut out of the mountain without hands, which should roll until it filled the whole earth. [Daniel 2:34-35,44.] The God of heaven was to do this, but he would use men as his instruments. (*CR*, October 1901, pp.7-8.)

Anthon H. Lund: 1
There shall be a record kept among you

At the beginning of this revelation [Sec. 21] we were told that there should be a recorder in the Church, that records should be kept among the people. This important work in the Church, of keeping records, was commanded; and if we read farther we will find that John Whitmer was appointed to be Church recorder, to write the events of the

Church. I mention this to show you how important this part of our Church government is, to keep history, to keep a record of what takes place. (CR, April 1913, p.11.)

Orson F. Whitney: 1
A seer

A seer is greater than a prophet. [Mosiah 8:15.] One may be a prophet without being a seer; but a seer is essentially a prophet — if by "prophet" is meant not only a spokesman, but likewise a foreteller. Joseph Smith was both prophet and seer.

A seer is one who sees. But it is not the ordinary sight that is meant. The seeric gift is a supernatural endowment. Joseph was "like unto Moses"; and Moses, who saw God face to face, explains how he saw him in these words: "Now mine own eyes have beheld God; but not my natural, but my spiritual eyes, for my natural eyes could not have beheld; for I should have withered and died in his presence; but his glory was upon me; and I beheld his face, for I was transfigured before him." (Moses 1:11.) Such is the testimony of the ancient seer, as brought to light by the seer of the latter days. (*Saturday Night Thoughts*, 1921, p. 39.)

Ezra T. Benson: 1
A translator

When Brother Joseph commenced this work, he used to translate by means of the Urim and Thummim, as we read that the prophets and seers did anciently. Did he do this in the latter part of his career? No; he did not, and by the Holy Ghost he could see the very secrets of a man's heart. He could translate other languages, and he did it by the gift and power of the Holy Ghost. I wish to bring this matter to your minds, I want you to understand what it is. (*Ezra T. Benson*, 1856, pp. 227-28.)

Anthony W. Ivins: 1
A prophet

The word Prophet defined in the Hebrew language means one who has been called to denounce sin and foretell the consequences and punishment of it. He is to be above all else a preacher of righteousness, to call the people back from idolatry to faith in the living God, and when moved upon by the Spirit of the Lord, to foretell coming events. But more particularly a prophet is to be an expounder of present duties and an interpreter of the meaning and application of the written word. (CR, October 1933, p. 84.)

Anthon H. Lund: 1
A prophet

Joseph Smith was a Prophet of God. His teachings prove that what he taught was divinely inspired. Some of his prophecies have been fulfiled, and others remain to be fulfilled. His predictions have not been guesswork. In 1832 he looked down and saw the fate of the Church. [Sec. 101:17-22; 103:5-7.] Now it is reasonable to suppose that if the Lord raised up a prophet, that prophet would say something in regard to these two important things: the nation and the Church, and he did. He told how the Church would be persecuted and driven, and that even the blood of some should be spilt and should cry unto heaven against those who had shed it. [Sec. 87:7.] He prophesied that the Church should go to the Rocky Mountains, and he was so much impressed with the spirit of this that he appointed a committee to go and search for a place to locate the saints. He did not live to see this accomplished, but we have seen this prophecy fulfilled. In regard to the nation, he plainly foretold where the Rebellion (Civil War) should begin and what its results should be. [Sec. 87:1-3.] Everyone can see plainly that part of that revelation has been fulfilled and the other part remains to be fulfilled. (CR, October 1899, pp. 13-14.)

Marion G. Romney: 4-6

I would like now to suggest some tests which can safely be used to distinguish the genuine from the counterfeit. . . .

Anything purporting to pertain to the Gospel of Jesus Christ may be put to the following four simple tests:

1. Does it purport to originate in the wisdom of men or

was it revealed from heaven? If it originated in the wisdom of men, it is [John 3:3-5; 7:16; 2 Nephi 9:28-29; 1 Cor. 2:14] not of God. . . .

2. Does the teaching bear the proper label? . . . [3 Nephi 27:4-8.]

From the foregoing it is perfectly plain that if any teaching purporting to be from Christ comes under any label other than that of Jesus Christ, we can know it is not of God.

3. The last phrase of the above quotation gives us the third test. "But if it be called in my name then it is my church, if it so be that they are built upon my gospel." The teaching must not only come under the proper label, but it must also conform to the other teachings of the gospel of Jesus Christ.

4. Now the fourth and last test I shall mention is: Does it come through the proper Church channel? . . .

In the revelation the Lord gave to the Prophet in answer to his inquiry about the stone which Hiram Page had, he said, speaking of the president of the Church [Sec. 21:4-5, quoted].

Such is the obligation of this Priesthood with respect to our present Prophet, Seer, and Revelator, President David O. McKay. [Sec. 21:6, quoted.]

Now . . . if we will keep these things in mind, we shall not be deceived by false teachings. I remember years ago when I was a bishop, I had President [Heber J.] Grant talk to our ward. After the meeting I drove him home. . . . Standing by me, he put his arm over my shoulder and said:"My boy, you always keep your eye on the President of the Church, and if he ever tells you to do anything, and it is wrong, you do it, and the Lord will bless you for it." Then, with a twinkle in his eye, he said, "But you don't need to worry. The Lord will never let his mouthpiece lead the people astray." (CR, October 1960, pp. 76-78.)

Anthon H. Lund: 6
The gates of hell

The Lord, in comforting the saints, told them that if they would listen to his counsel, the gates of hell should not

253

have power over them, and this promise is the same to you and to me inasmuch as we listen to the counsels of inspired men. As I understand that expression, "the gates of hell," it means those things which lead to hell, in fact, are the entrances to it. How many things are there that lead to those gates? How many things we have to be warned against and which we have to watch out for, because if we yield to them, they will lead us to the gates of hell! Let us each and every one examine ourselves and know well the path in which we are walking and avoid everything that we know is wrong, and forbidden by the Lord, well knowing that if we yield to such we have not the promise that the gates of hell shall not have power over us; on the other hand, if we perform our duty, live according to the testimony which God has given us, we need not fear, for he will lead us in the paths of righteousness that lead to eternal life. (CR, April 1913, pp. 10-11.)

George Albert Smith: 9

A hundred years ago yesterday the Lord commenced this work. At that time he gave certain information. I shall not take time to read that [Sec. 21], but I call attention to the fact that in it the Lord said: [Sec. 21:9, quoted.]

I call attention to the fact that he made a promise that he would bless all those who labored in his vineyard, and since that time thousands of men and women have gone into the world to advocate the truth. I have met and visited with hundreds, yes, and with thousands of them myself, and I have never heard one bear any other testimony than that the Lord had blessed him and given him great joy when he labored in his service. (CR, April 1930, p. 66.)

Brigham Young: 9
By the Comforter

I have proven to my satisfaction, according to the best knowledge I can gather, that a man can be deceived by the sight of the natural eye, he can be deceived by the hearing of the ear, and by the touch of the hand; that he can be deceived in all of what are called the natural senses. But there is one thing in which he cannot be deceived. What is that? It is the operations of the Holy Ghost, the Spirit and power of God upon the creature. It teaches him of heavenly things; it directs him in the way of life; it affords him the key by which he can test the devices of man, and which recommends the things of God. (*JD*, September 17, 1876, 18:230.)

Anthon H. Lund: 10-11

Joseph had informed the little flock that gathered there when the Church was organized of what the Lord commanded, and it was proposed to them that Joseph Smith be the first Elder of the Church, and Oliver the second. Then Joseph ordained Oliver and Oliver ordained Joseph to the office of an Elder. This was not bestowing the Melchizedek Priesthood on either of them. They held that before. It had been conferred upon them by Peter, James and John. [Sec. 27:12-13.] It was not given to them by the authority of those present. The Lord had revealed to them, through his servant, and had conferred upon them the Melchizedek Priesthood, but there was no Church organized as yet, and hence there were no officers needed in the Church, but when the Church was organized, on April the 6th, 1830, then it was necessary that men should fill official positions in the Church, and do this by the consent of those over whom they were to exercise authority. As yet, the office of a High Priest had not been given, but Elders had been voted for, and had been ordained, and they took charge of the meeting. (*CR*, April 1913, pp. 9-10.)

George Q. Cannon: 12

The first public meeting of the Church after the day of its organization was held at the house of Peter Whitmer in Fayette, on the 11th day of April, 1830. On that occasion, Oliver Cowdery, under Joseph's direction, proclaimed the word of God for the comfort and instruction of saints and strangers. The appointment for this meeting had gone forth through all the neighborhood; and many persons came to hear what wonderful things were to be spoken by the men who professed to be called directly of God to the ministry. This was the first public discourse delivered by an authorized servant of God in these last days. At the conclusion of the services a number of persons demanded baptism and membership among the people of God. (*Life of Joseph Smith*, 1907, p. 61.)

SECTION 22

Revelation given through Joseph Smith the Prophet, to The Church of Jesus Christ of Latter-day Saints, which was established in these last days, in the year of our Lord one thousand eight hundred and thirty. Given at Manchester, New York, April, 1830, in consequence of some who had previously been baptized desiring to unite with the Church without re-baptism. – The indispensability of baptism in the way prescribed and through the authority given by the Lord is set forth.

1. Behold, I say unto you that all old covenants have I caused to be done away in this thing; and this is a new and an everlasting covenant, even that which was from the beginning.

2. Wherefore, although a man should be baptized an hundred times it availeth him nothing, for you cannot enter in at the strait gate by the law of Moses, neither by your dead works.

3. For it is because of your dead works that I have caused this last covenant and this church to be built up unto me, even as in days of old.

4. Wherefore, enter ye in at the gate, as I have commanded, and seek not to counsel your God. Amen.

Joseph Smith: *Introduction*

Several persons who had attended the above meeting [April 6, 1830] became convinced of the truth and came forward shortly after, and were received into the Church. ... Revelation to the Church of Jesus Christ which was established in these last days, in the year of our Lord, one thousand eight hundred and thirty. Given at Manchester, New York, April, 1830, in consequence of some desiring to unite with the Church without re-baptism, who had previously been baptized. [Section 22, follows.] (*HC* 1:79, April 1830.)

James E. Talmage: 1-4

In this restored Church has been placed, by divine ministration and ordinance, the authority of the Lesser and the Greater — or of the Aaronic and of the Melchizedek

Priesthoods, with the several offices thereof and the several duties, responsibilities and powers pertaining to each office as of old.

That it was and is something new, and yet something old, as it is in fact eternal, was set forth by the Lord in a revelation given in April, 1830, just after the organization of the Church. [Sec. 22.] There were people who had joined other churches. Many of them had been and were devout. They had been baptized, some of them by sprinkling and some of them by pouring, but they called it baptism, and some of them by immersion; and they raised the question as to whether they could not become members of this Church now by application and profession of faith alone, affirming that it was unjust that they should be required to be baptized again. In this claim they plainly forgot that the outward form of baptism can be performed by anybody, but that baptism as an ordinance acceptable unto the Lord requires the power and the authority of the Priesthood which he has given. Therefore the Lord said: [Sec. 22:1-4, quoted.] . . .

Isn't that in line with the declaration our Lord made while he talked in the flesh, even the Christ, known as Jesus of Nazareth, who was acknowledged as a marvelous prophet whose teachings were full of wisdom? On one occasion, amidst circumstances which the rest of the chapter will give unto you, he spoke these words recorded in the 9th chapter of Matthew, beginning with the sixteenth verse:

> No man putteth a piece of new cloth unto an old garment, for that which is put in to fill it up taketh from the garment, and the rent is made worse.
> Neither do men put new wine into old bottles; else the bottles break, and the wine runneth out, and the bottles perish, but they put new wine into new bottles, and both are preserved. (CR, October 1922, pp. 71-72.)

Joseph Fielding Smith: 1
A new and an everlasting covenant

I am reminded of an expression that occurs in one of the early revelations (Sec. 22) shortly after the organization of the Church, when the Lord said that he had given unto the

Church "a new and an everlasting covenant, even that which was from the beginning." Those words are very significant. It was a new and everlasting covenant, and yet it had always existed, for it was from the beginning, and so this new commandment that we should love one another has always been. The truth does not grow old. Some people, you know, are extremely progressive. They want a change in this and a change in that, and a change in the other thing, but the principles of the gospel never change. (CR, October 1920, p. 55.)

Rudger Clawson: 2
Baptized

Baptism, then, may be said to be the door that leads into the kingdom of God, or into the Church and kingdom of God. How beautiful that is! I am not spiritualizing. There is an earthly work to do. And then when one gets into the kingdom of God there is a greater work to do because it is word upon word, line upon line, precept upon precept, that one must learn by experience after he comes into the Church and kingdom of God. A man is not saved by baptism altogether, but he must exercise that power and do the work that is necessary. (CR, October 1932, pp. 9-10.)

Anthon H. Lund: 4
Enter ye in at the gate

There are so many religious denominations in the world, and the question arises, How shall I find the correct one? Paul tells us there is but one true faith, that none is allowed to preach any other gospel than the one he preached: for if one should do so, he says, "Let him be accursed." [Gal. 1:6-8.] It is therefore of vital consequence to know which is the true religion. The Lord has not left us without means to show this for ourselves. We have his word, which we can study, and it was written by men inspired by the Holy Ghost. While we are convinced of this, we do not believe that the word of God as contained in the sacred books is able to authorize men to officiate in the ordinances of the Gospel. The word of God is for our guidance, but we need the living oracles to direct and guide us and to administer the ordinances. . . .

The true Church must be established by authority of God, and there must be the life of the Holy Spirit in it. The Holy Ghost must be conferred upon the members by the ordinance ordained for its bestowal [Sec. 20:41], and when the Spirit is received it will testify unto the recipients that they have obeyed the demands of the true Gospel. (CR, October 1915, p. 10.)

SECTION 23

Revelation given through Joseph Smith the Prophet, at Manchester, New York, April, 1830, to Oliver Cowdery, Hyrum Smith, Samuel H. Smith, Joseph Smith, Sen., and Joseph Knight, Sen. As the result of earnest desire on the part of the five persons named, the Prophet inquired of the Lord, and received this revelation in response.

1. Behold, I speak unto you, Oliver, a few words. Behold, thou art blessed, and art under no condemnation. But beware of pride, lest thou shouldst enter into temptation.

2. Make known thy calling unto the church, and also before the world, and thy heart shall be opened to preach the truth from henceforth and forever. Amen.

3. Behold, I speak unto you, Hyrum, a few words; for thou also art under no condemnation, and thy heart is opened, and thy tongue loosed; and thy calling is to exhortation, and to strengthen the church continually. Wherefore thy duty is unto the church forever, and this because of thy family. Amen.

4. Behold, I speak a few words unto you, Samuel; for thou also art under no condemnation, and thy calling is to exhortation, and to strengthen the church; and thou art not as yet called to preach before the world. Amen.

5. Behold, I speak a few words unto you, Joseph; for thou also art under no condemnation, and thy calling also is to exhortation, and to strengthen the church; and this is thy duty from henceforth and forever. Amen.

6. Behold, I manifest unto you, Joseph Knight, by these words, that you must take up your cross, in the which you must pray vocally before the world as well as in secret, and in your family, and among your friends, and in all places.

7. And, behold, it is your duty to unite with the true church, and give your language to exhortation continually, that you may receive the reward of the laborer. Amen.

Joseph Smith: *Introduction*

The following persons being anxious to know of the Lord what might be their respective duties in relation to this work, I inquired of the Lord, and received for them the following:

Revelation to Oliver Cowdery, Hyrum Smith, Samuel

H. Smith, Joseph Smith, Sen., and Joseph Knight, Sen. Given at Manchester, New York, April 1830. [Section 23, follows.] (HC 1:80, April 1830.)

Joseph Fielding Smith: 1-5

First the Lord spoke to Oliver Cowdery informing him that he was under no condemnation, but that he was to beware of pride, lest thou shouldst enter into temptation. This was one of Oliver Cowdery's besetting sins. If he could have humbled himself in the troubled days of Kirtland he would not have lost his place and membership in the Church. That which had been bestowed upon him was exceedingly great and had he been willing to humble himself, it was his privilege to stand with the Prophet Joseph Smith through all time and eternity, holding the keys of the Dispensation of the Fulness of Times. However, at this particular time when this word was sought, he was free from condemnation. He was commanded to make known his calling to both the Church and also to the world, and while doing this his heart would be opened to teach them the truth from henceforth and forever. His great mission was to stand shoulder to shoulder with the Prophet Joseph Smith holding the keys of salvation for this dispensation. It was also his duty to bear witness to all mankind of the restoration of the Gospel.

The Lord also told Hyrum Smith that he was free from condemnation and that his heart was opened, his tongue loosed, and his calling was to exhortation, and to strengthen the Church continually. In a later revelation the Lord said of Hyrum Smith that he loved him "because of the integrity of his heart, and because he loved that which is right before me, saith the Lord." Because of his integrity and because his heart was right, he had conferred upon his head all that once was given to Oliver Cowdery. (D&C 124:15, 94-96.) There is another thing of great significance in this brief blessing to Hyrum Smith (Sec. 23:3), which is: "Wherefore thy duty is unto the church forever, and this because of thy family. Amen." It is doubtful if the Prophet Joseph fully understood the meaning of this expression when this revelation was given. In later years it was made clear. Evidently it has reference to the office of Patriarch, and in this office it was his duty and that of his family forever.

To Samuel Smith the Lord said it was his duty also to strengthen the Church, although he was not yet called to preach before the world. It will be recalled that Samuel was the third person baptized in this dispensation. He was one of the first to be ordained to the office of Elder, and it was not long after this revelation when he was sent forth to teach, which he did with marked success, far beyond his own realization.

To Joseph Smith, Sen., who was so faithful and devoted to his son in the commencement of this marvelous work, the Lord said: He was not under any condemnation, and he also was called to exhort, and to strengthen the Church, and this was his duty from henceforth and forever. (CHMR, 1947, 1:112-13.)

James E. Talmage: 6
Take up your cross

The cross to be taken up may be heavy, perhaps to be dragged because too burdensome to be borne. We are apt to assume that self-denial is the sole material of our cross; but this is true only as we regard self-denial in its broadest sense, comprising both positive and negative aspects. One man's cross may consist mostly in refraining from doings to which he is inclined, another's in doing what he would fain escape. One's besetting sin is evil indulgence; his neighbor's a lazy inattention to the activities required by the Gospel of Jesus Christ, coupled perchance with puritanical rigor in other observances.

But the great question, striking home to every thoughtful soul, is that of the Master — "For what is a man profited, if he shall gain the whole world and lose his own soul?" (Matt. 16:26.)

It is possible then for a man to lose his own soul. To deny is to reject the Lord's own doctrine. The safeguard against such incalculable loss is specifically indicated — to follow the Savior; and this can mean only keeping his commandments, whatever the temporary suffering or worldly sacrifice may be. (*The Vitality of Mormonism*, 1919, p. 353.)

Joseph F. Merrill: 6
Pray vocally . . . as well as in secret

I was reared in a family where prayer, night and morning, was always the order. I have seen my father sometimes too busy to eat his breakfast, but never too busy to kneel with his family in prayer before he left, to thank the Lord for the prospects of the day, for the rest of the night, and to ask his direction and help in the labors of the day. I was taught to pray at my mother's knee, and when I would say my own little prayers, I was taught that it was my prayer; it should be said in secret, or at least to myself. (*CR*, April 1944, p. 151.)

Charles C. Rich: 7

In the first instructions we received from the Elders, we were told we must repent of our sins and be baptized, in order to receive the Holy Spirit, and that we had no claims upon the Lord for his Spirit until we had complied with the requirements made of us. [Sec. 36:2-3.] I remember very well my feelings upon this subject before I obeyed the Gospel. I studied carefully, anxiously, and prayerfully, that I might know if it were the Church of Jesus Christ. I did not want to run any risk in the matter, and remain in uncertainty. I was willing to do anything that would give me a knowledge of the truth. I was willing to receive it through the ministration of an angel, through direct revelation, or by any other way, but I did not want to be deceived. Every time I reflected carefully upon the subject I came to this point: the conditions upon which the promises have been made are repentance, baptism, and imposition of hands. The spirit would then whisper, You have not been baptized, you have not obeyed the Gospel; but when I had complied with the law, then I had a perfect claim to the blessings and the promises, and did receive them, and obtained a perfect knowledge of the truth, and then could bear a testimony of it to all the world. I mention these things to show you the principles we have to act upon in order to obtain the blessings of salvation and eternal life. And I can testify that the Lord has fulfilled his promises, and has poured out his Spirit upon the people, through baptism and the laying on of hands. . . .We must comply with the principles of the eternal law in order to obtain eternal blessings. [Sec. 130:20-21.] I want to impress these principles upon your minds, for there is no "think so" and "guess so" about these things, for the Lord himself has decreed them, and I bear record that they are true. (JD, February 10, 1878, 19:250-51.)

First Presidency (David O. McKay, Stephen L Richards, J. Reuben Clark, Jr.): 7
Unite with the true church

We hold out to all men the promise that if they will accept the Lord's revealed truth and conform their lives to the commandments and revelations of the Father, they will acquire testimony convincing to their souls of the divinity of the mission of the Lord Jesus Christ and the restoration of his Holy Gospel in this Dispensation of the Fulness of Times, which is to precede the second coming of our Lord and Savior. The Lord will bring to those who accept his truth and the way of life he has given — happiness, contentment, satisfaction, and a peace that passeth understanding. [Sec. 59:23.] (DN, December 16, 1953.)

SECTION 24

Revelation given to Joseph Smith the Prophet and Oliver Cowdery, at Harmony, Pennsylvania, July 1830. Though less than four months had elapsed since the Church was organized, persecution had become intense, and the leaders had to seek safety in partial seclusion. See History of the Church, vol. 1, p. 101. – The Lord combines encouragement with reproof – Gives individual commandments to Joseph and Oliver respectively.

1. Behold, thou wast called and chosen to write the Book of Mormon, and to my ministry; and I have lifted thee up out of thine afflictions, and have counseled thee, that thou hast been delivered from all thine enemies, and thou hast been delivered from the powers of Satan and from darkness!

2. Nevertheless, thou art not excusable in thy transgressions; nevertheless, go thy way and sin no more.

3. Magnify thine office; and after thou hast sowed thy fields and secured them, go speedily unto the church which is in Colesville, Fayette, and Manchester, and they shall support thee; and I will bless them both spiritually and temporally;

4. But if they receive thee not, I will send upon them a cursing instead of a blessing.

5. And thou shalt continue in calling upon God in my name, and writing the things which shall be given thee by the Comforter, and expounding all scriptures unto the church.

6. And it shall be given thee in the very moment what thou shalt speak and write, and they shall hear it, or I will send unto them a cursing instead of a blessing.

7. For thou shalt devote all thy service in Zion; and in this thou shalt have strength.

8. Be patient in afflictions, for thou shalt have many; but endure them, for, lo, I am with thee, even unto the end of thy days.

9. And in temporal labors thou shalt not have strength, for this is not thy calling. Attend to thy calling and thou shalt have wherewith to magnify thine office, and to expound all scriptures, and continue in laying on of the hands and confirming the churches.

10. And thy brother Oliver shall continue in bearing my name before the world, and also to the church. And he shall not suppose that he can say enough in my cause; and lo, I am with him to the end.

11. In me he shall have glory, and not of himself, whether in weakness or in strength, whether in bonds or free;

12. And at all times, and in all places, he shall open his mouth and declare my gospel as with the voice of a trump, both day and night. And I will give unto him strength such as is not known among men.

13. Require not miracles, except I shall command you, except casting out devils, healing the sick, and against poisonous serpents, and against deadly poisons;

14. And these things ye shall not do, except it be required of you by them who desire it, that the scriptures might be fulfilled; for ye shall do according to that which is written.

15. And in whatsoever place ye shall enter, and they receive you not in my name, ye shall leave a cursing instead of a blessing, by casting off the dust of your feet against them as a testimony, and cleansing your feet by the wayside.

16. And it shall come to pass that whosoever shall lay their hands upon you by violence, ye shall command to be smitten in my name; and, behold, I will smite them according to your words, in mine own due time.

17. And whosoever shall go to law with thee shall be cursed by the law.

18. And thou shalt take no purse nor scrip, neither staves, neither two coats, for the church shall give unto thee in the very hour what thou needest for food and for raiment, and for shoes and for money, and for scrip.

19. For thou art called to prune my vineyard with a mighty pruning, yea, even for the last time; yea, and also all those whom thou hast ordained, and they shall do even according to this pattern. Amen.

George Q. Cannon: Introduction

Accompanied by his wife and three of the Elders, he [Joseph Smith] went again to Colesville. Here they found many people awaiting baptism. Joseph prepared to accede to their demand. A suitable portion of a little stream in that locality was prepared for the purpose of the administration of the ordinance; but in the night sectarian priests, fearful of losing their congregations and their hire, instigated evil men to desecrate the spot and to destroy all the preparations of the Elders. . . . A few days later the ordinance was administered by Oliver Cowdery to thirteen persons at Colesville....

While the baptisms were in progress an angry mob collected, and threatened destruction to the Elders and believers. The mob surrounded the house of Joseph Knight and his son Newel and railed with devilish hatred at the inmates. The Prophet spoke to them and made an effort to calm their passions, but without avail. Wearied with their own impotent wrath, the mobs departed; but only to concoct new plots.

That night a meeting was to be held, and when the believers and sympathizers had assembled, and Joseph was about to offer them instruction and consolation, a constable approached and arrested him on a warrant charging him with being a disorderly person, for setting the country in an uproar by circulating the Book of Mormon and by preaching a gospel of revelation....

A court was convened to consider the strange charges brought against the young man, Joseph Smith; and hateful lies, of every form which the father of falsehood could devise, were circulated to create popular dislike.... The bitter feeling of endangered priestcraft was visible throughout the trial; but all the accusations which were made were but lies, and none were sustained. The court declared an acquittal. The evidence in the trial was a high tribute to the character of Joseph Smith....

This paper [a warrant] was secured on the oath of a sectarian bigot; and no sooner was Joseph acquitted by the court in Chenango County than he was seized under the new warrant and dragged back to Colesville....

When the morning came, Joseph was arraigned before the magistrate's court of Colesville. Arrayed against him were some of the people who had been discomfited at the trial in Chanago County. This time they were determined to secure a conviction. By the side of the Prophet were his friends and advocates who had aided him in the former trial. Despite the vindictive effort of the mob, the court discharged the Prophet, declaring that nothing was shown to his dishonor. (*Life of Joseph Smith*, 1907, pp. 64-67.)

Joseph Smith: *Introduction*

After our departure from Colesville, after the trial, the Church there was very anxious, as might be expected, concerning our again visiting them, during which time Sister Knight, wife of Newel Knight, had a dream which enabled her to say that we would visit them that day, which really came to pass, for a few hours afterwards we arrived; and thus was our faith much strengthened concerning dreams and visions in the last days, foretold by the ancient Prophet Joel [Joel 2:28-29]; and although we this time were forced to seek safety from our enemies by flight, we did feel confident that eventually we should come off victorious, if we only continued faithful to him who had called us forth from darkness into the marvelous light of the everlasting Gospel of our Lord Jesus Christ.

Shortly after our return home we received the following commandments: [Sections 24, 25, and 26, follow.] (HC 1:101, July 1830; Harmony, Pennsylvania.)

Joseph Fielding Smith: 1-9

Early in July [1830] another revelation was given to Joseph Smith and Oliver Cowdery in Harmony, Pennsylvania. They were commanded to return to the saints in Colesville, Manchester, and Fayette, and the members would support them. They should expound the scriptures and devote their time exclusively to the cause of Zion, and if the members should not support them in these labors, then would the Lord withdraw his blessings. [Sec. 24:8, quoted.] The afflictions surely came, for Joseph Smith was called on to suffer as few men have had to suffer. He was to attend to his calling, for the Lord would withhold his power in temporal things that he should not have strength. (*Essentials in Church History*, 1950, pp. 106-7.)

George Q. Cannon: 2

Thou art not excusable in thy transgressions

Instead of being lifted up by the favor which had been

shown to him, Joseph was made to feel his own weaknesses. Chosen to be a prophet and the leader of God's people, he was conscious that he was only human, subject to human temptations and human frailties. Having the honesty and courage inspired by the Spirit of the Lord, he dared to confess this openly; and, under the same inspiration, acknowledge his transgression and make his contrition known. He was not above any law which applied to his fellow-man. Of his responsibility to God and his brethren of the Church, he was required by the law revealed through himself to the Church, to give as strict an account as any other member. They who participated with him in authority owed it not to him as an individual, but to the eternal power to which they were alike responsible. (*Life of Joseph Smith*, 1907, pp. 58-59.)

Charles W. Penrose: 3
Magnify thine office

Everyone who is called to the ministry is growing up to him, and we are bulding up the Church and the Kingdom of our God unto Christ, our Redeemer, and he will be the King and Lord of all. . . . So, while we dwell on the earth . . . let us devote ourselves to the building up of this Kingdom, unto him, and when he comes we will receive our share of the reward. . . . Now let us perform our work and do our part, no matter what it may be, great or small, and unite together in one spirit. . . . (CR, April 1913, p. 65.)

Charles W. Penrose: 5
Calling upon God in my name

When we pray, we are told directly how to pray, and a sample is given to us in the blessing of the bread and of the water in the sacrament: "O God, the Eternal Father, we ask Thee in the name of Jesus Christ, Thy Son," so and so; that is the pattern for our prayers. [Sec. 20:77, 79.] We pray to the Eternal Father, whom we have named Elohim. We pray to him in the name of Jesus Christ for Jesus Christ is his Word. (CR, April 1916, pp. 22-23.)

Joseph Fielding Smith: 10-19

The second half of this revelation [Sec. 24] is to Oliver Cowdery. The Prophet was instructed to tell him to continue in bearing witness before the world, and he was not supposed to think he could say enough in the Lord's cause. If he would do this the Lord would be with him to the end, and in the Lord he should have glory, and that not of himself. At all times and in all places he was to open his mouth and declare the Gospel as with the voice of a trump, both day and night, and in this the Lord would give him strength such as is not known among men. He was to require no miracles, except as the Lord should call on him, to cast out devils, to heal the sick, and against poisonous serpents and against deadly poisons. [Sec. 24:14, quoted.]

Oliver was instructed that as he went forth with the voice of the trump, that where he was received he should leave a blessing; where he was rejected he was to leave a cursing. [Sec. 24:13-16, quoted.] He was told that if anyone took him to law, they would be cursed. He was to travel. [Sec. 24:18, quoted.]

This was a wonderful commission given to Oliver Cowdery as a witness for the truth, and the promises of the Lord to him were very great. Had he gone forth in this spirit all the time, as he did in the first half-dozen years of the history of the Church, he surely would have accomplished a wonderful work. He was sent to "prune the vineyard for the last time." This is also true of all others who have been ordained. The Lord has declared that the Gospel is here, in this dispensation, to stay. The vineyard (world) is to be pruned. To do this pruning laborers are needed, for the time is short.

While the Lord has instructed the Elders who go forth, just as he instructed Oliver Cowdery, to cleanse their feet, or wash them, as a witness against those who persecute them or in bitterness reject their message, yet the performance of such a responsibility should not be done unless the Spirit of the Lord indicates that it should be done. [Sec. 11:12-14.] (CHMR, 1947, pp. 114-15.)

Parley P. Pratt: 13

When the miracles and gifts of the divine Spirit ceased from among men, Christianity ceased, the Christian ministry ceased, the Church of Christ ceased.

That ministry which sets aside modern inspiration, revelation, prophecy, angels, visions, healings, etc., is not ordained of God, but is anti-Christian in spirit. In short, it is that spirit of priestcraft and kingcraft by which the world, for many ages, has been ruled as with a rod of iron. [Sec. 1:15-16, 33-34.] (*Key to the Science of Theology*, 1938, pp. 109-10.)

Brigham Young: 13
Require not miracles

You will recollect that I have often told you that miracles would not save a person, and I say that they never should. If I were to see a man come in here this day, and say, "I am the great one whom the Lord has sent," and cause fire to come down in our sight, through the ceiling that is over our heads, I would not believe any more for that. It is no matter what he does, I cannot believe any more on that account. [Rev. 16:13-14.] What will make me believe? What made the Twelve Apostles of Jesus Christ witnesses? What constituted them Apostles, special witnesses to the world? Was it seeing miracles? No. What was it? The visions of their minds were opened, and it was necessary that a few should receive light, knowledge, and intelligence, that all the powers of earth and hell could not gainsay or compete with. [Matt. 16:13-18; Gal. 1:11-12.] (*JD*, February 17, 1856, 3:206.)

George Q. Cannon: 13
Casting out devils

Newel, a son of Joseph Knight, became much interested in the Prophet's words. Many serious conversations ensued, and Newel became so far convinced of the divinity of the work that he gave a partial promise that he would arise in meeting and offer supplication to God before his friends and neighbors. But at the appointed moment he failed to respond to Joseph's invitation. Later he told the Prophet that he would pray in secret, and thus seek to resolve his doubts and gain strength. On the day following, Newel went into the woods to offer his devotions to heaven; but was unable to give utterance to his feelings, being held in bondage by some power which he could not define. He returned to his home ill in body, and depressed in mind. His appearance alarmed his wife, and in a broken voice he requested her to quickly find the Prophet and bring him to his bedside. When Joseph arrived at the house, Newel was suffering most frightful distortions of his visage and limbs, as if he were in convulsions. Even as the Prophet gazed at him, Newel was seized upon by some mysterious influence and tossed helpless about the room. Through the gift of discernment, Joseph saw his friend was in the grasp of the evil one, and that only the power of God could save him from the tortures under which he was suffering. He took Newel's hand and gently addressed him. Newel replied, "I am possessed of a devil. Exert your authority, I beseech you, to cast him out." Joseph replied, "If you know that I have power to drive him from your soul, it shall be done." And when these words were uttered, Joseph rebuked the destroyer and commanded him in the name of Jesus Christ to depart. The Lord condescended to honor his servant, in thus exercising the power which belonged to his Priesthood and calling, for instantly Newel cried out with joy that he felt the accursed influence leave him and saw the evil spirit passing from the room.

Thus was performed the first miracle of the Church. . . .

Since that hour thousands of miracles have been performed by the Elders of the Church, through the power of the Priesthood restored from heaven and in fulfillment of the promises made by the Lord Jesus. (*Life of Joseph Smith*, 1907, pp. 61-63.)

George Albert Smith in Behalf of the Council of the Twelve: 13

Healing the sick

When the sick have faith and make a request, those

holding the Melchizedek Priesthood should, first, anoint with oil; second, lay their hands on the sick person's head; and third, bless him and offer a prayer in his behalf. [Sec. 42:44; James 5:14-15.]

The anointing with the oil and the confirming of the anointing and sealing the blessing upon the sick person should be done in the name of the Lord, and by the power of the Priesthood. [Sec. 84:63, 65, 68.] The Elders should pray earnestly and exercise all the faith possible.

The promises and blessings that are pronounced should be prompted by the Spirit of the Lord. Therefore, it is important that Elders should carefully heed the promptings of the Holy Ghost that the right things might be said. Faith to heal the sick is one of the great and desirable gifts of the Spirit [Sec. 46:20], and Elders should be willing at all times to exercise their faith and give their services in performing this important ordinance.... [Sec. 24:14, quoted.](*The Missionary Handbook*, 1944, pp. 142-43.)

SECTION 25

Revelation given through Joseph Smith the Prophet, at Harmony, Pennsylvania, July, 1830. – The word of the Lord directed to Emma Smith, the Prophet's wife – Her duties defined, and glorious possibilities of achievement set forth – The Lord's admonitions are applied to all.

1. Hearken unto the voice of the Lord your God, while I speak unto you, Emma Smith, my daughter; for verily I say unto you, all those who receive my gospel are sons and daughters in my kingdom.

2. A revelation I give unto you concerning my will; and if thou art faithful and walk in the paths of virtue before me, I will preserve thy life, and thou shalt receive an inheritance in Zion.

3. Behold, thy sins are forgiven thee, and thou art an elect lady, whom I have called.

4. Murmur not because of the things which thou hast not seen, for they are withheld from thee and from the world, which is wisdom in me in a time to come.

5. And the office of thy calling shall be for a comfort unto my servant, Joseph Smith, Jun., thy husband, in his afflictions, with consoling words, in the spirit of meekness.

6. And thou shalt go with him at the time of his going, and be unto him for a scribe, while there is no one to be a scribe for him, that I may send my servant, Oliver Cowdery, whithersoever I will.

7. And thou shalt be ordained under his hand to expound scriptures, and to exhort the church, according as it shall be given thee by my Spirit.

8. For he shall lay his hands upon thee, and thou shalt receive the Holy Ghost, and thy time shall be given to writing, and to learning much.

9. And thou needest not fear, for thy husband shall support thee in the church; for unto them is his calling, that all things might be revealed unto them, whatsoever I will, according to their faith.

10. And verily I say unto thee that thou shalt lay aside the things of this world, and seek for the things of a better.

11. And it shall be given thee, also, to make a selection of sacred hymns, as it shall be given thee, which is pleasing unto me, to be had in my church.

12. For my soul delighteth in the song of the heart; yea, the song of the righteous is a prayer unto me, and it shall be answered with a blessing upon their heads.

13. Wherefore, lift up thy heart and rejoice, and cleave unto the covenants which thou hast made.

14. Continue in the spirit of meekness, and beware of pride. Let thy soul delight in thy husband, and the glory which shall come upon him.

15. Keep my commandments continually, and a crown of righteousness thou shalt receive. And except thou do this, where I am you cannot come.

16. And verily, verily, I say unto you, that this is my voice unto all. Amen.

[Revelation given through Joseph Smith the Prophet to Emma Smith, at Harmony, Pennsylvania, July, 1830. See "Introduction" to Section 24.]

Joseph Fielding Smith: 1-9

This revelation was given to Emma Smith, wife of Joseph Smith. She was the daughter of Isaac and Elizabeth Lewis Hale, and was born July 10, 1804. She was married to the Prophet in 1827, while he was under the tutelage of the Angel Moroni. She believed in the Prophet, although her parents did not, and she was baptized by Oliver Cowdery in June, 1830. Her life from that time on was a very trying one, due to constant persecution and mobbings. She passed through these trials with her husband and shared them, as did the faithful wives of the leaders of the Church. The calling given to Emma Smith in this revelation was an important one, and was fulfilled.

Emma Smith was human, possessing many of the characteristics which are found in most of us. Being the wife of the man whom the Almighty had blessed, she felt, as most women would have felt under like circumstances, that she was entitled to some special favors. It was difficult for her to understand why she could not view the plates, the Urim and Thummim, and other sacred things, which view had been given to special witnesses. At times this human thought caused her to murmur and ask the questions of the Prophet why she was denied this privilege. In this revelation the Lord admonishes her and tells her that it is for a wise purpose to be made known in time to come, why she and the world were deprived of this privilege. Her duty was to be obedient to her husband, hearken to him in faith, and she should have an inheritance in Zion. Even greater blessings were in store for her; she should be a daughter of God . . . in his kingdom, and a crown of righteousness should she receive. Moreover, she was told that her duty was to be a comfort with consoling words to her huband in his afflictions, for he should have many. (D&C 24:8.) Any man who has had afflictions knows what a comfort a confiding wife can be. How much better it is to be a comfort than to be a nagger and to murmur! . . .

"And thou shalt be ordained under his hand to expound scriptures, and to exhort the church." Like the expression "elect lady," so also has this saying led to speculation and misunderstanding. The term "ordain" was used generally in the early days of the Church in reference to both ordination and setting apart, and, too, correctly according to the meaning of the word. Men holding the Priesthood were said to have been "ordained" to preside over branches and to perform special work. Sisters also were said to have been "ordained" when they were called to some special duty or responsibility. In later years we developed a distinction between ordain and setting apart. Men are ordained to offices in the Priesthood and set apart to preside over stakes, wards, branches, missions, and auxiliary organizations. The sisters are set apart — not ordained — as presidents of auxiliary organizations, to missions, etc. This saying that Emma Smith was "ordained" to expound scripture does not mean that she had conferred upon her the Priesthood, but that she was set apart to this calling, which found its fulfillment in the Relief Society of the Church. (CHMR, 1947, 1:117-18.)

Brigham Young: 1
All those who receive my gospel are sons and daughters

By what means shall the people of this generation become the sons and daughters of the Almighty? By believing in the Lord Jesus Christ? [Sec. 11:30; 34:1-4; 35:2.]

Yes. How shall they know that they believe in him? By yielding obedience to the Gospel as it is revealed to us in this generation, at the same time believing in all that has been revealed to others until now concerning the children of men, the character of God, the creation of the earth, the ordinances of the Lord's house, the oracles of truth — believing in all things that have been revealed to mankind from the time that the Lord first began to reveal his will to them. (*JD*, November 17, 1867, 12:101.)

Joseph Smith: 3
Thou art an elect lady

I assisted in commencing the organization of "The Female Relief Society of Nauvoo" in the Lodge Room. Sister Emma Smith, President, and Sister Elizabeth Ann Whitney and Sarah M. Cleveland, Counselors. I gave much instruction, read in the New Testament, and Book of Doctrine and Covenants, concerning the Elect Lady, and showed that the elect meant to be elected to a certain work, etc., and that the revelation was then fulfilled by Sister Emma's election to the Presidency of the Society, she having previously been ordained to expound the Scriptures. [Sec. 25:3, 7.] Emma was blessed, and her counselors were ordained by Elder John Taylor. (*HC* 4:552-53, March 17, 1842.)

John Taylor: 7
And thou shalt be ordained . . . to expound scriptures

I was in Nauvoo at the time the Relief Society was organized by the Prophet Joseph Smith, and I was present on the occasion. At a later meeting of the Society held in Salt Lake City I was present, and I read from a record called the Book of the Law of the Lord, the minutes of that meeting. At that meeting the Prophet called Sister Emma to be an elect lady. That means that she was called to a certain work; and was in fulfillment of a certain revelation concerning her. [Sec. 25:13.] She was elected to preside over the Relief Society, and she was ordained to expound the scriptures. In compliance with Brother Joseph's request, I set her apart and also ordained Sister Whitney, wife of Bishop Newel K. Whitney, and Sister Cleveland, wife of Judge Cleveland, to be her counselors. Some of the sisters have thought that these sisters mentioned were in this ordination ordained to the Priesthood. And for the information of all interested in this subject I will say, it is not the calling of these sisters to hold the Priesthood, only in connection with their husbands, they being one with their husbands. (*JD*, August 8, 1880, 21:367-68.)

John A. Widtsoe: 10

I remember the man who baptized me into the Church, a very common, ordinary man to begin with, a ropewalker with a jug of beer two or three times a day, a glass of whiskey a little later, and a cud of tobacco mostly all day long, living a useless, purposeless life, except for three meals a day, and the satisfaction of some of the carnal appetites. He heard the Gospel and accepted it. It was good. It was something he had been longing for. The man grew in power and stature in the Church. As I recall it, he filled five or six missions and presided over one of the missions of the Church. He was the same man, with the same arms, same feet, same body, same mind, but changed because of the Spirit that comes with the acceptance of eternal truth. Have we not seen this in our own families and friends, in the little towns in which we live? Have not we felt our own strength grow mightier in love for our fellow men, in love for our daily tasks, in love for all the good things of life? (*CR*, April 1952, p. 34.)

Hyrum M. Smith: 10

It is folly to suppose that you gain a salvation in the kingdom of God while you are breaking the commandments of God. It is folly to suppose that the broad way, and those roads that meander and curve and turn away from the straight and narrow path will lead to that gate which entereth into life. . . . We must take all the words of the Savior; live by every word that proceedeth from the mouth of God, following the paths of truth, and keep the Lord's commandments; then there will be salvation for us. [James 1:22.] (*CR*, April 1906, p. 51.)

George Albert Smith: 11-12

Not only does the spoken word touch the hearts of the

children of men, but our Heavenly Father, knowing the importance of appropriate singing in worship, called Emma Smith and appointed her to select the hymns that were published in the first hymn book of The Church of Jesus Christ of Latter-day Saints. They have been added to from time to time, until today the songs of Zion are sung in many lands, and the words of the Gospel of Jesus Christ have been interpreted in many lands, not only by the spoken word, but by the hymns that are sung from the hearts of those who accept the Gospel of our Lord. (CR, October 1938, pp. 27-28.)

Reed Smoot: 12
The song of the righteous is a prayer unto me

In a revelation given through the Prophet Joseph Smith in July, 1830, the Lord, in speaking to Joseph's wife, Emma, said: [Sec. 25:12, quoted.] . . .

I believe that we can worship in song as acceptably to him as in any other way. . . . I know of no people on earth who have written into their songs the principles of the Gospel they believe in more than have the Latter-day Saints. . . .

"Come, come ye Saints, no toil nor labor fear,
        But with joy wend your way.
Though hard to you this journey may appear,
        Grace shall be as your day,"

is filled with inspiration. Brother William Clayton, the author of this song, was inspired to write it, at a time when the people were crossing the plains, careworn, disheartened and in need of encouragement. President [Brigham] Young realized their condition and knew that music would inspire them to renewed energy. He therefore asked William Clayton to write a hymn suitable to the conditions, and the result was the hymn "Come, Come, Ye Saints." It was inspired by God, and it has been an inspiration to God's people ever since.

I believe that Sister Snow, when she composed that immortalized song, "O My Father, Thou that dwellest in the high and glorious place," was inspired of God the Eternal Father. The idea that we had a Mother, as well as a Father, in heaven was first taught in this dispensation by the Prophet Joseph Smith. Sister Snow was convinced that he was right in so teaching, and embodied that principle of the Gospel in the song. I believe that hymn, "O My Father," has been the means of causing thousands of people of the world to investigate "Mormonism." (CR, October 1912, pp. 50-51.)

Joseph F. Smith: 12
It shall be answered . . . upon their heads

Good music is gracious praise of God. It is delightsome to the ear, and it is one of our most acceptable methods of worshipping God. And those who sing in this choir and in all the choirs of the saints should sing with the spirit and with the understanding. They should not sing merely because it is a profession, or because they have a good voice; but they should sing also because they have the spirit of it and can enter into the spirit of prayer and praise to God who gave them their sweet voices. (CR, October 1899, p. 69.)

Boyd K. Packer: 12
It shall be answered with a blessing upon their heads

This is what I would teach you. Choose from among the sacred music of the Church a favorite hymn, one with words that are uplifting and music that is reverent, one that makes you feel something akin to inspiration. Remember President Lee's counsel: perhaps "I am a Child of God" would do. Go over it in your mind carefully. Memorize it. Even though you have had no musical training, you can think through a hymn.

Now, use this hymn as the place for your thoughts to go. Make it your emergency channel. Whenever you find these shady actors have slipped from the sidelines of your thinking onto the state of your mind, put on this record, as it were.

As the music begins and as the words form in your thoughts, the unworthy ones will slip shamefully away. It will change the whole mood on the stage of your mind. Because it is uplifting and clean, the baser thoughts will disappear. For while virtue, by choice, *will not* associate with filth, evil *cannot* tolerate the presence of light.

In due time you will find yourself, on occasion, humming the music inwardly. As you retrace your thoughts, you discover some influence from the world about you encouraged an unworthy thought to move on stage in your mind, and the music almost automatically began. . . .

There are many references in the scriptures, both ancient and modern, that attest to the influence of righteous music. The Lord, Himself, was prepared for His greatest test through its influence, for the scripture records: "And when they had sung an hymn, they went out into the mount of Olives." (Mark 14:26.) (CR, October 1973, pp. 24-25.)

John Taylor: 13
Cleave unto the covenants which thou hast made

The covenants which men enter into generally are of a transitory nature, and pertain to time, and when time ceases with them these obligations terminate. Our covenants, however, are of another character. We enter into eternal covenants with God to serve him faithfully here on the earth, and then we expect to be associated with him in the heavens. Having entered into covenants of this kind, we feel that there are certain responsibilities and obligations resting upon us, which it is our bounden duty to perform. [Sec. 101:39-40.] (JD, January 12, 1873, 15:284.)

George Albert Smith: 15
Keep my commandments continually

I have many times repeated what my grandfather said. . . . In advising his family he said, "There is a line of demarcation, well defined. On one side of the line is the Lord's territory. On the other side of the line is the devil's territory." And he said, "If you will stay on the Lord's side of the line, you are perfectly safe, because the adversary of all righteousness cannot cross the line."

What does that mean? It means to me that those who are living righteous lives, keeping all the commandments of our Heavenly Father, are perfectly safe, but not those who trifle with his advice and counsel. (CR, September 1949, pp. 5-6.)

SECTION 26

Revelation given to Joseph Smith the Prophet, Oliver Cowdery, and John Whitmer, at Harmony, Pennsylvania, July, 1830. – Instructions as to immediate duty – Reaffirmation of the principle of common consent in Church affairs.

1. Behold, I say unto you that you shall let your time be devoted to the studying of the scriptures, and to preaching, and to confirming the church at Colesville, and to performing your labors on the land, such as is required, until after you shall go to the west to hold the next conference; and then it shall be made known what you shall do.

2. And all things shall be done by common consent in the church by much prayer and faith, for all things you shall receive by faith. Amen.

Charles W. Penrose: 2
All things shall be done by common consent

It may seem rather a dry and formal matter to some of the people to come together and lift up their hands to sustain the authorities of the Church, but it is a necessary duty and if we look at it properly, we shall take pleasure therein. It may seem a little monotonous, but as I have said, it is necessary, for it was designed by the Almighty in the organization of this Church, that the voice of the people should respond to the voice of the Lord. It is the voice of the Lord and the voice of the people together in this Church that sanctions all things therein. [Sec. 20:63-66.] In the rise of the Church the Lord gave a revelation which said that "all things shall be done by common consent." And the Lord designs that every individual member shall take upon him or her the spirit of the Church, and be an active living member of the body. (JD, November 29, 1879, 21:45-46.)

Joseph F. Smith: 2
All things shall be done . . . by much prayer and faith

President Smith . . . presented the authorities of the Church, first remarking that "we desire that the brethren and sisters will all feel the responsibility of expressing their feelings in relation to the propositions that may be put before you. We do not want any man or woman who is a member of the Church to violate their conscience. Of course, we are not asking apostates or non-members of the Church to vote on the authorities of the Church. We are only asking for members of the Church in good standing to vote on the propositions that shall be put before you, and we would like all to vote as they feel, whether for or against." (CR, October 1902, p. 83.)

SECTION 27

Revelation given to Joseph Smith the Prophet, at Harmony, Pennsylvania, August, 1830. In preparation for a religious service at which the sacrament of bread and wine was to be administered, Joseph set out to procure wine for the occasion. He was met by a heavenly messenger, and received this revelation, the first four paragraphs of which were written at the time, and the remainder in the September following. Water is commonly used instead of wine in the sacramental services of the Church. – Warning against the use of wine of unassured purity in the sacrament – Many ancient prophets named, with whom, as with the latter-day prophets, the Lord promises to partake at a time yet to come – The prior ordination of Joseph Smith, Jun., and Oliver Cowdery to the Apostleship avowed – Encouraging admonition given.

1. Listen to the voice of Jesus Christ, your Lord, your God, and your Redeemer, whose word is quick and powerful.

2. For behold, I say unto you, that it mattereth not what ye shall eat or what ye shall drink when ye partake of the sacrament, if it so be that ye do it with an eye single to my glory — remembering unto the Father my body which was laid down for you, and my blood which was shed for the remission of your sins.

3. Wherefore, a commandment I give unto you, that you shall not purchase wine neither strong drink of your enemies;

4. Wherefore, you shall partake of none except it is made new among you; yea, in this my Father's kingdom which shall be built up on the earth.

5. Behold, this is wisdom in me; wherefore, marvel not, for the hour cometh that I will drink of the fruit of the vine with you on the earth, and with Moroni, whom I have sent unto you to reveal the Book of Mormon, containing the fulness of my everlasting gospel, to whom I have committed the keys of the record of the stick of Ephraim;

6. And also with Elias, to whom I have committed the keys of bringing to pass the restoration of all things spoken by the mouth of all the holy prophets since the world began, concerning the last days;

7. And also John the son of Zacharias, which Zacharias he (Elias) visited and gave promise that he should have a son, and his name should be John, and he should be filled with the spirit of Elias;

8. Which John I have sent unto you, my servants, Joseph Smith, Jun., and Oliver Cowdery, to ordain you unto the first priesthood which you have received, that you might be called and ordained even as Aaron;

9. And also Elijah, unto whom I have committed the keys of the power of turning the hearts of the fathers to the children, and the hearts of the children to the fathers, that the whole earth may not be smitten with a curse;

10. And also with Joseph and Jacob, and Isaac, and Abraham, your fathers, by whom the promises remain;

11. And also with Michael, or Adam, the father of all, the prince of all, the ancient of days;

12. And also with Peter, and James, and John, whom I have sent unto you, by whom I have ordained you and confirmed you to be apostles and especial witnesses of my name, and bear the keys of your ministry and of the same things which I revealed unto them;

13. Unto whom I have committed the keys of my kingdom, and a dispensation of the gospel for the last times; and for the fulness of times, in the which I will gather together in one all things, both which are in heaven, and which are on earth;

14. And also with all those whom my Father hath given me out of the world.

15. Wherefore, lift up your hearts and rejoice, and gird up your loins, and take upon you my whole armor, that ye may be able to withstand the evil day, having done all, that ye may be able to stand.

16. Stand, therefore, having your loins girt about with truth, having on the breastplate of righteousness, and your feet shod with the preparation of the gospel of peace, which I have sent mine angels to commit unto you;

17. Taking the shield of faith wherewith ye shall be able to quench all the fiery darts of the wicked;

18. And take the helmet of salvation, and the sword of my Spirit, which I will pour out upon you, and my word which I reveal unto you, and be agreed as touching all things whatsoever ye ask of me, and be faithful until I come, and ye shall be caught up, that where I am ye shall be also. Amen.

Joseph Smith: *Introduction*

Early in the month of August, Newel Knight and his wife paid us a visit at my place in Harmony, Pennsylvania; and as neither his wife nor mine had been as yet confirmed, it was proposed that we should confirm them and partake together of the sacrament, before he and his wife should leave us. In order to prepare for this I set out to procure some wine for the occasion, but had gone only a short distance when I was met by a heavenly messenger, and received the following revelation, the first four paragraphs of which were written at this time, and the remainder in September following: [Sec.27.] (HC 1:106, August 1830.)

Heber C. Kimball: 1-4

When Christ instituted this supper he enjoyed its continuance upon the disciples, and we have been instructed to observe it in this generation. Jesus remarked at his last supper: "With desire I have desired to eat this passover with you before I suffer: For I say unto you, I will not any more eat thereof, until it is fulfilled in the kingdom of God. And he took the cup, and gave thanks, and said, Take this, and divide it among yourselves: For I say unto you, I will not drink of the fruit of the vine until the kingdom of God shall come. And he took bread, and gave thanks, and brake it, and gave unto them, saying, This is my body which is given for you: this do in remembrance of me. Likewise also the cup after supper, saying, This cup is the new testament in my blood, which is shed for you." (Luke 22:15-20.)

To some it may be a curiosity that we partake of water instead of wine. (Pres. B. Young: Tell them that the Lord told Joseph that he would accept of water.) Yes, the Lord has warned us against taking impure wine, and in a revelation given to Joseph Smith as early as September, 1830, he revealed his will on this subject in the following language: [Sec.27:1-2, quoted.] . . . let us be faithful and remember in partaking of this ordinance we renew our covenants, and we have a promise that we shall receive a renewal of the Holy Spirit, to enable us to be humble and to perform the duties that are enjoined upon us as saints. (JD, July 19, 1863, 10:244-45.)

Brigham Young: 3-4

By some it is very well understood that in the days of ancient Israel, while in the land of Palestine, they were not blessed so profusely as we are with the crystal streams from the mountains. They were in the habit of drinking a great deal of wine, and among the few who have continued to inhabit that land, this habit I believe has been kept up to the present time. It is a wine country. But the Lord has said to us it mattereth not what we partake of when we administer the cup to the people, inasmuch as we do it with an eye single to the glory of God; it is then acceptable to him. Consequently we use water as though it were wine; for we are commanded to drink not of wine for this sacred purpose except it be made by our own hands. (JD, August 19, 1877, 19:92.)

David W. Patten: 5-13

Now the thing to be known is, what the fulness of times means, or the extent or authority thereof. It means this, that the dispensation of the fulness of times is made up of all the dispensations that have been given since the world began, until this time. Unto Adam first was given a dispensation. It is well known that God spake to him with his own voice in the garden, and gave him the promise of the Messiah. [Moses 4:14-21; 5:9.] And unto Noah also was a dispensation given; for Jesus said, "As it was in the days of Noah, so shall it be also in the days of the Son of Man" [Matt. 24:37]; and as the righteous were saved then, and the wicked destroyed, so it will be now. And from Noah to Abraham, and from Abraham to Moses, and from Moses to Elias, and from Elias to John the Baptist, and from them to Jesus Christ, and from Jesus Christ to Peter, James and John, the Apostles — all received in their time a dispensation by revelation from God, to accomplish the great scheme of restitution spoken of by all the holy prophets since the world began; the end of which is the dispensation of the fulness of times, in the which all things shall be fulfilled that have been spoken of since the earth was made. [Sec. 128:20-21.]

Now the question is, unto whom is this dispensation to be given? Or by whom to be revealed? The answer is, to the deliverer that is to come out of Zion, and be given to him by the angel of God. "And I saw another angel fly in the midst of heaven, having the everlasting gospel to preach unto them that dwell on the earth, and to every nation, and kindred, and tongue, and people, saying with a loud voice, Fear God, and give glory to him: for the hour of his judgment is come: and worship him that made heaven and earth, and the sea, and the fountains of waters."(Revelation 14:6-7.) Now observe, this angel delivers the everlasting Gospel to man on the earth, and that, too, when the hour of the judgments of God had come on the generation in which the Lord should set his hand the second time to gather his people, as stated above. [Isa. 11:11.] Now we have learned that this deliverer must be clothed with the power of all the other dispensations, or his dispensation could not be called the dispensation of the fulness of times, for this it means, that all things shall be revealed both in heaven and on earth [Eph. 1:9-10]; for the Lord said there is nothing secret that shall not be revealed, and this may with propriety be called the fulness of times. . . . For those holy men are angels now, and these are they who make the fulness of times complete with us; and they who sin against this authority given to him (the aforementioned man of God), sin not against him only, but against Moroni, who holds the keys of the stick of Ephraim [Book of Mormon], and also Elias, who holds the keys of bringing to pass the restitution of all things. . . . [Sec. 27:7-13, quoted.] (HC 3:51-53, July 31, 1838.)

Joseph Smith: 5-13

Most generally, when angels have come, or God has revealed himself, it has been to individuals in private, in their chamber, in the wilderness or fields, and that generally without noise or tumult. The angel delivered Peter out of prison in the dead of night [Acts 5:9]; came to Paul unobserved by the rest of the crew [Acts 27:23-24]; appeared to Mary and Elizabeth without the knowledge of others [Luke 1:28-30]; spoke to John the Baptist whilst the people around were ignorant of it. [John 5:36-38.] (HC 5:31, June 15, 1842.)

Joseph F. Smith: 5-13

It is the extreme of foolishness for a man to rise up and say, because those who have gone to the beyond have not appeared to him, therefore they have not returned, that no one has returned from the great beyond to prove we do go on, and to teach such nonsense in his ignorance to the people, because it appeals to his reason. He never will receive such visitations and knowledge as long as he holds to such views, and rejects the Lord Jesus Christ as the Redeemer of the world. (CR, April 1916, p. 72.)

Joseph Smith: 5-13

The dispensation of the fulness of times will bring to light the things that have been revealed in all former dispensations; also other things that have not been before revealed. [Sec. 124:41.] (HC 4:426, October 2, 1841.)

James E. Talmage: 5
I will drink of the fruit of the vine with you

Can a resurrected being eat food of earth? [Luke 24:39-43.] A resurrected being can function upon any lower plane. A resurrected personage can do anything that a mortal personage can do, and much besides. (CR, April 1928, p. 93.)

Joseph Fielding Smith: 7
Which Zacharias he (Elias)

It was Gabriel who appeared to Zacharias and promised him a son, and who appeared to Mary and announced the coming of the Son of God as recorded by Luke. It was also Gabriel as an Elias who is mentioned in the Doctrine and Covenants, Section 27, verse 7, and was Gabriel or Noah, who stands next to Michael or Adam in the Priesthood. (CR, April 1960, p. 72.)

John Taylor: 13
A dispensation . . . for the fulness of times

It is called the "dispensation of the fulness of times," wherein God will gather together all things in one, whether they be things in the heavens or things in the earth. It is a dispensation in which all the holy prophets that ever lived upon the face of the earth are interested. They prophesied about it as the grand and great consummation in the accomplishment of the purposes of God [Acts 3:19-21]; purposes which he designed before the morning stars sang together, or the sons of God shouted for joy, or this world itself rolled into existence. It is a work in which we, our progenitors and our posterity are especially interested. . . . We are indebted to God for the revelation of all those principles that we today possess, whether they relate to the Church of God, to the Zion of God, or to the kingdom of God; so far as any principles thereof have been made manifest and developed unto us they are truly, positively and unequivocally the gift of God our Heavenly Father. They did not originate with us. They did not originate with any man that lived on the earth, for no man knew them. They did not originate with Joseph Smith, or with Brigham Young, or with myself, or with the Apostles, or with any class of men in this Church. They are the gift of God to his people, to his children who dwell upon the earth. (JD, June 24, 1883, 24:260-61.)

Lorenzo Snow: 14

No matter what condition we are in, we ought to have that understanding that we can do all our labors, whatever they may be, as the Lord pleases that we should to them. . . . Those who endure unto the end shall sit upon thrones as Jesus hath overcome and sat down upon his Father's throne. All things shall be given unto such men and women, so we are told in the revelations we have received. [Sec. 76:58-60; 84:38.] In view of these prospects, what should we not be willing to sacrifice when duty requires? It is a great thing, we say, for a man to be an Apostle; yet there are things you can look forward to which are greater than his. . . . The glory that is before us is open to every man and every women, through this Gospel, which is the power of God unto salvation, glory and exaltation, in the fulness thereof. (CR, October 1898, pp. 55-56.)

Brigham Young: 15-18

The men and women who desire to obtain seats in the

celestial kingdom will find that they must battle with the enemy of all righteousness every day. "Stand therefore, having your loins girt about with truth, and having on the breastplate of righteousness; and your feet shod with the preparation of the gospel of peace; above all, taking the shield of faith, wherewith ye shall be able to quench all the fiery darts of the wicked. And take the helmet of salvation, and the sword of the Spirit, which is the work of God: Praying always with all prayer and supplication in the Spirit, and watching thereunto with all perserverance and supplication for all saints." [Eph. 6:14-18.] Thus let every saint protect and guard his little castle against every effort of the enemy to assail and secure a foothold therein. Let us see to it that we are ready for the enemy to baffle him at every point, contending bravely against him until he is successfully repulsed. (JD, December 11, 1864, 11:14.)

Harold B. Lee: 15-18

We have the four parts of the body that . . . [are] the most vulnerable to the powers of darkness. The loins, typifying virtue, chastity. The heart, typifying our conduct; our feet, our goals or objectives in life; and finally, our head, our thoughts. . . .

We should have our loins girt about with truth. What is truth? Truth, the Lord said, is knowledge of things as they are, things as they were, and things as they are to come.[Sec. 93:24.] What is going to guide us along the path of proper morals or proper choices? It will be the knowledge of truth. There must be a standard by which we measure our conduct, else how shall we know which is right? And how shall we know which is wrong? How do we know it is wrong to steal? How do we know it is wrong to lie? How do we know it is wrong to kill, unless we have a knowledge of the truth, that written by the finger of God on tables of stone were the divine injunctions, thou shalt not. "Our loins shall be girt about with truth," the prophet said.

And the heart, what kind of breastplate shall protect our conduct in life? We shall have over our hearts a breastplate of righteousness. Well, having learned truth we have a measure by which we can judge between right and wrong, and so our conduct will always be gauged by that thing which we know to be true. Our breastplate to cover our conduct shall be the breastplate of righteousness.

By what shall we protect our feet, or by what shall we gauge our objectives or our goals in life? . . ."Your feet shall be shod with the preparation of the gospel of peace." [Eph. 6:15.] Interesting? What is the gospel of peace? The whole core and center of the gospel of peace was built around the person of him who was cradled in the manger, of whom on that night the angels sang, "Glory to God in the highest, and on earth, peace, good will to men." Or to put it even more correctly, "on earth peace to men of good will." Our feet should be shod with the preparation of the gospel of peace to them of good will. . . .

"Train a child in the way he shall go and when he is old he will not depart from it" [Proverbs 22:6], the old adage said. . . . How fortunate are you if in your childhood in the home of your father and mother you were taught the doctrine of repentance, faith in Christ, the Son of the living God, the meaning of baptism and what you gain by the laying on of hands for the gift of the Holy Ghost. Fortunate is the child who has been taught to pray and who has been given those steps to take on through life. Feet shod with the preparation of the gospel of peace! . . .

And then finally, the helmet of salvation. Did you ever hear of what kind of helmet? The helmet of salvation. What is salvation? Salvation is to be saved. Saved from what? Saved from death and saved from sin. . . .

A helmet of salvation shall guide our thinking all through our days. Well, as we think that through, let me review them again for just a moment, to get the full significance. Truth to safeguard our virtue; righteousness to keep our conduct right; the preparation of the gospel of peace to guide our course and to set our standards and aims in life; salvation, a return back to the presence of the Lord, shall be the inhibiting promise and a motivating objective to guide us on to the victory of life over death. That is what it means. . . .

... [The] armoured man holds in his hand a shield and in his other hand a sword, which were the weapons of those days. The shield was the shield of faith and the sword was the sword of the spirit, which is the Word of God. I can't think of any more powerful weapons than faith and a knowledge of the scriptures, in which are contained the Word of God. One so armoured and one so prepared with those weapons is prepared to go out against the enemy that is more to be feared than the enemies that strike in the darkness of the night, that we can't see with our eyes. (*BYU Speeches of the Year*, November 9, 1954.)

Francis M. Lyman: 18

By observance of the laws of the Lord we are led in the straight and narrow way, and the Holy Spirit alone can keep us there. We have power to so live that the Spirit of the Lord may dwell with us. We cannot be Latter-day Saints without the Spirit of the Lord; and should not try to live without it. Do not try to speak without the Spirit of the Lord; do not try to build up the kingdom of God without the direction of his Spirit. If we endeavor to do these things by our own wisdom we will be sure to go astray and make mistakes. It is the office and calling of the Spirit of the Lord to dwell with you always; to be in your homes, with your families; in your neighborhoods, and in your business affairs, on the Sabbath day and throughout the week, and every day in the year, if you do right. (CR, April 1904, p. 13.)

SECTION 28

Revelation given through Joseph Smith the Prophet, to Oliver Cowdery, at Fayette, New York, September, 1830. Hiram Page, a member of the Church, had a certain stone and professed to be receiving revelations by its aid concerning the upbuilding of Zion and the order of the Church. Several members had been deceived by these claims, and even Oliver Cowdery was wrongly influenced thereby. Just prior to an appointed conference, the Prophet inquired earnestly of the Lord concerning the matter and this revelation followed. See History of the Church, vol. 1, p. 109. – Joseph's position of presidency defined – Oliver warned against undue assumption – Oliver's mission to the Lamanites stated – He to labor with Hiram Page, whom Satan had deceived – Hiram Page not appointed by the Lord nor accepted by the people as a revelator to the Church.

1. Behold, I say unto thee, Oliver, that it shall be given unto thee that thou shalt be heard by the church in all things whatsoever thou shalt teach them by the Comforter, concerning the revelations and commandments which I have given.

2. But, behold, verily, verily, I say unto thee, no one shall be appointed to receive commandments and revelations in this church excepting my servant Joseph Smith, Jun., for he receiveth them even as Moses.

3. And thou shalt be obedient unto the things which I shall give unto him, even as Aaron, to declare faithfully the commandments and the revelations, with power and authority unto the church.

4. And if thou are led at any time by the Comforter to speak or teach, or at all times by the way of commandment unto the church, thou mayest do it.

5. But thou shalt not write by way of commandment, but by wisdom;

6. And thou shalt not command him who is at thy head, and at the head of the church;

7. For I have given him the keys of the mysteries, and the revelations which are sealed, until I shall appoint unto them another in his stead.

8. And now, behold, I say unto you that you shall go unto the Lamanites and preach my gospel unto them; and inasmuch as they receive thy teachings thou shalt cause my church to be established among them; and thou shalt have revelations, but write them not by way of commandment.

9. And now, behold, I say unto you that it is not revealed, and no man knoweth where the city Zion shall be built, but it shall be given hereafter. Behold, I say unto you that it shall be on the borders by the Lamanites.

10. Thou shalt not leave this place until after the conference; and my servant Joseph shall be appointed to preside over the conference by the voice of it, and what he saith to thee thou shalt tell.

11. And again, thou shalt take thy brother, Hiram Page, between him and thee alone, and tell him that those things which he hath written from that stone are not of me and that Satan deceiveth him;

12. For, behold, these things have not been appointed unto him, neither shall anything be appointed unto any of this church contrary to the church covenants.

13. For all things must be done in order, and by common consent in the church, by the prayer of faith.

14. And thou shalt assist to settle all these things, according to the covenants of the church, before thou shalt take thy journey among the Lamanites.

15. And it shall be given thee from the time thou shalt go, until the time thou shalt return, what thou shalt do.

16. And thou must open thy mouth at all times, declaring my gospel with the sound of rejoicing. Amen.

Joseph Smith: *Introduction*

To our great grief, however, we soon found that Satan had been lying in wait to deceive, and seeking whom he might devour. Brother Hiram Page had in his possession a certain stone, by which he had obtained certain "revelations" concerning the upbuilding of Zion, the order of the Church, etc., all of which were entirely at variance with the order of God's house as laid down in the New Testament, as well as in our late revelations. As a conference meeting had been appointed for the 26th day of September, I thought it wisdom not to do much more than to converse with the brethren on the subject, until the conference should meet. Finding, however, that many, especially the Whitmer family and Oliver Cowdery, were believing much in the things set forth by this stone, we thought best to inquire of the Lord concerning so important a matter; and before conference convened, we received the following: [Section 28.] (*HC* 1:109-10, September 1830; Fayette, New York.)

First Presidency (Joseph F. Smith, Anthon H. Lund, Charles W. Penrose): 1-7

To the officers and members of The Church of Jesus Christ of Latter-day Saints:

From the days of Hiram Page (D&C 28), at different periods there have been manifestations from delusive spirits to members of the Church. Sometimes these have come to the men and women who, because of transgression, became easy prey to the arch-deceiver. At other times people who pride themselves on their strict observance of the rules and ordinances and ceremonies of the Church are led astray by false spirits, who exercise an influence so imitative of that which proceeds from a divine source that even these persons, who think they are "the very elect," find it difficult to discern the essential difference. Satan himself has transformed himself to be apparently "an angel of light." [Sec. 129:8.]

When visions, dreams, tongues, prophecy, impressions or any extraordinary gift of inspiration, convey something out of harmony with accepted revelations of the Church or contrary to the decisions of its constituted authorities, Latter-day Saints may know that it is not of God, no matter how plausible it may appear. Also, they should understand that directions for the guidance of the Church will come, by revelation, through the head. All faithful members are entitled to the inspiration of the Holy Spirit for themselves, their families, and for those over whom they are appointed and ordained to preside. But anything at discord with that which comes from God through the head of the Church is not to be received as authoritative or reliable. In secular as well as spiritual affairs, saints may receive divine guidance and revelation affecting themselves, but this does not convey authority to direct others, and is not to be accepted when contrary to Church covenants, doctrine or discipline, or to known facts, demonstrated truths, or good common sense. [Sec. 42:13; 97:8.] No person has the right to induce his fellow members of the Church to engage in speculations or take stock in ventures of any kind on the specious claim of divine revelation, or vision, or dream, especially when it is in opposition to the voice of recognized authority, local or general. The Lord's Church "is a house of order." [Sec. 132:8.] It is not governed by individual gifts or manifestations, but by the order and power of the Holy Priesthood as sustained by the voice and vote of the Church in its appointed conferences. [Sec. 124:143-44.]

The history of the Church records many pretended revelations claimed by imposters or zealots who believed in the manifestations they sought to lead other persons to accept, and in every instance, disappointment, sorrow and disaster have resulted therefrom. Financial loss and sometimes utter ruin have followed. We feel it our duty to warn the Latter-day Saints against fake mining schemes which have no warrant for success beyond the professed spiritual manifestations of their projectors and the influence gained over the excited minds of their victims. We caution the saints against investing money or property in shares of stock which bring no profit to anyone but those who issue and trade in them. Fanciful schemes to make money for the alleged purpose of "redeeming Zion" or providing means for "the salvation of the dead" or other seemingly worthy objects, should not deceive anyone acquainted with the order of the Church, and will result only in waste of time and labor, which might be devoted now to doing something tangible and worthy and of record on earth and in heaven.

Be not led by any spirit or influence that discredits established authority and contradicts true scientific principles and discoveries, or leads away from the direct revelations of God for the government of the Church. The Holy Ghost does not contradict its own revealings. Truth is always harmonious with itself. Piety is often the cloak of error. [Sec. 52:14-16.] The counsels of the Lord through the channel he has appointed will be followed with safety, therefore, Oh! ye Latter-day Saints, profit by these words of warning. (*IE*, September 1913, 16:1148-49.)

John A. Widtsoe: 1-7

For a number of years I was engaged in reading the sermons of Brigham Young, having in mind a compilation of his wise sayings for the benefit of the saints. I was amazed to note how closely, how carefully, he followed the doctrine laid down by the Prophet Joseph Smith, who himself only taught the pure, unchanged Gospel of the Lord Jesus Christ. As I read on, studying the teachings of those who came after Brigham Young, I found the same thing to be true. I have listened in this tabernacle, for many years, to the words of President Heber J. Grant, and I have found him likewise a teacher of the same doctrine that was taught by Joseph Smith, by Brigham Young, and by the others who have preceded President Grant in his high office. There has been no deviation in his teachings from fundamental truth; not by a hair's breadth.

In this changelessness of fundamental teaching lies not only a testimony of the truth of this great work, but also a principle of comfort to all who belong to the Church. I belong to various scientific societies. In them I find that theories come and go. We all belong to various organizations, political parties, and we observe that from day to day the principles that guide the membership of these associations seem to vary, to change. I can cling safely to the Church, to the Gospel of Jesus Christ; it has steadying power, it does not change nor vary. It is the same today, yesterday and forever. . . .

Do not misunderstand me as I speak on this theme. Every man clothes his ideas in his own words. Joseph Smith did not speak as Heber J. Grant speaks. The principles, the ideas were the same, but the words used, the forms of expression, belong to the speaker; and every man has a right to express as best he can in the words God gives him, the eternal truths that he may obtain from a divine source.

Again, do not misunderstand me. I do not mean that this Church and kingdom is static, that we stand still. I believe in a living, growing Church, which is in need of and does receive revelation from day to day. Nothing is more certain to me than that we are founded on revelation from God, and that we are guided daily by such revelation. We shall have revelation for our guidance to the end of time; but such new revelations as may come will never supersede, destroy or abrogate the fundamental principles upon which this Church rests its body of doctrine. A new revelation merely adds and develops and more nearly completes that which has formerly been given.

The conditions of our people, the Latter-day Saints, in the days of Ohio, Missouri and Illinois, were as different from the conditions of today, almost as night is from day. Our people then lived under pioneer conditions, with no knowledge of the things which have given us the most remarkable mechanical civilization of all earthly time. We cannot expect that the exact application of the eternal principles of the Gospel should be the same today as in the days of Ohio or Missouri, but we do expect that any new revelation will be very largely the application of the eternal principles of truth to present needs. I rejoice that, as far as I have been able to read the history of the Church and as I have lived life in the Church, I have seen from day to day such application of fundamental eternal unchanging laws of the Gospel to the needs of the changing existing today. (CR, October 1934, pp. 9-10.)

George Q. Cannon: 5
Thou shalt not write by way of commandment

Oliver Cowdery . . . received at the same time that the Prophet Joseph did the Aaronic Priesthood. . . . He afterwards received, in common with Joseph, the administration of those who held the keys of the Apostleship in the flesh on the earth — that is, Peter, James and John. They administered unto him at the same time that they administered unto Joseph, upon the same occasion, and he became an Apostle with Joseph, being the second Apostle in The Church of Jesus Christ of Latter-day Saints. Now, it might be thought a man thus favored, favored to receive the Aaronic Priesthood, favored with the privilege of baptizing the Prophet of God, I say, that a man thus favored would have stood alongside of the Prophet and been of equal authority in giving the word of God in writing unto the people. But no. God drew a distinction and plainly told Oliver Cowdery that that which he wrote to this Church should not be by way of commandments to the Church, but by wisdom. The Lord said to him [Sec. 28:4, quoted]. It was only one man's privilege, one man's authority to stand pre-eminent in the earth at one time, holding the keys and giving the commandments of God — or rather the Lord — giving his commandments through him in writing to the Church. (JD, December 2, 1883, 24:363-64.)

Joseph Smith: 6
Thou shalt not command him who is at thy head

I will inform you that it is contrary to the economy of God for any member of the Church, or anyone, to receive instructions for those in authority, higher than themselves; therefore, you will see the impropriety of giving heed to them; but if any person have a vision or a visitation from a heavenly messenger, it must be for his own benefit and instruction, for the fundamental principles, government, and doctrine of the Church are vested in the keys of the kingdom. (HC 1:388, April 13, 1833.)

George Q. Cannon: 13

God gave revelations unto this Church in exceeding great plainness, and there was one principle that was emphatically dwelt on and enforced, namely, that there was but one channel, one channel alone, through which the word of God and the commandments of God should come to this people. The word of God was not to come from the people up. It was not *vox populi, vox dei,* but it was to be *vox dei, vox populi* — that is, the voice of God and then the voice of the people — from God downward through the channel that he should appoint, by the means that he should institute, that word should come to the people, and when obeyed by the people would bring the union and love and the strength consequent upon union and love. And this has been the peculiarity and the excellence of this work of God thus far in the earth. Its excellence has consisted in this. Its power, its glory, the glory that we have as a people, the glory that belongs to the Church of God consists in this peculiar feature, that the word of God to us comes from God and not from the people. It is received by the people, accepted by the people, submitted to by the people, and this has produced the union and the love, as I have said, that have characterized the word thus far in its progress in the earth. (JD, December 2, 1883, 24:362-63.)

Delbert L. Stapley: 13

If the members of the Church will follow this counsel and act together in prayer and true faith, the Holy Ghost will not permit them to yield to the influence of error and false teachings of those who seek to overthrow the work of God. The great Nephite prophet, Mosiah, warning his people against kingcraft, counseled them concerning the manner in which judges to govern them should be selected, and wisely advised:

"Now it is not common that the voice of the people desireth anything contrary to that which is right; but it is common for the lesser part of the people to desire that which is not right; therefore, this shall ye observe and make it your law — to do your business by the voice of the people." (Mosiah 29:26.)

All wavering and disaffected individuals should remember the safeguards to faith and testimony given by the Lord through revelation, and, recognizing and working through constituted channels of priesthood authority, submit their views or claims and be willing to abide by the voice of the people, who, conforming to the above-quoted revelation [Sec. 26:27], are to decide the matter after exercising much faith and prayer. If they would do this before permitting themselves to follow a deviating or contrary course, and manifest the faith to abide by the voice of the Saints, they would not go astray nor depart from the right way, and their souls and those of their posterity would, through obedience to the commandments, be saved in the kingdom of God. (CR, October 1959, p. 73.)

SECTION 29

Revelation given through Joseph Smith the Prophet, in the presence of six Elders, at Fayette, New York, September, 1830. This revelation was given some days prior to the conference beginning September 26, 1830. — The gathering of the elect specified — The imminence of the Lord's advent affirmed — Calamities incident to the sinful state of the world — The Millennium and scenes of judgment to follow — Distinction between the spiritual and temporal creations — Purpose of the mortal probation — The agency of man — The assured redemption of children who die in infancy.

1. Listen to the voice of Jesus Christ, your Redeemer, the Great I AM, whose arm of mercy hath atoned for your sins;

2. Who will gather his people even as a hen gathereth her chickens under her wings, even as many as will hearken to my voice and humble themselves before me, and call upon me in mighty prayer.

3. Behold, verily, verily, I say unto you, that at this time your sins are forgiven you, therefore ye receive these things; but remember to sin no more, lest perils shall come upon you.

4. Verily, I say unto you that ye are chosen out of the world to declare my gospel with the sound of rejoicing, as with the voice of a trump.

5. Lift up your hearts and be glad, for I am in your midst, and am your advocate with the Father; and it is his good will to give you the kingdom.

6. And, as it is written — Whatsoever ye shall ask in faith, being united in prayer according to my command, ye shall receive.

7. And ye are called to bring to pass the gathering of mine elect; for mine elect hear my voice and harden not their hearts;

8. Wherefore the decree hath gone forth from the Father that they shall be gathered in unto one place upon the face of this land, to prepare their hearts and be prepared in all things against the day when tribulation and desolation are sent forth upon the wicked.

9. For the hour is nigh and the day soon at hand when the earth is ripe; and all the proud and they that do wickedly shall be as stubble; and I will burn them up, saith the Lord of Hosts, that wickedness shall not be upon the earth;

10. For the hour is nigh, and that which was spoken by mine apostles must be fulfilled; for as they spoke so shall it come to pass;

11. For I will reveal myself from heaven with power and great glory, with all the hosts thereof, and dwell in righteousness

with men on earth a thousand years, and the wicked shall not stand.

12. And again, verily, verily, I say unto you, and it hath gone forth in a firm decree, by the will of the Father, that mine apostles, the Twelve which were with me in my ministry at Jerusalem, shall stand at my right hand at the day of my coming in a pillar of fire, being clothed with robes of righteousness, with crowns upon their heads, in glory even as I am, to judge the whole house of Israel, even as many as have loved me and kept my commandments, and none else.

13. For a trump shall sound both long and loud, even as upon Mount Sinai, and all the earth shall quake, and they shall come forth — yea, even the dead which died in me, to receive a crown of righteousness, and to be clothed upon, even as I am, to be with me, that we may be one.

14. But, behold, I say unto you that before this great day shall come the sun shall be darkened, and the moon shall be turned into blood, and the stars shall fall from heaven, and there shall be greater signs in heaven above and in the earth beneath;

15. And there shall be weeping and wailing among the hosts of men;

16. And there shall be a great hailstorm sent forth to destroy the crops of the earth.

17. And it shall come to pass, because of the wickedness of the world, that I will take vengeance upon the wicked, for they will not repent; for the cup of mine indignation is full; for behold, my blood shall not cleanse them if they hear me not.

18. Wherefore, I the Lord God will send forth flies upon the face of the earth, which shall take hold of the inhabitants thereof, and shall eat their flesh, and shall cause maggots to come in upon them;

19. And their tongues shall be stayed that they shall not utter against me; and their flesh shall fall from off their bones, and their eyes from their sockets;

20. And it shall come to pass that the beasts of the forest and the fowls of the air shall devour them up.

21. And the great and abominable church, which is the whore of all the earth, shall be cast down by devouring fire, according as it is spoken by the mouth of Ezekiel the prophet, who spoke of these things, which have not come to pass but surely must, as I live, for abominations shall not reign.

22. And again, verily, verily, I say unto you that when the thousand years are ended, and men again begin to deny their God, then will I spare the earth but for a little season;

23. And the end shall come, and the heaven and the earth shall be consumed and pass away, and there shall be a new

heaven and a new earth.

24. For all old things shall pass away, and all things shall become new, even the heaven and the earth, and all the fulness thereof, both men and beasts, the fowls of the air, and the fishes of the sea;

25. And not one hair, neither mote, shall be lost, for it is the workmanship of mine hand.

26. But, behold, verily I say unto you, before the earth shall pass away, Michael, mine archangel, shall sound his trump, and then shall all the dead awake, for their graves shall be opened, and they shall come forth — yea, even all.

27. And the righteous shall be gathered on my right hand unto eternal life; and the wicked on my left hand will I be ashamed to own before the Father;

28. Wherefore I will say unto them — Depart from me, ye cursed, into everlasting fire, prepared for the devil and his angels.

29. And now, behold, I say unto you, never at any time have I declared from mine own mouth that they should return, for where I am they cannot come, for they have not power.

30. But remember that all my judgments are not given unto men; and as the words have gone forth out of my mouth even so shall they be fulfilled, that the first shall be last, and that the last shall be first in all things whatsoever I have created by the word of my power, which is the power of my Spirit.

31. For by the power of my Spirit created I them; yea, all things both spiritual and temporal—

32. First spiritual, secondly temporal, which is the beginning of my work; and again, first temporal, and secondly spiritual, which is the last of my work—

33. Speaking unto you that you may naturally understand; but unto myself my works have no end, neither beginning; but it is given unto you that ye may understand, because ye have asked it of me and are agreed.

34. Wherefore, verily I say unto you that all things unto me are spiritual, and not at any time have I given unto you a law which was temporal; neither any man, nor the children of men; neither Adam, your father, whom I created.

35. Behold, I gave unto him that he should be an agent unto himself; and I gave unto him commandment, but no temporal commandment gave I unto him, for my commandments are spiritual; they are not natural nor temporal, neither carnal nor sensual.

36. And it came to pass that Adam, being tempted of the devil — for, behold, the devil was before Adam, for he rebelled against me, saying, Give me thine honor, which is my power; and also a third part of the hosts of heaven turned he away from me

because of their agency;

37. And they were thrust down, and thus came the devil and his angels;

38. And, behold, there is a place prepared for them from the beginning, which place is hell.

39. And it must needs be that the devil should tempt the children of men, or they could not be agents unto themselves; for if they never should have bitter they could not know the sweet—

40. Wherefore, it came to pass that the devil tempted Adam, and he partook of the forbidden fruit and transgressed the commandment, wherein he became subject to the will of the devil, because he yielded unto temptation.

41. Wherefore, I, the Lord God, caused that he should be cast out from the Garden of Eden, from my presence, because of his transgression, wherein he became spiritually dead, which is the first death, even that same death which is the last death, which is spiritual, which shall be pronounced upon the wicked when I shall say: Depart, ye cursed.

42. But, behold, I say unto you that I, the Lord God, gave unto Adam and unto his seed, that they should not die as to the temporal death, until I, the Lord God, should send forth angels to declare unto them repentance and redemption, through faith on the name of mine Only Begotten Son.

43. And thus did I, the Lord God, appoint unto man the days of his probation — that by his natural death he might be raised in immortality unto eternal life, even as many as would believe;

44. And they that believe not unto eternal damnation; for they cannot be redeemed from their spiritual fall, because they repent not;

45. For they love darkness rather than light, and their deeds are evil, and they receive their wages of whom they list to obey.

46. But behold, I say unto you, that little children are redeemed from the foundation of the world through mine Only Begotten;

47. Wherefore, they cannot sin, for power is not given unto Satan to tempt little children, until they begin to become accountable before me;

48. For it is given unto them even as I will, according to mine own pleasure, that great things may be required at the hand of their fathers.

49. And, again, I say unto you, that whoso having knowledge, have I not commanded to repent?

50. And he that hath no understanding, it remaineth in me to do according as it is written. And now I declare no more unto you at this time. Amen.

Joseph Fielding Smith: *Introduction*

In these early days of the Church the Lord revealed to the Prophet for the benefit of the members, line upon line and precept upon precept, thus unfolding to them the great truths of the Gospel. This revelation [Sec. 29] was given a few days before the conference of September 26, 1830, and in anticipation of that gathering. The Lord had commanded Oliver Cowdery to tarry [Sec. 28:10] until after this conference should be held, before departing on his mission to the Lamanites. The wonderful doctrines explained in this revelation were of such importance that it was well for Oliver and his companions to know them that they might teach the people on their way, and to the Lamanites when they arrived at their destination, with a more complete comprehension of the plan of Salvation than they otherwise would have had. This revelation is very comprehensive. (*CHMR*, 1947, 1:130.)

James E. Talmage: 1
The Great I AM

Jesus of Nazareth, who in solemn testimony to the Jews declared himself the *I Am* or *Jehovah*, who was God before Abraham lived on earth, was the same Being who is repeatedly proclaimed as the God who made covenant with Abraham, Isaac, and Jacob; the God who led Israel from the bondage of Egypt to the freedom of the promised land, the one and only God known by direct and personal revelation to the Hebrew prophets in general.

The identity of Jesus Christ with the Jehovah of the Israelites was well understood by the Nephite prophets, and the truth of their teachings was confirmed by the risen Lord who manifested himself unto them shortly after his ascension from the midst of the apostles at Jerusalem. This is the record: "And it came to pass that the Lord spake unto them saying: Arise and come forth unto me, that ye may thrust your hands into my side, and also that ye may feel the prints of the nails in my hands and in my feet, that ye may know that I am the God of Israel, and the God of the whole earth, and have been slain for the sins of the world." (3 Nephi 11:13-14.) (*Jesus the Christ*, 1916, p. 38.)

Franklin D. Richards: 2
Who will gather his people

Looking on down to our own time, we see that we live in the dispensation of the fulness of times, in which the Lord has promised to gather together in one all things which are in Christ, both which are in heaven and which are upon earth. This is according to scripture, and this is what we are working at. As soon as the Gospel was first preached to the people, they felt the spirit of gathering. When the Presidency, from the Kirtland Temple, sent Elders over to the old country and instructed them not to teach gathering particularly at present, why the people got to dreaming about gathering and about Zion. It could not be kept from them. The spirit of the work was upon them. Thus the spirit of gathering comes upon the Saints wherever the Gospel is preached to them, and there arises within them an inclination to want to leave where they have become strangers, to go to people whose faith is like their own, with whom they are acquainted in the Lord and have fellowship together. (CR, April 1899, p. 44.)

Francis M. Lyman: 4
Ye are chosen... to declare my gospel

You know that your mission in the world is for the salvation of the souls of the children of men, including your own souls. You are not allowed to be wicked and corrupt. If you are a thief we deal with you for your fellowship . Dishonesty, unvirtuous conduct, lying and thieving are not tolerated among the Latter-day Saints. We have not gone into the world to gather people who indulge in such evil practices; but we have labored all the time to gather the honest, the conscientious, the upright, and those who would be obedient and pure in their lives. If they are not willing to submit to these requirements, we do not want them. We cannot save them in their sins; they must repent and reform. If they do not do this, the Gospel has no chance to save them. The atonement wrought out by the Savior has relieved us of the sin of our first parents, and has brought us into communion with the Lord; but we are responsible for our own transgressions. We must repent of them. Baptism is unavailing without repentance. Faith that does not produce repentance is unavailing. But the faith that has been restored to us through the mission of the Prophet Joseph Smith is a vital faith. It moves men to repentance and reformation, and to keeping the commandments of the Lord. It opens the way that we may know the Father and the Son; that we may know the Prophets, and that we may comprehend the principles of the Gospel. (CR, April 1901, pp. 48-49.)

Franklin D. Richards: 5
It is his good will to give you the kingdom

The Lord says, in the Book of Doctrine and Covenants, that it is his good pleasure to give to his people the kingdom. He told the early Elders to be of good cheer; "it is your Father's good pleasure to give you the kingdom." Now the kingdom of God has come; that is today, the government, the priesthood, the ordinances and the principles of salvation are revealed to us to build up the Church of Christ, as we may have it to build up until the Savior shall come, or until the prophets shall come and reveal to us more than we have already attained to.

I recollect very distinctly hearing the Prophet Joseph say that the kingdom had come, but the will was not done yet on the earth as it was done in heaven; and in order that the sisters especially might understand it, he said, "You sisters can understand it by this little similitude. When you scald out your milk pan, you have the milk pan." "Yes." "But it is not full of milk?" "No, of course not." "Now, here the kingdom has come, but his will is not done on earth yet as it is done in heaven. The milkpan is not filled up yet in doing the will of God." We are here to learn and to toil to this end; not only those who are grey-haired and bald-headed, but the boys and girls. It is for all of us to do the works of righteousness and faith, that the will of God may be done on earth as it is done in heaven, so that there may not only be a milkpan, but a pan of milk. (CR, April 1899, p. 47.)

LeGrand Richards: 7-8

In September 1830, only five months after the Church was organized, and five and a half years before Moses brought the keys of the gathering of Israel and committed them to Joseph Smith and Oliver Cowdery, the Lord, in a revelation to the Prophet Joseph Smith, made a very definite statement on this subject: [Sec. 29:7-8, quoted.]

Thus, the first elders of the Church were "called to bring to pass the gathering of mine elect," so that from the very beginning of the Church, the Latter-day Saints have been "gathering." Their first place of gathering was at Kirtland, Ohio. . . .

While the Lord has indicated that his Zion of the latter-days, to which Israel should be gathered, should be in the land of America, and that the New Jerusalem (Ether 13:1-13) should be built upon this land, it is obvious that such a gathering could not be to but one city. In fulfilment of the command of the Lord in this matter, the Latter-day Saints have built over six hundred cities, to which have been gathered converts to the new faith from many countries. This gathering has been continuous from the organization of the Church unto the present time. (*A Marvelous Work and a Wonder*, 1950, pp. 181, 183.)

George Q. Cannon: 7
Mine elect hear my voice

There is an absence of moral purity in the people. Nearly all have gone astray, and have corrupted themselves to such an extent as to drive that portion of the Spirit of God from them with which every man and woman is endowed who comes into the world. Where people are pure and chaste in their thoughts and actions, the Spirit of God has such power with them that they readily perceive and comprehend the truth. It is by this means that the best among the children of God are being gathered out from the nations. Truth cleaves to truth, light to light and purity to purity. [Sec. 88:40.] The Gospel gathers within its influence those who love its principles; and if any should be gathered in who cannot abide its requirements, they pass off and mingle with the elements that are congenial to the spirit they possess. (MS, 1863, 25:169.)

John Taylor: 8
They shall be gathered ... upon the face of this land

And when you have gathered, many of you think it is a curious kind of Zion, don't you? It is; for while the net gathers in the good, it brings in all kinds as well, good and bad. We have some very good fish, and some very bad ones, and some a kind of half and half, and some feel like saying "Good Lord and good devil," as they do not know into whose hands they may fall. Nevertheless, this is the order, and the wheat and tares, I suppose, have got to grow together until the harvest comes, and that is not quite here yet, and hence we are jostling one against another and some of us hardly know whether it is us or somebody else. Difficulties and trials beset us, and we are amazed. But we are here, and we are here according to the command of God and according to the operation of the Spirit of God that rests upon us, and did rest upon us, and led us here, and I was going to say, we are here because we could not help it. (JD, January 14, 1880, 21:67.)

James E. Talmage: 9-11

This Church proclaims the doctrine of the impending return of the Christ to earth in literal simplicity, without mental or other reservation in our interpretation of the scriptural predictions. He will come with the body of flesh and bones in which his Spirit was tabernacled when he ascended from Mount Olivet. One of the characteristic features of the Church concerning that great, and in the language of the scripture, both glorious and terrible event, is its nearness. It is close at hand. The mission of the Church is to prepare the earth for the coming of its Lord. Biblical prophecies are numerous [Luke 21:7-28; Mark 8:38; Acts 1:11; 1 Thess. 4:16]; the Book of Mormon prophecies are abundant, respecting the return of the Christ. [1 Ne. 22:24; Mosiah 15:20; 3 Ne. 21:25; 29:2.] His own words, both before and after his crucifixion and resurrection are unambiguous, definite, convincing, and convicting unto those

who do not close their ears wilfully against the truth. Refer-
ring to himself the Savior said: "For the Son of man shall
come in glory of his Father with his angels; and then he shall
reward every man according to his works." Read the context
in the 16th chapter of Matthew. The Prophets who lived
before the meridian of time said comparatively little, though
their testimony is abundant and all sufficient, concerning
the return of the Christ; for they were devoted to the teaching of the doctrine of his first coming in the flesh, to live
among men, to suffer and to die among men, to be resurrected from the dead. But after his resurrection and ascension the words of inspired teachers were definite in foretelling the certainty of his return; and in this day and age of the
world he has spoken with his own voice unto his prophets,
impressing upon them the fact that the time of his coming in
judgment is near at hand. [Sec. 34:7, 8, 12; 63:34; 133:17.]
Thus, within a few months after the Church was organized,
in the year 1830, as recorded in the 29th section of the
Doctrine and Covenants, the Lord Jesus Christ said unto his
Prophet Joseph Smith: [Sec. 29:9-11, quoted.] (CR, April
1916, pp. 126-27.)

Charles A. Callis: 11

Now the great day of the Lord is coming. It is going to be
a terrible day. The wicked are going to be destroyed and
when I say the wicked I do not mean everybody outside the
Mormon Church. There will be countless millions of people
not of this Church spared because they are not ripe in
iniquity and to them we will preach the everlasting Gospel
and bring them unto Christ. When Jesus Christ comes there
is going to be a glorious resurrection of the dead. [Sec. 88:97;
133:56.] The millennium will be inaugurated and men in
every land and every clime shall live in peace. [Isa. 11:6-9;
65:25.] (CR, April 1935, p. 18.)

John Taylor: 12
The Twelve . . . shall . . . judge the whole house of Israel

We may here state that Christ is called the judge of the
quick and the dead, the judge of all the earth. We further

read that the Twelve Apostles who ministered in Jerusalem "shall sit upon twelve thrones, judging the twelve tribes of Israel." (Matt. 19:28.)

And Nephi writes in the Book of Mormon:

And the angel spake unto me, saying, Behold the twelve disciples of the Lamb, who are chosen to minister unto thy seed; And he said unto me, Thou rememberest the twelve apostles of the Lamb? Behold, they are they who shall judge the twelve tribes of Israel; wherefore, the twelve ministers of thy seed shall be judged of them; for ye are of the house of Israel. And these twelve ministers, whom thou beholdest, shall judge thy seed. And, behold, they are righteous forever; for because of their faith in the Lamb of God their garments are made white in his blood. (1 Nephi 12:8-10.)

This exhibits a principle of adjudication or judgment in the hands, firstly, of the Great High Priest and King, Jesus of Nazareth, the Son of God; secondly, in the hands of the Twelve Apostles on the continent of Asia, bestowed by Jesus himself; thirdly, in the Twelve Disciples on this continent, to their people, who it appears are under the presidency of the Twelve Apostles who ministered at Jerusalem; which presidency is also exhibited by Peter, James and John, the acknowledged presidency of the Twelve Apostles; they, holding this Priesthood first on the earth, and then in the heavens. Being the legitimate custodians of the keys of the Priesthood, they came and bestowed it upon Joseph Smith and Oliver Cowdery. It is also further stated that the Saints shall judge the world. Thus Christ is at the head, his apostles and disciples seem to take the next prominent part; then comes the action of the Saints, or other branches of the Priesthood, who it is stated shall judge the world. This combined Priesthood, it would appear, will hold the destiny of the human family in their hands and adjudicate in all matters pertaining to their affairs; and it would seem to be quite reasonable, if the Twelve Apostles in Jerusalem are to be the judges of the Twelve Tribes, and the Twelve Disciples on this continent are to be the judges of the descendants of Nephi, then that the brother of Jared and Jared should be the judges of the Jaredites, their descendants; and, further, that the First Presidency and Twelve who have officiated in our age, should operate in regard to mankind in this dispensation, and also in regard to all matters connected with them, whether they relate to the past, present, or future, as the aforementioned have done in regard to their several peoples; and that the Patriarchs, the Presidents, the Twelve, the High Priests, the Seventies, the Elders, the Bishops, Priests, Teachers and Deacons should hold their several places behind the veil, and officiate according to their calling and standing in that Priesthood. In fact, the Priesthood is called an everlasting Priesthood; it ministers in time and in eternity. (*Mediation and Atonement*, pp. 152-53.)

James E. Talmage: 13

I am just simple-minded enough to stand upon the rock of assurance that not one jot or tittle of the word of the Lord shall fail. Do not allow yourselves to think that the coming of the Christ means merely the spread of different or more advanced ideas among men, or simply the progress and advancement of society as an institution. These shall be but incidents of the great consummation of this particular stage or epoch of the Lord's work. The Lord Jesus Christ shall come in the clouds of heaven, accompanied by the heavenly hosts, and his advent shall be marked by a great extension of the resurrection of the just, which has been in progress since that resurrection Sunday on which he came forth from the tomb and took up the wounded, pierced body which he had laid down; and those who are not able to bear the glory of his coming because of their wickedness, their foulness, and wilful state of sin, shall by natural means, perish. (CR, April 1916, pp. 130-31.)

Wilford Woodruff: 14-21

No man can contemplate the truth concerning the nations of the earth without sorrow, when he sees the wailing, the mourning, and death, that will come in consequence of judgments, plagues, and war. It has already begun, and it will continue to multiply and increase until the scene is ended, and wound up. . . .

Do I delight in the destruction of the children of men? No. Does the Lord? No. He gives them timely warning, and if they do not listen to his counsel, they must suffer the consequences of their wicked acts. (*JD*, February 25, 1855, 2:201.)

Orson Hyde: 14-21

When I was young I used to read about a day that should burn as an oven, and all the proud and they that do wickedly shall be as stubble. [Mal. 4:1.] I then had an idea that a sheet of fire would come down from heaven and burn up the ungodly; that the sun would be darkened and the moon turned to blood and the stars fall from heaven. I look at things in another point of light now; I now consider that the elements, the agents of destruction, are right here to accomplish that work, and the revelations of God will be fulfilled; for God has put in their hearts to fulfil his will, and they shall make the whore of all the earth desolate and naked, and shall eat her flesh and burn her with fire. [Ezek. 37:14-23; Rev. 18.] That great day of burning is beginning; we have had a few drops before the shower; it will wax worse and worse, and men will continue to deceive and be deceived until the earth shall burn up. The word of the Lord is, "Come out from her, my people, that ye be not partakers of her sins and receive not of her plagues." [Rev. 18:4.] (*JD*, October 7, 1865, 11:154.)

Joseph Smith: 14-21

I will prophesy that the signs of the coming of the son of Man are already commenced. One pestilence will desolate after another. We shall soon have war and bloodshed. The moon will be turned to blood. I testify of these things, and that the coming of the Son of Man is nigh, even at your doors. If our souls and our bodies are not looking forth for the coming of the Son of Man; and after we are dead, if we are not looking forth, we shall be among those who are calling for the rocks to fall upon them. (*HC* 3:390, July 2, 1839.)

Charles A. Callis: 17

My blood shall not cleanse them if they hear me not

On the cross our Savior paid the debt that made mankind free. He bought us with the price of his precious blood. We are not our own for we are bought with a price. [Acts 20:28.] His blood atones for all our sins, through obedience to righteousness, but it shall not cleanse those who obey not his commandments. The manner of our redemption calls forth our love and affection. (CR, October 1937, p. 122.)

Joseph Fielding Smith: 22-25

The Lord created all things for a purpose. Nothing has he created to be destroyed, but that all things might endure forever. This mortal condition with all its changes and eventual death, is part of the great plan of eternal progress. . . .

In one of the revelations to Joseph Smith the Lord said to the Church and to all who are willing to receive it: [Sec. 29:22, quoted.]

The Lord here is speaking of his second coming, of the millennial reign which shall be followed by a short period of wickedness and then the end. The revelation continues: [Sec. 29:23, quoted.]

This does not mean that this earth shall pass away and another take its place, and the heaven thereof shall pass away, and another heaven shall take its place, but that the earth and its heaven, shall, after passing away, through death, be renewed again in immortality. This earth is living and must die, but since it keeps the law it shall be restored through the resurrection by which it shall become celestialized and the abode of celestial beings. The next verse of this revelation explains this as follows: [Sec. 29:24-25, quoted.]

So we see that the Lord intends to save, not only the earth and the heavens, not only man who dwells upon the earth, but all things which he has created. The animals, the fishes of the sea, the fowls of the air, as well as man, are to be re-created, or renewed, through the resurrection, for they too are living souls. (CR, October 1928, pp. 99-100.)

Orson Pratt: 24
All things shall become new

When this world was formed, no doubt, it was a very beautiful creation, for God is not the author of anything imperfect. If we have imperfections in our world God has had nothing to do with their introduction or origin; man has brought them upon himself and upon the earth he inhabits. But however long or short may have been the period of the construction of this earth, we find that some six thousand years ago it seems to have been formed, something after the fashion and in the manner in which it now exists, with the exception of the imperfections, evils, and curses that exist on the face of it. Six thousand years, according to the best idea that we have of chronology, are now about completed; we are living almost on the eve of the last of the six millenniums — a thousand years are called a millennium, and tomorrow, we may say, we will be in the seventh; that is the seventh period, the seventh age or seventh time; or we can call it a day — the seventh day, the great day of rest wherein our globe will rest from all wickedness, when there will be no sin or transgression upon the whole face of it, the curses that have been brought upon it being removed, and all things being restored as they were before the Fall. The earth will then become beautified, not fully glorified, not fully redeemed, but it will be sanctified, and purified, and prepared for the reign of our Savior, whose death and sufferings we have this afternoon commemorated. He will come and personally reign upon it, as one of the mansions of his Father; and after the thousand years have passed away, and wickedness is permitted again, for a short season, to corrupt the face of the earth, then will come the final change which our earth, or this mansion of our Father, will undergo. A change which will be wrought, not by a flood of waters, or baptism, as in the days of Noah, cleansing it then from all its sins; but by a baptism of fire and of the Holy Ghost, which will sanctify and purify the very elements themselves. After the seventh millennium has passed away the elements will be cleansed, or in other words, they will be resolved into their original condition — as they were before they were brought together in the formation of this globe. Hence John says, in the 20th chapter of Revelation: "I saw a great white throne and him that sat on it, from whose face the earth and heaven fled away; and there was found no place for them." [V. 11.]

We might say, with great propriety, when a man is martyred or burned at the stake, his body has fled away, its present organization is dissolved, and its elements are resolved into their original condition, and perhaps united with and dispersed among many other elements of our globe; but in the resurrection these elements are brought together again and the body reorganized, not into a temporal or mortal tabernacle, but into an eternal house or abiding place for the spirit of man. So the earth will pass away, and its elements be dispersed in space; but, by the power of that Almighty Creator who organized it in the beginning, it will be renewed, and those elements which now enter into the composition of our globe, will again enter into the composition of the new heavens and the new earth, for says the Prophet John, "I saw a new heaven and a new earth: for the first heaven and the first earth were passed away." [Rev. 21:1.] (JD, August 20, 1871, 14:235-36.)

Parley P. Pratt: 23

A new heaven and a new earth are promised by the sacred writers. Or, in other words, the planetary systems are to be changed, purified, refined, exalted, and glorified, in the similitude of the resurrection, by which all physical evil or imperfections will be done away. (Key to the Science of Theology, 1943, p. 60.)

Charles W. Penrose: 26-27

There is a heresy getting abroad in what is named "the Christian church," throughout so-called Christendom, and it is emphasized by scientists, that it is an utter impossibility for the body to be brought together again, that the atoms cannot be re-collected; that death is the end of man, so far as the body is concerned. When he dies his body is gone forever. But that is a fearful heresy; for one of the very fundamental principles of real Christianity is the resurrection from the dead. Jesus the Christ declares, himself, "I am the resurrection and the life. He that believeth in me, though he were dead, yet shall he live." [John 11:25.] Further he says, "Marvel not at this, for the hour is coming in the which all that are in the graves" — not the spirits of men merely — "all that are in the graves, shall hear the voice of the Son of God, and shall come forth" [Ibid., 5:28-29], some in the resurrection of life, and others in the resurrection of damnation, or just condemnation, a resurrection of the just and a resurrection of the unjust. But all shall be raised from the graves, as we read in the twenty-ninth section of our book of Doctrine and Covenants. The Lord declares that "they shall all come forth — yea, *even all.*" This truth is made plain in ancient as well as modern scripture, that all shall be raised. "As in Adam all die, even so in Christ shall all be made alive." [1 Cor. 15:22.] Then, when we do come forth we will recognize one another, because we will be the same persons. There is something in the substratum, so to speak, of our bodies that will be quickened by the celestial or other glory, quickened by spirit instead of blood, and there will be in them particles that belong one to another, just as we will belong one to another through the ordinances of the gospel — the wife to the husband, the husband to the wife, the parents to the children, families grouped together again, to go in an everlasting existence. So will it be with these bodies of ours. . . .

I want to impress . . . the fact that the resurrection will prove to be just as natural as birth; that the coming together of those particles that belong to us and belong to one another, each in a distinct organization, although similar in many respects to others, and the formation or reformation of our own personality, is just as sure as that we lay down our lives. As we rise in the morning from our night's rest, so it will be with us in the resurrection. (*IE*, July 1919, 22:752, 754.)

Joseph Smith: 29
Never . . . have I declared . . . that they shall return

Say to the brothers Hulet and to all others, that the Lord never authorized them to say that the devil, his angels

[Sec. 76:44-48] or the sons of perdition, should ever be restored; for their state of destiny was not revealed to man, is not revealed, nor ever shall be revealed, save to those who are made partakers thereof: consequently those who teach this doctrine, have not received it of the Spirit of the Lord. Truly Brother Oliver [Cowdery] declared it to be the doctrine of devils. We therefore command that this doctrine be taught no more in Zion. (HC 1:366, June 4, 1833.)

Charles W. Penrose: 30-33

In the twenty-ninth section of the Doctrine and Covenants, God says that he made all things. He speaks there of the earth and the animals upon it, and the vegetation that grows out of the ground, and of the material things which men handle. The Lord says he created them all by the word of his power, "firstly spiritual, and secondly temporal;" and the last of his works will be "firstly temporal, and secondly spiritual." But he explains further, that to him all these things are spiritual, because they are eternal. The elements are eternal, and therefore God calls them spiritual; for the things that are temporal are those that pass away, and the things that are spiritual are those that remain. So we will find by and by, when we understand things as God understands them, that they are all eternal in his sight; for his eyes penetrate to the essence of things, while we can only see things on the surface. The things that pass away from our gaze, caught up as it were in the air and passing out of sight, like the vapors of the sea drawn up by the sun — the elements of these things remain and abide, and cannot be annihilated. Not one particle of matter can be annihilated; not one particle of spirit can be annihilated; for they are eternal. They always were, in their essential particles, in their primary elements, and they always will abide, though their forms may be changed by the power of the great Creator. (CR, April 1905, p. 71.)

Orson Pratt: 30-33

In the work of creation the first is last and the last first. God made the spirit part of this creation during these six days' work that we read of (Gen., chapters 1-2); then he commenced the temporal work on the seventh day. He planted the garden on the seventh day; he placed man in that garden on the seventh day; formed the beasts and brought them before the man on the seventh day, all this being the temporal work, the first being spiritual. Not so in the last of his work — the great work that is to come. When the seventh millennium shall arrive the Lord will redeem man and bring him forth from the grave, and he will begin to redeem this creation not making it entirely immortal and spiritual, like a sea of glass. It will exist for a thousand years in a temporal condition, as it was before the Fall. This will be the first of his temporal work in the last days. By and by when the millennium has passed, and the earth passes away and dies and its elements are melted with fervent heat, and there is no place found for it as an organized body, he will again speak and there will be another creation — a creation of this earth out of the old materials; in other words a resurrection of the earth, a literal resurrection. That will be the last of his work. In the morning of creation spiritual first, and lastly temporal. But in the ending temporal first in the redemption, and lastly spiritual, which will be the perfection or ending of his work. (JD, December 29, 1872, 15:265.)

Albert E. Bowen: 34-35

We have a very practical religion. It pertains to our lives now. And the reward of observance of the law is not altogether postponed to a future on the other side of the grave. Building up the kingdom involves some very practical things. It is not altogether concerned with the non-material lying out in the ethereal realm. The building of meetinghouses, places of worship, schools, temples, for example, clearly is for spiritual purposes. But they involve a large element of the material. They are essential to the building up of the kingdom of God. And where would you classify the beautifying of your home; the making of refined surroundings? It is necessary to provide the things that sustain life, to master the arts and crafts and trades that meet the needs of progress and improvement. I do not think I can find the line that divides the spiritual from the temporal. (CR, April 1951, p. 124.]

John A. Widtsoe: 35
For my commandments are spiritual

The all-important thing in life, after all, is to find a place in the universal scheme of things, for all the acts of our lives. There is a spiritual meaning of all human acts and earthly events. The Lord has specifically declared "Not at any time have I given unto you a law which was temporal." It is the business of man to find the spiritual meaning of earthly things. I pay my tithing, for many reasons, perhaps, but the one great reason is that by so doing, I am advancing this great cause, this great purpose, this great plan to which I am committed. I keep the Word of Wisdom also, because by so doing I make myself an abler co-laborer with God in carrying onward this great work. I grow sugar beets, not merely because I want clothing and food for my family, but because the cultivation of the soil and the consequent increased prosperity among the people, add to the onward progress and nearer fulfilment of the purposes of Almighty God, of the great explanation of explanations, beginning in the vast Before and ending in the vast Hereafter. No man is quite so happy, I think, as he who backs all his labors by such a spiritual interpretation and understanding of the acts of his life. A piece of silver always has a certain value as it passes from hand to hand; it is weighed and we sell it in the market place; but, when that piece of silver is coined into a dollar, it receives the stamp of government service; it becomes a coin of the realm, and it moves from hand to hand to accomplish the work of the realm. So, every act of man, the moment it is fitted into the great plan, the plan of salvation, receives spiritual coinage, and passes from hand to hand, from mind to mind, to accomplish the great work of God. (CR, April 1922, pp. 96-97.)

George Q. Morris: 36-45

This being "conceived in sin" (Moses 6:55), as I understand it, is only that they are in the midst of sin. They come into the world where sin is prevalent, and it will enter into their hearts, but it will lead them "to taste the bitter, that they may know to prize the good." And then with further emphasis on the matter of agency, the Lord says," . . . it is given to them to know good from evil; wherefore they are agents unto themselves." (Moses 6:56.)

This matter of agency is the very essence of our existence. The Lord said unto Enoch:

> Behold these thy brethren; they are the workmanship of mine own hands, and I gave unto them their knowledge, in the day I created them; and in the Garden of Eden, gave I unto man his agency. (*Ibid.*, 7:32.)

Also the revelation in the 93rd section of the Doctrine and Covenants emphasizes again this matter of agency. We are intelligences, and the Lord says,

> All truth is independent in that sphere in which God has placed it, to act for itself, as all intelligence also; otherwise there is no existence. (D&C 93:30.)

If we take away their free agency we nullify the purpose of the existence of mankind in the world. Satan attempted to do that.

By these revelations we see why sin is in the world and adversities and evils of various kinds. We can picture the plight of Adam and Eve. They had been condemned to sorrows, woes, troubles, and labor, and they were cast out from the presence of God, and death had been declared to be their fate. A pathetic picture, indeed. But now a most important thing happened. Adam and Eve had explained to them the gospel of Jesus Christ. What would be their reaction? When the Lord explained this to them, that a redemption should come through Jesus Christ, the Only Begotten of the Father, Adam exclaimed:

> Blessed be the name of God, for because of my transgression my eyes are opened, and in this life I shall have joy, and again in the flesh I shall see God. (Moses 5:10.)

And what was the response of Eve, his wife? She heard all of these things, and was glad, saying: "Were it not for our transgression we never should have had seed, and never should have known good and evil, and the joy of our redemption, and . . . eternal life." (*Ibid.*, 5:11.)

There is the key to the question of evil. If we cannot be good, except as we resist and overcome evil, then evil must be present to be resisted.

So this earth life is set up according to true principles, and these conditions that followed the transgression were not, in the usual sense, penalties that were inflicted upon us. All these that I have named to you that seem to be sad inflictions of punishment, sorrow, and trouble are in the end not that. They are blessings. We have attained a knowledge of good and evil, the power to prize the sweet, to become agents unto ourselves, the power to obtain redemption and eternal life. These things had their origin in this transgression. The Lord has set the earth up so we have to labor if we are going to live, which preserves us from the curse of idleness and indolence; and though the Lord condemns us to death — mortal death — it is one of the greatest blessings that comes to us here because it is the doorway to immortality, and we can never attain immortality without dying.

So these are all real blessings. We come to the earth with all these conditons arranged as they are so that we have to struggle constantly against evil, struggle to preserve our lives, struggle for everything of true value — that is the thing for us to understand — this is the course of life that is most desirable, and for our good. We have no need to find fault with these conditions. The Lord has ordained them all for our welfare and happiness. The truth as I understand and feel about it is simply that circumstances placed Adam in a position where by a technical transgression he could come into mortal life, moving out of immortality into these earth conditions for his blessings, for the blessing of the race, without which no immortality and eternal life and exaltation could ever come. And in doing this, also, of course, his body, taken from the earth, was made mortal — an absolute essential. There is no salvation or exaltation except through the possession of a body of flesh and blood.

In conclusion I want to give this inspired declaration by the Prophet Lehi.

For it must needs be, that there is an opposition in all things. If not so . . . righteousness could not be brought to pass, neither wickedness, neither holiness nor misery, neither good nor bad. Wherefore, all things must needs be a compound in one; . . .

And now, behold, if Adam had not transgressed he would not have fallen, but he would have remained in the garden of Eden. And all things which were created must have remained in the same state in which they were after they were created; and they must have remained forever, and had no end.

And they would have had no children; wherefore they would have remained in a state of innocence, having no joy, for they knew no misery; doing no good, for they knew no sin.

But behold, all things have been done in the wisdom of him who knoweth all things.

Adam fell that men might be; and men are, that they might have joy. (2 Nephi 2:11, 22-25.)

The answer to all the problems in the world is the gospel of Jesus Christ, which enables us to overcome all adversities, sin, and death, and go back into the presence of God fit to dwell in his presence, through the Lord Jesus Christ, our Redeemer. (CR, April 1958, pp. 38-40.)

George F. Richards: 36-40

I call attention to the war that took place in heaven of which we read in the Bible, the 12th chapter of Revelation, and the Pearl of Great Price [Moses 4:1-4], where one of our Father's sons who was regarded as a noble and great one, presented a plan for our salvation that would oblige us to comply with the law without the exercise of our agency, and he would take away from our Father in heaven his honor and his glory. In that council in heaven the Firstborn of the Father in the spirit came forward with a simple but forceful declaration: "Father, thy will be done, and the glory be thine forever."

The battle was fought, whatever its nature, upon this platform of principles, and we have reason to believe that we were among those who stood with the Savior, our Elder Brother, true and faithful, and those who rebelled were cast out and down, and God's purposes and his will are made to obtain in the plan of man's salvation. The Savior is our great exemplar and we are instructed by Scripture that we should walk in the light as he is in the light, with the promise that we will have fellowship one with another, and his blood will cleanse us from all sin. [1 John 1:7.] We have good reason to believe that the principle which the Savior presented in the council of heaven, pertained not to the spirit life alone, but to our existence here on the earth.

Of course the earth was not framed at that time, but the end is known unto God even from the beginning. Provision was made even at that time for redeeming mankind from a fall that had not yet taken place, through the atonement of Christ, and that was one of the purposes of his being chosen, and that we might all have forgiveness of sin through obedience to the laws and ordinances of the Gospel. The Father gave the Son, and the Son gave himself, the greatest gift that ever was given, the greatest sacrifice that ever was made, the greatest service that ever was rendered. (CR, October 1941, pp. 20-21.)

Orson Pratt: 36-40

Suppose we were created in the celestial world without a knowledge of that which we term pain, could we learn to sense it by seeing others suffer? No, no more than a person born in a dungeon and kept there until he reached the years of manhood, without the least gleam of light, could, while in that condition, be instructed about the principle of light. Why could he not be instructed? Because it is something he never has experienced. You tell him that light produces beautiful colors, such as red, blue, green, etc., what would he know about these colors? Nothing at all; his experience has not been called to grasp them; such a thing as a ray of light never penetrated his dungeon. But when he is permitted to experience the nature of light, when he sees the various colors, he then learns something which he never could reason out. So with regard to ourselves. We, in our first state of existence, never having seen misery among any of the immortal beings, and never experiencing it in our spiritual personages, how could we know anything about it? I do not think we could possibly comprehend the nature of it. We could not reason out the difference between happiness and misery. Why? For the want of experience. It was for this reason that God the Father caused the tree bearing forbidden fruit to be placed in the garden. This tree was not placed beyond Adam's reach, but it was found in a conspicuous place — in the midst of the garden, so that man, by his agency, might bring upon himself his own misery, and by that means he would be able to distinguish between happiness and misery. The Lord prepared everything, and he made special reference to the tree of knowledge of good and evil, forbidding Adam to eat of it, saying that in the day he ate the fruit of that tree he should surely die. But then, what did Adam know about death? Such a penalty could not be understood by him; the only way possible for him to conceive of it was through vision, and the probability is he did not know anything about it. But he was his own agent, and he exercised that agency by putting forth his hand and partaking of the fruit: both he and his wife ate the fruit, and thus transgressed the law of God. Then the earth became fallen, and all the inhabitants thereof have inherited the effects of the fall, through these two fallen beings. Death is not something we bring upon ourselves, we are sure to die because our first parents rendered themselves mortal; before that they were immortal. They made themselves mortal by partaking of the forbidden fruit, transgressing the law of heaven, and we are the inheritors of these calamities and these penalties, the same as children are susceptible of parental diseases, and frequently inherit, for many generations, evils that their forefathers were in possession of. We learn quite an experience here: we learn what it is to be miserable, we learn what it is to be unhappy, and we can now contrast misery with happiness; and we can say in our hearts, if I could only get rid of sickness, and pain, and sorrow, the effects of this death, now I could appreciate it! We often give expression to such feelings, when we are deeply afflicted. The Lord intends to free us, if we keep his commandments, after having suffered sufficiently long through this state of sickness and feebleness, this state of suffering and sorrow, which we have endured for so many years. . . . Yes, suppose the Lord were to appoint to you a kingdom; suppose he were to say to you, "Son, yonder are materials which you may organize by my power into a world; and you may place upon it your own offspring, as I do my offspring upon the world upon which you dwelt." What kind of person would you be if you had no experience? What? Go and create a world, and then people that world with your own offspring, and not know the difference between good and evil, between sickness and health, between pain and happiness, having no knowledge of these by experience. I think that such a one would not be fit to be entrusted with a world that was to undergo and pass through the same ordeals that our creation is now experiencing. (JD, 1878, 19:288-89.)

Jedediah M. Grant: 39

I have always felt that no Saint fully comprehends the power of Satan as well as God's Prophet; and again I have thought that no Saint could fully understand the power of God unless he learn the opposite. I am not myself acquainted with any happiness that I have not learned the opposite of. You may perhaps enjoy a great deal, the opposite of which you known nothing of, you may be constituted different to me, your feelings may be different, you may have learned to enjoy without first experiencing the opposite; but I may say with safety, nearly all the blessings I enjoy and highly prize are most appreciated after I have learned their opposite; and I am of opinion that all Saints sooner or later will have to learn the opposite of good, they will have to partake of the bitter in order to properly appreciate the sweet, they will have to be impressed with pain that they may appreciate pleasure. (JD, February 19, 1854, 2:11.)

Brigham Young: 40
Adam . . . transgressed the commandment

How did Adam and Eve sin? Did they come out in direct opposition to God and to his government? No. But they transgressed a command of the Lord, and through that transgression sin came into the world. The Lord knew they would do this, and he had designed that they should. (JD, June 12, 1864, 10:312.)

James E. Talmage: 40
Adam . . . partook of the forbidden fruit

Here let me say, that therein consisted the fall — the eating of things unfit, the taking into the body of things that made of that body a thing of earth; and I take this occasion to raise my voice against the false interpretation of scripture, which has been adopted by certain people, and is current in their minds, and is referred to in a hushed and half-secret way, that the fall of man consisted in some offense against the laws of chastity and of virtue. Such a doctrine is an abomination. What right have we to turn the scriptures from their proper sense and meaning? What right have we to declare that God meant not what he said? The fall was a natural process, resulting through the incorporation into the bodies of our first parents of the things that came from food unfit, through the violation of the command of God regarding what they should eat. Don't go around whispering the fall consisted in the mother of the race losing her chastity and her virtue. It is not true; the human race is not born of fornication. These bodies that are given unto us are given in the way that God has provided. Let it not be said that the patriarch of the race, who stood with the Gods before he came here upon the earth, and his equally royal consort were guilty of any such foul offense. The adoption of that belief has led many to excuse departures from the path of chastity and the path of virtue, by saying that it is the sin of the race, it is as old as Adam. It was not introduced by Adam. It was not committed by Eve. It was the introduction of the devil and came in order that he might sow the seeds of early death in the bodies of men and women, that the race should degenerate as it has degenerated, whenever the laws of virtue and of chastity have been transgressed.

Our first parents were pure and noble, and when we pass behind the veil we shall perhaps learn something of their high estate, more than we know now. But be it known that they were pure; they were noble. It is true that they disobeyed the law of God, in eating things they were told not to eat; but who amongst you can rise up and condemn? (CR, October 1913, pp. 118-19.)

Joseph F. Smith: 41-45

In this natural body are the seeds of weakness and decay, which, when fully ripened or untimely plucked up, in the language of scripture, is called "the temporal death." The spirit is also subject to what is termed in the scriptures and revelation from God, "spiritual death." The same as that which befell our first parents, when through disobedience and transgression they became subject to the will of Satan, and were thrust out from the presence of the Lord and became spiritually dead, which the Lord says, "is the first death, even that same death which is the last death, which is spiritual, which shall be pronounced upon the wicked when I shall say, Depart ye cursed!" And the Lord further says, [Sec. 29:42-44, quoted]. From the natural death, that is the death of the body, and also from the first death, "which is spiritual," there is redemption through belief on the name of the "only Begottn Son," in connection with repentance and obedience to the ordinances of the Gospel declared by holy angels.... If man will not repent and come unto Christ, through the ordinances of his Gospel, they cannot be redeemed from their spiritual fall, but must remain forever subject to the will of Satan and the consequent spiritual darkness or death into which our first parents fell, subjecting all their posterity thereto, and from which none can be redeemed but by belief or faith on the name of the "only Begotten Son" and obedience to the laws of God. But, thanks be to the Eternal Father through the merciful provisions of the Gospel, all mankind will have the opportunity of escape or deliverance from this spiritual death either in time or in eternity, for not until they are freed from the first can they become subject unto the second death, still if they repent not "they cannot be redeemed from their spiritual fall," and will continue subject to the will of Satan, the first spiritual death, so long as "they repent not." I have been speaking of those who repent not, and thereby reject Christ and his Gospel....

The "temporal death" is one thing, and the "spiritual death" is another thing. The body may be dissolved and become extinct as an organism, although the elements of which it is composed are indestructible or eternal, but I hold it as self-evident that the spiritual organism is an eternal, immortal being, destined to enjoy eternal happiness and a fullness of joy, or suffer the wrath of God, and misery — a just condemnation, eternally. Adam became spiritually dead, yet he lived to endure it until freed therefrom by the power of the atonement, through repentance, etc. Those upon whom the second death shall fall, will live to suffer and endure it, but without hope of redemption. The death of the body or natural death is but a temporary circumstance to which all were subjected through the fall and from which all will be restored or resurrected by the power of God, through the atonement of Christ. (JD, June 18, 1882, 23:169-71.)

George F. Richards: 43
He might be raised in immortality unto eternal life

The word immortal means not mortal; that is, not subject to the power of death. I would define immortality as being that state to which we attain in the progress of life when we have passed through death and the resurrection, the spirit and body being reunited and inseparably connected, constituting the soul of man prepared to receive a fulness of the glory of God. Immortality is a means to an end, the end being the accomplishment of man's eternal salvation and glory. In support of this statement I call attention to the word of the Lord to the Prophet Joseph, as recorded in the Doctrine and Covenants, Sec. 93, verses 33 and 34, as follows: "For man is spirit. The elements are eternal, and spirit and element, inseparably connected, receive a fulness of joy; And when separated, man cannot receive a fulness of joy." Hence the importance of bringing about the immortality of man.

The eternal life referred to means something more than that man shall not cease to live. I read the word of the Lord from Docrine and Covenants, Sec. 14, verse 7, as follows: "And, if you keep my commandments and endure to the end, you shall have eternal life, which gift is the greatest of all the gifts of God." The revelations of the Lord indicate to us the height, depth and grandeur of the glory of God to which the righteous may attain. Eternal life, as here used, being the greatest gift of God, must include a fulness of glory of God, in his celestial kingdom. [Sec. 76:54-60; 132:20-24.]

The Lord uses the expressions "eternal life" and "salvation" synonymously (see Doctrine and Covenants, Sec. 6:13): "If thou wilt do good, yea, and hold out faithful to the end, thou shalt be saved in the kingdom of God, which is the greatest of all the gifts of God; for there is no gift greater than the gift of salvation." (CR, April 1916, p. 52.)

Wilford Woodruff: 46-48

Children are taken away in their infancy, and they go to the spirit world. They come here and fulfill the object of their coming, that is, they tabernacle in the flesh. They come to receive a probation and an inheritance on the earth; they obtain a body or tabernacle, and that tabernacle will be preserved for them, and in the morning of the resurrection the spirits and bodies will be reunited, and as here we find children of various ages in a family, from the infant at the mother's breast to manhood, so will it be in the family organization in the celestial world. Our children will be restored to us as they are laid down if we, their parents, keep the faith and prove ourselves worthy to obtain eternal life; and if we do not so prove ourselves worthy to obtain eternal life; and if we do not so prove ourselves our children will still be preserved, and will inherit celestial glory. This is my view in regard to all infants who die, whether they are born to Jew or Gentile, righteous or wicked. They come from their eternal Father and their eternal Mother unto whom they were born in the eternal world, and they will be restored to their eternal parentage; and all parents who have received children here according to the order of God and the holy priesthood, no matter in what age they may have lived will claim those children in the morning of the resurrection, and they will be given unto them and they will grace their family organizations in the celestial world. . . .

With regard to the growth, glory, or exaltation of children in the life to come, God has not revealed anything on that subject to me, either about your children, mine or anybody else's any further than we know they are saved. And I feel that we have to put our trust in the Lord in these afflictions, we have to lean upon his arm and to look to him for comfort and consolation. We do not mourn under these afflictions as those who have no hope; we do not mourn the loss of our children as though we were never going to see them again, because we know better. The Lord has taught us better, and so has the Gospel; the revelations of Jesus Christ have shown us that they will be restored to us in the resurrection of the just. (*JD*, June 24, 1875, 18:32, 34.)

Joseph F. Smith: 46-48

Of course it is nice to say that all is well with little children, that they are redeemed by the blood of Christ from the sins of the world, and that when they pass away they return to a Father from whence they came. If we have received the testimony of the Spirit of truth in our souls we know that all is well with our little children who pass away, that we could not, if we would, better their condition, and least of all would it better their condition if we could call them back here, for the reason that so long as man is in the world, clothed with mortality, surrounded by the evils that are in the world, he runs chances, and is subject to risks, and there are responsibilities resting upon him which may prove fatal to his future prosperity, happiness, and exaltation. . . . But, with little children who are taken away in infancy and innocence before they are capable of committing sin, the Gospel reveals to us the fact that they are redeemed, and Satan has no power over them; neither has death any power over them. They are redeemed by the blood of Christ, and they are saved just as surely as death has come into the world through the fall of our first parents. . . . Joseph Smith declared that the mother who laid down her little child, being deprived of the privilege, the joy, and the satisfaction of bringing it up to manhood or womanhood in this world, would, after the resurrection, have all the joy, satisfaction and pleasure, and even more than it would have been possible to have had in mortality, in seeing her child grow to the full measure of the stature of its spirit. (MS, June 20, 1845, 57:388-89.)

Francis M. Lyman: 46-48

We know too, that our children particularly are secured to us; if we are but worthy of them, and can obtain and retain the favor of Heaven in regard to our family associations, we know that our children will be ours hereafter. The only question is in regard to ourselves, not in regard to our children. Their security and salvation is without question. The Savior, our Elder Brother, has secured the salvation of all children, whether they be the children of the Christian or the children of the heathen. They are secured by the atonement of the Savior. [Mosiah 3:16.] The redemption that he has worked out has brought salvation to all children. We feel confident and we know that their salvation is complete, so we know that we can add nothing to little children by baptism, by confirmation, by ordinations, or anything else [Moroni 8], more than to bless them, as the pattern was set by the Savior. The Savior has said: "Suffer little children to come unto me, and forbid them not: for of such is the kingdom of heaven." [Luke 18;16.] When our children have finished their life in mortality, we know that they have passed beyond the possibility of temptations by Satan, that they have passed by his reach. . . . I have not the least doubt but we would be greatly astonished if we could get only a glimpse of what will be reached by this boy [four-and-one-half-year-old son of Heber J. Grant] who is not developed here; his tabernacle is not developed; his faculties are not developed; he has not been enlarged in this life as he is to be enlarged hereafter, for he is not to lose anything by passing away as he has done prematurely. His power, his glory, his salvation, his exaltation, his enlargement, are not to be sacrificed and cut short because his life has been taken when he has only had two or three years of existence in mortality. There is ample time and opportunity in securer paths than in this life, where he will be beyond the power of Satan, and have the possibility of enlargement equal to any. I do not believe for one moment that the child is to be the loser because he is cut down in the morning of life; I do not belive that he is to be cut short in his final development, enlargement, and attainments. (MS, June 13, 1845, 57:371-72.)

George Q. Cannon: 46-48

Many other things did the Prophet see and hear. [Kirtland Temple, Jan. 21, 1836.] He beheld that all children who died before reaching years of accountability are saved in the celestial kingdom of our God. [See commentary on Sec. 76:67-70.] A holy comfort this, which takes the place of all the black threats concerning infantile damnation. (*Life of Joseph Smith*, 1907, p. 189.)

Hyrum G. Smith: 46-48

There are many of our Latter-day Saint mothers who have mourned the loss of their little children, and many mothers have felt that they themselves had committed some great sin, else their little ones would not be taken from them. Now, to such mothers let me say, do not accuse the Lord of taking your little ones from you, nor feel that you have committed any great sin, that those little ones are taken from you, because the Lord loves little children and he will not treat them unkindly, nor without mercy, for through the blood of his atonement they shall come forth in the morning of the resurrection with his saints, and they shall be glorified according to the words they would have accomplished in the earth had they lived. (CR, April 1917, pp. 70-71.)

Joseph F. Smith:49

"Who is there," says the Lord, "that hath understanding, that I have not called to repentance." There is not one that God has not called to repentance, which means the forsaking of sin, a departure from evil to do righteousness and walk in the way of life and salvation. I understand that unless we do this we will be weighed in the balance and found wanting. Can you take any other view of these matters? How can man excuse himself for drunkenness, when he knows that it is injurious to himself, to his family and others, and is forbidden by the law of God, and is a violation of the most sacred covenants he can make? How can a man excuse himself under these circumstances? What reason will he be able to give before God? How can he escape the damnation that awaits the wicked? It is written that "not every one that saith unto me, Lord, Lord, shall enter into the kingdom of heaven." [Matt. 7:21.] No; but those who keep the commandments of God, who walk righteously before him; they shall say "Lord, Lord," and the Lord will hearken unto them. (CR, April 1880, p. 36.)

Joseph Fielding Smith: 49-50

We have good reason to believe that all spirits while in the preexistence were perfect in form, having all their faculties and mental powers unimpaired. It is difficult to believe that in that existence spirits were deficient, for that was a perfect world notwithstanding each spirit had his or her free agency. The reason for these deformities in body and mind are therefore physical. In other words they are confined to the mortal existence, and they are due to physical injury or impairment which comes because of accident or sickness before birth. . . .

The Lord has made it known by revelation that children born with retarded minds shall receive blessings just like little children who die in infancy. They are free from sin, because their minds are not capable of of a correct understanding of right and wrong. Mormon, when writing to his son Moroni on the subject of baptism, places deficient children in the same category with little children who are under the age of accountability, they do not require baptism for the atonement of Jesus Christ takes care of them equally with little children who die before the age of accountability, as follows:

> For behold that all little children are alive in Christ, and also all they that are without the law. For the power of redemption cometh on all them that have not law; wherefore, he that is not condemned, or he that is under no condemnation, cannot repent; and unto such baptism availeth nothing. (Moroni 8:22.)

Again the Lord has stated: [Sec. 29;45-50, quoted.]

Therefore The Church of Jesus Christ of Latter-day Saints considers all deficient children with retarded capacity to understand, just the same as little children under the age of accountability. they are redeemed without baptism and will go to the celestial kingdom of God, there, we believe, to have their faculties or other deficiencies restored according to the Father's mercy and justice. (*IE*, February 1959, 62:80-81.)

SECTION 30

Revelation given through Joseph Smith the Prophet, to David Whitmer, Peter Whitmer, Jun., and John Whitmer, at Fayette, New York, September, 1830, following the three days' conference at Fayette, but before the Elders of the Church had separated. See History of the Church, vol. 1, p. 115. – Individual instruction is given, and the fact of Oliver Cowdery's mission to the Lamanites is reiterated.

1. Behold, I say unto you, David, that you have feared man and have not relied on me for strength as you ought.

2. But your mind has been on the things of the earth more than on the things of me, your Maker, and the ministry whereunto you have been called; and you have not given heed unto my Spirit, and to those who were set over you, but have been persuaded by those whom I have not commanded.

3. Wherefore, you are left to inquire for yourself at my hand, and ponder upon the things which you have received.

4. And your home shall be at your father's house, until I give unto you further commandments. And you shall attend to the ministry in the church, and before the world, and in the regions round about. Amen.

5. Behold, I say unto you, Peter, that you shall take your journey with your brother Oliver; for the time has come that it is expedient in me that you shall open your mouth to declare my gospel; therefore, fear not, but give heed unto the words and advice of your brother, which he shall give you.

6. And be you afflicted in all his afflictions, ever lifting up your heart unto me in prayer and faith, for his and your deliverance; for I have given unto him power to build up my church among the Lamanites;

7. And none have I appointed to be his counselor over him in the church, concerning church matters, except it is his brother, Joseph Smith, Jun.

8. Wherefore, give heed unto these things and be diligent in keeping my commandments, and you shall be blessed unto eternal life. Amen.

9. Behold, I say unto you, my servant John, that thou shalt commence from this time forth to proclaim my gospel, as with the voice of a trump.

10. And your labor shall be at your brother Philip Burroughs', and in that region round about, yea, wherever you can be heard, until I command you to go from hence.

11. And your whole labor shall be in Zion, with all your soul, from henceforth; yea, you shall ever open your mouth in my cause, not fearing what man can do, for I am with you. Amen.

Joseph Smith: *Introduction*

At length our conference assembled. The subject of the stone previously mentioned was discussed (Section 28), and after considerable investigation Brother Page, as well as the whole Church who were present, renounced the said stone, and all things connected therewith, much to our mutual satisfaction and happiness. We now partook of the Sacrament, confirmed and ordained many, and attended to a great variety of Church business on the first of the two following days of the conference, during which time we had much of the power of God manifested amongst us; the Holy Ghost came upon us, and filled us with joy unspeakable; and peace, and faith, and hope, and charity abounded in our midst.

Before we separated we received the following: [Sections 30 and 31, follow.] (*HC* 1:115, September 1830; Fayette, New York.)

Joseph Fielding Smith: *1-4*

A revelation was given (Sec. 30) to David, Peter, Jr., and John Whitmer, and intruction was given to each. To David Whitmer the Lord said: [Sec. 30:1-3, quoted.] He was further commanded to remain at his father's home and mend his ways and attend to his ministry in the Church. It seems a little strange that so soon after the wonderful manifestation which he had received and the witnessing of the outpouring of the Spirit at other times, that he would forget, but human nature is such that all of us need constant reminding of our responsibilities or we are likely to lapse into some indifference. The need of constant prayer and concentration of our thoughts on the things of the kingdom, and sincere attention to duty, is apparent with most of us, lest we slip. How frequently the Lord has had to caution his people against the weaknesses of the flesh! (*CHMR*, 1947, 1:136.)

Marriner W. Merrill: *2*
You have not given heed... to those who were set over you

According to my education and experience in the Church, and according to the teachings I have had and the suggestions through the inspiration of the Holy Ghost, there is no man, I don't care what his standing is; he may be a president of a stake, or an apostle, no matter, he cannot safely gainsay the counsel of the Priesthood. If he does he will have it to meet some day just as sure as the sun rises and sets. . . . We must observe the will of Lord; we must observe the counsels of the Priesthood, no matter what the world may think in regard to these things; and we can do this in all humility and maintain our right and manhood, and maintain our fellowship with each other and with the Lord: but when we turn away from these things we are like the sow that was washed and returned to her wallowing in the mire. The Lord has established his work; he is about to establish his Kingdom; he has revealed the everlasting Gospel; and he has revealed the principle by which you and I may go back into his presence; but when we turn a deaf ear to these things, through some motive or other that may arise in our minds, we will have to atone for it sooner or later. (CR, April 1899, p. 16.)

Joseph Fielding Smith: 5-8

To Peter Whitmer, Jr., the Lord gave a commandment that he should take his journey with Oliver Cowdery on a mission to the Lamanites. From the very beginning the attention of the Prophet and his brethren had been drawn to the Lamanites. This was due, of course, to the fact that great promises had been made to them in the Book of Mormon that the Gospel would be given to them in this dispensation and eventually they would be restored to full fellowship and favor before the Lord. The enthusiasm of the brethren may have been premature, but nevertheless the Lord commanded such a mission at that time. It seems that it was not so much for the benefit of the Indians, or Lamanites, although that factor was very great, but to carry the message to the land which later was to be revealed as the land of Zion, where the City Zion will eventually be built. Peter Whitmer, Jr., was also one of the eight witnesses of the Book of Mormon.

Peter was informed that he was to heed the words of his brother, Oliver Cowdery, and he was to share with him in all his afflictions, lifting his heart to the Lord in prayer and faith, for their deliverance. "I have given unto him power to build up my church among the Lamanites." Moreover, Peter was informed that there was none appointed to be Oliver's counselor, except Joseph Smith. Thus Peter understood that it was his duty to take, not to give, counsel while on this journey. The fact that Oliver Cowdery had shared with Joseph Smith in the conferring of Priesthood and authority on all occasions naturally gave to him the authority to stand second in the Church to Joseph Smith in the government of the Church. (*CHMR*, 1947, 1:136.)

George Q. Cannon: 8

Our only safety lies in diligently keeping the commandments of him who has hitherto been our protector, and in living such a life of holiness as will meet with his favour and approbation. (*MS*, January 3, 1863, 25:9.)

Joseph Fielding Smith: 9-11

John Whitmer was commanded to proclaim the Gospel from that time henceforth as with the voice of a trump. His "whole life was to be in Zion" and he was not to fear man but devote his entire time to the cause of the Gospel. Later he was to be called to take the responsibility of keeping the history from the shoulders of Oliver Cowdery [Sec. 47:1-4]. (*CHMR*, 1947, 1:136-37.)

George Q. Cannon: 11

I say to you this day, in the presence of God and the holy angels and of this assembly, if we expect to attain the fulfillment of the promises God has made to us, we must be self-sacrificing. There is no sacrifice that God can ask of us or his servants whom he has chosen to lead us that we should hesitate about making. In one sense of the word it is not sacrifice. We may call it so because it comes in contact with our selfishness and our unbelief; but it ought not to come in contact with our faith. (*CR*, April 1899, p. 65.)

SECTION 31

Revelation given through Joseph Smith the Prophet, to Thomas B. Marsh, September, 1830. Thomas B. Marsh had been baptized earlier in the month, and had already been ordained an Elder in the Church when this revelation was given. – Commended for obedience and faithfulness – Assured as to the welfare of his family – Appointed to preach and administer – Promised the guidance of the Comforter in his ministry.

1. Thomas, my son, blessed are you because of your faith in my work.

2. Behold, you have had many afflictions because of your family; nevertheless, I will bless you and your family, yea, your little ones; and the day cometh that they will believe and know the truth and be one with you in my church.

3. Lift up your heart and rejoice, for the hour of your mission is come; and your tongue shall be loosed, and you shall declare glad tidings of great joy unto this generation.

4. You shall declare the things which have been revealed to my servant, Joseph Smith, Jun. You shall begin to preach from this time forth, yea, to reap in the field which is white already to be burned.

5. Therefore, thrust in your sickle with all your soul, and your sins are forgiven you, and you shall be laden with sheaves upon your back, for the laborer is worthy of his hire. Wherefore, your family shall live.

6. Behold, verily I say unto you, go from them only for a little time, and declare my word, and I will prepare a place for them.

7. Yea, I will open the hearts of the people, and they will receive you. And I will establish a church by your hand;

8. And you shall strengthen them and prepare them against the time when they shall be gathered.

9. Be patient in afflictions, revile not against those that revile. Govern your house in meekness, and be steadfast.

10. Behold, I say unto you that you shall be a physician unto the church, but not unto the world, for they will not receive you.

11. Go your way whithersoever I will, and it shall be given you by the Comforter what you shall do and whither you shall go.

12. Pray always, lest you enter into temptation and lose your reward.

13. Be faithful unto the end, and lo, I am with you. These words are not of man nor of men, but of me, even Jesus Christ, your Redeemer, by the will of the Father. Amen.

First Presidency (Joseph F. Smith, John R. Winder, Anthon H. Lund): 9

Revile not against those that revile

Let no one suppose that "Mormonism," so-called, is here to make war upon men, or upon creeds, governments, and institutions that men revere. It sustains law, order, liberty and truth, the world over. The Latter-day Saints are friends, not enemies, to mankind. That we have a message to deliver we know; and, God being our helper, we will deliver it, come life or death, come weal or woe! But we purpose doing this in the spirit of peace, in the spirit of patience and brotherly love, forgiving our enemies, and returning good for evil; oppressing no man for refusing to listen to our testimony, nor ridiculing what he holds sacred, however false or foolish it may appear to us. The liberty of conscience is inviolable and we stand ready to defend all men in the exercise of this sacred, God-given right. We may be abused and slandered for exercising this right ourselves, but heaven forbid that we should ever deny it to others! Despite the human weakness that all men possess, and which prompts them to retaliate when they feel themselves wronged, we will endeavor, with the help of the Lord, to follow his divine injunction: "When men revile you, revile not again." [1 Peter 2:23.] Our plain and simple duty is the preaching of the Gospel, the gathering of scattered Israel, the redemption of Zion, and the salvation of the living and the dead. We have no warfare to wage against our fellow men, no wrongs that we wish to avenge. We leave that to him who has said, "Vengeance is mine; I will repay." [Rom. 12:19.] May he be merciful to those who misrepresent and bring trouble upon his people. (*DN*, December 1907.)

George A. Smith: 9

Govern your house in meekness, and be steadfast

The wife of Thomas B. Marsh, who was then President of the Twelve Apostles, and Sister Harris concluded they would exchange milk, in order to make a little larger cheese then they otherwise could. To be sure to have justice done, it was agreed that they should not save the strippings, but that the milk and strippings should all go together. Small matters to talk about here, to be sure, two women's exchanging milk to make cheese.

Mrs. Harris, it appeared, was faithful to the agreement and carried to Mrs. Marsh the milk and strippings, but Mrs. Marsh, wishing to make some extra good cheese, saved a pint of strippings from each cow and sent Mrs. Harris the milk without the strippings.

Finally, it leaked out that Mrs. Marsh had saved strippings, and it became a matter to be settled by the Teachers. They began to examine the matter, and it was proved that Mrs. Marsh had saved the strippings, and consequently had wronged Mrs. Harris out of that amount.

An appeal was taken from the Teacher to the Bishop, and a regular Church trial was had. President Marsh did not consider that the Bishop had done him and his lady justice, for they decided that the strippings were wrongfully saved, and that the woman had violated her covenant.

Marsh immediately took an appeal to the High Council, who investigated the question with much patience, and I assure you they were a grave body. Marsh, being extremely anxious to maintain the character of his wife, as he was the President of the Twelve Apostles, and a great man in Israel, made a desperate defense, but the High Council finally confirmed the Bishop's decision.

Marsh, not being satisfied, took an appeal to the First Presidency of the Church, and Joseph and his counselors had to sit upon the case, and they approved the decision of the High Council.

This little affair, you will observe, kicked up a considerable breeze, and Thomas B. Marsh then declared that he would sustain the character of his wife, even if he had to go to hell for it.

The then President of the Twelve Apostles, the man who should have been the first to do justice and cause reparation to be made for wrong, committed by any member of his family, took that position, and what next? He went before the magistrate and swore that the "Mormons" were hostile towards the State of Missouri.

The affidavit brought from the government of Missouri an exterminating order, which drove some 15,000 Saints from their homes and habitations, and some thousands perished through suffering the exposure consequent on this state of affairs. (JD, April 6, 1856, 3:282-84.)

Francis M. Lyman: 11-13

Those who enter into covenant with the Lord, having humbled themselves before him and repented of their sins, as a result of their faith, and have taken upon them the name of Jesus Christ, and have undertaken to serve him to the end, having repented of all their sins, they receive that witness and testimony, and that Spirit abides with them always through their faithfulness. It gives them stability of charac-ter; it gives them understanding and light that is not pos-sessed otherwise, and that does not remain with Latter-day Saints unless they continue to be faithful and very humble, meek and lowly of heart. The Spirit of the Lord is easily offended, easily grieved, and it is quite an undertaking for men to so live that that Spirit can always be a fountain of inspiration, of revelation and light to them. (CR, October 1912, pp. 42-43.)

Heber C. Kimball: 12

What good do your prayers do when your works do not correspond? Men may talk about praying, and exhort the people to pray; and if you do not live in a manner to fulfill your prayers, what do they avail you? Faith is dead without works, just as much as my body is dead without my spirit. When my spirit leaves my body, my body is dead; but put them together, and they make a soul — a spirit in a taberna-cle. What is the use of our professing to be Saints unless we live our religion? By our faithfulness and by our good works we shall obtain knowledge. . . .

About the time he [Thomas B. Marsh] was preparing to leave this Church, he received a revelation in the Printing Office. He retired to himself, and prayed, and was humble, and God gave him a revelation, and he wrote it. There were from three to five pages of it; and when he came out he read it to Brother Brigham [Young] and me. In it, God told him what to do, and that was to sustain Brother Joseph and to believe that what Brother Joseph had said was true. But no; he took a course to sustain his wife and oppose the Prophet of God, and she led him away. . . .

Thomas B. Marsh was once the President over the Quorum of the Twelve — over Brother Brigham, me, and others; and God saw fit to give him a revelation to forewarn him of the course he would take; and still he took that course. We told him that if he would listen to that revelation he had received, he would be saved; but he listened to his wife, and away he went. His wife is now dead and damned. She led him some eighteen years; and as soon as she died, he came to Winter Quarters — now Florence — and has written to us, pleading for mercy. We have extended it to him, and he will probably be here this season or the next. (JD, July 12, 1857, 5:28-29.)

Thomas B. Marsh: 12-13

Many have said to me, "How is it that a man like you, who understood so much of the revelations of God as recorded in the Book of Doctrine and Covenants, should fall away?" I told them not to feel too secure, but to take heed lest they also should fall, for I had no scruples in my mind as to the possibility of men falling away. [Sec. 20:32-34.]

I can say, in reference to the Quorum of the Twelve, to which I belonged, that I did not consider myself a whit behind any of them, and I suppose that others had the same opinion; but, let no one feel too secure; for, before you think of it, your steps will slide. You will not then think nor feel for a moment as you did before you lost the Spirit of Christ; for when men apostatize, they are left to grovel in the dark. . . .

Had I known as much of the Church of Jesus Christ and its doctrines before I apostatized as I now know, I think I could not have back-slidden. . . .

I see the propriety of God's vesting the authority in one man, and in having a head, or something tangible to see, hear, and understand the mind and will of God. When I saw this, I said, it is consistent: Christ is the great head of the

Church. Christ is the head of his Church in the same relationship as every head is to the body to which it belongs; for every head must have eyes to see, a mouth to speak, and ears to hear. Well, Jesus Christ is the head of the Church, and he has got a man to represent him on earth — viz., President Brigham Young. Jesus Christ is still the head of the Church; and his will to men on the earth is known by means of the mouthpiece of God, the Prophet, and Seer. (*JD*, September 6, 1857, 5:206, 208-9.)

SECTION 32

Revelation given through Joseph Smith the Prophet, to Parley P. Pratt and Ziba Peterson, October, 1830. Great interest and yearning desires were felt by the Elders respecting the Lamanites, of whose predicted blessings the Church had learned from the Book of Mormon. In consequence, supplication was made that the Lord would indicate his will as to whether Elders should be sent at that time to the Indian tribes in the West. The revelation followed. See History of the Church, vol. 1, p. 118. – The missionaries admonished to confine themselves to the expounding of the written word, as they shall be given understanding thereof.

1. And now concerning my servant Parley P. Pratt, behold, I say unto him that as I live I will that he shall declare my gospel and learn of me, and be meek and lowly of heart.

2. And that which I have appointed unto him is that he shall go with my servants, Oliver Cowdery and Peter Whitmer, Jun., into the wilderness among the Lamanites.

3. And Ziba Peterson also shall go with them; and I myself will go with them and be in their midst; and I am their advocate with the Father, and nothing shall prevail against them.

4. And they shall give heed to that which is written, and pretend to no other revelation; and they shall pray always that I may unfold the same to their understanding.

5. And they shall give heed unto these words and trifle not, and I will bless them. Amen.

George Q. Cannon: *Introduction*

The revelation formerly given through the Prophet to Oliver Cowdery [Sec. 28:14-16], enunciating the divine decree concerning the Lamanites and the work to be accomplished among them, created great interest in the minds of the Elders of the Church. The desire to learn more of this important matter was intensified by the harmony which prevailed during the conference [Sept. 1830], and the flow of the Spirit resulting therefrom. Joseph and his brethren realized the purposes of God toward the Indians of this land were great and far-reaching, and that the time would come when they must receive the Gospel and enjoy its blessings.

Many of the Elders expressed a desire to take up the work of the ministry among their brethren bound in darkness and ignorance through the curse laid upon their fathers; but before appointing anyone to aid Oliver and Peter Whitmer in this mission, Joseph inquired of the Lord. [Oct. 1830.] (*Life of Joseph Smith*, 1907, pp. 78-79.)

George Q. Cannon: 1-5

His [the Lord's] answer was a revelation appointing unto Parley P. Pratt and Ziba Peterson that they should go with Oliver and Peter into the wilderness, among the Lamanites. Our Lord and Savior promised them that he would go with them and be in their midst, and that nothing should prevail against them; but they were commanded to pretend to no power or revelation except that which was given to them by God, and unfolded by the Holy Spirit to their understanding. (*Life of Joseph Smith*, 1907, p. 79.)

John A. Widtsoe: 2
He shall go with my servants . . . among the Lamanites

These missionaries [Oliver Cowdery, Parley P. Pratt, Peter Whitmer, Jr., Ziba Peterson], left in the fall of 1830. On the way they stopped at Kirtland, Ohio, and the neighboring villages. There they preached the newly restored gospel with astonishing results. In Kirtland and neighborhood were hundreds of settlers who were seekers after truth. Alexander Campbell and his flock were there. Some of these, Lyman Wight, Isaac Morley, and Titus Billings, belonged to a group which attempted to have all things in common. There also Parley P. Pratt presented to Sidney Rigdon, his old friend and teacher, a copy of the Book of Mormon.

Before long several persons applied for baptism. Sidney Rigdon, a Campbellite writer and eloquent preacher, entered the waters of baptism. Branches were organized. The field there seemed fertile for the preaching of the restored gospel. The missionaries spent several weeks in the Kirtland territory to expound the gospel to interested listeners.

However, the missionaries had been called to go to the

Indian territory. Winter was coming, so about November 1st, they left the congenial Kirtland area and moved westward. On the way they proselyted and left copies of the Book of Mormon here and there.

Then the winter of 1830-31, the severest in the memories of men, descended upon them. The Mississippi River was frozen over, and the usual carriage or riding travel was impossible. But despite the weather, and under great suffering, they walked through snow and over ice for three hundred miles.

At last they reached Independence, Missouri. Since they had disposed of all their copies of the Book of Mormon, Parley P. Pratt was selected to return for a new supply.

Meanwhile, under restrictions set up by the Indian agents, the missionaries had little access to the Indians. But they preached long and loud to the Missouri settlers. To support themselves they did such work as was available. They set up a tailor shop in Independence; some of their patrons became defenders of the Latter-day Saints later when persecution raged.

All in all, this mission bore rich fruit. (*Joseph Smith*, 1951, pp. 136-37.)

John Taylor: 4

We, as Latter-day Saints, are indebted to the revelations of God, given unto Joseph Smith, for the knowledge of the very first principles of the doctrine of Christ, and he could not have known it unless it had been revealed to him. One thing I did know of myself before I came into this Church, and that is more than a great many know of themselves, namely that I was a fool, and did not know anything unless God revealed it. It takes a great deal of hammering to get that into some men's minds. The main questions in my mind, when this Gospel came were, "Is this true?" "Is this from God or is it not?" "Has God indeed spoken as this man says he has?" If he has not, it is all a fiction, and a farce, and delusion, like the other "isms" that exist in the world; if he has, it is for me to obey, no matter what the consequences may be.

There is one thing that has always been satisfactory to my mind in relation to this Gospel, namely, there has never been one principle revealed, at any time, but what has been instructive and in accordance with the Scripture, which we consider to be of divine origin. Never one principle but what could be substantiated by the word of God, although we did not know it before, and the world does not know it now. (*JD*, May 6, 1870, 13:225-26.)

SECTION 33

Revelation given through Joseph Smith the Prophet, to Ezra Thayre and Northrop Sweet, at Fayette, New York, October, 1830. In recording this revelation the Prophet avers that the Lord is ever ready to instruct such as diligently seek in faith. – The corrupted state of the world declared – Call for laborers in the ministry – Bringing forth of the Church from the wilderness and its establishment by the Lord – Commission of the Elders to proclaim repentance and baptism – Imminence of the Lord's coming.

1. Behold, I say unto you, my servants Ezra and Northrop, open ye your ears and hearken to the voice of the Lord your God, whose word is quick and poweful, sharper than a two-edged sword, to the dividing asunder of the joints and marrow, soul and spirit; and is a discerner of the thoughts and intents of the heart.

2. For verily, verily, I say unto you that ye are called to lift up your voices as with the sound of a trump, to declare my gospel unto a crooked and perverse generation.

3. For behold, the field is white already to harvest; and it is the eleventh hour, and the last time that I shall call laborers into my vineyard.

4. And my vineyard has become corrupted every whit; and there is none which doeth good save it be a few; and they err in many instances because of priestcrafts, all having corrupt minds.

5. And verily, verily, I say unto you, that this church have I established and called forth out of the wilderness.

6. And even so will I gather mine elect from the four quarters of the earth, even as many as will believe in me, and hearken unto my voice.

7. Yea, verily, verily, I say unto you, that the field is white already to harvest; wherefore, thrust in your sickles, and reap with all your might, mind, and strength.

8. Open your mouths and they shall be filled, and you shall become even as Nephi of old, who journeyed from Jerusalem in the wilderness.

9. Yea, open your mouths and spare not, and you shall be laden with sheaves upon your backs, for lo, I am with you.

10. Yea, open your mouths and they shall be filled, saying: Repent, repent, and prepare ye the way of the Lord, and make his paths straight; for the kingdom of heaven is at hand;

11. Yea, repent and be baptized, every one of you, for a remission of your sins; yea, be baptized even by water, and then cometh the baptism of fire and of the Holy Ghost.

12. Behold, verily, verily, I say unto you, this is my gospel; and remember that they shall have faith in me or they can in nowise be saved;

13. And upon this rock I will build my church; yea, upon this rock ye are built, and if ye continue, the gates of hell shall not prevail against you.

14. And ye shall remember the church articles and covenants to keep them.

15. And whoso having faith you shall confirm in my church, by the laying on of the hands, and I will bestow the gift of the Holy Ghost upon them.

16. And the Book of Mormon and the holy scriptures are given of me for your instruction; and the power of my Spirit quickeneth all things.

17. Wherefore, be faithful, praying always, having your lamps trimmed and burning, and oil with you, that you may be ready at the coming of the Bridegroom—

18. For behold, verily, verily, I say unto you, that I come quickly. Even so. Amen.

Joseph Smith: *Introduction*

The Lord, who is ever ready to instruct such as diligently seek in faith, gave the following revelation at Fayette, New York; [Section 33, follows.] (*HC* 1:126, October 1830.)

George Q. Cannon: *Introduction*

In this same month of October a revelation was given through the Prophet to Ezra Thayre and Northrop Sweet, calling them to labor in the vineyard, for the eleventh hour had come. They were promised that speech sacred and powerful should be given unto them, if they would have faith to open their mouths before congregations. (*Life of Joseph Smith*, 1907, p. 79.)

Hugh B. Brown: 2-5

And still there are some who say it matters little or not at all which church one joins, which gospel one preaches, whether it be the gospel of Luther, Knox, or Calvin, whether one belongs to the Roman or Greek Catholic church, to one of the numerous Protestant denominations, or to some group which emphasizes some one aspect of the gospel, such as faith healing, mode of baptism, which day is the Sabbath, etc. Unfortunately, the world is faced with a variety of religious denominations which in some measure neutralize each other's influence in the minds of the people.

The question then arises, "Where shall we find that gospel?" The Church of Jesus Christ of Latter-day Saints makes certain definite statements with respect to what the gospel is. A commission was appointed in England recently by the Archbishops of Canterbury and York to make a complete survey of modern evangelism, and they were asked to seek and discover, if they could, the causes for the wide and deep gulf that exists between the church and the people. This commission in the preamble of their report, emphasized the irrelevance of the church in the life and thought of the community in general.

The most arresting observation made by the commission was, "We believe that the tendency to preach another gospel, or a partial gospel, has been the weakness (not to say the sin) of the church." This observation reminds us of Paul's warning and anathema which for emphasis he repeated:

"As we said before, so say I now again, if any man preach any other gospel unto you than that ye have received, let him be accursed." (Gal. 1:9.)

What gospel did Paul preach? All will agree that he was converted to the gospel of Jesus Christ as now taught in the New Testament through personal communication and instruction. He became one of its chief exponents, most effective and fearless defenders, and finally one of its martyrs. Many are asking, "Where can one find a church which teaches the gospel as Paul taught it?" Any search for the true gospel leads at once to the matter of origin and authority.

In a brief consideration of that subject we shall not challenge the claims of other churches unless our claim that we have the gospel is taken as a challenge. The Catholic church bases its claims to authority on the long line of apostolic succession. Many of the other churches began with a protest against or an attempted reformation of the so-called mother church. As the great reformers failed to change or reform the false teachings and undesirable conditions they claimed to have discovered, and as they were successively excommunicated, some of them undertook to establish new churches without claiming new revelation or authoritative ordination.

The restored gospel of Jesus Christ does not base its claim to authority on apostolic succession, nor did it begin with a protest against or attempt to reform other churches. Furthermore, this Church did not have its beginning in scholarly analysis of the gospel as taught in the Bible. Its founder, at the time of the first vision, did not claim to be a profound student of theology, and he knew little of the writings of the early church fathers. His message came as a direct revelation from heaven. (CR, April 1958, pp. 108-9.)

Joseph Fielding Smith: 3
The last time

By the "last time" the Lord meant the Dispensation of the Fulness of Times. (CR, April 1946, p. 155.)

George Albert Smith: 4
There is none which doeth good save it be a few

The condition that has come upon the earth is not the result of righteousness; it is the result of disobedience to the laws of our Father in heaven, and we as members of this Church have been warned of what is to come. We have not only been warned by the scriptures that were given in the days of the Savior and prior to his time, and those that were given after him, but in our own day and age the Lord has spoken and the revelations of our Heavenly Father are found in the Doctrine and Covenants. If we will read these revelations we will learn that the experiences through which we are passing were predicted, that the very promises that the Lord made are now being fulfilled. [P. of G. P., Joseph Smith, 1:21-55; D&C 45:25-34.]

It does seem strange that so many of our Father's children think they are finding satisfaction in doing things that are wrong. The distress of the world today is very largely because men have turned from the teachings of the Lord. (CR, April 1932, p. 43.)

Hyrum M. Smith: 4
All having corrupt minds

Let me explain, when I use the term "corrupt" with reference to these ministers of the gospel, that I use it in the same sense that I believe the Lord used it when he made that declaration to Joseph Smith, the Prophet, in answer to the Prophet's prayer. He did not mean, nor do I mean, that the ministers of religion are personally unvirtuous or impure. I believe as a class they, perhaps in personal purity, stand a little above the average order of men. When I use the term "corrupt" I mean, as I believe the Lord meant, that they have turned away from the truth, the purity of the truth, the beauty of the truth, and have turned to that which is false. A false doctrine is a corrupt doctrine; a false religion is a corrupt religion; a false teacher is a corrupt teacher. Any man who teaches a false doctrine, who believes in and practices and teaches a false religion is a corrupt professor, because he teaches that which is impure and not true. That is the trouble with Christianity today. It is not true. (CR, October 1916, p. 43.)

Anthon H. Lund: 6
Even so will I gather mine elect

We look upon this as the land of Zion, and the principle of gathering, though a unique one, has been one that has pervaded the teachings and belief of the Latter-day Saints from the beginning. Even before the Elders in their missionary labors have said anything about a Zion, the Spirit of God has witnessed to the spirits of those who have received the Gospel that there would be a gathering, but that God would have a people of his own and that they would be gathered in one place. From the very beginning of the Gospel being sent to England we have evidence to prove this. I have seen in my administrations how quickly this spirit has taken possession of the Saints. And while we do not urge gathering today, feeling that the work will be strengthened by most of the

Saints remaining in the branches for a time and helping the Elders carry the warning message of the Gospel, yet the principle of gathering is just as true as ever it has been. (*CR*, October 1899, p. 13.)

Anthony W. Ivins: 8-18

I will read . . . a word or two from one of the revelations given in the year 1830, in October of that year, the portion to which I refer reads as follows: [Sec. 33:10-18, quoted.] . . .

In the first place, in order that a man may be saved in the kingdom of God he must have faith in our Lord and Savior Jesus Christ, he must accept him and believe that he is indeed the Son of God and the Redeemer of the world. When he knows that, repents of his sins, and is baptized for the remission of his sins, then it is his duty to continue in well doing, remembering, as stated here, the Church articles and covenants to keep them; and the Book of Mormon and the Holy Scripture, which contain in great part these articles and covenants. For the Lord declares they are given of him for our instruction by the power of the Spirit, which quickeneth all things. . . .

Now, the Lord has revealed unto us in these modern scriptures as well as in scriptures that were given in ancient times, the necessary articles and covenants by which we may be guided and directed in church government and understand the truth of the Gospel. Through the faith, diligence and heed we give to these instructions, we may know that the Lord and Savior of this world is indeed our Redeemer and the Son of God. We may know this provided our studies and faithfulness are guided by prayer, for in this same commandment the Lord declared that we should pray always. [Sec. 33:17, quoted.]

There is no reason in the world why each member of the Church should not have a thorough understanding of the principles of the Gospel, of the order of the Church, and the government of the Church, so that none need be led astray by any wind of doctrine, or notion, that prevails among the children of men, which may come to their attention. If we are firmly grounded in the faith and built upon the rock, we will know the truth, the truth which will make us free. (CR, October 1918, pp. 53-54.)

Charles W. Penrose: 11-15

It is a glorious work to carry this message of salvation, to bring souls, honest souls, into the knowledge of the truth and into the Church of Christ, to baptize them for the remission of their sins, and their sins are washed away; as the water washes their bodies, so their souls are cleansed, their spiritual being is cleansed and revived, and they are born unto Christ Jesus, and become part of him, or of his body, the Church; and then by the laying on of hands to confer upon them the gift of the Holy Ghost as a gift from God, the Holy Spirit to be with them as a constant witness, as the abiding testimony, as the light of God, lit up in their souls, and to enable them to come near to the Lord and receive the revelations of his will concerning themselves, but not to govern the Church unless they are so appointed.... People of different languages and countries and customs, to whom I have had the privilege of bearing my testimony, who have embraced the Gospel, have received this one spirit, which gives the testimony of Jesus, and it is a reality.... It is the light from the Sun of Righteousness. It is the glory of God that shines around about them. It fills the soul with peace. It gives them an abiding witness of the life and death and atonement of the Lord Jesus Christ, of the divine authority of the elders of Israel who bear this priesthood, and it is a real thing in the soul of man. (CR, October 1918, p. 20.)

Rudger Clawson: 12
This is my gospel

We mean by the Gospel just what Paul said about it. He said: "I am not ashamed of the gospel of Christ; for it is the power of God unto salvation, to every one that believeth." [Rom. 1:16.] The Savior said that those who rejected it and would not have the Gospel would be damned, or, in other words, would come under very great condemnation. If you do not like the word damned, use the word condemnation, because both words mean exactly the same thing, only one is a little more expressive than the other. And so we find that salvation is to come through obedience to the Gospel. (CR, October 1932, p. 8.)

Lorenzo Snow: 13
The gates of hell shall not prevail against you

The Church of Christ today is built upon the same principle [revelation] and the gates of hell shall not prevail against it. They did not prevail against us in our infancy; they did not in our boyhood; they did not in our early manhood; and I will assure you they will not now that we are seventy years old.

This Church will stand because it is upon a firm basis. It is not from man; it is not from the study of the New Testament or the Old Testament; it is not the result of the learning that we received in the colleges nor seminaries, but it has come directly from the Lord. The Lord has shown it to us by the revealing principle of the Holy Spirit of light, and every man can receive this same spirit. (CR, April 1900, p. 3.)

First Presidency (Brigham Young, Heber C. Kimball): 17
Having your lamps trimmed and burning

Let the Church, therefore, prepare as a bride to receive her bridegroom; let the Saints have on their wedding garments, and have their lamps well supplied with oil, trimmed and burning; let all things be made ready for the reception of our Savior and Redeemer, even our Lord the Christ. Let all the Saints throughout the world live their religion, that they may be worthy to enjoy his presence and have converse with the angels of our God; let them gird up their loins and step forth in the power and might of Elijah's God to do battle in this great cause, and armed with high heaven's panoply, even the armour of salvation and the helmet of righteousness, go forth conquering and to conquer, until the gospel shall be sounded to every nation, kindred, tongue and people, and the pure in heart, the meek of the earth, the Israel of our God, be gathered out from the wicked nations and brought to inherit and worship under their own vines and fig trees, and learn of him whose glory will rest upon his temple as a cloud by day and a pillar of fire by night. (MS, January 26, 1856, 18:49-55.)

Francis M. Lyman: 17
Praying always, having . . . oil with you

The Lord requires his people to bow the knee before him every night and morning, and to remember him in their secret prayers. Every Latter-day Saint who neglects this requirement has not that supply of oil which is necessary to prepare him for the coming of the Son of Man. The Lord requires us to be obedient to the counsels of the Priesthood, and to look to them for counsel. Every Latter-day Saint who is obdurate in his feelings and will not listen to the counsels of the servants of the Lord shows a lack of oil. The Lord requires that we shall meet together on the fast day, fasting, praying, and remembering our offerings for the relief of the poor. Every Latter-day Saint who follows his daily avocation and neglects this duty shows a lack of oil. The Lord requires us to love our wives, our husbands, our children, and to love our neighbors. The Latter-day Saint who does not do this shows a dearth of that oil that is necessary to enable him to stand and be prepared for the coming of the Son of Man. The Lord requires us to preach the Gospel to all the world, and for this reason above all others has endowed us with his divine authority. If we neglect to honor and magnify the Priesthood, as we ought to do every day of our lives, we evidence a lack of oil. (CR, April 1901, p. 46.)

SECTION 34

Revelation given through Joseph Smith, the Prophet, to Orson Pratt, at Fayette, New York, November 4, 1830. The recipient was nineteen years old at the time. He had been converted and baptized when he first heard the preaching of the restored Gospel by his brother, Parley P. Pratt, six weeks before. See History of the Church, vol. 1, p. 127. – Commended for obedience – Commanded to preach and to prophesy as the Holy Ghost shall give utterance – Certainty of the Lord's advent.

1. My son Orson, hearken and hear and behold what I, the Lord God, shall say unto you, even Jesus Christ your Redeemer;

2. The light and the life of the world, a light which shineth in darkness and the darkness comprehendeth it not;

3. Who so loved the world that he gave his own life, that as many as would believe might become the sons of God. Wherefore you are my son;

4. And blessed are you because you have believed;

5. And more blessed are you because you are called of me to preach my gospel—

6. To lift up your voice as with the sound of a trump, both long and loud, and cry repentance unto a crooked and perverse generation, preparing the way of the Lord for his second coming.

7. For behold, verily, verily, I say unto you, the time is soon at hand that I shall come in a cloud with power and great glory.

8. And it shall be a great day at the time of my coming, for all nations shall tremble.

9. But before that great day shall come, the sun shall be darkened, and the moon be turned into blood; and the stars shall refuse their shining, and some shall fall, and great destructions await the wicked.

10. Wherefore, lift up your voice and spare not, for the Lord God hath spoken; therefore prophesy, and it shall be given by the power of the Holy Ghost.

11. And if you are faithful, behold, I am with you until I come—

12. And verily, verily, I say unto you, I come quickly. I am your Lord and your Redeemer. Even so. Amen.

Joseph Smith: *Introduction*

In the fore part of November, Orson Pratt, a young man nineteen years of age, who had been baptized at the first preaching of his brother, Parley P. Pratt, September 19th (his birthday), about six weeks previous, in Canaan, New York, came to inquire of the Lord what his duty was and received the following answer: [Section 34, follows.] (*HC* 1:127-28, November 1830; Fayette, New York.)

Joseph F. Smith: 1-3
My son Orson. . . . Wherefore you are my son

The Gospel has been preached to us, and we have essayed to obey it, that we might become the sons and daughters of God — heirs of God and joint-heirs with his Son. We can never attain to the blessings of the Gospel by merely becoming acquainted with it and then sitting down and doing nothing ourselves to stem the current of evil that is preying upon us and upon the world. (*CR*, April 1900, p. 40.)

Orson Pratt: 4
Blessed are you because you have believed

I remained therefore, apart from all of them [churches], praying continually in my heart that the Lord would show me the right way.

I continued this for about one year; after which, two Elders of this Church came into the neighborhood. I heard their doctrine, and believed it to be the ancient Gospel; and as soon as the sound penetrated my ears, I knew that if the Bible was true, their doctrine was true. They taught not only the ordinances, but the gifts and blessings promised the believers, and the authority necessary in the Church in order to administer the ordinances. All these things I received with gladness. Instead of feeling, as many do, a hatred against the principles, hoping they were not true, fearing and trembling lest they were, I rejoiced with great joy, believing that the ancient principles of the Gospel were restored to the earth — that the authority to preach it was also restored. I rejoiced that my ears were saluted with these good tidings while I was yet a youth, and in the day, too, of the early rising of the kingdom of God. I went forward and was baptized. I was the only individual baptized in that country for many years afterward. I immediately arranged my business and started off on a journey of two hundred and thirty miles to see the Prophet. I found him in the house of old father Whitmer, in Fayette, Seneca County, State of New York, — the house where this Church was first organized, consisting of only six members. I also found David Whitmer, then one of the three witnesses who saw the angel and the plates. . . .

I called upon the Lord with more faith than before, for I had then received the first principles of the Gospel. The gift of the Holy Ghost was given to me; and when it was shed forth upon me, it gave me a testimony concerning the truth of this work that no man can ever take from me. It is impossible for me, so long as I have my reasoning faculties and powers of mind, to doubt the testimony I then received as among the first evidences that were given, and that, too, by the gift and power of the Holy Ghost. (*JD*, July 10, 1859, 7:177-78.)

Orson Pratt: 5-10

He [Joseph Smith] inquired of the Lord, and obtained a revelation for your humble servant. He retired into the chamber of old Father Whitmer, in the house where this Church was organized in 1830. John Whitmer acted as his scribe, and I accompanied him into the chamber, for he had told me that it was my privilege to have the word of the Lord; and the Lord in that revelation, which is published here in the Book of Doctrine and Covenants, made a promise which to me, when I was in my youth, seemed to be almost too great for a person of as humble origin as myself ever to attain to. After telling in the revelation that the great day of the Lord was at hand, and calling upon me to lift up my voice among the people, to call upon them to repent and prepare the way of the Lord, and that the time was near when the heavens should be shaken, when the earth should tremble, when the stars should refuse their shining, and when great destructions awaited the wicked, the Lord said to your humble servant: "Lift up your voice and prophesy, and it shall be given by the power of the Holy Ghost." This was a particular point in the revelation that seemed to me too great for me ever to attain to, and yet there was a positive command that I should do it. I have often reflected upon this revelation, and have oftentimes inquired in my heart — "Have I fulfilled the commandment as I ought to have done? Have I sought as earnestly as I ought to obtain the gift of prophecy, so as to fulfill the requirement of heaven?" And I have felt sometimes to condemn myself because of my slothfulness and because of the little progress that I have made in relation to this great heavenly and divine gift. I certainly have had no inclination to prophesy to the people unless it should be given to me by the inspiration and power of the Holy Ghost; to prophesy out of my own heart is something perfectly disagreeable to my feelings, even to think of, and hence I have oftentimes, in my public discourses, avoided, when a thing would come before my mind pretty plain, uttering or declaring it for fear that I might get something out before the people in relation to the future that was wrong. (JD, February 7, 1875, 17:290-91.)

Brigham Young: 5-6

And I wish we had more Elders to go and preach just such sermons by the power of God, that is, "I know that Joseph Smith is a Prophet of God, that this is the Gospel of salvation, and if you do not believe it you will be damned, every one of you."

That is one of the most important sermons that ever was preached, and then if they could add anything by the power of the Spirit, it would be all right. When a man teaches that doctrine by the power of God in a congregation of sinners, it is one of the loudest sermons that was ever preached to them, because the Spirit bears testimony to it. That is the preaching which you hear all the time, viz. — to live so that the voice of God's Spirit will always be with you, and then you know that what you hear from the heads of the people is right. (JD, March 29, 1857, 4:298-99.)

Wilford Woodruff: 7-9

War, pestilence, famine, earthquakes and storms await this generation. These calamities will overtake the world as

God lives, and no power can prevent them. Therefore I say to the Elders of Israel, be faithful. We have had the priesthood given to us, and if we fail to use it right, we shall be brought under condemnation. Therefore, let us round up our shoulders and bear off the kingdom. (*JD*, June 1880, 21:127.)

Orson Pratt: 7-12

In regard to the future, it has been a duty devolving upon me, in connection with hundreds of others, to declare not only the Gospel, but to portray before the people future events. There are great things in the future, and we are sometimes apt to forget them. We have been looking, for some time past, for the Lord to accomplish and fulfill the times of the Gentiles; or the times allotted to them, during which the testimonies of his servants should go forth among them; or in other words, the times of the warning of the Gentile nations, the gathering out of their midst, a few here and there, of the believing instructions that are to be poured out without measure upon the Gentile nations. These things have been sounded so long in the ears of the Latter-day Saints that I have sometimes thought they have become like a pleasing song, or like a dream, and that they scarcely realize that these great events are at hand, even at the doors. But if we can depend upon the word of the Lord, if we can depend upon modern revelation which God has given — there is a time of tribulation, of sorrow, of great judgment, of great wrath and indignation, to come upon the nations of the earth, such as has not been since the foundation of the world. And these things are not far off, but are near at hand, and who, in that day, that has any sympathy in their hearts, any feelings of humanity but will mourn and sorrow over the calamities that will fall upon the nations. I know that these things are true. (CR, April 1880, p. 86.)

SECTION 35

Revelation given to Joseph Smith the Prophet, and Sidney Rigdon, December, 1830. As a preface to his record of this revelation the Prophet wrote: In December Sidney Rigdon came to inquire of the Lord, and with him came Edward Partridge; the latter was a pattern of piety, and one of the Lord's great men. See History of the Church, vol. 1, p. 128. – How men may become sons of God – Sidney is promised that through him the Holy Ghost shall be given, as by the Apostles of old – Directed to assist the Prophet Joseph, and assured of the eventual redemption of Israel.

1. Listen to the voice of the Lord your God, even Alpha and Omega, the beginning and the end, whose course is one eternal round, the same today as yesterday, and forever.

2. I am Jesus Christ, the Son of God, who was crucified for the sins of the world, even as many as will believe on my name, that they may become the sons of God, even one in me as I am one in the Father, as the Father is one in me, that we may be one.

3. Behold, verily, verily, I say unto my servant Sidney, I have looked upon thee and thy works. I have heard thy prayers, and prepared thee for a greater work.

4. Thou are blessed, for thou shalt do great things. Behold thou wast sent forth, even as John, to prepare the way before me, and before Elijah which should come, and thou knewest it not.

5. Thou didst baptize by water unto repentance, but they received not the Holy Ghost;

6. But now I give unto thee a commandment, that thou shalt baptize by water, and they shall receive the Holy Ghost by the laying on of the hands, even as the apostles of old.

7. And it shall come to pass that there shall be a great work in the land, even among the Gentiles, for their folly and their abominations shall be made manifest in the eyes of all people.

8. For I am God, and mine arm is not shortened; and I will show miracles, signs, and wonders, unto all those who believe on my name.

9. And whoso shall ask it in my name in faith, they shall cast out devils; they shall heal the sick; they shall cause the blind to receive their sight, and the deaf to hear, and the dumb to speak, and the lame to walk.

10. And the time speedily cometh that great things are to be shown forth unto the children of men;

11. But without faith shall not anything be shown forth except desolations upon Babylon, the same which has made all nations drink of the wine of the wrath of her fornication.

12. And there are none that doeth good except those who are ready to receive the fulness of my gospel, which I have sent forth unto this generation.

13. Wherefore, I call upon the weak things of the world, those who are unlearned and despised, to thrash the nations by the power of my Spirit;

14. And their arm shall be my arm, and I will be their shield and their buckler; and I will gird up their loins, and they shall fight manfully for me; and their enemies shall be under their feet; and I will let fall the sword in their behalf, and by the fire of mine indignation will I preserve them.

15. And the poor and the meek shall have the gospel preached unto them, and they shall be looking forth for the time of my coming, for it is nigh at hand—

16. And they shall learn the parable of the fig-tree, for even now already summer is nigh.

17. And I have sent forth the fulness of my gospel by the hand of my servant Joseph; and in weakness have I blessed him;

18. And I have given unto him the keys of the mystery of those things which have been sealed, even things which were from the foundation of the world, and things which shall come from this time until the time of my coming, if he abide in me, and if not, another will I plant in his stead.

19. Wherefore, watch over him that his faith fail not, and it shall be given by the Comforter, the Holy Ghost, that knoweth all things.

20. And a commandment I give unto thee — that thou shalt write for him; and the scriptures shall be given, even as they are in mine own bosom, to the salvation of mine own elect;

21. For they will hear my voice, and shall see me, and shall not be asleep, and shall abide the day of my coming; for they shall be purified, even as I am pure.

22. And now I say unto you, tarry with him, and he shall journey with you; forsake him not, and surely these things shall be fulfilled.

23. And inasmuch as ye do not write, behold, it shall be given unto him to prophesy; and thou shalt preach my gospel and call on the holy prophets to prove his words, as they shall be given him.

24. Keep all the commandments and covenants by which ye are bound; and I will cause the heavens to shake for your good, and Satan shall tremble and Zion shall rejoice upon the hills and flourish;

25. And Israel shall be saved in mine own due time; and by the keys which I have given shall they be led, and no more be confounded at all.

26. Lift up your hearts and be glad, your redemption draweth nigh.

27. Fear not, little flock, the kingdom is yours until I come. Behold, I come quickly. Even so. Amen.

George Q. Cannon: *Introduction*

In December, 1830, two men came from Kirtland, Ohio, to visit the Prophet at Fayette. They were Sidney Rigdon and Edward Partridge. Both had accepted the gospel, as declared to them by the western missionaries, and Sidney Rigdon had been baptized. After reaching Fayette, Edward Partridge demanded and received baptism under the Prophet's hands. These two men offered to Joseph, for the work of the Lord, their time, their talents, and all they possessed. Like all the early members of the Church, having not yet gained full understanding of the purposes of God, having not yet gained confidence in their own ability to rightly determine their conduct, they desired that the Lord should give them his special commands. Joseph prayed for revelation on their behalf, and was speedily answered. (*Life of Joseph Smith*, 1907, p. 83.)

Brigham Young: 2
As the Father is one in me . . . we may be one

How is it that the Latter-day Saints feel and understand alike, are of one heart and one mind, no matter where they may be when they receive the Gospel, whether in the north or the south, the east or the west, even to the uttermost parts of the earth? They receive that which was promised by the Savior when he was about to leave the earth, namely, the Comforter, the holy unction from on high which recognizes one God, one faith and one baptism, whose mind is the will of God the Father, in whom there dwelleth unity of faith and action, and in whom there cannot be division or confusion; when they receive this further light, it matters not whether they have seen each other or not, they at once become brothers and sisters, having been adopted into the family of Christ through the bonds of the everlasting covenant, and all can then exclaim, in the beautiful language of Ruth, "Thy people shall be my people, and thy God my God!" [Ruth 1:16.] (*JD*, October 8, 1876, 18:259.)

Charles W. Penrose: 2
Jesus Christ . . . who was crucified for the sins of the world

Now, we want to teach these things to our children, train them up to believe in the living and true God, the Author of our being, our Father in heaven, and in Jesus Christ, his Son, who died for us, and without whose redemption, as we read in the Book of Mormon, our spirits would have been banished forever from the divine presence, and our bodies would have mouldered in the dust forever. But through that atonement wrought out by Jesus Christ, and by our obedience to his commandments, we shall come forth from the dust and stand upon our feet and have all things that we have made ourselves fit for by our own acts. Forgiveness of sins, redemption from personal sin, is a doctrine of Christ to be obtained in the way that he has appointed. He died that we might live, and thus he atoned for the sin of Adam. He died that we might live and attain glory if we would repent and obey his commandments and receive the blessings in the way he has appointed; and our mission in the world here, what we have come on the earth to do, is to live that gospel and carry it to the ends of the earth and send it forth to all people, that all nations may hear the glorious sound of the glad tidings of salvation to the human race. (CR, April 1898, pp. 20-23.)

Charles W. Penrose: 2
As the Father is one in me

There is the oneness of Deity, the three in one; not as some preachers try to expound it, in the doctrines of the outside world, in the Article of Faith that they have, making them one immaterial spirit, no body, no real personage, no substance. On the contrary, they are three individuals, one in spirit, one in mind, one in intelligence united in all things that they do, and it takes the Father, and the Son, and the Holy Ghost, to make the perfect Trinity in one, three persons and one God or Deity, one Godhead. (CR, April 1921, pp. 13-14.)

Matthias F. Cowley: 3-6

A striking instance of divine purpose in the labors of men outside the true Church is pointed out in a revelation given in December, 1830, to Joseph Smith, Jr., and Sidney Rigdon. The Lord said: [Sec. 35:3-6, quoted.]

The revelation given December, 1830, from which the above is quoted, was upon the occasion of the first visit of Sidney Rigdon and Edward Partridge to the Prophet Joseph Smith. The labors of Sidney Rigdon, referred to in the quotation, must have alluded to his ministry in the Campbellite church, for he had been in the Church of Christ only about six weeks when this revelation was given, having embraced the Gospel at the hands of Parley P. Pratt and fellow missionaries near Kirtland, Ohio, late in October or early November, 1830.

As is well understood, the followers of Alexander Campbell preach faith, repentance and baptism by immersion for the remission of sins. These views Sidney Rigdon espoused as being better than what he already had, and when the true Gospel, in its fulness, with authority from God to administer the ordinances thereof, found him, he gladly obeyed the same. In about three weeks from the time Brother Pratt and co-laborers entered Kirtland, 127 persons were baptized. Subsequently the numbers were augmented to about 1,000 souls. In the providence of the Lord, Kirtland soon became the gathering place of the Saints, the facilities there being greatly enhanced by so many people embracing the Gospel and thus making a foothold for the Prophet Joseph Smith and the Saints who should follow him from the East. There the Kirtland Temple was built. (*Cowley's Talks on Doctrine*, 1902, pp. 447-78.)

Franklin D. Richards: 5-6

A man cannot preach with effect and power to another the forgiveness of sins through faith in the Lord Jesus Christ, or baptism for the remission of sins unless he has himself been baptized for the remission of sins and has faith in the Lord Jesus Christ himself. No man can administer in the ordinances of the Gospel of Christ with effect and with power unless he has first been made partaker of them himself. (*CR*, October 1897, pp. 24-25.)

Joseph F. Smith: 5-6

It is well, in my judgment, that the Latter-day Saints do not lose sight of the great privilege that has been bestowed upon them. No man can become a citizen of the Kingdom of God but by entering in at the door: there are thousands, tens of thousands, aye, millions of people who will never become citizens of the Kingdom of God in this world because they fail to exercise the agency and the power that has been given to them in the right direction. Nevertheless, they enjoy many of the blessings that are bestowed upon the world in common. The sun shines upon the evil and the good; but the Holy Ghost descends only upon the righteous and upon those that are forgiven of their sins. The rain descends upon the evil and upon the good; but the rights of the Priesthood are conferred, and the doctrine of the Priesthood distills as the dews of heaven upon the souls of those only that receive it in God's own appointed way. The favor of heaven, the acknowledgement of the Almighty of his children upon the earth as his sons and his daughters can only be secured through obedience to the laws which he has revealed. Riches or the wealth of the world cannot purchase these things. (*JD*, 1883, 24:175-76.)

George Q. Cannon: 5-6

A great many, to prove that baptism and laying on of hands are not necessary, have cited the case of Cornelius, who, though he was not baptized, received the Holy Ghost. [Acts 10.] The case of Cornelius is the only case of the kind on record, and there were strong reasons why it should be as it was with him. The Gospel and its ordinances were administered only to the Jews; Cornelius was a Gentile, and between the two races strong prejudices existed, the Jews looking upon the Gentiles as inferior to them. Cornelius and his household were the first Gentiles to whom the Gospel was preached. They received it, and the Lord, to show the Apostles that the Gentiles were entitled to the ordinances of salvation as well as the Jews if they were willing to comply with the requirements of the Gospel, conferred the Holy Ghost upon Cornelius and his family. When Peter saw this family he said, "Of a truth I perceive that God is no respecter of persons, but in every nation he that heareth him and worketh righteousness is accepted with him." [*Ibid.*, 10:34-35.] And when afterwards, he heard them speak with tongues and magnify God, he said, "Can any man forbid water that these should not be baptized which have received the Holy Ghost as well as we." [*Ibid.*, 10:47.] And he commanded them to be baptized in the name of the Lord. Peter did not say, Cornelius, you have received the Holy Ghost as well as we have, and there is no necessity for you to obey any further ordinances, which, under the circumstances, if he had considered baptism or the laying on of hands non-essential, he would have been very likely to do; but instead of that, he commanded them to be baptized. Peter took this, as the Lord intended it, as an evidence that the Gentiles as well as the House of Israel were entitled to the Gospel. And he had them baptized, and without doubt laid his hands upon them to confirm upon them the gift they had received. Had Cornelius, at that hour, stood upon his dignity and said, "There is no necessity for me to be baptized for the remission of my sins, God having given me the Holy Ghost without obeying that ordinance, and having already received the Holy Ghost, I have no need to have hands laid upon me," there is not a doubt in my mind but what that precious and inestimable gift would have been withdrawn from him, and he would not have enjoyed it after. It could only be continued to him on condition of his obeying the ordinances which God had placed in his Church and which he required all the inhabitants of the earth to submit to without hesitation; and without doubt Cornelius wisely went forward and obeyed those ordinances.

This was the manner in which the Apostles preached the Gospel to the inhabitants of the earth in those days. They did not say to the people, "You must seek the Holy

Ghost and probably the Lord will give it to you if you will only exercise faith enough"; they would comply with certain requirements if they should receive the Holy Ghost. The only condition was their sincerity and faithfulness in obeying the requirements. (JD, August 15, 1869, 14:50-51.)

George F. Richards: 6
They shall receive the Holy Ghost . . . even as the apostles of old

The people of the world of mankind today have not that Holy Ghost that was enjoyed by those holy men of God who gave the scriptures. If they had the Holy Ghost in the same degree of power that was had by those holy men who gave us the scriptures, then they would understand the scriptures just as did those men who gave the scriptures to us.

We are not only to receive the Holy Ghost, being born again, the way the Lord has designed that it should be and has been in the days of the primitive Church, but we are to live and labor as to have the constant companionships of the Holy Ghost, and he will not dwell in unholy tabernacles. (CR, October 1944, p. 88.)

Orson F. Whitney: 7-11

They who doubt the possibility of miracles are indeed without the power to perform them. But this does not prove that believers lack that power. Miracles are the fruits of faith — "These signs shall follow them that believe." [Mark 16:17.] The gist of the matter is this: These doubters have done away with God, or have tried to do away with him, and consequently are unable to conceive of a higher power than they themselves possess. . . .

Miracles are extraordinary results flowing from superior means and methods of doing things. When a man wants light he strikes a match, or presses a button, or turns a switch, and lo! there is light. When God wants light, he says: "Let there be light." It is simply a matter of knowing how to do things in a superior way, and having the power to do them. Man is gradually acquiring this power. It is a far call from the tallow dip to the electric light. But the end is not yet. Improvements will continue to be made, and some day, perhaps men may be able to make light just as the Lord makes it. Paradoxically, it might be said that the time will come when miracles will be so common that there will be none.

The Latter-day Saints are not strangers to the miraculous workings of divine power. Our history as a people is replete with such occurrences. I could relate many experiences of my own in support of this assertion, and so could these, my brethren, seated here upon the stand. . . .

Some years ago I was engaged to deliver a lecture in one of the towns south of this city, and was on my way to the lecture hall when I received a message from the bishop of the ward, asking me to come and administer to his little daughter, who was critically ill. Her doctor had said that she could not live till morning. Taking with me another elder, I proceeded to the bishop's home, and we administered to the dying girl. Next morning a telephone message informed me that a marvelous change had taken place. The young patient, who had not slept for days prior to being blessed by us, immediately thereafter had sunk into a sweet and refreshing slumber. She slept twelve hours, and woke up normal, and continued so. The doctor was astounded, and the parents, of course, were overjoyed. The girl, then fifteen years of age, and now twenty-four, is an active member of the ward in which she resides, has a good position and goes to and from her work as well and as happy as if she had never known a day's illness.

Her physician had said that she could not live till morning and no doubt he was right, from his viewpoint. Medical science had so decreed, and but for the interposition of Divine Providence, that decree would probably have gone into effect. According to the lesser law, she should not live. But a greater law said: "She shall live." And the lesser could not operate in the presence of the greater.

Miracles belong to no particular time or place. Wherever and whenever there is a legitimate demand for the exercise of divine power, that power will act, and marvels will result. We worship a God of miracles, and he changeth not, but is the same yesterday, today and forever. (Mormon

9:11, 17-20.) There is but one valid reason for the absence of miracles among any people, and that is the absence of faith. "All things are possible to them that believe." [Mark 9:23.] (CR, April 1925, pp. 17, 20-22.)

Jedediah M. Grant: 8-9

I want to bear my testimony that mine eyes have seen the sick healed in the way the Gospel recommends; I have seen the ears of the deaf opened, and they have heard; I have seen the lame man walk, and leap like a hart; and I have seen others rise up suddenly from their sickbed, healed of a consuming fever.

In Montrose, near Nauvoo, hundreds of families were sick nigh unto death, and some were given up to die. The Prophet Joseph Smith took some of the Elders with him, and went over there, and said to the sick, "I command you, in the name of the Lord God, to rise up and walk." And he went from house to house, and made every man, woman, and child to walk, and they followed him to the next sick family, and they are witnesses here to testify to it. There are men now upon the face of the earth who, by the visions of the Almighty, have seen convoy after convoy of angels. Can you find these things outside of the Latter-day Saint Church? No; you cannot. (JD, December 17, 1854, 2:232.)

Heber C. Kimball: 8-9

As to the circumstance [above] Brother Jedediah M. Grant was speaking of in Montrose, I was with Brother Joseph, and so was Brother Brigham and many others, and hundreds were healed, and leaped out of their beds, and followed us. If you do not believe it, call on many of those that were sick nigh unto death at that time, and are now living in these valleys, enjoying good health. How many sick have been healed in old England? I have been many a time in houses where people were sick nigh unto death with smallpox and with other complaints, and they were healed by the power of God; I have taken them to the water, when they have been on the verge of the grave, and baptized them, and they have been healed. "What, of the smallpox?" Yes; and there are numbers of people here that were sick nigh unto death, and Brother Orson Hyde is a witness that they were just ready to die, and they are now here in a robust state of health. (Orson Hyde, "It is true.") True? Yes, as true as that God reigns in the heavens; and there are thousands more in the Church who know it is true. The testimony of Brother Grant and other men is just as true, and will be valid just as much as the testimony of Peter, James, and John, for they speak the truth as it is in Jesus Christ. . . .

I wanted to bear testimony, in connection with Brother Grant, of the truth of his statements with regard to the healing power of God manifested in Montrose, for I went with the Prophet, and am an eyewitness. Has not this Gospel the same power it had eighteen hundred years ago? It has, for God has renewed it unto us, and conveyed it to us through Joseph Smith, by the ministration of an angel. (*JD*, December 17, 1854, 2:233-34.)

Luke Johnson: 9
They shall heal the sick

Soon after Joseph Smith moved from the state of New York my father, mother and Ezra Booth, a Methodist minister, went to Kirtland to investigate "Mormonism." My mother had been laboring under an attack of chronic rheumatism in the shoulder, so that she could not raise her hand to her head for about two years; the Prophet laid hands upon her, and she was healed immediately. (MS, December 31, 1864, 26:834.)

Joseph F. Smith: 12

There are . . . certain blessings which God bestows upon the children of men only upon the condition of the rightful exercise of this agency. For instance, no man can obtain a remission of his sins but by repentance and baptism by one having authority. If we would be free from sin, from its effects, from its power, we must obey this law which God has revealed, or we never can obtain a remission of sins. Therefore, while God has bestowed upon all men, irrespective of condition, this agency to choose good or evil, he has not and will not bestow upon the children of men a remission of sins but by their obedience to law. Therefore the whole world lies in sin and is under condemnation, inasmuch as light has come unto the world and men will not avail themselves of that light to put themselves in a proper position before the Lord. And this condemnation rests with tenfold force upon all those that have yielded obedience to this law, and have once received a remission of their sins, but have returned unto sin, and have forgotten or disregarded the covenants they made in the waters of baptism. (*JD*, April 8, 1883, 24:175.)

Hugh B. Brown: 12

While the Church, which was organized under divine direction, is the kingdom of God on earth, its membership consists of men and women who are not yet made perfect. It is a mixed society with an international complexion, subject in varying degrees to the weaknesses of humanity. It does not claim to be a picture gallery where every portrait is a masterpiece; therefore, Church membership requires continued tolerance, charity, and love of fellow men.

We do not claim to have achieved perfection; we often fall short of our ideals; but with additional revelations from the Lord, and with the gift of the Holy Ghost to help us, we hope it may be said of The Church of Jesus Christ of Latter-day Saints what Peter said to the Church of Jesus Christ of former-day Saints:

"But ye are a chosen generation, a royal priesthood an holy nation, a peculiar people; that ye should shew forth the praises of him who hath called you out of darkness into the marvelous light." [1 Peter 2:9.] (*CR*, April 1958, pp. 109-10.)

Joseph Fielding Smith: 13-14

How wonderfully this promise has been fulfilled! [Sec. 35:13-14.] There have not been many of the great and mighty, according to the notions of the world, who have come into the Church. Most of those who have arisen to prominence have been humble and from the ranks of the poor. Educated men today, as in the days of Paul, seem to think that the "marvelous work and wonder" which the Lord has revealed is beneath their notice. They cannot be bothered with "purported" revelations from the Lord, or with foolish ordinances such as the Lord requires.

> For ye see your calling, brethren, how that not many wise men after the flesh, not many mighty, nor many noble, are called:
> But God hath chosen the foolish things of the world to confound the wise; and God hath chosen the weak things of the world to confound the things which are mighty.
> And base things of the world, and things which are despised, hath God chosen, yea, and things which are not, to bring to nought things that are:
> That no flesh should glory in his presence. (1 Cor. 1:26-29.)

Never in the history of the world has this truth been so greatly manifest as in the preaching of the Gospel by the weak and humble Elders of the Church. They have gone forth into strength which the Lord promised them and they have confounded the wisdom of the wise and the understanding of their prudent men has been hid. (Isa. 29:14.) Think of the Prophet Joseph Smith, who was without training or education, only in the simple grades, so far as the learning of the world is concerned. Yet the Lord called him and educated him and he has confounded the entire religious world and brought to naught their false doctrines. (*CHMR*, 1947, 1:149.)

Wilford Woodruff: 17-18

How could he, an illiterate boy, do that which the whole of the learning of the Christian world for seventeen centuries failed to do? Because he was moved upon by the power of God, he was instructed by those men who, when in the flesh, had preached the same Gospel themselves, and in doing this he fulfilled that which Father Adam, Enoch, Moses, Elias, Isaiah, Jeremiah and Jesus and his Apostles all prophesied about. . . .

Here is laid the foundation of the fulfillment of that mighty flood of prophecy delivered since the days of Father

Adam down to the last Prophet who breathed the breath of life. There has been more prophecy fulfilled in the last forty-three years upon the face of the earth, than in two thousand years before. These mighty prophecies . . . like a band of iron, governed and controlled Joseph Smith in his labors while he lived on the earth. He lived until he received every key, ordinance and law ever given to any man on the earth, from Father Adam down, touching this dispensation. He received powers and keys from under the hands of Moses for gathering the House of Israel in the last days; he received under the hands of Elias the keys of sealing the hearts of the fathers to the children, and the hearts of the children to the fathers; he received under the hands of Peter, James and John, the Apostleship, and everything belonging thereto; he received under the hands of Moroni all the keys and powers required of the stick of Joseph in the hands of Ephraim; he received under the hands of John the Baptist the Aaronic Priesthood, with all its keys and powers, and every other key and power belonging to this dispensation, and I am not ashamed to say that he was a Prophet of God, and he laid the foundation of the greatest work and dispensation that has ever been established on the earth. (JD, October 8, 1873, 16:266-67.)

John Taylor: 19
The Holy Ghost, that knoweth all things

This same Comforter has been given, in connection with the Gospel in these days, for our enlightenment, for our instruction, for our guidance, that we may have a knowledge of things that are past, of the dealings of God with the human family, of the principles of truth that have been developed in the different ages, of the position of the world and its relationship to God in those different ages, of its position in years that are past and gone, and of its present status. It is also given for our enlightenment, that we may be enabled to conduct all things according to the mind and will of God, and in accordance with his eternal laws and those principles which exist in the heavens and which have been provided by God for the salvation and exaltation of a fallen world; also for the manifestation of principles which have been and will be developed in the interest of man, not only pertaining to this world, but also that which is to come; through which medium the Lord will make known his plans and designs to his Priesthood and his people in his own due time. (*JD*, May 18, 1884, 25:178-79.)

George Q. Cannon: 20

The Lord revealed many comforting and exalting truths to Sidney Rigdon and Edward Partridge. To Sidney he gave a special command that he should write for Joseph. The Lord made known to Sidney what Joseph already understood — that the Scriptures should be given, even as they were in God's own bosom, to the salvation of his elect. And soon after this time, Joseph began a new translation of the Scriptures. While he labored, many truths, buried through scores of ages, were brought forth to his understanding, and he saw in their purity and holiness all the doings of God among his children, from the days of Adam unto the birth of our Lord and Savior. (*Life of Joseph Smith*, 1907, pp. 83-84.)

George Q. Cannon: 21

If men and women will be pure before the Lord in all things, to the extent of their ability, their progress in the Church of God and in the knowledge of God will be very rapid. Pure-minded people readily comprehend every principle that is advanced. They have no difficulty in understanding the truth when presented before them, nor in obeying its principles. Such persons never apostatize. God is bound by his promise to preserve them, and they can put unlimited confidence in him, knowing that he will deliver them from every evil. (MS, March 14, 1863, 25:169.)

John Taylor: 25

Why is it that you are here today? and what brought you here? Because the keys of the gathering of Israel from the four quarters of the earth have been committed to Joseph Smith, and he has conferred those keys upon others that the gathering of Israel may be accomplished, and in due time the same thing will be performed to the tribes in the land of the north. (*JD*, May 1884, 25:179.)

Brigham Young: 27
Fear not

Do you know that it is the eleventh hour of the reign of Satan on the earth? Jesus is coming to reign, and all you who fear and tremble because of your enemies, cease to fear them, and learn to fear to offend God, fear to transgress his laws, fear to do any evil to your brother, or to any being upon the earth, and do not fear Satan and his power, nor those who have only power to slay the body, for God will preserve his people. (*JD*, October 6, 1863, 10:250.)

Charles W. Penrose: 27
The kingdom is yours

I rejoice in the knowledge that God has set up his Church and Kingdom on the earth in the last days for the last time, and has so organized it that it shall continue and abide and shall not be overcome. The Lord says, "It is my good pleasure, little flock, to give unto you the Kingdom"; and the Kingdom is ours if we will obey these precepts and these commandments and counsels, and walked in the way of life, and be guided by those who are appointed. Let those who are appointed to labor in this ministry labor with all diligence, and give this Church all their powers and strength. (*CR*, April 1913, p. 64.)

Francis M. Lyman: 27
Behold, I come quickly

Can we not afford to do this now ["to be good, conscientious and honest with the Lord"], so that when the Bridegroom comes we shall be prepared to meet him: for he will come, he has always come when he has promised. He has visited the earth in this dispensation and has established his authority and power among men, and the millennium, the reign of righteousness, is to be ushered in; and it is liable to come in our day. The redemption of Zion is also liable to come in our day. There is doubtless a set time for the redemption of Zion and for the coming of the Son of Man. The time has not been made known to us, and is not likely to be until he comes. . . . We hope to be prepared, and we hope the people will be prepared, but it will come suddenly, and you will know it as soon as we know it. We have the spirit of that coming, and we have the spirit of the redemption of Zion. We have the spirit that indicates that in the near future the Lord will appear. (CR, April 1900, p. 8.)

SECTION 36

Revelation given through Joseph Smith the Prophet, to Edward Partridge, December, 1830. See heading to Section 35. – The recipient instructed to preach – Every man may be commissioned in the ministry if he will comply with the Lord's requirements.

1. Thus saith the Lord God, the Mighty One of Israel: Behold, I say unto you, my servant Edward, that you are blessed, and your sins are forgiven you, and you are called to preach my gospel as with the voice of a trump;

2. And I will lay my hand upon you by the hand of my servant Sidney Rigdon, and you shall receive my Spirit, the Holy Ghost, even the Comforter, which shall teach you the peaceable things of the kingdom;

3. And you shall declare it with a loud voice, saying: Hosanna, blessed be the name of the most high God.

4. And now this calling and commandment give I unto you concerning all men—

5. That as many as shall come before my servants Sidney Rigdon and Joseph Smith, Jun., embracing this calling and commandment, shall be ordained and sent forth to preach the everlasting gospel among the nations—

6. Crying repentance, saying: Save yourselves from this untoward generation, and come forth out of the fire, hating even the garments spotted with the flesh.

7. And this commandment shall be given unto the elders of my church, that every man which will embrace it with singleness of heart may be ordained and sent forth, even as I have spoken.

8. I am Jesus Christ, the Son of God; wherefore, gird up your loins and I will suddenly come to my temple. Even so. Amen.

Joseph Smith: *Introduction*

In December Sidney Rigdon came to inquire of the Lord, and with him came Edward Partridge; the latter was a pattern of piety, and one of the Lord's great men. Shortly after the arrival of these two brethren, thus spake the Lord: [Section 35.] And the voice of the Lord to Edward Partridge was: [Section 36, follows.] (*HC* 1:128, 131, December 1830; Kirtland, Ohio.)

First Presidency (Brigham Young, Heber C. Kimball, Jedediah M. Grant): 2

Incomparable delight and happiness fill the soul of the faithful Saint, who has the testimony of Jesus and the Spirit of the living God to enlighten his understanding. Happiness supreme and love divine fill his bosom, as he seeks to impart the gladsome intelligence to his fellow species, that they may also be partakers with him in the glorious cause, and share in its blessings. Thus our holy religion absorbs every feeling, desire, ambition, motive, and action of our natures, and renders every association in life tributary thereto; it forms the vitality of our very existence; it enters not only into our spiritual but also into our temporal organization, and controls us in all our affairs. This is true of every person who has tasted the good work of life, has received the Holy Ghost, and continues to walk in the light, and be led by its gentle influence. This is salvation in the kingdom of God, it is glory celestial, and exaltation. This is the work that makes angry the adversary, who fears the overthrow of his kingdom and power upon the earth, that causes Satan to rage and seek to destroy the Saints of the Most High, as he did in the days of Jesus and of his Apostles and followers. (MS, August 11, 1855, 17:497-504.)

David O. McKay: 2
The peaceable things of the kingdom

The peace of Christ does not come by seeking the superficial things of life, neither does it come except as it springs from the individual's heart. Jesus said to his disciples: "Peace I leave with you. My peace I give unto you; not as the world giveth, give I unto you." [John 14:27.] Thus the Son of Man as the executor of his own will and testament gave to his disciples and to mankind the "first of all human blessings." It was a bequest conditioned upon obedience to the principles of the Gospel of Jesus Christ. It is thus bequeathed to each individual. No man is at peace with himself or his God who is untrue to his better self, who transgresses the law of right either in dealing with himself by indulging in passion, in appetite, yielding to temptations against his accusing conscience, or in dealing with his fellow men, being untrue to their trust. Peace does not come to the transgressor of law; peace comes by obedience to law, and it is that message which Jesus would have us proclaim among men. (CR, October 1938, p. 133.)

Joseph Fielding Smith: 6

He [Edward Partridge] was baptized by the Prophet in December 1830, while on the visit to Fayette, and was commanded to proclaim the Gospel with a loud voice along with others who were ordained, to cry repentance saying: [Sec. 36:6, quoted.] This expression is found in Jude (3), and the Lord said to John (Rev. 3) "Thou hast a few names even in Sardis which have not defiled their garments; and they shall walk with me in white; for they are worthy." This is symbolic language yet is plain to understand. This is an untoward generation, walking in spiritual darkness and the punishment for sin is spoken of as punishment in fire. Garments spotted with flesh are garments defiled by the practices of carnal desires and disobedience to the commandments of the Lord. We are commanded to keep our garments unspotted from all sin, from every practice that defiles. We are therefore commanded to come out of the world of wickedness and forsake the things of this world. Every man who will embrace the truth and receive it in humility of heart was entitled to be ordained and set forth, to teach the truth. (CHMR, 1947, 1:150.)

Rudger Clawson: 8
My temple

We have two great churches, one in heaven, the other upon earth. They are moving along parallel lines, and the temple of God, as it appears to me, is the connecting link that connects the heavens with the earth, because it is through the temple that we will be able to reach our dead, and not otherwise. To pray for the dead may not be of any real assistance to them. To actually help them we must do a work for them. (CR, April 1933, pp. 77-78.)

SECTION 37

Revelation given to Joseph Smith the Prophet, and Sidney Rigdon, December, 1830. Herein is given the first commandment respecting gathering in this dispensation. – The future migration of the Church westward – Duties of the Elders in strengthening the Church.

1. Behold, I say unto you that it is not expedient in me that ye should translate any more until ye shall go to the Ohio, and this because of the enemy and for your sakes.

2. And again, I say unto you that ye shall not go until ye have preached my gospel in those parts, and have strengthened up the church whithersoever it is found, and more especially in Colesville; for, behold, they pray unto me in much faith.

3. And again, a commandment I give unto the church, that it is expedient in me that they should assemble together at the Ohio, against the time that my servant Oliver Cowdery shall return unto them.

4. Behold, here is wisdom, and let every man choose for himself until I come. Even so. Amen.

Joseph Smith: *Introduction*

It may be well to observe here, that the Lord greatly encouraged and strengthened the faith of his little flock, which had embraced the fulness of the everlasting Gospel, as revealed to them in the Book of Mormon, by giving some more extended information upon the Scriptures, a translation of which had already commenced. Much conjecture and conversation frequently occurred among the Saints, concerning the books mentioned, and referred to, in various places in the Old and New Testaments, which were now nowhere to be found. [Jude 3, 14, 15; Colossians 4:16; 1 Corinthians 5:9.] The common remark was, "They are *lost books!*" but it seems the Apostolic Church had some of these writings, as Jude mentions or quotes the Prophecy of Enoch, the seventh from Adam. To the joy of the little flock, which in all, from Colesville to Canandaigua, New York, numbered about seventy members, did the Lord reveal the following doings of olden times, from the prophecy of Enoch: [Moses, ch. 7, quoted.]

Soon after the words of Enoch were given, the Lord gave the following commandment: [Section 37, follows.] (HC 1:131-39, December 1830; Fayette, New York.)

George Q. Cannon: 1-4

But before the close of December 1830, after Sidney had been aiding Joseph some little time, the Lord required the Prophet to temporarily cease his work of translation. The enemy of all truth was drawing his forces around about Fayette to achieve the destruction of the Prophet, and the downfall of the newly-founded Church. But they were to be foiled. Fayette was not the region where the Lord designed his people to settle. Joseph's mind had been led to look to the western country for that purpose. Contact with Sidney Rigdon and Edward Partridge confirmed his inclination in that direction. The time had now arrived when it appeared necessary for the accomplishment of God's purposes, that his people (now increased to several score,) should have an abiding-place. It was made known to Joseph by revelation from the Lord, where this new resting-place should be. [V. 3.] He himself, did not expect to escape personal suffering or persecution by this new move; nor was this in the providence of God concerning him. But he knew that every migration made by him under the direction of the Almighty had been followed by prosperity and increase to the work, and he, therefore, obeyed the command to move to the place designated by the Lord without hesitation or doubt.

In the revelation now referred to [Sec. 37], it was commanded that the people of God should assemble in the State of Ohio, and there await the return of Oliver Cowdery and his fellow-missionaries from their eventful journey into the wilderness. Thus early in the history of the Church was the destiny of the people outlined. Kirtland was to be a stake of Zion: blessed by the presence of God's anointed Prophet and the Apostles of our Lord Jesus Christ: glorified by a temple built to the name of the Most High; and worthy to receive the ministrations in person of the Only Begotten Son of the Eternal Father. And yet it was to be but a temporary resting-place; for even while the Saints were to gather to Kirtland, the western missionaries were viewing the region in Missouri, yet to be known as the centre stake of Zion, which was to be built up and beautified for the visible presence of our Lord. (*Life of Joseph Smith*, 1907, pp. 84-85.)

John A. Widtsoe: 1

The use of the Bible by L.D.S. missionaries led, however, to one of the most notable labors of Joseph Smith. The teachings of the Book of Mormon, and the revelations he had received, convinced Joseph that in the Bible were many errors, such as unauthorized additions, incomplete statements, and faulty translations. This seemed to him, a lover and expounder of truth, out of keeping with the sacred nature of the volume.

Therefore, after placing the matter before the Lord he began the so-called "inspired translation" of the Bible. In June, 1830, less than three months after the Church was organized, there was revealed to him the "Visions of Moses," which gave a more complete account of the events mentioned in the book of Genesis, and set forth many lost doctrines; for example, the meaning of the fall of Adam and Eve, long misunderstood because of the imperfections of existing translations of the Bible, was cleared, and shown to be a necessary act in the development of the Lord's plan of salvation. [Moses, chapters 2-8.]

Towards the end of the year 1830, with Sidney Rigdon as assistant, he began a somewhat full "explanation and review" of the Old and New Testaments. The work then done is a convincing evidence of Joseph's inspiration.

Thousands of the changes were made, all conforming to common sense, and many in full harmony with later modern scholarship. Disputed meanings were made clear, and new doctrines expounded.

Here are some examples: The Bible says about conditions in the days of Noah: "It repented the Lord that he had made man on earth, and it grieved him at his heart." [Gen. 6:6.] The inspired translation reads: "It repented Noah, and his heart was pained, that the Lord had made man on earth, and it grieved him at his heart." [Moses 8:25.] The Bible says that "Melchizedek . . . without father, without mother, without descent, having neither beginning of days, nor end of life; but made like unto the Son of God; abideth a priest continually." [Heb. 7:3.] The inspired translation clears up this mass of confusion by saying: "For this Melchizedek was ordained a priest after the order of the Son of God, which order was without father, without mother, without descent, having neither beginning of days nor end of life. And all those who are ordained unto this priesthood are made like unto the Son of God, abiding a priest continually." Melchizedek, confusedly mentioned in the Bible, was given intelligent, biographical notice. Other like explanations abound in this really amazing document.

Joseph Smith may well be accounted one of the early students who sought to restore the Bible to its original form and simplicity. All this which came as helps to the missionaries in the field was opposed by the ministers whose Bible teaching left the people confused and in a state of uncertainty. (*Joseph Smith*, 1951, pp. 138-40.)

SECTION 38

Revelation given through Joseph Smith the Prophet, at Fayette, New York, January 2, 1831, at a conference of the Church. – Jesus Christ proclaims himself as the Creator – Doom of the wicked depicted – Goodly inheritance promised to the righteous – Definite promise of endowment with power from on high – The riches of eternity extolled – Diligent service required of every member of the Church.

1. Thus saith the Lord your God, even Jesus Christ, the Great I AM, Alpha and Omega, the beginning and the end, the same which looked upon the wide expanse of eternity, and all the seraphic hosts of heaven, before the world was made;

2. The same which knoweth all things, for all things are present before mine eyes;

3. I am the same which spake, and the world was made, and all things came by me.

4. I am the same which have taken the Zion of Enoch into mine own bosom; and verily, I say, even as many as have believed in my name, for I am Christ, and in mine own name, by the virtue of the blood which I have spilt, have I pleaded before the Father for them.

5. But behold, the residue of the wicked have I kept in chains of darkness until the judgment of the great day, which shall come at the end of the earth;

6. And even so will I cause the wicked to be kept, that will not hear my voice but harden their hearts, and wo, wo, wo, is their doom.

7. But behold, verily, verily, I say unto you that mine eyes are upon you. I am in your midst and ye cannot see me;

8. But the day soon cometh that ye shall see me, and know that I am; for the veil of darkness shall soon be rent, and he that is not purified shall not abide the day.

9. Wherefore, gird up your loins and be prepared. Behold, the kingdom is yours, and the enemy shall not overcome.

10. Verily I say unto you, ye are clean, but not all; and there is none else with whom I am well pleased;

11. For all flesh is corrupted before me; and the powers of darkness prevail upon the earth, among the children of men, in the presence of all the hosts of heaven—

12. Which causeth silence to reign, and all eternity is pained, and the angels are waiting the great command to reap down the earth, to gather the tares that they may be burned; and, behold, the enemy is combined.

13. And now I show unto you a mystery, a thing which is had in secret chambers, to bring to pass even your destruction in process of time, and ye knew it not;

14. But now I tell it unto you, and ye are blessed, not because of your iniquity, neither your hearts of unbelief; for verily some of you are guilty before me, but I will be merciful unto your weakness.

15. Therefore, be ye strong from henceforth; fear not, for the kingdom is yours.

16. And for your salvation I give unto you a commandment, for I have heard your prayers, and the poor have complained before me, and the rich have I made, and all flesh is mine, and I am no respecter of persons.

17. And I have made the earth rich, and behold it is my footstool, wherefore, again I will stand upon it.

18. And I hold forth and deign to give unto you greater riches, even a land of promise, a land flowing with milk and honey, upon which there shall be no curse when the Lord cometh;

19. And I will give it unto you for the land of your inheritance, if you seek it with all your hearts.

20. And this shall be my covenant with you, ye shall have it for the land of your inheritance, and for the inheritance of your children forever, while the earth shall stand, and ye shall possess it again in eternity, no more to pass away.

21. But, verily I say unto you that in time ye shall have no king nor ruler, for I will be your king and watch over you.

22. Wherefore, hear my voice and follow me, and you shall be a free people, and ye shall have no laws but my laws when I come, for I am your lawgiver, and what can stay my hand?

23. But, verily I say unto you, teach one another according to the office wherewith I have appointed you;

24. And let every man esteem his brother as himself, and practise virtue and holiness before me.

25. And again I say unto you, let every man esteem his brother as himself.

26. For what man among you having twelve sons, and is no respecter of them, and they serve him obediently, and he saith unto the one: Be thou clothed in robes and sit thou here; and to the other: Be thou clothed in rags and sit thou there — and looketh upon his sons and saith I am just?

27. Behold, this I have given unto you as a parable, and it is even as I am. I say unto you, be one; and if ye are not one ye are not mine.

28. And again, I say unto you that the enemy in the secret chambers seeketh your lives.

29. Ye hear of wars in far countries, and you say that there will soon be great wars in far countries, but ye know not the hearts of men in your own land.

30. I tell you these things because of your prayers; wherefore, treasure up wisdom in your bosoms, lest the wickedness of men reveal these things unto you by their wickedness, in a manner which shall speak in your ears with a voice louder than that which shall shake the earth; but if ye are prepared ye shall not fear.

31. And that ye might escape the power of the enemy, and be gathered unto me a righteous people, without spot and blameless—

32. Wherefore, for this cause I gave unto you the commandment that ye should go to the Ohio; and there I will give unto you my law; and there you shall be endowed with power from on high;

33. And from thence, whosoever I will shall go forth among all nations, and it shall be told them what they shall do; for I have a great work laid up in store, for Israel shall be saved, and I will lead them whithersoever I will, and no power shall stay my hand.

34. And now, I give unto the church in these parts a commandment, that certain men among them shall be appointed, and they shall be appointed by the voice of the church;

35. And they shall look to the poor and the needy, and administer to their relief that they shall not suffer; and send them forth to the place which I have commanded them;

36. And this shall be their work, to govern the affairs of the property of this church.

37. And they that have farms that cannot be sold, let them be left or rented as seemeth them good.

38. See that all things are preserved; and when men are endowed with power from on high and sent forth, all these things shall be gathered unto the bosom of the church.

39. And if ye seek the riches which it is the will of the Father to give unto you, ye shall be the richest of all people, for ye shall have the riches of eternity; and it must needs be that the riches of the earth are mine to give; but beware of pride, lest ye become as the Nephites of old.

40. And again, I say unto you, I give unto you a commandment, that every man, both elder, priest, teacher, and also member, go to with his might, with the labor of his hands, to prepare and accomplish the things which I have commanded.

41. And let your preaching be the warning voice, every man to his neighbor, in mildness and in meekness.

42. And go ye out from among the wicked. Save yourselves. Be ye clean that bear the vessels of the Lord. Even so. Amen.

George Q. Cannon: *Introduction*

Before organizing his company for the migration from Seneca County, New York, into Ohio, the Prophet called a conference of the Church to be held in Fayette on the 2nd day of January, 1831. With the opening of the year, the Prophet saw a glorious prospect for the welfare of the kingdom. And at this conference all present seemed to partake of his faith and of the power of the Holy Spirit. In a revelation [Section 38] given for the comfort and sustenance of the Saints on this occasion, the Lord made known that in secret chambers there was much plotting for the destruction of the Saints of God. The command was renewed that they should go into Ohio, and some of the reasons for this movement were made known. Encouragement was also given to the people that the Lord intended to give unto them a land of promise — a land upon which there should be no curse when the Lord should come. If they would seek it with all their hearts the Lord made a covenant with them that it should be the land of inheritance for themselves and their children, not only while the earth shall stand, but in eternity, no more to pass away. It is upon this and kindred promises that is founded the hope so tenaciously clung to by the Latter-day Saints amid all the vicissitudes of their checkered career, that they will yet inherit that land where the centre stake of Zion is to be built. (*Life of Joseph Smith*, 1907, p. 85.)

First Presidency (Joseph F. Smith, Anthon H. Lund, Charles W. Penrose): 1-4

In all his dealings with the human family, Jesus the Son has represented, and yet represents Elohim his father in power and authority. This is true of Christ in his pre-existent, antemortal, or unembodied state, in which he was known as Jehovah; also during his embodiment in the flesh; and during his labors as a disembodied spirit in the realm of the dead; and since that period in his resurrected state. To the Jews he said: "I and my Father are one" (John 10:30; see also 17:11, 22); yet he declared "My Father is greater than I" (John 14:28); and further, "I am come in my Father's name"

(John 5:43; see also 10:25). The same truth was declared by Christ himself to the Nephites (see 3 Nephi 20:32 and 28:10), and has been reaffirmed by revelation in the present dispensation. (D&C 50:43.) Thus the Father placed his name upon the Son; and Jesus Christ spoke and ministered in and through the Father's name; and so far as power and authority, and Godship are concerned his words and acts were and are those of the Father.

We read, by way of analogy, that God placed his name upon or in the Angel who was assigned to special ministry unto the people of Israel during the exodus. Of that Angel the Lord said: "Beware of him, and obey his voice, provoke him not; for he will not pardon your transgressions: for my name is in him." (Exodus 23:21.) (AF, 1924, pp. 470-71.)

Joseph Smith: 1-3

The great Jehovah contemplated the whole of the events connected with the earth, pertaining to the plan of salvation, before it rolled into existence, or ever "the morning stars sang together" for joy; the past, the present, and the future were and are, with him, one eternal "now"; he knew of the fall of Adam, the iniquities of the antediluvians, of the depth of iniquity that would be connected with the human family, their weakness and strength, their power and glory, apostasies, their crimes, their righteousness and iniquity; he comprehended the fall of man, and his redemption; he knew the plan of salvation and pointed it out; he was acquainted with the situation of all nations and with their destiny; he ordered all things according to the council of his own will; he knows the situation of both the living and the dead, and has made ample provision for their redemption, according to their several circumstances, and the laws of the kingdom of God, whether in this world, or in the world to come. (HC 4:597, April 15, 1842.)

James E. Talmage: 2
The same which knoweth all things

Divine revelation of what is to come is proof of foreknowledge. God, therefore, knows, and has known from the beginning, what shall be, even to the end of the world. The transgression of Adam was foreknown. . . . The earthly life, ministry, and sacrificial death of the Savior were all foreseen, and their certainty was declared by the mouths of holy prophets. . . .

But who will venture to affirm that foreknowledge is a determining cause? God's omniscience concerning Adam cannot reasonably be considered the cause of the Fall. Adam was free to do as he chose to do. God did not force him to obey the divine command. Neither did God's knowledge compel false Judas to betray the Christ, nor the recreant Jews to crucify their Lord.

Surely the omniscience of God does not operate to make of men automatons; nor does it warrant the superstition of fatalism. The chief purpose of earth life, as a stage in the course of the soul's progression, would be nullified if man's agency was after all but a pretense, and he a creature of circumstance compelled to do as he does. . . .

By way of illustration, consider the man versed in meteorology, who by due consideration of temperature, air-pressure, humidity, and other essential data, is able to forecast weather conditions. He speaks with the assurance of long experience in foretelling a storm. The storm comes, bringing benefit or injury, contributing to the harvest perhaps or destroying the ripening grain; but, whether it be of good or ill effect, can he who prophesied of the approaching storm be held accountable for its coming? . . .

The Father of our spirits has a full knowledge of the nature and disposition of each of his children, a knowledge gained by observation and experience in the long ages of our primeval childhood, when we existed as unembodied spirits, endowed with individuality and agency — a knowledge compared with which that gained by earthly parents through experience with their children in the flesh is infinitesimally small. In that surpassing knowledge God reads the future of child and children, of men individually and of men collectively. He knows what each will do under given conditions, and sees the end from the beginning. His foreknowledge is based on intelligence and reason. He foresees the future of men and nations as a state that naturally and surely will be;

not as a state of things that must be because he has arbitrarily willed that it shall be.

"Known unto God are his works from the beginning of the world." (Acts 15:18.) (*The Vitality of Mormonism*, 1919, pp. 318-20.)

Joseph Fielding Smith: 1-3

The Lord has stated that his progression is in building worlds and bringing to pass the immortality and eternal life of man, and this goes on forever thus increasing his power, dominion and glory, but not his intelligence or knowledge, or virtue, or wisdom, or love, for these things are, as the scriptures teach, in a state of perfection. (*CHMR*, 1947, 1:156.)

John Taylor: 1
The Great I AM

He is called in Scripture the I AM, in other words, I AM THAT I AM [Ex. 3:14], because of those inherent principles, which are also eternal and unchangeable; for where those principles exist, he exists. (*Mediation and Atonement*, 1950, pp. 161-62.)

Joseph Smith: 2
The same which knoweth all things

. . . God is the only supreme governor and independent being in whom all fulness and perfection dwell; who is omnipotent [all-powerful], omnipresent [everywhere present], and omniscient [all-knowing]; without beginning of days or end of life; and that in him every good gift and every good principle dwell. . . .

. . . Without the knowledge of all things, God would not be able to save any portion of his creatures; for it is by reason of the knowledge which he has of all things, from the beginning to the end, that enables him to give that understanding to his creatures by which they are made partakers of eternal life; and if it were not for the idea existing in the minds of men that God has all knowledge it would be impossible for them to exercise faith in him. (*Lectures on Faith*, Lecture 2, Paragraph 2; Lecture 4, Paragraph 11.)

Wilford Woodruff: 4
The Zion of Enoch

He [Enoch] perfected a city, which was called the city of the Zion of God. But behold and lo, the nations of the earth awoke and found that Zion had fled! [Moses 7:69.] The Lord took it to himself; took it away from the earth. The people were righteous; they had become sanctified and the Lord took them away out of the power of the wicked. Zion could not remain on the earth; there was not power sufficient to withstand the assaults of the wicked; or if there was, the time had not come when the Lord would make use of the children of men; or there were not enough of the children of men willing to take hold and manifest those principles in their lives so that they could remain on earth. (JD, December 12, 1869, 13:162.)

Anthon H. Lund: 4.
By the virtue of the blood which I have spilt

This earth was prepared for us; this was the school we had to pass through; and the Lord, seeing what would take place, prepared the Lamb, "slain from the foundation of the world" [Rev. 18:8] to atone for men and regain all that was lost in the fall. Jesus accepted of this mission. The sacrifice that was to be made for the human family could only be made by one who had not sinned himself. It would have to be done by One who voluntarily offered to do this, in order that justice might be satisfied and mercy be extended to the sinner. We learn in the revelations of the Lord that the fall extended to all, and that the grievous consequences of the fall were both temporal and spiritual. Jesus came; he made the sacrifice. He did it willingly. He was without blemish or fault. No sin was found in him, and as such he was proper subject for the sacrifice. (CR, April 1912, p. 12.)

Brigham Young: 6

Every departed spirit is subject to the laws that govern the spirit world. There are wicked men in the spirit world. Millions of them will have the privilege of receiving the Gospel in the spirit, that they may be judged according to men in the flesh, and no doubt but many will reject the Gospel there. (*JD*, December 10, 1868, 13:76.)

Joseph Fielding Smith: 7-9

If we would carry out that which the Lord revealed, as he had revealed it, then all things would be perfect; for the organization is a perfect organization, the theory of it, the plan of it, is without flaw, and if we followed all the orders that have been given to us in the priesthood and otherwise, if we would put into practice the great doctrines which have been revealed in the revelations contained in the Holy Scriptures, it would only be a matter of a very short time until this great people would be in the same condition, absolutely, as were the people in the city of Enoch. We would be able to walk with God, we would be able to behold his face, because then faith would abound in the hearts of the people to the full extent that it would be impossible for the Lord to withold himself, and he would reveal himself unto us as he has done in times past. (*CR*, April 1921, p. 40.)

John Taylor: 9
Be prepared

We never ought to do a thing that we would be afraid of God seeing us do; and if we are not afraid of God seeing us, we should not be afraid of man seeing us. (*JD*, September 20, 1857, 5:263.)

Joseph Fielding Smith: 10-14

In January, 1831, a conference was held in Fayette. Ordinary business was transacted and a revelation given in which the Lord made known the reason for the removal of the Church to the West. [Sec. 38:12, quoted.] This was because "all flesh is corrupted" and the powers of darkness prevail. The Lord revealed that the wicked were plotting in secret chambers the destruction of Joseph Smith and the Church. (*Essentials in Church History*, 1950, p. 121.)

Wilford Woodruff: 10-12

There is no prophecy of Scripture of any private interpretation, but holy men of old spoke as they were moved upon by the Holy Ghost, and their words will be fulfilled to the very letter, and it certainly is time that we prepare ourselves for that which is to come. Great things await this generation — both Zion and Babylon. All these revelations concerning the fall of Babylon will have their fulfillment. Forty-five years ago, in speaking to the Church, the Lord said — [Sec. 38:10-11, quoted.] This causes silence to reign, and all eternity is pained. The angels of God are waiting to fulfill the great commandment given forty-five years ago, to go forth and reap down the earth because of the wickedness of men. How do you think eternity feels today? Why there is more wickedness, a thousand times over, in the United States now, than when that revelation was given. The whole earth is ripe in iniquity; and these inspired men, these Elders of Israel, have been commanded of the Almighty to go forth and warn the world, that their garments may be clear of the blood of all men. (JD, October 8, 1875, 18:128.)

Joseph F. Smith: 10
Ye are clean, but not all

I do not suppose that you think or that anyone will think that we esteem ourselves as perfect, or as different and apart from other people of the world. We are, indeed, I am sorry to say, altogether too much like the rest of the world in many respects. We are people with like passions, like weaknesses, like imperfections — no doubt, results of human nature — as the rest of mankind. But the difference lies here: We have made a covenant in our hearts with God, the Eternal Father, that we will forsake sin; that we will eschew the very appearance of evil, as far as we possibly can; that we will overcome to the utmost our weakness and proneness to evil and wrong-doing; that we will seek light from all sources of light and intelligence; that we will seek knowledge that comes from above, and hold our ears open to listen to the words of truth, to the voice of understanding, and to the voice of inspiration that comes from the Lord, or that may come from man, inspiring men to do better, to improve, to advance in the scale of righteousness and of intelligence in the world; and that we will keep ourselves, as far as it is

possible for us to do so, clean and pure and unspotted from
the sins of the world. That is the difference. We have
covenanted with God that we will do this, and we expect
that God will require us to keep this covenant that we have
made with him, and that we will strive with all our might to
live consistent lives before the Lord and keep his laws. (CR,
April 1904, pp. 2-3.)

Melvin J. Ballard: 12
The angels are waiting. . . to gather the tares

I am willing to accept this statement. [Sec. 86:4-11.] I
believe it. I am convinced that the Latter-day Saints are the
"wheat," and they have been, and are being gathered out of
the midst of the "tares" of the earth. They are the salt of the
earth, and the gathering of the wheat from the midst of the
tares is almost completed. There remains but the gleaning of
the wheat; and when the wheat is gathered the tares shall be
bound in bundles, and the burning time remaineth for them.
The Lord gathered this people out from the midst of the
nations of the earth to preserve them from the desolations
that would come.

I bear witness to you that the angels of God, who hold
the power delegated to them to pour out his judgments upon
the wicked, marvel at God's leniency and patience to this
generation. That is why they cried: "Why are we not permitted to go forth?" They are stayed and held back. (CR,
October 1920, p. 78.)

Brigham Young: 16-20

All those who wish to possess true riches, desire the
riches that will endure. Then look at the subject of salvation,
where you will find true riches. They are to be found in the
principles of the Gospel of salvation, and are not to be found
anywhere else. . . . The only true riches in existence are for
you and me to secure for ourselves a holy resurrection; then
we have command of the gold and the silver, and can place it
where we please, and in whose hands we please. . . .

The power which belongs to the true riches is gained by
pursuing a righteous course, by maintaining an upright de-

portment towards all men, and especially towards the household of faith, yielding to each other, giving freely of that which the Lord has given to you, thus you can secure to yourselves eternal riches; and gain influence and power over all your friends, as well as your enemies. . . .

Remember, that true riches — life, happiness, and salvation, is to secure for ourselves a part in the first resurrection, where we are out of the reach of death, and him that hath the power of it; then we are exalted to thrones, and have power to organize element. Yes, they that are faithful, and that overcome, shall be crowned with crowns of eternal glory. They shall see the time when their cities shall be paved with gold; for there is no end to the precious metals, they are in the native element, and there is an eternity of it. If you want a world of the most precious substance, you will have nothing to do but say the word, and it is done. You can then say to the elements, "produce ye the best oranges, lemons, apples, figs, grapes, and every other good fruit." (JD, August 14, 1853, 1:269, 272, 273, 276.)

Rudger Clawson: 16

So, my brethren and sisters, if there are to be distinctions among us, they must not be based on our financial condition, but rather upon the principle of righteousness. One man is better than another if he is more righteous than the other. One man is more acceptable to the Lord than another if he lives nearer to the Lord than the other.

The prophet Jacob points out very clearly the manner in which it would be safe for his people to seek after riches. First seek the kingdom of God and its righteousness, and all other things will be added. Then if we seek for riches we will do it with the intent to accomplish good and to use them for the benefit and blessing of mankind and for the establishment and upbuilding of the Church and Kingdom of God.

The poor we have always with us. It was said by Abraham Lincoln that God must love the poor because he has made so many of them. The Savior seemed to think a great deal of the poor. He came to preach the Gospel to them, to administer to their wants, to heal the sick, to cast out devils, to open the eyes of the blind. His life and his ministry was devoted to the poor. You will find, if you study closely the revelations of God found in the Book of Covenants, that a great amount of space is devoted to the poor. [Secs. 42:30-42, 71; 56:16-18; 58:8-11; 78:3; 82:12; 83:6; 109:55; 136:8.] We are reminded of them continually; that we shall divide our substance with them. The fast day has been instituted, in part, for that purpose. It has been estimated that if the entire people of the Latter-day Saints would give to the poor the value of the two meals that they refrain or should refrain from partaking of upon that day, the poor of this church would be well provided for. (CR, April 1899, p. 4.)

George Q. Cannon: 16
The poor have complained before me

When wealth multiplies, the people get lifted up in the pride of their hearts, and they look down on their poor brethren and despise them, because they are better educated, have better manners, and speak better language — in a word, because they have advantages which their poor brethren and sisters have not. There is sin in this, and God is angry with a people who take this course. He wants us to be equal in earthly things, as we are in heavenly. He wants no poor among his people; he does not want the cry of the oppressed to ascend from the midst of the Latter-day Saints, and God forbid that it ever should! God forbid that the cry of any should ever ascend from the midst of the Latter-day Saints because of oppression or because of the lack of any blessing necessary for comfort! God wants us to feed the hungry, clothe the naked, and impart our substance for their support. But he does not want the poor to envy the rich. That is just as great a sin on their part as for the rich to oppress them. They must not envy the rich; they must not look on their brethren and sisters and envy them that which they have. [Sec. 56:17-18.] That is sinful, that is wrong, and the man or woman who indulges in it, indulges in a wrong spirit. God wants us to build each other up in righteousness. He wants us to love one another and to seek one another's benefit. This is the spirit of the Gospel of Jesus Christ. He has revealed it unto us, and we must cultivate it. (JD, September 8, 1872, 15:156.)

James E. Talmage: 21-22

We have seen that according to the words of holy prophets ancient and modern, Christ is to come in a literal sense and so manifest himself in person in the last days. He is to dwell among his saints, "Yea, even I will be in the midst of you." [3 Nephi 20:22; 21:25.] He declared to the people on this continent, whom he promised to establish in the land of the New Jerusalem; and similar assurances were given through the prophets of the east. [Ezek. 37:26-27; 2 Cor. 6:16.] In this prospective ministration among his gathered saints, Jesus Christ is to be at once their God and their King. His government is to be that of a perfect theocracy; the laws of righteousness will be the code, and control will be administered under one authority, undisputed because indisputable. . . .

The kingdom of heaven including the Church, and comprising all nations, will be set up with power and great glory when the triumphant King comes with his heavenly hosts to personally rule and reign on the earth, which he has redeemed at the sacrifice of his own life.

As seen, the kingdom of heaven will comprise more than the Church. The honorable and honest among men will be accorded protection and the privileges of citizenship under the perfect system of government which Christ will administer; and this will be their lot whether they are members of the Church or not. Law-breakers and men of impure heart will receive judgment according to their sin; but those who live according to the truth as they have been able to receive and comprehend it will enjoy the fullest liberty under the benign influences of a perfect administration. The special privileges and blessings associated with the Church, the right to hold and exercise the Priesthood with its boundless possibilities and eternal powers, will be, as now they are, for those only who enter into the covenant and become part of the Church of Jesus Christ. (AF, 1950, pp. 363, 368.)

Joseph Fielding Smith: 21

The commandment came to the members of the Church in January, 1831: [Sec. 38:21, quoted.] This will be when he descends in the clouds of heaven in power and glory. Let all people know that the parable of the fig tree is being fulfilled today. The tree puts forth its leaves and the summer is nigh. We are told that when we see these things we may know that in this generation, when these things take place, all that has been said concerning the coming Christ will be fulfilled. (*Progress of Man*, 1940, p. 490.)

First Presidency (Brigham Young, Heber C. Kimball, Jedediah M. Grant): 27

In union there is strength, but how can a people become united while their interests are diversified? How can they become united in spiritual matters, and see eye to eye, which they can only partly understand, until they become united in regard to temporal things, which they do comprehend? (MS, July 8, 1854, 16:427.)

Francis M. Lyman: 27

It is a great mystery to the people of the world how the Latter-day Saints hold so unitedly together as a people, why there is such a fraternal, binding feeling existing between them. Quite generally they look upon it as the result of compulsory power, exercised by the leaders of the Church. How incorrect this idea is! What holds this people together so solidly, and what makes them willing to labor for the salvation of the children of men, at the sacrifice of their own worldly affairs and interests, is answered in the text I have just read to you. [3 Nephi 11:20-36.] The Lord has spoken to us today by the inspiration of his Spirit. He has been present with us by his Spirit. Every Latter-day Saint has been moved upon by that same Spirit, and record has been borne in our hearts that we have listened to the word and the will of the Lord. That is the power, the secret power, that binds our hearts together and makes them respond as one, no matter where we may be. We may be thousands of miles apart, yet we are in unison, because bound together and inspired by the one Spirit. It is the same Spirit which binds the Father and the Son and makes them one. As the Father and the Son are one, so are we one. This is accomplished through our faith, repenting of our sins, cleansing our hearts, and living lives of purity before him. We may make a good start, but if we fail to continue in our good works and in our devotion to the Lord, that Spirit will diminish within us, and as his influence grows less within us, we are inclined to divide one against the other and receive the spirit of the world. Then it is that every man is for himself, following the imaginations of his own heart instead of being guided by the inspiration of the Holy Ghost. I would like us to understand and realize this. (CR, April 1904, pp. 10-11.)

George Q. Cannon: 27

The Lord desires to have us a united people, the people that will listen to his voice. And what does this mean? Does it mean tyranny? Does it mean oppression? Does it mean the taking away of any human being's rights? Does it encroach upon the liberty of any soul? No, it does not. It never has. It never will, because the Priesthood of the Son of God is not a tyrant. The operations of that Priesthood are beneficent under all circumstances. Look at the prosperity of this people. See how God has blessed them when they have listened to counsel and been guided aright. All our prosperity is traceable to this. Our misfortunes are traceable to our disobedience and neglect. Everyone knows this that has any faith whatever in the work of God. There is nothing asked of any man that he cannot do with the utmost pleasure and with the freest exercise of his agency. It has been so from the beginning, and it will be so to the end. (CR, April 1898, p. 35.)

Harold B. Lee: 27

I refer to the importance of unity and oneness of the Latter-day Saints.

As I have pondered the importance of this matter, I have recalled some of the blessings we could enjoy if we would be united as a people. If we would be united in paying our fast offerings and observing the law of the fast as fully as the Lord has taught it, and if we were united in carrying out the principles of the welfare program as they have been given to us by our leaders today, we would be free from want and distress and would be able fully to care for our own. Our failure to be united would be to allow our needy to become the pawns of politicians in the public mart.

If we were fully united as a people in our missionary work, we would rapidly hasten the day when the gospel would be preached to all people without and within the boundaries of the organized stakes of Zion. If we are not united, we will lose that which has been the lifeblood and which has fed and stimulated this Church for a generation.

If we were fully united in keeping the law of sacrifice and paying our tithes as we have been schooled today, we would have sufficient to build our temples, our chapels, our schools of learning. If we fail to do that, we will be in the bondage of mortgage and debt.

If we were united as a people in electing honorable men to high places in our civil government, regardless of the political party with which we have affiliation, we would be able to safeguard our communities and to preserve law and order among us. Our failure to be united means that we permit tyranny and oppression and taxation to the extent of virtual confiscation of our own property.

If we are united in supporting our own official newspapers and magazines which are owned and operated by the Church and for Church members, there will always be in this Church a sure voice to the people, but if we fail to be united in giving this support, we permit ourselves to be subject to abuse, slander, and to misrepresentation without any adequate voice of defense.

If we were united in safeguarding our youth from promiscuous associations that foster marriages out of the Church and out of the temples, by having socials and recreations as a united people, as has been the practice from our pioneer days, we would be building all our Latter-day Saint homes on a sure and happy foundation. Our failure to be united in these things will be our failure to receive eternal blessings that otherwise could be ours.

If we were united in safeguarding the Church from false doctrines and error and in standing as watchmen upon the tower as teachers and leaders in watching over the Church, then we would be free from these things that cause many to stumble and fall and lose their faith. If we are not thus united, the wolves among us will be sowing the seeds of discord, disharmony, all tending to the destruction of the flock.

If we were united in our temple work and in our genealogical research work, we would not be satisfied with the present temples, only, but we would have sufficient work for temples yet to come, to the unlocking of the doors of opportunity to those beyond who are our own kin, and thus ourselves become saviors on Mount Zion. Our failure to be united will be our failure to perpetrate our family homes in the eternity. So we might multiply the blessings that could come to this people if they were fully united in the purposes of the Lord. . . .

If we are not united, we are not his. Here unity is the test of divine ownership as thus expressed. If we would be united in love and fellowship and harmony, this Church would convert the world, who would see in us the shining example of these qualities which evidence that divine ownership. Likewise, if in that Latter-day Saint home the husband and wife are in disharmony, bickering, and divorce is threatened, there is an evidence that one or both are not keeping the commandments of God.

If we, in our wards and our branches, are divided, and there are factions not in harmony, it is but an evidence that there is something wrong. If two persons are at variance, arguing on different points of doctrine, no reasonable, thinking persons would say that both were speaking their different opinions by the Spirit of the Lord. . . .

If it is so important, then, that this people be a united people, we might well expect that upon this principle the powers of Satan would descend for their greatest attack. We might well expect, also, that if there be those of apostate mind among us, they would be inclined to ridicule and to scorn this principle of oneness and unity as being narrow-minded or as being unprogressive. We would likewise expect that those who are enemies would also seek to fight against that principle. . . .

May I test your unity as Latter-day Saints? Have you received a witness of the Spirit to your souls testifying that this is the truth; that you know this is the Church and kingdom of God; that you have received by baptism and by the laying on of hands the power of the Holy Ghost by which that unity of testimony might be accomplished? Have you that testimony in your souls?

May I ask you another question? Are you living each day so to improve your lives by living the principles and ordinances of the gospel that you are moving toward that day when you will overcome all things?

Finally, do you believe that these men whom we have sustained in this conference are the men through whom the channels of communication from our Heavenly Father are open? Do you believe — as Enos, the grandson of the great prophet Lehi, declared in his writing when he said he went into the mountain and prayed and " . . . the voice of the Lord came into my mind, again saying:" (Enos 1:10.) — Do you believe that the voice of the Lord comes into the minds of these men? If you do, then you believe what the Lord said that:

"Whatsoever they shall speak when moved upon by the Holy Ghost shall be scripture, shall be the will of the Lord, shall be the mind of the Lord, shall be the word of the Lord, shall be the voice of the Lord, and the power of God unto salvation." (D&C 68:4.)

Some there are who are prone to say, "We will follow their counsel in spiritual matters but not in temporal affairs. If they counsel us in other than that which pertains strictly to the spiritual welfare of the people, we will not follow them." Have any of you ever heard such comments? (CR, April 1950, pp. 96-100.)

Joseph F. Smith: 28

The hatred of the wicked always has and always will follow the Priesthood and the saints. The devil will not lose sight of the power of God vested in man — the Priesthood.

He fears it, he hates it, and will never cease to stir up the hearts of the debased and corrupt in anger and malice towards those who hold this power, and to persecute the saints, until he is bound. (*JD*, April 2, 1877, 19:24.)

Wilford Woodruff: 29

We cannot know the hearts of men, nor the will of God concerning nations, kingdoms and people only as it is revealed to us by the gift and power of the Holy Ghost. (*JD*, June 12, 1863, 10:215.)

James E. Talmage: 30
Treasure up wisdom in your bosoms

It is not fair to blame the Lord, even in thought, because he gives us warning of what is to come. It is most irrational and illogical so to do. He, with his omniscience, knows what is to come to individuals and nations, and he gives warnings. Many of us take that warning to be an expression of divine determination to punish and to afflict. Well, others besides the Lord are subjects of ill-directed blame sometimes. I have suffered from it. On one occasion I undertook to warn a merry party of intending picnickers not to set out on their jaunt, because a storm was coming, a violent storm. I had consulted the instruments that told of its coming. But they knew better and they went, and they came back in some fashion. I wish you could have seen them. But the tragical part of it was they blamed it all on me.

Shall it be that because the storm is predicted we should believe that the pre-knowledge so used is a determining cause? You know better. Let us be thankful for the warnings that the Lord has given and is giving, and prepare ourselves aginst the tempest.

Oh, Latter-day Saints, we have to bear the conditions that have been foretold, and that are now being realized. Let us do it with faith and resignation, never faltering, knowing that the Lord will bring out all things well, for his word shall not fail, nor shall his purposes be turned aside. (*CR*, April 1933, p. 109.)

Stephen L Richards: 30
Treasure up wisdom in your bosoms

We all prize wisdom. It is said to be the greatest of gifts. It is really the power to apply beneficent knowledge in all the decisions and vicissitudes of life. How we need wisdom in the composition of the troubles and difficulties of the world! How we need wisdom in our own affairs, with our families, our business and our associations. Almost every day is a day of decision — what to do; what choice to make. I don't know of a better way to secure the wisdom that we need than by keeping the commandments. We are enjoined by the commandments to study, to pray, to work and to serve, and be humble and contrite of spirit. The great promises are to the meek who shall inherit the earth. Wisdom is not to be found among the arrogant, the haughty and self-sufficient, nor among the sinful and the anti-Christs of the world. Wisdom is a gift to the prayerful student, to the faithful and the obedient, to those who repose their trust in the counsels of the spirit and the Priesthood of God. (CR, April 1949, pp. 143-44.)

Joseph F. Smith: 30
Ye shall not fear

No man need fear in his heart when he is conscious of having lived up to the principles of truth and righteousness as God has required it at his hands, according to his best knowledge and understanding. (CR, April 1904, p. 2.)

Joseph Fielding Smith: 32-37

They [Saints] were commanded to assemble in Ohio, and there he would give unto them his law, and these things should be made known. They were to dispose of their property as best they could; farms that could not be sold should be rented, and men of wisdom were to be appointed to look after the interests of the poor and needy and send them forth to the place the Lord commanded them. (*Essentials in Church History*, 1950, p. 122.)

Wilford Woodruff: 39

Remember, my brethren, the greatest gift that God can bestow upon us [is] eternal life, and it is worth more than all the houses and lands or the gold and the silver upon the earth. For by and by we will go to the grave, and that puts an end to wordly possessions, as far as our using them is concerned. The grave finds a home for all flesh, and no man can take his houses and lands, his gold and silver, or anything else of a worldly character with him. We brought none of these things with us when we came from our previous state. As Bishop Hunter says, babies are born without shoes and stockings. All the knowledge that we can accumulate from experience and observation, and from the revelations of God to man, goes to show that the riches of this world are fleeting and transitory; while he that has eternal life abiding in him is rich indeed. [Sec. 6:7.] (*JD*, June 26, 1881, 22:234.)

George Q. Cannon: 39

There is something in the human heart of that character that when human beings are prospering they are apt to be lifted up in pride and to forget the cause or the source of their prosperity; and they are apt to forget God, who is the fountain of all their blessings, and to give glory to themselves. It requires a constant preaching of the word of God, a constant pleading with the people, a constant outpouring of the Spirit of God upon the people to bring them to a true sense of their real condition. Is it right that we should be prudent, that we should take care of those gifts and blessings which God has given unto us, that we should husband our resources, that we should be economical, and not extravagant? Certainly; this is right, this is proper; we should be culpable if we are not so. But with this there is also something else required, and that is, to keep constantly in view that the management and care of these things is not the object that God had in sending us here, that is not the object of our probation. . . . I have been in reduced circumstances; have been on missions when I did not know where to get a mouthful to eat; turned away by the people who dare not entertain me because of the anger that was kindled against us. I could stand by and weep, being a boy and away from all my friends. But I, nevertheless, was happy. I never enjoyed myself in my life as I did then. I know that happiness does not consist in the possession of worldly things. Still it is a great relief when people have the means necessary for the support of themselves and families. If they possess these things and the Spirit of God with them, they are blessed. (JD, July 25, 1880, 22:100-1.)

Anthon H. Lund: 39

If one man acquire more of this world's goods than another, let it not lift him up and make him feel that it makes him better than his brother. Remember that the Lord withstands the proud; and purse-pride I think is meaner than any other pride. Yet it is natural to us. There should not arise class distinctions among the Latter-day Saints. We should love one another, and be one. You do not see any class distinction between those who labor in the Temples. The Temple is a place where the atmosphere is entirely free from a feeling of one being above another. When our missionaries go out to preach the Gospel, sometimes a young man of rich parents will be associated with the son of poor parents, but they do not feel that there is any distinction between them. They go out tracting and holding meetings together, they pray together, and live together as brethren. The difference between them in worldly means is forgotten, and they try to be united in the work they have in hand. Now, as the missionaries feel abroad, as you feel when you go into the Temples of God, so you should feel in your everyday lives. (CR, April 1901, pp. 21-22.)

Joseph F. Smith: 40-41

The one thing now that I desire to impress upon the minds of my brethren of the Holy Priesthood is that we should live so near to the Lord, be so humble in our spirits, so tractable and pliable, under the unfluence of the Holy Spirit, that we will be able to know the mind and will of the Father concerning us as individuals and as officers in the Church of Christ under all circumstances. And when we live so that we can hear and understand the whisperings of the still small voice of the Spirit of God, let us do whatsoever that Spirit directs, without fear of the consequences. It does not make any difference whether it meet the minds of carpers or critics, or of the enemies of the kingdom of God, or not. Is it agreeable to the will of the Lord? Is it compatible with the spirit of the great latter-day work in which we are engaged? Is the end aimed at likely to advance the Church and to strengthen it in the earth? If its trend is in that direction, let us do it, no matter what men say or think. (CR, October 1903, p. 86.)

George F. Richards: 40

One might ask: Why all the activity we see in the Church, in the ministry abroad, in the ministry at home, in the stakes and wards, in the priesthood quorums and auxiliary associations, in genealogy and temple work, in Church school and seminary work, etc.? The answer might be briefly given thus: The salvation of man depends upon it. It is the work and glory of God to accomplish the salvation of his children, by the plan of the Gospel which he has revealed. The religious activities seen in the Church and in which we are engaged are for the purpose, and are assisting the Lord in the noblest work, the most important service in which man may be engaged. If we be not called officially into the service, there are many things we can do of our own volition which will contribute to our happiness and salvation and to the happiness and salvation of others. (CR, April 1936, p. 79.)

David O. McKay: 40

In the Church, increased participation in Church activity indicates a desire to be a partaker of spirituality, the highest acquisition of the soul, and young people desire it. (CR, April 1961, p. 7.)

Franklin D. Richards: 40
Prepare and accomplish the things which I have commanded

I recollect the first time I went to stop with President

[Brigham] Young. When it came to prayer time, he asked Brother Franklin to pray. I was but a boy, and I turned to him and said, "President Young, I would rather you pray; you can pray better than I can." " Oh! Well," said he, "you can pray well enough; you try it." So I knelt down and prayed the best I could. Thus we have to prepare ourselves and be ready for every duty as we go along. (CR, April 1899, p. 46.)

Charles W. Penrose: 42

[The gospel] must be proclaimed to every nation, kindred, tongue and people: to professors of religion and non-professors, to preachers and their congregations, to pastors and their flocks, to the king upon his throne and to the peasant in his cottage, to the presidents of republics, and in fact to all peoples on the face of the earth. All must hear the warning voice: Repent of your sins, O ye inhabitants of the earth! Turn away from your corruptions wherewith you have defiled yourselves and the earth on which you dwell, or woe unto you, for I the Lord God will cleanse the earth as with the besom of destruction. Repent, before judgment shall overtake you. Repent and be baptized every one of you, in the name of the Lord Jesus, and you shall be cleansed from sin, and a new heart shall be put into you. You shall be born of the water and be made new creatures in Christ Jesus. You shall be born of the Spirit, the Holy Ghost shall be given unto you as a gift from God, which shall be a light to your feet and a lamp to your path, by which you can be brought into communion with the Father and the Son and the heavenly hosts, by which light and intelligence can be flashed from the celestial kingdom to your souls, and by which you may know you are accepted of God! This Gospel must be preached to all the world by the servants of God. (JD, July 17, 1881, 22:167.)

SECTION 39

Revelation given through Joseph Smith the Prophet, to James Covill, at Fayette, New York, January 5, 1831. James Covill covenanted that he would obey any command that the Lord would give to him through Joseph the Prophet. See History of the Church, vol. 1, p. 143. – The Lord Jesus Christ specifies the conditions under which men may become his sons – James Covill promised blessing beyond all he had ever known, conditioned on his obedience to the Lord's commandments.

1. Hearken and listen to the voice of him who is from all eternity to all eternity, the Great I AM, even Jesus Christ—

2. The light and the life of the world; a light which shineth in darkness and the darkness comprehendeth it not;

3. The same which came in the meridian of time unto mine own, and mine own received me not;

4. But to as many as received me, gave I power to become my sons; and even so will I give unto as many as will receive me, power to become my sons.

5. And verily, verily, I say unto you, he that receiveth my gospel receiveth me; and he that receiveth not my gospel receiveth not me.

6. And this is my gospel — repentance and baptism by water, and then cometh the baptism of fire and the Holy Ghost, even the Comforter, which showeth all things, and teacheth the peaceable things of the kingdom.

7. And now, behold, I say unto you, my servant James, I have looked upon thy works and I know thee.

8. And verily I say unto thee, thine heart is now right before me at this time; and, behold, I have bestowed great blessings upon thy head;

9. Nevertheless, thou hast seen great sorrow, for thou hast rejected me many times because of pride and the cares of the world.

10. But, behold, the days of thy deliverance are come, if thou wilt hearken to my voice, which saith unto thee: Arise and be baptized, and wash away your sins, calling on my name, and you shall receive my Spirit, and a blessing so great as you never have known.

11. And if thou do this, I have prepared thee for a greater work. Thou shalt preach the fulness of my gospel, which I have sent forth in these last days, the covenant which I have sent forth to recover my people, which are of the house of Israel.

12. And it shall come to pass that power shall rest upon thee; thou shalt have great faith, and I will be with thee and go before thy face.

13. Thou art called to labor in my vineyard, and to build up my church, and to bring forth Zion, that it may rejoice upon the hills and flourish.

14. Behold, verily, verily, I say unto thee, thou art not called to go into the eastern countries, but thou art called to go to the Ohio.

15. And inasmuch as my people shall assemble themselves at the Ohio, I have kept in store a blessing such as is not known among the children of men, and it shall be poured forth upon their heads. And from thence men shall go forth into all nations.

16. Behold, verily, verily, I say unto you, that the people in Ohio call upon me in much faith, thinking I will stay my hand in judgment upon the nations, but I cannot deny my word.

17. Wherefore lay to with your might and call faithful laborers into my vineyard, that it may be pruned for the last time.

18. And inasmuch as they do repent and receive the fulness of my gospel, and become sanctified, I will stay mine hand in judgment.

19. Wherefore, go forth, crying with a loud voice, saying: The kingdom of heaven is at hand; crying: Hosanna! blessed be the name of the Most High God.

20. Go forth baptizing with water, preparing the way before my face for the time of my coming;

21. For the time is at hand; the day or the hour no man knoweth; but it surely shall come.

22. And he that receiveth these things receiveth me; and they shall be gathered unto me in time and in eternity.

23. And again, it shall come to pass that on as many as ye shall baptize with water, ye shall lay your hands, and they shall receive the gift of the Holy Ghost, and shall be looking forth for the signs of my coming, and shall know me.

24. Behold, I come quickly. Even so. Amen.

Joseph Smith: *Introduction*

Not long after this conference of the 2nd of January closed, there was a man came to me by the name of James Covill, who had been a Baptist minister for about forty years, and covenanted with the Lord that he would obey any command that the Lord would give to him through me, as his servant, and I received the following: [Section 39, follows.] (HC 1:143, January 5, 1831, Fayette, New York.)

Joseph Fielding Smith: 1-18

This revelation [Section 39] contains the usual greetings with which the Lord addressed others who came for counsel. He declared that he is [Sec. 38:2-4, quoted]. Moreover, he was told that the Lord would receive all who are willing to receive his Gospel. We may well believe that much of this doctrine was new to James Covill. The Lord stated that he knew his works and he knew him, and that at this particular time his heart was right, and the Lord had placed great blessings upon him. He had seen great sorrow, and many times he had rejected the Lord because of his pride and the cares of the world.

He was promised that the day of his deliverance had come, if he would hearken unto the voice of the Lord. It seems from this commandment and promise that there had been times when Mr. Covill had received a desire to join the Church, but had weakened because of his pride and the love of the world. Now, however, he had come seeking the truth, and the Lord informs him that is to him the day of deliverance from these wordly cares if he will now abide in the truth. The voice of the Spirit of the Lord had said to him on other occasions that he should rise and be baptized, and wash away his sins. This commandment was now renewed with the promise if he did so he would receive the Spirit as he had never had it before. "If thou do this, I have prepared thee for a greater work," the Lord said to him. He was to proclaim the Gospel in its fulness, and the covenant which had been sent forth to recover the house of Israel. The power of the Lord would rest upon him and he would be given great faith, for the Lord would be with him and go before him. He was called not to go to the "eastern countries," but to the Ohio, where the Lord had commanded his people to assemble, and where blessings had been kept in store such as had not been known among the children of men. And from thence the blessings and the Gospel should go forth to all nations. [Sec. 39:16-17, quoted.]

It seems that the people in Ohio, like many other people of today, thought the Lord could stay his hand, and revoke the judgments upon mankind even if they would not repent. The Lord declared to the contrary, that his hand could not be stayed, except in the case that the people would repent; otherwise the judgments were bound to follow. They would bring them upon themselves because of their wickedness, and it was a matter of their agency. (*CHMR*, 1947, 1:158-59.)

Reed Smoot: 1

How often I have been asked, and in all sincerity I might add, if the Mormon Church believes in Jesus Christ? My answer has always been, "Perhaps to a greater degree than any other Church organization in the world." We believe Jesus Christ to be the actual Son of God — the second in the Godhead, foreordained to his birth, his mission and crucifixion. The spirit of Christ is the spirit of salvation, of blessing to do good, to prepare us all for the presence of our Eternal Father and to enjoy the glory of his kingdom. (*CR*, April 1933, p. 18.)

Joseph Fielding Smith: 3
In the meridian of time

Moreover, our Savior came in the meridian of time. That dispensation is called the dispensation of the meridian of time. This means that it was about half-way from the *beginning of "time" to the end of "time."* Anyone who desires can figure it for himself, that our Lord came about 4,000 years from the time of the fall. The millennium is to come some time following the 2,000 years after his coming. Then there is to be the millennium for 1,000 years, and following that a *"little season,"* the length of which is not revealed, but which may *bring "time" to its end* about 8,000 years from the beginning. (*Doctrines of Salvation*, 1954, 1:181.)

George Teasdale: 4

We say to all the world, Repent, obey the Gospel, receive the remission of your sins, become sanctified through the precious blood of Jesus Christ, receive the gift of the Holy Ghost, and be one with us in our glorious brotherhood in

Christ Jesus, adopted into the family of our Father in heaven. (CR, April 1902, p. 68.)

Henry D. Moyle: 6

In all generations of time those who have been baptized according to the plan laid down by the Father, justified by the Son and recognized and approved by both the Father and the Holy Ghost, have, after baptism, received the Holy Ghost through the laying on of hands by those who are in authority — the Holy Ghost, the Comforter, which Christ promised his disciples would be sent to them by the Father upon his ascension on high. Those who seek after the Comforter can be assured, through obedience to the laws and ordinances of the Gospel, never to be left alone, but always to have the influence, power, and inspiration of a member of the Godhead ever present. (CR, April 1961, p. 101.)

Parley P. Pratt: 6
The Holy Ghost... which... teacheth the peaceable things

The gift of the Holy Ghost adapts itself to all these organs or attributes. It quickens all the intellectual faculties, increases, enlarges, expands and purifies all the natural passions and affections, and adapts them, by the gift of wisdom, to their lawful use. It inspires, develops, cultivates and matures all the fine-toned sympathies, joys, tastes, kindred feelings and affections of our natures. It inspires virtue, kindness, goodness, tenderness, gentleness and charity. It develops beauty of person, form and features. It tends to health, vigor, animation and social feeling. It invigorates all the faculties of the physical and intellectual man. It strengthens and gives tone to the nerves. In short, it is as it were, marrow to the bone, joy to the heart, light to the eyes, music to the ears, and life to the whole thing. (*Key to the Science of Theology*, 1843, p. 100.)

Hyrum M. Smith: 6
The Comforter which... teacheth

When [the convert] has so received the gift of the Holy

Ghost, or the Holy Ghost as a gift from God, he has received a comforter to his soul, a light to his path, a spirit that giveth understanding and knowledge, that brightens the mind, quickens the intellect and gives a proper comprehension of the things of God that have been revealed through the prophets, and are written in the holy scriptures. A man with this spirit, reading the scriptures will understand them. He will not wrest them to his own condemnation. . . . And he will not attempt to spiritualize it or to interpret the word of God into meaning something else. . . . As he reads the scriptures all things spoken by the prophets of old shall be understood by him, by virtue of his possessing the Spirit of truth, and they will be clear to his understanding; and, as the multitude read who are possessed of this spirit, having been spiritualized in this manner, they shall see and understand, believe and know alike, and there shall be no difference of opinion nor of understanding upon . . . great fundamental truths of the gospel of salvation. He, the Spirit of truth, shall guide them into all truth, and shall abide with the faithful forever. (CR, October 1912, pp. 55-56.)

Brigham Young: 12
Faith

I know nothing about faith in the Lord, without works corresponding therewith; they must go together, for without works you cannot prove that faith exists. We might cry out, until the day of our death, that we love the Savior, but if we neglect to observe his sayings he would not believe us. (JD, April 18, 1874, 17:40.)

George Teasdale: 19
Go forth, crying with a loud voice

We take our lives in our hands and go forth to the nations of the earth with this glad message of great joy to the people, that God hath spoken and that he has restored to the earth his holy Gospel. We promise them that if they will obey the Gospel and live the principles of righteousness they shall have a living testimony and shall know, as we know, that God lives, that Jesus is the Christ, that Joseph Smith was a true Prophet sent of God, that the dispensation of the fulness of times is being ushered in, and that the people are being prepared for everlasting life, or for death, for a glorious resurrection of the just and the resurrection of the unjust. How could we expect a part in the resurrection of the just unless we were just to our God and to each other? (CR, October 1899, pp. 21-22.)

Wilford Woodruff: 21
For the time is at hand

This is a great day, an important time — a time in which great events await the world — Zion, Babylon, Jew, Gentile, saint and sinner, high and low, rich and poor. Great and important events will follow each other in quick succession before the eyes of this generation. No generation that ever lived on the earth lived in a more interesting period than the one in which we live; and when we consider that our eternal destiny depends upon the few short years that we spend here, what manner of persons ought we to be? Men spend their lives for what they call wealth or happiness, but they seek not after the way of life, and in a few years they lie down and die, and open their eyes in the spirit world, and they will come forth at some time and be judged according to the deeds done in the body. (JD, April 7, 1873, 16:36.)

SECTION 40

Revelation given to Joseph Smith the Prophet and Sidney Rigdon, at Fayette, New York, January, 1831. Preceding the record of this revelation, the Prophet wrote: As James Covill rejected the word of the Lord, and returned to his former principles and people, the Lord gave unto me and Sidney Rigdon the following revelation:

1. Behold, verily I say unto you, that the heart of my servant James Covill was right before me, for he covenanted with me that he would obey my word.

2. And he received the word with gladness, but straightway Satan tempted him; and the fear of persecution and the cares of the world caused him to reject the word.

3. Wherefore, he broke my covenant, and it remaineth with me to do with him as seemeth me good. Amen.

Joseph Smith: *Introduction*

As James Covill rejected the word of the Lord, and returned to his former principles and people, the Lord gave unto me and Sidney Rigdon the following revelation, explaining why he obeyed not the word: [Section 40 follows.] (HC 1:145, January 6, 1831, Fayette, New York.)

Joseph Fielding Smith: 1-3

This man James Covill received a most wonderful revelation and blessing, provided he would turn to the Lord and in humility and faith seek to bring forth and establish Zion. "And again," the Lord said to him in conclusion, "it shall come to pass that on as many as ye shall baptize with water, ye shall lay your hands, and they shall receive the gift of the Holy Ghost, and shall be looking forth for the signs of my coming and shall know me. Behold, I come quickly. Even so. Amen." [Sec. 39:23-24.]

We are led to believe that in this promised blessing, this foolish man was convinced of the truth, for it is clear that the Lord revealed to him things which he and the Lord alone knew to be the truth. However, when he withdrew from the influence of the Spirit of the Lord and had time to consider the fact that he would lose the fellowship of the world, and his place and position among his associates, he failed and rejected the promises and blessings which the Lord offered him. In a revelation explaining why he failed, the Lord said: [Sec. 40:1-3, quoted.]

How many others there have been, and now are, who have rejected the word of the Lord because of the love of the world and the fear of men, to mortals may never be made known. Evidently they are legions, some have frankly admitted, others have turned away and have developed a spirit of extreme bitterness towards the Church. (*CHMR*, 1947, 1:159-60.)

George Q. Cannon: 1-3

The Apostle says, "Where no law exists there is no transgression" [Rom. 4:15], but when the Gospel came in its purity and plainness, and they did not receive it, then commenced their condemnation. This was the condemnation of the people in the days of Jesus. When light came into the world they were condemned because they rejected it. "This is condemnation," says Jesus, "that light is come into the world and men loved darkness rather than light, because their deeds were evil." [John 3:19.] Ministers of religion and others who have been partly convinced of the truth when they have looked at the difficulties they would have to encounter and the sacrifices, as they considered them, which they would have to make, have shrunk from it, not having the courage to take upon them, I was going to say the shame of Jesus Christ, but they have been afraid and ashamed to take upon them his name, and to bear the odium which is cast upon the servants of God. There are many instances, doubtless, in your own experience of this kind; and they have gone backward from the time they rejected the truth; they have lost the favor of man, which they rejected the truth to obtain, have been disgraced in the sight of their fellow men and have met with the very things they desired to shun. Because of the rejection of the truth by men, the anger of the Lord is kindled against them and his judgments come upon them. (*MS*, February 21, 1863, 25:118.)

Orson F. Whitney: 2
Fear of persecution

There are still others who love the truth and who recognize it, but they dare not espouse it; they are afraid of the social consequences. This whole broad land, this whole broad world, is sprinkled with such people. When the principles of the Gospel are presented to them they say, in surprise and astonishment: "Is that Mormonism? I never dreamed it. Why, that is true — I believe it with all my heart." And the tears spring to their eyes as they acknowledge it. But they don't come out in the open and fight for it. Why not? Judge ye.

"They are slaves who fear to speak
For the fallen and the weak;
They are slaves who will not choose
Hatred, scoffing and abuse,
Rather than in silence shrink
From the truth they needs must think;
They are slaves who dare not be
In the right with two or three."

(CR, April 1915, p. 102.)

Joseph F. Smith: 2
The cares of the world caused him to reject the word

That there are many good people in the world who believe the principles of the gospel as taught by the Latter-day Saints, and yet, through circumstances and environment, are not prepared to publicly accept the same, is evidenced by the following letter written by a reverend gentleman to a kinsman and a member of the Church in Idaho, and which the *Era* is permitted to use. The names of the parties immediately interested, for obvious reasons, are omitted. The letter follows:

". . . Fortunately or unfortunately for me, I say, I believe you people are right in following the word given with such wonderful power and certainty as witnessed by the disinterested men who saw with their own eyes and heard with their own ears, at the beginning. Who can believe these, with Joseph and Hyrum Smith, were all liars and worse? I cannot. But here, dear cousin, is a question for you, and your elders: What is to become of such as me, who believes this about you, and yet are tied and bound by circumstances such as mine? Here I have been a minister for fifty-five years, and an ordained priest in the English church, the church of our forefathers, thirty-eight years. I have exercised this ministry all those years, unbroken — I cannot change now if I would. I am an old man seventy-eight years next birthday (March 10, 1835, I was born). Yes, let there be no mistake about my belief. I preach three sermons every week and execute other ministerial duties, but I never preach anything contrary to the doctrine of 'Mormonism,' not designedly but necessarily, because I see the fundamentals of Holy Scripture are the same as those restored by what people call 'Mormonism' . . ."

In answer to the question, "What is to become of such as me?" Let it be said that every person will receive his just reward for the good he may do and for his every act. But let it be remembered that all blessings which we shall receive, either here or hereafter, must come to us as a result of our obedience to the laws of God upon which these blessings are predicated. Our friend will not be forgotten for the kindness he has extended to the work and the servants of the Lord, but will be remembered of him and rewarded for his faith and for every good deed and word. But there are many blessings that result from obeying the ordinances of the gospel, and acknowledging the priesthood authorized of the Father and restored to The Church of Jesus Christ of Latter-day Saints, that cannot be obtained until the person is willing to comply with the ordinances and keep the commandments revealed in our day for the salvation of mankind. The true searcher will see and understand this truth and act upon it, either in this world or the world to come, and not until then, of course, may he claim all the blessings. The earlier he accepts, the earlier will he obtain the blessings, and if he neglects to accept the laws in this world, knowing them to be true, it is reasonable to suppose that disadvantages will result that will cause him deep regret. (IE, November 1912, 16:70-72.)

SECTION 41

Revelation given through Joseph Smith the Prophet, to the Church, at Kirtland, Ohio, February 4, 1831. The Kirtland branch of the Church at this time was rapidly increasing in numbers, and the Saints generally were striving to live according to the commandments of the Lord; but, the Prophet states, some strange notions and false spirits had crept in among them. See History of the Church, vol. 1, p. 146. – Commandment regarding the observance of the law of the Lord – Promise of greater knowledge as to the government of the Church – Edward Partridge named as the first Bishop unto the Church.

1. Hearken and hear, O ye my people, saith the Lord and your God, ye whom I delight to bless with the greatest of all blessings, ye that hear me; and ye that hear me not will I curse, that have professed my name, with the heaviest of all cursings.

2. Hearken, O ye elders of my church whom I have called, behold I give unto you a commandment, that ye shall assemble yourselves together to agree upon my word;

3. And by the prayer of your faith ye shall receive my law, that ye may know how to govern my church and have all things right before me.

4. And I will be your ruler when I come; and behold, I come quickly, and ye shall see that my law is kept.

5. He that receiveth my law and doeth it, the same is my disciple; and he that saith he receiveth it and doeth it not, the same is not my disciple, and shall be cast out from among you;

6. For it is not meet that the things which belong to the children of the kingdom should be given to them that are not worthy, or to dogs, or the pearls to be cast before swine.

7. And again, it is meet that my servant Joseph Smith, Jun., should have a house built, in which to live and translate.

8. And again, it is meet that my servant Sidney Rigdon should live as seemeth him good, inasmuch as he keepeth my commandments.

9. And again, I have called my servant Edward Partridge; and I give a commandment, that he should be appointed by the voice of the church, and ordained a bishop unto the church, to leave his merchandise and to spend all his time in the labors of the church;

10. To see to all things as it shall be appointed unto him in my laws in the day that I shall give them.

11. And this because his heart is pure before me, for he is like unto Nathanael of old, in whom there is no guile.

12. These words are given unto you, and they are pure before me; wherefore, beware how you hold them, for they are to be answered upon your souls in the day of judgment. Even so. Amen.

George Q. Cannon: *Introduction*

In the latter part of January, 1831, Joseph departed for Kirtland. . . .

The branch of the Church at Kirtland had become numerically strong, for it numbered nearly one hundred members. But they had been led into strange errors and darkness. False spirits had crept in and had manifested themselves in the subjugation of the physical and mental power of their victims — as Newel Knight had formerly been controlled and possessed by the evil powers at Colesville. [See Sec. 24:13.] The Saints at Kirtland, not having had experience to enable them to distinguish between the powers of light and the powers of darkness, and believing these things to be divine manifestations, were yielding to them and imperiling their earthly and eternal salvation, when the Prophet came and by his presence and prayers and faith of those Elders who accompanied him, banished all these dark influences from the congregation of the Saints. When the faith of the Saints was aroused and exercised, the miracle which had been wrought at Colesville was here repeated. Joseph, by the power of God, rebuked the vile one and his crew; and his brother Hyrum, under the Prophet's direction, laid his hands on the sufferers' heads and cast out the devils.

Immediately following the reconciliation wrought among the Saints of God by their faith and these miracles, a revelation [Section 41] was given from the Lord directing what the Elders should do to receive his law, that they might know how to govern his Church, and informing them that he who received his law and doeth it is his disciple; but he that saith he receiveth it and doeth it not, is not his disciple, and should be cast out from among them; and also appointing unto Edward Partridge that he should be ordained a bishop, to leave his own affairs and devote his time to the service of the Lord. This was on the 4th of February 1831. (*Life of Joseph Smith,* 1907, pp. 85-87.)

Orson F. Whitney: *Introduction*

Another instance of Joseph's use of the seeric gift connects with the occasion of his arrival at Kirtland, Ohio, where the Church at an early day established its headquarters. A few months prior to that time, Oliver Cowdery and three other Elders on their way to preach the Gospel to the Lamanites, or Indians, had tarried for a season at Kirtland, where they converted a number of the white dwellers in that region. Among these were Sidney Rigdon, Newel K. Whitney, and others who became prominent in the "Mormon" community. The Saints in Ohio, learning that the Church would probably move westward, began to pray for the coming of the Prophet.

The prayer was soon answered. About the first of February, 1831, a sleigh, driven into Kirtland from the East, drew up in front of the mercantile store of Gilbert and Whitney. A stalwart young man alighted and walked into the store. Approaching the junior partner and extending his hand cordially, as if to an old and familiar acquaintance, he saluted him thus: "Newel K. Whitney, thou art the man!"

The merchant was astonished. He had never seen this person before. "Stranger," he said, "you have the advantage of me; I could not call you by name as you have me."

"I am Joseph the Prophet," said the stranger, smiling. "You have prayed me here, now what do you want of me?"

Joseph Smith, while in the State of New York, had seen Newel K. Whitney, in the State of Ohio, praying for his coming to Kirtland, and therefore knew him when they met. The purpose of this vision, in all probability, was to pave the way for a meeting between the Prophet and the man who was to have the honor of entertaining him during the first weeks after his arrival in Ohio. (*Saturday Night Thoughts*, 1921, pp. 42-43.)

Joseph F. Smith: 1-4

I desire now to read a few words in relation to the duty which devolves upon the men who have been speaking during this conference. I will read a portion of the 41st Section of the Doctrine and Covenants. [Sec. 41:1-4, quoted.]

The Lord here especially demands of the men who stand at the head of this Church and who are responsible for the guidance and direction of the people of God, that they shall see to it that the law of God is kept. It is our duty to do this. . . . The Lord requires of us that we shall see that his law is kept among the people. This is one of the principal reasons why we are talking to you as we are. (CR, October 1899, p. 41.)

Joseph Fielding Smith: 4

"I will be your ruler." In the Church of Jesus Christ, it is our Redeemer who is the ruler. Many times we have heard President Joseph F. Smith, and other Presidents, say, when they have been addressed, or spoken of, as being the head of the Church, that this was not the case. No man stands at the head of the Church but Jesus Christ, whose Church it is. This is vital to the true Church. The President of the Church on earth is the representative and "mouthpiece" of our Lord, appointed to conduct the affairs of the Church in this mortal sphere. "I will be your ruler when I come," said the Lord. In the meantime his officers are to see that his law is kept. Here we may apply the parable of the talents. It is the duty of his servants to magnify his work through their diligence, faith and obedience to every principle and commandment; and this responsibility does not rest solely upon the President of the Church, neither upon the general authorities of the Church, but it must be shared by every man who holds the Priesthood. In fact, it goes beyond even this, for every member of the Church, both men and women, share in this responsibility, by obedience and righteous living and the teaching of the truth by example as well as by precept. (CHMR, 1947, 1:164.)

Howard W. Hunter: 5
He that receiveth my law . . . is my disciple

The pathway to exaltation is well defined. We are told to have faith — faith in the Lord Jesus Christ — and repent of those things which are not according to his teachings. After this change of mental attitude, and with firm resolution, we must declare ourselves by going into the waters of baptism, thereby making a covenant with the Lord to keep his commandments. Can we thereafter be a secret disciple? Can we stand on the sidelines and merely observe? This is a day for action. This is the time for decision, not tomorrow, not next week. This is the time to make our covenant with the Lord. Now is the time for those who have been non-committal or who have had a half-hearted interest to come out boldly and declare belief in Christ and be willing to demonstrate faith by works. (CR, October 1960, p. 109.)

Joseph Smith: 6

To every ordained member, and to all, we say, be merciful and you shall find mercy. Seek to help save souls, not to destroy them: for verily you know that "there is more joy in heaven over one sinner that repents than there is over ninety and nine just persons that need no repentance." [Luke 15:7.] Strive not about the mysteries of the kingdom; cast not your pearls before swine, give not the bread of the children to dogs, lest you and the children should suffer, and you thereby offend your righteous judge. (HC 2:230, June 1835.)

Joseph Fielding Smith: 7-8

After the Prophet arrived in Kirtland, and away from the opposition and hate that was so prevalent in and around Fayette, New York, the Lord called upon him to commence a very important work, that of revising the Bible and restoring to the words of the ancient Hebrew prophets many of the things that had been taken away. He was without a home and without any kind of office. For a time he boarded with the Whitney family. The Lord said to the members of the Church: [Sec. 41:7, quoted.] It was also necessary that Sidney Rigdon be cared for in some manner, as he was to be scribe for the Prophet in his great undertaking. Under all the conditions, some of them very unfavorable, it is remarkable what was accomplished. (CHMR, 1947, 1:164-65.)

John Taylor: 9

Called . . . appointed by the voice of the Church

We believe in two principles — one is the voice of God,

the other is the voice of the people. For instance, we believe that nobody but God could set the religious world right, we believe that none but God could have given any man correct information in regard to doctrine and ordinances. We believe that God did instruct Joseph Smith in relation to both, and also pertaining to the government of his people here on the earth. How are this people selected and set apart? Joseph Smith was selected by the Lord, and set apart, and ordained by holy angels. How with the others? By the authority which God conferred on Joseph he selected, set apart, and ordained others to the various orders and organizations of the Priesthood. . . . The position we occupy is this: the Holy Ghost, which has been given to all who have obeyed the Gospel and have lived faithful to its precepts, takes of the things of God and shows them forth through a living Priesthood to a people enlightened and instructed by the spirit of revelation from God, and the people thus enlightened, instructed and blessed by the spirit of light, voluntarily and gladly sustain the Priesthood who minister unto them. When Joseph Smith was upon the earth, he did not force himself upon the people as these kings and emperors do, but he presented himself before them every six months, at the annual or semi-annual conference, and the people had a chance to lift up their hands to receive or reject him. That was the position occupied by Joseph Smith, and those associated with him, in guiding the affairs of the Church and kingdom of God upon the earth, and it is precisely so with President [Brigham] Young. He stands here as the representative of God to the people, as the President of The Church of Jesus Christ of Latter-day Saints. He is, or ought to be, full of light, life, revelation and the power of God, and he is, and bears testimony to it. He ought to be able to lead the people in the paths of life, and he is. He is the choice of God, and what more? He is the choice of the people of God. Has he a right to say, "I am chosen, I am elected, I am President, and I will do as I darned please, and help yourselves"? No, he presents himself before you, and if there is, say, a man who has ought against him, he has the privilege of holding up his hand to signify the same. That is the position of our President — he is brought to a test every six months, as it rolls around, before the assembled conference of The Church of Jesus Christ of Latter-day Saints. It is the same with the Twelve, the President of the Stake, the High Council, the Presidents of Seventies, and with all the leading officers of the Church — they are all put to this test twice a year, and the people have the privilege of voting for or against them, just as they please. (JD, October 7, 1872, 15:215-16.)

Brigham Young: 12

Read the history of the world and you will find that when God has blessed a people and placed his name upon them, and they afterwards became disobedient, the whole catalogue of curses pronounced by him upon his unworthy children have come upon them and they have been blotted out. Those who do not profess to know anything of the Lord are far better off than we are, unless we live our religion, for we who know our Master's will and do it not will be beaten with many stripes; while they who do not know the Master's will and do it not will be beaten with few stripes. This is perfectly reasonable. We cannot chastise a child for doing that which is contrary to our wills, if he knows no better; but when our children are taught better and know what is required of them, if they then rebel, of course, they expect to be chastised, and it is perfectly right that they should be. (JD, June 27, 1873, 16:111-12.)

Joseph F. Smith: 12
These words . . . beware how you hold them

We know that every man will be judged according to the deeds done in the body; and whether our sin be against our own peace and happiness alone or whether it affects that of others, as the Lord lives we will have to make satisfaction or atonement; God requires it, and it is according to his providences and we cannot escape it. (JD, December 7, 1879, 21:13.)

GENERAL AUTHORITIES QUOTED IN THIS VOLUME

Presidents of the Church

JOSEPH SMITH, JR.: *December 23, 1805-June 27, 1844*
Received the Melchizedek Priesthood from Peter, James, and John in 1829; sustained as First Elder of the Church April 6, 1830; sustained as President of the High Priesthood January 25, 1832.

BRIGHAM YOUNG: *June 1, 1801-August 29, 1877*
Ordained an apostle February 14, 1835; sustained as President of the Church December 27, 1847.

JOHN TAYLOR: *November 1, 1808-July 25, 1887*
Ordained an apostle December 19, 1838; sustained as President of the Church October 10, 1880.

WILFORD WOODRUFF: *March 1, 1807-September 2, 1898*
Ordained an apostle April 26, 1839; sustained as President of the Church April 7, 1889.

LORENZO SNOW: *April 3, 1814-October 10, 1901*
Ordained an apostle February 12, 1849; sustained as President of the Church September 13, 1898.

JOSEPH F. SMITH: *November 13, 1838-November 19, 1918*
Ordained an apostle July 1, 1866; sustained as President of the Church October 17, 1901.

HEBER J. GRANT: *November 22, 1856-May 14, 1945*
Ordained an apostle October 16, 1882; sustained as President of the Church November 23, 1918.

GEORGE ALBERT SMITH: *April 4, 1870-April 4, 1951*
Ordained an apostle October 8, 1903; sustained as President of the Church May 21, 1945.

DAVID O. McKAY: *September 8, 1873-January 18, 1970*
Ordained an apostle April 9, 1906; sustained as second counselor in the First Presidency October 6, 1934; also

sustained as second counselor to President George Albert Smith May 21, 1945; sustained as President of the Church April 9, 1951.

JOSEPH FIELDING SMITH: *July 19, 1876-July 2, 1972*
Ordained an apostle April 7, 1910; sustained as counselor in the First Presidency October 29, 1965; sustained as President of the Church January 23, 1970.

HAROLD B. LEE: *March 18, 1899-December 26, 1973*
Ordained an apostle April 10, 1941; sustained as first counselor to President Joseph Fielding Smith January 23, 1970; sustained as President of the Church July 7, 1972.

SPENCER W. KIMBALL: *March 28, 1895-*
Ordained an apostle October 7, 1943; sustained as President of the Church December 30, 1973.

Second Elder and Assistant Counselor
OLIVER COWDERY: *October 3, 1806-March 3, 1850*
Received the Melchizedek Priesthood from Peter, James, and John in 1829; sustained as second elder of the Church April 6, 1830; sustained as assistant counselor in the First Presidency September 3, 1837. Excommunicated April 11, 1839; rebaptized November 12, 1848.

Counselors in the First Presidency
SIDNEY RIGDON: *February 19, 1793-July 14, 1876*
Set apart as first counselor to President Joseph Smith March 18, 1833; excommunicated September 8, 1844.

HYRUM SMITH: *February 9, 1800-June 27, 1844*
Sustained as assistant counselor to the First Presidency September 3, 1837; sustained as second counselor November 7, 1837; called to be Patriarch to the Church and Assistant President January 24, 1841.

HEBER C. KIMBALL: *June 14, 1801-June 22, 1868*
Ordained an apostle February 14, 1835; sustained as first counselor to President Brigham Young December 27, 1847.

WILLARD RICHARDS: *June 24, 1804-March 11, 1854*

Ordained an apostle April 14, 1840; sustained as second counselor to President Brigham Young December 27, 1847.

JEDEDIAH M. GRANT: *February 21, 1816-December 1, 1856*
Set apart as one of the first seven presidents of the Seventy December 2, 1845; ordained an apostle April 7, 1854; sustained as second counselor to President Brigham Young April 7, 1854.

DANIEL H. WELLS: *October 27, 1814-March 24, 1891*
Set apart as second counselor to President Brigham Young January 4, 1857; released at the death of President Young August 29, 1877; sustained as counselor to the Twelve Apostles October 6, 1877.

GEORGE A. SMITH: *June 26, 1817-September 1, 1875*
Ordained an apostle April 26, 1839; sustained as first counselor to President Brigham Young October 7, 1868.

GEORGE Q. CANNON: *January 11, 1827-April 12, 1901*
Ordained an apostle August 26, 1860; sustained as first counselor to President John Taylor October 10, 1880; to President Wilford Woodruff April 7, 1889; to President Lorenzo Snow September 13, 1898.

JOHN R. WINDER: *December 11, 1821-March 27, 1910*
Sustained as first counselor to President Joseph F. Smith October 7, 1901.

ANTHON H. LUND: *May 15, 1844-March 2, 1921*
Ordained an apostle October 7, 1889; sustained as second counselor to President Joseph F. Smith October 17, 1901; sustained as first counselor April 7, 1910; sustained as first counselor to President Heber J. Grant November 22, 1918.

JOHN HENRY SMITH: *September 18, 1848-October 13, 1911*
Ordained an apostle October 27, 1880; sustained as second counselor to President Joseph F. Smith April 7, 1910.

CHARLES W. PENROSE: *February 4, 1832-May 16, 1925*
Ordained an apostle July 7, 1904; sustained as second counselor to President Joseph F. Smith December 7, 1911; sus-

tained as second counselor to President Heber J. Grant November 23, 1918, and as first counselor March 10, 1921.

ANTHONY W. IVINS: *September 16, 1852-September 23, 1934*
Ordained an apostle October 6, 1907; sustained as second counselor to President Heber J. Grant March 10, 1921, and as first counselor May 28, 1925.

CHARLES W. NIBLEY: *February 5, 1849-December 11, 1931*
Sustained as Presiding Bishop December 4, 1907; sustained as second counselor to President Heber J. Grant May 28, 1925.

J. REUBEN CLARK, JR.: *September 1, 1871-October 6, 1961*
Sustained as second counselor to President Heber J. Grant April 6, 1933; sustained as first counselor October 6, 1934; ordained an apostle October 11, 1934; sustained as second counselor to President David O. McKay April 9, 1951, and as first counselor June 13, 1959.

STEPHEN L RICHARDS: *June 18, 1879-May 19, 1959*
Ordained an apostle April 10, 1947; sustained as first counselor to President David O. McKay April 9, 1951.

HENRY D. MOYLE: *April 22, 1889-September 18, 1963*
Ordained an apostle April 10, 1947; sustained as second counselor to President David O. McKay June 12, 1959, and as first counselor October 12, 1961.

HUGH B. BROWN: *October 24, 1883-December 2, 1975*
Sustained as Assistant to the Council of the Twelve October 4, 1953; ordained an apostle April 10, 1958; sustained as second counselor to President David O. McKay October 12, 1961; sustained as first counselor October 4, 1963; released January 18, 1970.

N. ELDON TANNER: *May 9, 1898-*
Sustained as an Assistant to the Council of the Twelve October 8, 1960; ordained an apostle October 11, 1962;

sustained as second counselor to President David O. McKay October 4, 1963; sustained as second counselor to President Joseph Fielding Smith January 23, 1970; sustained as first counselor to President Harold B. Lee July 7, 1972; sustained as first counselor to President Spencer W. Kimball December 30, 1973.

MARION G. ROMNEY: *September 19, 1897-*
Sustained as an Assistant to the Council of the Twelve April 6, 1941; ordained an apostle October 11, 1951; sustained as second counselor to President Harold B. Lee July 7, 1972; sustained as second counselor to President Spencer W. Kimball December 30, 1973.

The Twelve Apostles of the Church

THOMAS B. MARSH: *November 1, 1799-January 1866*
Ordained an apostle April 26, 1835; excommunicated March 17, 1839; returned to the Church July 1857.

DAVID W. PATTEN: *November 14, 1799-October 25, 1838*
Ordained an apostle February 15, 1835.

ORSON HYDE: *January 8, 1805-November 28, 1878*
Ordained an apostle February 15, 1835.

PARLEY P. PRATT: *April 12, 1807-May 13, 1857*
Ordained an apostle February 21, 1835.

LUKE S. JOHNSON: *November 3, 1807-December 9, 1861*
Ordained an apostle February 15, 1835; excommunicated April 13, 1838; returned to the Church 1846.

ORSON PRATT: *September 19, 1811-October 3, 1881*
Ordained an apostle April 26, 1835.

EZRA T. BENSON: *February 22, 1811-September 3, 1869*
Ordained an apostle July 16, 1846.

CHARLES C. RICH: *August 21, 1809-November 17, 1883*
Ordained an apostle February 12, 1849.

ERASTUS SNOW: *November 9, 1818-May 27, 1888*
Ordained an apostle February 12, 1849.

FRANKLIN D. RICHARDS: *April 2, 1821-December 9, 1899*
Ordained an apostle February 12, 1849.

BRIGHAM YOUNG, JR.: *December 18, 1836-April 11, 1903*
Ordained an apostle February 4, 1864.

FRANCIS M. LYMAN: *January 12, 1840-November 18, 1916*
Ordained an apostle October 27, 1880.

GEORGE TEASDALE: *December 8, 1831-June 9, 1907*
Ordained an apostle October 16, 1882.

MARRINER W. MERRILL: *September 25, 1832-February 6, 1906*
Ordained an apostle October 7, 1889.

ABRAHAM H. CANNON: *March 12, 1859-July 19, 1896*
Set apart as one of the first seven presidents of the Seventy October 9, 1882; ordained an apostle October 7, 1889.

MATTHIAS F. COWLEY: *August 25, 1858-June 16, 1940*
Ordained an apostle October 7, 1897; resigned October 28, 1905.

ABRAHAM O. WOODRUFF: *November 23, 1872-June 20, 1904*
Ordained an apostle October 7, 1897.

RUDGER CLAWSON: *March 12, 1857-June 21, 1943*
Ordained an apostle October 10, 1898.

REED SMOOT: *January 10, 1862-February 9, 1941*
Ordained an apostle October 24, 1901.

HYRUM M. SMITH: *March 21, 1872-January 23, 1918*
Ordained an apostle October 24, 1901.

GEORGE F. RICHARDS: *February 23, 1861-August 8, 1950*
Ordained an apostle April 9, 1906.

ORSON F. WHITNEY: *July 1, 1855-May 16, 1931*
Ordained an apostle April 9, 1906.

JAMES E. TALMAGE: *September 21, 1862-July 27, 1933*
Ordained an apostle December 8, 1911.

MELVIN J. BALLARD: *February 9, 1873-July 30, 1939*
Ordained an apostle January 7, 1919.

JOHN A. WIDTSOE: *January 31, 1872-November 29, 1952*
Ordained an apostle March 17, 1921.

JOSEPH F. MERRILL: *August 24, 1868-February 3, 1952*
Ordained an apostle October 8, 1931.

CHARLES A. CALLIS: *May 4, 1865-January 21, 1947*
Ordained an apostle October 12, 1933.

ALONZO A. HINCKLEY: *April 23, 1870-December 22, 1936*
Ordained an apostle October 11, 1934.

ALBERT E. BOWEN: *October 31, 1875-July 15, 1953*
Ordained an apostle April 8, 1937.

SYLVESTER Q. CANNON: *June 10, 1877-May 29, 1943*
Set apart as Presiding Bishop of the Church June 11, 1925; ordained an apostle April 14, 1938.

EZRA TAFT BENSON: *August 4, 1899-*
Ordained an apostle October 7, 1943.

MARK E. PETERSEN: *November 7, 1900-*
Ordained an apostle April 20, 1944.

MATTHEW COWLEY: *August 2, 1897-December 13, 1953*
Ordained an apostle October 11, 1945.

DELBERT L. STAPLEY: *December 11, 1896-*
Ordained an apostle October 5, 1950.

LEGRAND RICHARDS: *February 6, 1886-*
Sustained as Presiding Bishop of the Church April 6, 1938; ordained an apostle April 10, 1952.

ADAM S. BENNION: *December 2, 1886-February 11, 1958*
Ordained an apostle April 9, 1953.

RICHARD L. EVANS: *March 23, 1906-November 1, 1971*
Sustained as a member of the First Council of Seventy

October 7, 1938; ordained an apostle October 8, 1953.

GEORGE Q. MORRIS: *February 20, 1874-April 23, 1962*
Sustained as Assistant to the Council of the Twelve October 6, 1951; ordained an apostle April 8, 1954.

HOWARD W. HUNTER: *November 14, 1907-*
Ordained an apostle October 15, 1959.

GORDON B. HINCKLEY: *June 23, 1910-*
Sustained as Assistant to the Council of the Twelve April 6, 1958; ordained an apostle October 5, 1961.

BOYD K. PACKER: *September 10, 1924-*
Sustained as Assistant to the Council of the Twelve September 30, 1961; ordained an apostle April 9, 1970.

MARVIN J. ASHTON: *May 6, 1915-*
Sustained as Assistant to the Council of the Twelve October 3, 1969; ordained an apostle December 2, 1971.

L. TOM PERRY: *August 1, 1922-*
Sustained as Assistant to the Council of the Twelve October 6, 1972; ordained an apostle April 7, 1974.

Patriarchs to the Church

HYRUM SMITH (*See "Counselors in the First Presidency"*)

JOHN SMITH: *July 16, 1781-May 23, 1854*
Ordained a patriarch January 10, 1844; set apart as Patriarch to the Church January 1, 1849.

JOHN SMITH: *September 22, 1832-November 6, 1911*
Ordained Patriarch to the Church February 18, 1855.

HYRUM G. SMITH: *July 8, 1879-February 4, 1932*
Ordained a high priest and Patriarch to the Church May 9, 1912.

JOSEPH F. SMITH: *January 30, 1899-August 29, 1964*
Ordained and set apart as Patriarch to the Church October 8, 1942; released October 6, 1946, due to ill health.

ELDRED G. SMITH: *January 9, 1907-*
Ordained and set apart as Patriarch to the Church April 10, 1947.

INDEX